Contents

Preface

This admirable book, combining both the unpublished letters and journals of Dr. Richard Pococke and Jeremiah Milles, is one of the most extensively documented collections of travel writing from the first decades of the eighteenth century. The editor, Dr. Rachel Finnegan, has judiciously selected the letters from three distinct tours of the continent and Eastern Mediterranean undertaken during the 1730s, which were written from Pococke to his mother, Elizabeth Pococke, and from Milles to his uncle, Thomas Milles, Bishop of Waterford. Parallel letters written on the same date by the travellers, contrast in tone between the more gossipy descriptions of social life written by Pococke to the very detailed scholarly accounts of Milles to his uncle. The journals of the two travellers are used to supplement the letters; in these, by contrast Pococke recorded the more scholarly descriptions, while Milles' lengthy discussions provide societal context. In her scholarly editing of the letters and journals, Rachel's own knowledge of the ancient Greek and Roman empires is manifest both in her introductory chapters and the footnotes, which are used to great effect to amplify and clarify the eighteenth-century writings.

While Rachel argues that the cousins, with eleven years between them travelled as equals, Milles' tone towards his elder cousin, a recent graduate of Oxford, is nevertheless deferential. It was most likely as a result of his pedagogical influence that Milles wrote such detailed letters, Pococke writing that the evenings were spent 'in reading of places and writing down what we see' (p.149). As you would expect, these travellers were well schooled in advance of their journeys and as Rachel points out, Pococke's posthumous sale catalogue reveals his ownership of publications which predate his first continental visit. At the outset of their first tour, their meeting with the great antiquarian Bernard de Montfaucon at St Germain-en-Laye, added to their scholarly

Letters from Abroad:

The Grand Tour Correspondence

of

Richard Pococke & Jeremiah Milles

Volume 1:

Letters from the Continent (1733-34)

Edited by Rachel Finnegan

Pococke Press 2011

Letters from Abroad, Volume 1

Published by
Pococke Press
Piltown, County Kilkenny, Ireland

Finnegan, Rachel

Letters from Abroad: The Grand Tour Correspondence of Richard Pococke & Jeremiah Milles
Volume 1, Letters from the Continent (1733-34)

Includes Bibliographical References & Index

ISBN 978-0-9569058-0-2

1. Travel correspondence - 18th century. 2. France - Description and travel. 3. Visitors, Foreign - France - History - 18th century. 4. Italy - Description and travel. 5. Visitors, Foreign - Italy - History - 18th century. 6. Travellers - Ireland - Biography. 7. Church of Ireland - History. 8. Bishop Richard Pococke - Biography - Travels - Memoirs. 9. Dean Jeremiah Milles - Biography - Travels - Memoirs. 10. Bishop Thomas Milles - Biography

Website: www.pocockepress.com

Printed and bound in Cashel, Ireland, by Lion Print

Cover design by Jon Stapleton, Lion Print, Cashel
Shows portrait of Richard Pococke by Jean-Etiènne Liotard (1740)
Courtesy of the Musée d'Art et d'Histoire de la Ville de Genève

pursuits, as he recommended them to visit such halls of learning as the ducal library in Modena. Rachel's suggestion that they may well have set out armed with literature, would have been consistent with the scholarly habits of other travellers of the period, such as Robert Wood of Palmyra fame, who in 1749 went so far as to charter a ship complete with a library on board to inform his travels of the Levant.

Characteristically for the period, the greatest part of the letters concern visits to classical antiquities, which are recorded in minute detail. At Arles the pair actually measured parts of the amphitheatre: 'we took the height of it and found it to be 44 feet' (p.104). In his letter of 21 March 1734, Pococke informed his mother that they had 'measured all parts' of the Colosseum and that they had gone to 'view and measure the Pantheon'. While at Rome, Milles wrote copiously and authoratively about the antiquities they visited during their stay such as the Baths of Diocletian and the Domus Aurea. Outside the city, while he surprisingly skims over a visit to Hadrian's Villa, Milles' descriptions of Tivoli, were perhaps where he was at his most poetical. Like most eighteenth-century travellers, their interest Medieval art was limited. Omissions in their writings from a twenty-first century view point, include the stained glass in Notre Dame in Paris and Giotto's Arena Chapel in Padua, consistent with contemporary aesthetic taste. As regards Renaissance works, it is surprising that in discussing the Sistine Chapel, Pococke mentioned the Michelangelo's *Last Judgement* but not the ceiling frescoes usually preferred by contemporary visitors.

Customs and fashion are regularly remarked on in the papers. In Paris, Pococke helps to explain why men are often shown with their hand tucked into their coat or waistcoat in eighteenth-century portraits. 'As the gentlemen never wear gloves, when they hand a Lady, they put their hand under the foreshirt of their coat or wastcoates' (p.92). Regarding their Eastern Mediterranean travels, Rachel's suggestion that the two travellers aimed to blend in with the locals, explains why Pococke appeared in Turkish dress in his exotic portrait by the Swiss painter Jean-Etiènne Liotard. Her suggestion that it was more for purposes of security than for aesthetic reasons is borne out by the earlier experience of Lady Mary Wortley Montagu, who set the fashion for appearing à la Turque in English and Irish portraits of the period.

In the publication of these volumes, Rachel has filled a major lacuna left by Pococke himself and she argues that he had intended to publish his journals but never did. Her reason for this assertion is based on the fact that his mother edited and produced perfectly legible copies of his letters, as if part of the process. While rival travel writers may have intimidated Pococke so that he did not complete the work, Milles, she suggests, did not publish his own travel letters, due to being preoccupied with the advancement of his ecclesiastical career and his later active involvement with the Royal Society of Antiquaries in London.

Like Michael McCarthy before her, the editor proves that Pococke was not the 'dullest man who ever travelled', as characterised by Mary Delany. Rachel's research, which also included reading the original letters, as opposed to those transcribed by his mother, exposes more of his character, than hitherto revealed. His gossipy letters to his mother were far from dull and it is upon Milles that we have to rely for lengthy descriptions of the Capitoline Museum in Rome, which had recently opened. Pococke's letters show that he was fascinated with everyday and whimsical details from mouse traps at Calais to watching carnival on the Corso in Rome, where the nobility in their 'Barkella's, made like boats finely gilt & carved without covering ... pelt one another with sugar plums' (p.152).

Rachel's passion for her subject bears fruit in this three-volumed work of considerable scholarship. The publication of these remarkable letters and journals will provide a rich banquet of thought and serve as source material to students from a wide variety of disciplines, ranging from classical and grand tour studies to the history of fashion and social customs.

Nicola Figgis
Art History and Cultural Policy, University College Dublin
May, 2011

Acknowledgements

I wish to thank the following individuals and organisations for their valuable assistance in the production of this book. First I thank the British Library for permission to transcribe the Milles/Pococke travel manuscripts (both correspondence and journals) and other manuscript sources used in this volume. Likewise, I am grateful to Gloucestershire Archives for providing copies of three manuscript letters from the Hartford Collection; The National Archives of the UK for providing me with the Milles/Pococke family Wills cited and transcribed in this volume; the Board of Trinity College Dublin for permission to quote from the manuscript of the Board Register; the Librarian of the Royal Irish Academy for giving me access to manuscript sources related to Dublin clubs; the Department of Manuscripts at the National Library of Ireland for permission to quote from a a twentieth-century photocopy of Richard Pococke's Will (originating from the National Archives of Ireland); and Donal Moore, Waterford City Archivist, for his assistance and advice relating to my research on Bishop Milles and Waterford City during the period.

I am grateful to the following for providing me with photographs and granting permission to reproduce illustrations for this volume: the Musée d'Art et d'Histoire de la Ville de Genève, for Jean-Etiènne Liotard's portrait of Richard Pococke; Donnchadh Ó Ccallacháin and Waterford Museum of Treasures for the painting of Waterford Cathedral; the National Portrait Gallery, London, for the portrait of Dean Jeremiah Milles; the Science Museum, London, for the medal commemorating Laura Maria Caterina Bassi; the British Library for Jeremiah Milles' sketch of an Alpine chair; Right Revd Michael Burrows, Bishop of Cashel & Ossory, for the 1765 portrait of Bishop Pococke, which hangs in the Bishop's Palace, Kilkenny; Tony Hand for his photographs of the Montgomery Monument, Ardbraccan; and David Kane, for other photographs appearing in this work.

I am grateful to Professor George L. Huxley for reading an earlier typescript of this book and for giving me helpful suggestions for its improvement; and I am extremely endebted to Dr. Nicola Figgis, School of Art History & Cultural Policy, University College Dublin, for kindly reading the final draft of this volume and for writing the Preface.

I also wish to thank the following colleagues at Waterford Institute of Technology: Mary Fenton, Head of Department of Adult & Continuing Education, for her support at the initial stages of this undertaking; Kevin O'Hanlon, Special Collections Librarian, for allowing me access to various rare books in the Christchurch Cathedral Collection; Dr. Séamus Ó Diollúin for proof-reading the final draft; Dr. William Donnelly, Head of the School of Research, for granting financial assistance towards the printing costs of this volume; and Susie Cullinane, Projects Manager, Research Support Unit, for her help.

I wish to honour the memory of the late Michael McCarthy, Emeritus Professor of Art History at University College, Dublin, who encouraged me to produce this edition and was extremely generous in providing me with typescripts and notes related to his own research on Pococke.

Finally, I thank my mother, Dr. Frances Finnegan, for her interest and support, and my husband David Kane for his assistance in formatting the text and designing the Pococke Press website.

Rachel Finnegan
School of Humanities, Waterford Institute of Technology
June, 2011

Introduction

Irish Grand Tour Studies

The discipline of Grand Tour Studies has, over the last few decades, become increasingly popular, largely through its appeal to students of art history and travel history but also through a general fascination with the study of eighteenth-century memoir.[1] Many first-hand accounts of the Grand Tour (whether published or unpublished) tend, by the very nature of such an elitist activity, to have been written by members of the aristocracy, particularly wealthy connoisseurs whose travels were generally more extensive, ambitious and extravagant than those of lesser means. Their appeal is often linked to an intrinsic interest in the families themselves, and the stately homes and gardens which the Grand Tourists created or "improved", decorating, furnishing, and landscaping them in the classical taste of the day.

Eighteenth-century travel to Italy (and further afield) was by no means limited to the aristocracy, but was a popular feature of life among members of the gentry and clergy. Nor, as can be seen from John Ingamells' magisterial *Dictionary of British and Irish Travellers in Italy, 1701-1800,*[2] was foreign travel a pursuit

---

[1] For general studies on the Grand Tour, the reader is directed to the following works: William Edward Mead, *The Grand Tour in the Eighteenth Century* (Boston & New York, 1914), Jeremy Black, *The British and the Grand Tour* (Croom Helm, 1985); Geoffrey Trease, *The Grand Tour* (Yale University Press, 1991, reprint 2003); Andrew Wilton & Ilaria Bignamini, *Grand Tour: The Lure of Italy in the Eighteenth-Century* (Tate Gallery Exhibition Catalogue, 1997); John Ingamells, *A Dictionary of British and Irish Travellers in Italy, 1701-1800* (Yale University Press, 1997); Edward Chaney, *The Evolution of the Grand Tour: Anglo-Italian Cultural Relations since the Renaissance,* 2nd ed. (London, 2000) ; Jeremy Black, *The British Abroad: The Grand Tour in the Eighteenth Century* (Sutton Publishing Ltd., 1992, reprint 2003); and Jeremy Black, *Italy and the Grand Tour* (Yale University Press, 2003)

[2] *Op.cit.* Henceforth, this will be abbreviated to "Ingamells"

confined to the English. Despite the scorn and scoffing it may have aroused among the English abroad, it had, by the middle of the century, become an integral part of upper-class Irish life, or the life of "the quality".[3] This is reflected in the amount of scholarship that has been devoted, in recent years, to Irish Grand Tour Studies, in particular to the travels of James Caulfeild, 4th Viscount Charlemont, whose seven-year sojourn abroad (1747-54) extended as far as the East, and whose resultant architectural gem, the "Casino", is one of the most important historic houses in Ireland.[4] Two other famous Anglo-Irish travellers who were later to become bishops, and whose travel memoirs have been published and otherwise documented, are Frederick Augustus Hervey, 4th Earl of Bristol and George Berkley. Bishop Hervey's frequent and lengthy spells in Italy (where he eventually died) spanned almost forty years of his life,[5] while Bishop Berkeley's travels, in which he accompanied St George Ashe(son of the Bishop of Clogher) to Italy in 1716, are recorded in a collection of note-books and formal letters written back to Alexander Pope and his friend and patron Sir John Percival.[6] Further evidence of the interest in aristocratic Anglo-Irish Grand Tours is in the recent publication of travel letters from William Fitzgerald, 1st Marquis of Kildare. In this collection of letters (which are interspersed with an explanatory narrative from the editor), Lord

---

[3]See Toby Barnard, *A New Anatomy of Ireland: The Irish Protestants, 1649-1770* (Yale University Press, 2003), who, in his chapter on "The Quality" (a word appearing frequently in the Milles/Pococke travel literature) discusses the scoffing and humiliation suffered by Irish Grand Tourists such as the "Hibernian Howards" (pp 68-69)

[4]See W.B. Stanford, "The Manuscripts of Lord Charlemont's Eastern Travels", in *Proceedings of the Royal Irish Academy,* Section C, Volume 80, Number 5 (1980) 69-90, W.B. Stanford and E.J. Finopoulos (eds), *The Travels of Lord Charlemont in Greece & Turkey,* 1749 (London, 1984), and Cynthia O'Connor, *The Pleasing Hours: The Grand Tour of James Caulfield, First Earl of Charlemont (1728-1799), Traveller, Connoisseur and Patron of the Arts* (Cork, 1999)

[5]See B. Fothergill, *The Mitred Earl: An Eighteenth-Century Eccentric: The Life of Frederick Hervey, Bishop of Derry* (London, 1974)

[6]For a fascinating essay on Berkeley's travels, see Edward Chaney, "Architectural Taste and the Grand Tour: George Berkley's evolving Canon", in *Journal of Anglo-Italian Studies* I (1991) 74-91; and Edward Chaney (2000, *op.cit.*), Chapter 13 (pp 314-76)

Offaly, as he was when he set out (or the Marquess of Kildare, as he became while abroad) describes to his mother his experiences in Italy from 1766-68.[7]

A further focus of Irish Grand Tour scholarship is artistic. One aspect of this field of study concerns patronage and the opportunities presented to Irish artists abroad to obtain commissions from Grand Tourists for portraits, landscapes and copies of old master paintings and sculptures. Another concerns the acquisition of works of art by Irish Grand Tourists who wished to adorn their recently built Palladian houses in Ireland.[8]

The same theme is also dealt with from a curatorial perspective, with exhibitions in art galleries and historic houses displaying not only the works of art and antiquities that Irish Grand Tourists acquired on or as a result of their travels, but also the portraits they and their companions sat for while abroad. Perhaps the most important example of this is the collection of the Leeson family of Russborough House, County Wicklow, who were ennobled in 1763 as Earls of Milltown. The famous collection of paintings, sculpture, furniture and silverware, acquired by Joseph Leeson senior and junior while abroad, was donated to the National Gallery of Ireland in 1902 and now forms part of the Milltown Wing. Sadly, there is no record of travel journals or correspondence from the Grand Tours of either the father (1711-83), who travelled from 1744-45 and 1750-51,[9] or

---

[7]See Elizabeth Fitzgerald, *Lord Kildare's Grand Tour 1766-1769* (Cork, 2000)
[8]To date, the most comprehensive study on this subject is Nicola Figgis' unpublished doctoral thesis, "Irish Artists, Dealers and Grand Tourists in Italy in the Eighteenth Century" (University College Dublin, 1994) in 3 volumes. Volume I (Text) includes chapters on the itineraries of Irish artists and collectors in Italy, Irish connections with academies of art in Italy, Irish artists & antiquity, techniques & studio practices, Irish patronage, Irish dealers & agents in Italy, and Irish collectors in Italy; Volume II (Biographies) is divided into three chapters on Irish artists, Irish dealers & agents, and Irish Grand Tourists; and Volume III (Plates) illustrates the thesis with maps, street plans, portraits of the Irish artists, dealers & Grand Tourists, landscapes, etc. It should also be noted that Dr. Figgis contributed to the Irish entries in Ingamells, *op.cit.*
[9]He is recorded as having been in Rome, in 1745, with his secretary Robert Wood. See N.Figgis, *op.cit.*, Vol.II, 165, and 203ff

the son (1730-1801), who travelled from 1750-51 and again in 1778.[10].

In the same way, the great collector and connoisseur Hon. William Ponsonby (1704-93), as he was when he set out on his Grand Tour (later being styled Viscount Duncannon, and 2nd Earl of Bessborough), left no written record of his travels. However, we are fortunate that a small collection of letters exists in the Bessborough family papers concerning his purchase of antiquities in later life. Some of this correspondence is from his old friend James Hamilton, 2nd Earl of Clanbrassill and 2nd Viscount of the City of Limerick, who wrote to him from France during the 1760s[11] in relation to antiquities on the market in Paris;[12] and the rest is from the famous dealer in Rome, Thomas Jenkins, who, over the course of several years, attempted to sell him ancient funerary urns and other "marbles" to adorn Roehampton Villa, one of the first commissions of Sir William Chambers.[13] These antiquities served to augment the large collection he had accumulated during his Grand Tour in the 1730s, during which he and the youthful Lord Sandwich made a voyage to the East, taking with them the little-known portrait painter Jean-Étienne Liotard. This artist remained in Constantinople for several years, producing stunning portraits of many English and Irish travellers in oriental dress,[14] and Lord Bessborough was to become his most important patron owning, at his death, more than seventy of his paintings.

---

[10]An exhibition devoted to their Grand Tours took place in the National Gallery of Ireland in 1997, entitled "The Milltowns - A Family Reunion". See the accompanying exhibition catalogue, S. Benedetti, *The Milltowns - A Family Reunion* (Dublin, 1997)

[11]His mother, Harriet Hamilton, Viscountess of Limerick, was in Italy in 1745. See N. Figgis, *op.cit.* Vol II, 153

[12]Though one letter on more general matters is from his estate in Dundalk

[13]For an account of this correspondence and Bessborough's collections of art and antiquities in general, see R. Finnegan, "The Classical Taste of William Ponsonby, 2nd Earl of Bessborough (1704-1793)", in *Irish Architectural and Decorative Studies: The Journal of the Irish Georgian Society,* Volume (VIII 2005) 12-43

[14]Including Lord Bessborough (who was to become his most important patron, owning more than seventy of his paintings at his death), Lord Sandwich and one of the subjects of this book, Richard Pococke (see cover)

The Grand Tours of Rev. Dr. Richard Pococke
& Mr. Jeremiah Milles

Two non-aristocratic voyagers associated with Ireland who did leave a prodigious record of their experiences abroad are Rev. Dr. Richard Pococke (1704-65) and his younger cousin Mr. Jeremiah Milles (1714-84).[15] Together they embarked upon two journeys to the Continent from 1733-34 and 1736-37, with Pococke, who was to become one of the most celebrated travel-writers of his age, extending the second tour, alone, to an intrepid exploration of the East, from which he did not return until 1741.[16] Since the nineteenth century, secondary sources have consistently confused the dates and circumstances of these travels, with Daniel William Kemp, for example, stating in 1887: "From 1733 to 1736 Dean Jeremiah Milles, D.D., and Dr. Pococke... travelled in company through France, Switzerland, Italy, Belgium, Holland, Hanover, Prussia, Austria, Greece, etc.".[17] More often, though, Milles' presence on the second tour of the Continent is completely overlooked.[18]

For the purposes of this book, which constitutes an edition of the combined and hitherto unpublished correspondence of these two travellers,[19] the eastern voyage is regarded as a third

---

[15]For purposes of simplification, and in order to differentiate them from all the other individuals with similar and sometimes identical names, the two travellers, who were known variously by the titles *Mr. Rev., Dr., Bishop, Archdeacon and Dean*, will be referred to henceforth as "Pococke" and "Milles", unless appearing as part of a quotation

[16]His fame was sealed by his publication of his "pioneering" book, *A Description of the East and of some other Countries, Vol. I, Observations on Egypt* (London 1743) & *A Description of the East and of some other Countries, Vol. II.1 Observations on Palaestina or the Holy Land, Syria, Mesopotamia, Cyprus and Candia; Vol. II. 2: Observations on the islands of the Archipelago, Asia Minor, Thrace, Greece, and some other parts of Europe* (London, 1745). Henceforth this book shall be abbreviated to *A Description of the East*, Vol. 1, 2 or 3

[17]*Tours in Scotland 1747, 1750, 1760, 1747, 1750, 1760* (Edinburgh, 1887; reprinted Maryland, 2003) xxxvi

[18]See, for instance, Ingamells (*op.cit.*), whose entries for Richard Pococke (779-80) and Jeremiah Milles (662) suggest that the second tour (1736 onwards) was undertaken by Pococke alone

[19]While the Milles/Pococke travel correspondence has never been published as a whole, either with or without the accompanying travel journals, two single letters from Pococke to his mother, and numerous brief excerpts from the

Grand Tour. As described below, the correspondence reproduced in this edition is supplemented by the extensive collections of unpublished journals also produced by Milles and Pococke during the course of their foreign travels.

Of English birth, and educated in England, both began their ecclesiastical careers (including ordination) in Ireland under the patronage of their uncle, Thomas Milles, Bishop of Waterford & Lismore (1671-1740).[20] While Milles returned to England after inheriting the bishop's estate, Pococke was to spend the remainder of his working life in Ireland and was dubbed, by one of his Victorian biographers, "an Englishman by birth, and an Irishman by adoption".[21] Both men were to become prominent in their clerical careers (Pococke being appointed successively as Bishop of Ossory, Elphin and Meath, and Milles as Dean of Exeter), and though eventually settling in different countries, the cousins maintained contact with each other throughout their lives, particularly in matters relating to their mutual passion for antiquity, church history and architecture. Furthermore, they

---

same source have appeared in print. James Joel Cartwright (ed.), in the preface to his book, *The Travels through England of Dr. Richard Pococke, successively Bishop of Meath and of Ossory during 1750, 1751, and later Years* (London, Camden Society, 1888-89) prints two letters from Pococke to his mother: the first was sent from Holyhead (13 July, 1734), at the end of their first Grand Tour and just as they were about to return to Ireland (see ii); and the second was sent from Dover (23 May, 1736), just before they departed from England on their second Grand Tour (see vii-xi). These two letters are reproduced (without Cartwright's errors) in the current edition. Curiously, and for no obvious reason, the former is also reproduced in Michael Quane, "Pococke School, Kilkenny", *The Journal of the Royal Society of Antiquaries of Ireland*, 80 (1950), Plate VII, facing p.43. Two other writers who include in their books brief excerpts from Pococke's letters (but not those of Jeremiah Milles) are Ingamells (*op.cit.*) and Jeremy Black. The latter uses these passages, in his seminal works on the Grand Tour, as examples to illustrate various aspects of foreign travel during the eighteenth century, rather than to provide the reader with a comprehensive account of Pococke's travels. A further writer who reproduces short extracts from five letters from Milles to his uncle (from June and July, 1737) is Catherine D. Carmichael, "Two Gentlemen Travelers in the Slovene Lands in 1737", in *Slovene Studies* 13/1 (1992) 19-26

[20]Henceforth, except in the section *Life of Bishop Thomas Milles (1697-1740)*, his name will be abbreviated to "Bishop Milles" or "the bishop"

[21]See Kemp, *op.cit.*, xxxi

became founding members of, and held offices, in the same clubs and learned societies in London (including the Egyptian Club and the Divan Club),[22] co-writing at least one scholarly work.[23] While neither Milles nor Pococke appear to have undertaken any further travels abroad, the latter is recognised as a notable traveller in Ireland, England and Scotland, though his accounts of these travels were not published until long after his death.[24]

Practicalities of the 1733-34 Tour

Milles does not refer, in any of his correspondence or memoirs, to his reasons for embarking on a Grand Tour, though of course it was by then a well established convention for such a voyage to be undertaken by young men of the upper classes as a means of completing their education, and in particular experiencing first-hand the wonders of the classical world. Clearly this was Milles' first opportunity for doing so, since he had only just graduated from Oxford with a BA, and was a mere nineteen years of age. Coincidentally, Pococke, at the time almost thirty, and therefore considerably older than was customary, had also just completed his studies at Oxford, on 28 June, 1733. Their travels began two months later, thus leaving very little time for preparations, which in Pococke's case possibly contributed to the financial difficulties he encountered while abroad. In his first letter to his mother after departing from England (Calais, 28 August, 1733), Pococke apologises for causing her anxiety on account of the journey he and Milles are about to take, and

---

[22]For further details on their membership of clubs, see R. Finnegan, "The Divan Club: an Eighteenth-Century Club for Travellers to the Ottoman Empire", in *Electronic Journal of Oriental Studies* IX (2006) 1-86

[23]*Inscriptionum Antiquarum Liber Alter - a supplement to Pococke's Inscriptionum Antiquarum Graec. et Latin. Liber* (1752)

[24]See Kemp, *op.cit.*; Cartwright, *op.cit.*, Rev. George Thomas Stokes (ed.), *Pococke's Tour in Ireland in 1753* (1891); Christopher J. Woods, "Pococke's Journey through County Down in 1760", in *Ulster Journal of Archaeology*, Vol. 48 (1985) 113-15; and John McVeagh, *Richard Pococke's Irish Tours* (Irish Academic Press, 1995) comprising an edition of all his tours in Ireland, including the previously unedited one through Connaught and Munster 1749. See also John McVeagh, '"Romantick" Ireland: Pococke's tour of Cork and Kerry, 1758', in *Éire-Ireland*, 25:2 (1990) 69–95

assures her that it "is undertaken for the improvement of ourselves, which is a good design & the same providence will I don't doubt, take care of us a broad, that would protect us at home..."[25] Unless this is false modesty on Pococke's part, it appears that the two were travelling as companions and equals, rather than according to the usual pupil/chaperone arrangement. Pococke even jokes about this unorthodox situation in the second letter to his mother, where he notes, "My pupil is very well, for I have been already taken for his preceptor".[26] Nevertheless, Pococke was highly educated, having graduated from Christ Church College, Oxford with a BA (1725), a BCL (1731) and a DCL (1733), and his sober character (for which he was noted, somewhat disparagingly, in later life) and good family connections would have made him an eminently suitable travelling companion for his younger relative.[27]

Though there is no record of Pococke having previously left the British Isles (which may have left his practical experience of foreign travel somewhat wanting), it is clear from the contents of his library that he owned a considerable amount of literature relevant to his intended travels.[28] The fact that the publication date of many of these volumes pre-dates or is concurrent with their first trip (1733-34) suggests that he had made some attempt to research the various cities and sites they were to visit on the Continent. Equally, he may well have set out armed with this literature, while some volumes, especially those published abroad, were certainly acquired during his travels.[29] He possessed, for example, numerous histories, "descriptions", travelogues and other works concerning the geography,

---

[25]Letter 1. British Library, Add. 22978. Henceforth, all British Library manuscript sources referred to in this book are abbreviated to Add, etc.

[26]Calais, 1-12 September, 1733. Add. 22978

[27]On the subject of agreeable companions, governors and tutors, see Richard Twiss, *A Tour in Ireland in 1775* (London, 1776) 177-80

[28]See L. Flin, *A Catalogue of the Library of the late Right Revd. Dr. Richard Pococke, Lord Bishop of Meath deceased* (Dublin, 1766). Henceforth this will be abbreviated to *A Catalogue of the Library*

[29]For example, when questioned by nuns in a church in Venice about the book on paintings they had with them, Pococke notes, "we buy such an one at almost every great city" (Letter 21. Add. 22978); and the pair regularly visited the book-sellers

architecture and antiquities of Italy, France, Germany and Hungary, together with various practical aids such as dictionaries, grammars and maps.

It appears that he was also academically prepared for his later eastern trip, since he had acquired similar literature relating to the East, including *Trotsii Lexicon Syriacum* (1645), an Arabic Grammar (undated), a Turkish Lexicon (1730), a Turkish Grammar (1729), a Thesaurus of ancient and modern Armenian language (1660), and a book entitled *Paradigmata de Ling. Arab. Armena, Syra, Athiop* (1660).[30] These, together with the rest of his collection of books, are listed in the sale catalogue of his library which (contrary to his Will, stipulating that they should be sold in London as they "will not sell here According to a just value"),[31] were actually sold by auction from "his late Dwelling-House in Henrietta Street", Dublin, on 10 March, 1766, from mid-day, "and to be Continued every Day until all are Sold".[32]

It is obvious from his occasional requests for money, promises to account for how he had spent it, and gratitude for having received "orders", that the young Milles obtained funding (at least for his first voyage) from the bishop who, being unmarried, and without children of his own, had already put his favourite nephew and future heir through Eton and Oxford. Milles responded to his uncle's generous patronage (and perhaps hoped to acquire more favours from him) by writing him numerous lengthy and very regular letters from abroad. The tone of these letters was formal yet solicitous, and reflected the gratitude he felt for his uncle's kind attentions to him. He also performed some useful services for his uncle from abroad. As is documented in several letters, both he and Pococke undertook to seek out, purchase and arrange for the binding, packing and dispatch of various scholarly books, at the bishop's request.

---

[30]For a detailed analysis of an Anglo-Irish traveller's private library, see R. Finnegan, "The Library of William Ponsonby, 2nd Earl of Bessborough, 1704-93", in *Hermathena*, No. 181 (Winter 2006) 149-87

[31]National Library of Ireland, Manuscript: D. 27, 161

[32]Pococke's *A Catalogue of the Library, op.cit.*, cover page

A theme that frequently emerged in Pococke's correspondence from the first tour was his lack of money.[33] While, by his own admission, he had a very good income from the Waterford diocese, and was owed the sum of £500, his funds were for some reason (perhaps, he suggests, through malice) being withheld from him. Nor did his bankers (Mr. Hoare in London and Mr. Bagwell in Clonmel) appear to be capable of sorting this out. As a result, he was forced to borrow from his cousin and seek favours from his ever obliging mother. Even without her generosity (though he made it clear that he would pay her back), his travel money had to be managed, and in many of his letters from abroad Pococke instructed his mother on how to arrange his finances, where to send "orders" and what messages to give to his bankers. Indeed, an important feature of the closing comments of numerous letters (as is common in other Grand Tour correspondence),[34] was to give a forwarding address for each new destination. He also, as we shall see in the correspondence, instructed his mother on how to deal with his personal effects, particularly towards the end of his first tour. Boxes of books, maps, etc., sent from Paris to London had to be shipped on to Waterford, and items such as cassocks, gowns, sermons and wigs, which he had stored at his mother's house while abroad, had to be sent to London for him to collect on his way back to Ireland.

Sources & Transmission of the Texts

We are fortunate both in the extent and variety of the primary sources for Pococke and Milles' continental and eastern travels. The documentary evidence spans an extensive collection of correspondence and numerous illustrated manuscript journals assiduously kept by each traveller. All of these manuscripts are

---

[33]This is not generally known since, as outlined below, passages concerning such details were deleted from the better-known copies of the correspondence and exist only in the more obscure originals

[34]Such as those of a contemporary English Grand Tourist, Rev. Joseph Spence, who undertook three Grand Tours with three different pupils in the years 1731-33, 1737-38 and 1739-41, while Professor of Poetry at Oxford. Like Pococke (whom he met in Rome during his third tour), he addressed the bulk of his letters to his mother. See S. Klima (ed.), *Letters from the Grand Tour* (Montreal & London, 1975)

housed in the British Library, with the exception of three original letters from the first Grand Tour (Milles to the bishop), which are located in the Gloucestershire Archives.[35] The focus of the present edition is the correspondence, which comprises several almost complete collections of detailed and very regular travel letters from Pococke to his mother, who resided in the parish of Newtown, near Southampton; from Pococke to his uncle, Bishop Milles, who occupied the Episcopal House in Waterford;[36] and from Milles to the same uncle. Though the travel journals are important in their own right, they are used here largely for comparative purposes and to supplement information where gaps in the correspondence occur, or where they provide additional points of interest. While these generally appear in footnotes, some larger passages from the journals (such as the pair's first impressions of Venice and Milles' essay on the character of the Italian people) are incorporated into the text itself.

The manuscript sources for the correspondence discussed and reproduced in Volume 1 are as follows:[37] a collection of three letters from Milles to the bishop (originals), dated 13/22 May, 1734, 15/26 May, 1734 and 30 May/10 June, 1734;[38] a collection of twenty-seven letters from Milles to the bishop (copies), covering the period 31 August, 1773 to 12/23 June, 1734;[39] a collection of fourteen letters from Pococke to his mother (originals), covering the period 10 December, 1733 to 13 July, 1734 (two of which do not appear in the volume of copies);[40] and

---

[35]Ref. D2663/Z8

[36]These relate to the second and third tours

[37]A complete listing appears in the manuscript section of the Bibliography

[38]Gloucestershire Archives, Ref. D2663/Z8. These letters were deposited in the archive by Gloucestershire County Library, 14 July 1971, originally from a collection belonging to Ernest Dixon Hartland, FSA (d.1931) and given to Gloucestershire County Library in 1936 by his widow, Mrs. Amy Georgina Hartland of Hardwicke Court, Chepstow

[39]Add. 15773. This totals 114 pages in the original form of pagination, which has been amended by an editor (presumably Milles himself) to 80 folios.

[40]Add. 19939. This manuscript also includes original letters from Pococke to his mother from the second tour (to be considered in Volume 2). It should be noted that the pagination for many of the sources (including those for the second tour) is problematic, in that the original numbering of the pages, applied by those who produced the copies, has subsequently been amended by an editor, causing a double pagination system. In order to avoid

a collection of twenty-two letters from Pococke to his mother (copies), covering the period 28 August, 1733 to 30 June, 1734.[41] The manuscript sources for the travel journals for Volume 1, all originals compiled in quarto volumes in very neat script, are as follows: three volumes by Jeremiah Milles: "An acct of some remarkable places between Paris, & Rome" (15 October, 1733 to 16 January, 1734);[42] "An Acct of My journey from Rome, to Venice" (11 May, 1734 to 13 June, 1734);[43] and "An Account of what I saw Remarkable between Venice & London";[44] and five volumes by Richard Pococke: "Travels Volume II From Antibes in France To Rome" (3 December, 1733 to 22 January, 1734);[45] "Travels Vol III Being A Description of Rome";[46] "Travels Vol

---

confusion, page numbers will not be used in citing letters - the place, date, and author being sufficient to identify the letter in question

[41] Add. 22978. The last letter in this series is from Dover and therefore has the simple O.S. date. In the same way that Milles has amended the pagination in the copies of his letters (see Note 6 above), an editor (presumably Pococke himself) has occasionally amended the pagination of these letters. The original number of pages is 164, amended to 93 quarto pages

[42] Add. 15762. A note on the cover states, "J: Milles bought at Paris October ye 12th 1733", for the price of 2 Livres. It also gives the dates at which he began and finished the volume. The journal is 213 pages in length and contains several prints of places visited. As with the letters, the pagination in the journals is invariably problematic, with a dual system in place. When cited, page numbers for the journals will be given, the preference being for the unedited pagination - that is, the one that has not been crossed out by the original editor

[43] Add. 15763. A note on the cover states, "Milles May ye 7th 1734 comprato in Roma prezo 3 pauli 7 Barocchi & mezza; Sapere aude... begun May 7e 11th finished June ye 13th 1734. The journal contains 131 pages of text

[44] Add. 60516. A note on the cover states, "J. Milles 1734 bought in Venice price 2 Livres 7 soldi. This volume consists of 130 pages of text with several prints illustrating places they visited. This volume, which continues up until their arrival in Dover (1 July, 1734), is a particularly important source as it fills a gap in the correspondence for Milles, whose last extant letter is dated June, 1734

[45] Add. 22979. This volume contains 114 pages of text and several prints

[46] Add. 22980. This is a very long manuscript of 226 pages, though containing only two or three printed illustrations. It differs from the earlier note-books in that it does not run like a journal, but is a volume arranged in seven thematic chapters, as follows: 1." Of Antient Rome according to it's Regions"; 2. "Of the Gates of Rome"; 3. "Of the Aqueducts of Rome"; 4. "Of the Bridges over the Tiber"; 5. "Of the Churches of Rome and First of St Peters"; 6. "Of The other Churches of Rome; 7. "Of the Palaces in

IV of The Places near Rome";[47] "Travels Vol. V. From Rome To Milan" (11-21 June, 1734);[48] and "Travels Vol VI Milan & from Milan to France" (21 June, 1734 to 1 July, 1734).[49]

We are again fortunate in the condition in which much of the correspondence has survived, since fair copies were made of most of the letters. The copies of letters sent to the bishop (by Milles in the first tour and by both nephews for their subsequent journeys) are composed in the same large neat hand, presumably that of a secretary or clerk,[50] and preserved in the form of large folio volumes.[51] Those sent to Mrs. Pococke by her son, both from the Continent and from the East, were neatly transcribed by her into several quarto volumes. In addition, she composed some of the letters into their present journal format,[52] with the date of entry being given for each section.[53] Pococke did not bother writing to his uncle on the first tour. In a letter sent from Paris, 25 September/6 October, 1733, Milles informed the bishop, "Dr. Pococke thinks it will be unnecessary for him to write any account at present to your Ldship, because I shall do that, but that he writes a full account to Newtown, wch he afterwards intends to copy out into a book when he returns home, whch at present he

---

Rome"; and 8. "Of the Piazzas, Fountains and some other Modern Works in Rome"

[47]Add. 22981. This is 77 pages, with no illustrations and, as with Vol. III, is divided into four thematic chapters, as follows: 1. "Of Things remarkable without the walls, & in the roads to Rome"; 2. "Of the Villas about Rome"; 3. "Of Tivoli, Prieneste, Frascati, Albano, & Places near them"; 4. "Of Porto Ostia, & the Places in the roads to Them"

[48]Add. 22982. This manuscript, which is 175 pages in length and contains a few prints, returns to the journal format, though the dates are difficult to make out as the author does not highlight them or included them in the margins. The date of arrival in Milan is not mentioned, though we know from the following volume that they reached this city on Monday, 21 June, 1734

[49]Add. 22983. This small volume, consisting of only 56 pages, covers a period of eleven days. Again, Pococke is not good about entering dates, but we know from the correspondence when they arrived in France

[50]The handwriting does not correspond with that of the bishop's letter to Mrs. Pococke, reproduced in Appendix 2

[51]In the British Library catalogue they are described as "Registers of Letters"

[52]From Letter 11 onwards in Add. 22978

[53]In the originals the text is completely free flowing, presumably because it was quicker and saved space

has not time to do."[54] Presumably he did not find time to do this on his return, which is why his mother ended up doing it for him.

Internal evidence gives some indication of when the copy letters were made. We know when Mrs. Pococke compiled the first volume of her son's letters since she made a note of the start and end date on the manuscript itself. Though this is not immediately obvious, being written in tiny script at the corner of the first and last page, it is clear that the neat quarto volume from the first tour (1733-34) was put together between 25 October and 25 November, 1745. This occurred more than a decade after his return from the first tour, four years after his return from the East, and immediately following the printing of *A Description of the East*. Internal evidence from Milles' correspondence suggests that the bishop had copies made as he went along. He advises his uncle in a letter from the second tour (1736-37), for example, "It will be better that this & the following letters be not transcribed till I have drawn out a perfect [account] of Venice for your Lordship."[55]

All of the letters reproduced in the present volume (both of Pococke and Milles), together with the journals, bear evidence of subsequent editing in the original author's hand. This includes the addition of page numbers, marginal notes, brackets, minor amendments, and comments written on the back of the pages. Furthermore, numerous words, lines and in some cases whole passages from Mrs. Pococke's copy letters have later been scored out with heavy black wavy lines, some to such an extent that the script on the previous and following pages of the manuscript have been obliterated by the ink. Bound into the folio volumes of Milles' letters and the journals of both writers are occasional pages from printed books (including Pococke's own publication) with maps, views and other illustrations relevant to the places they visited.[56]

---

[54]Add. 15773

[55]Letter from Treviso, 22 August/2 September, 1737 (Add. 15774). These are discussed in Volume 2 of this edition

[56]Some interesting examples appear in Milles' correspondence from the second tour (1736-37), where he inserts plates depicting Italian monuments from his cousin's book, noting underneath that these prints were taken from his original drawings. These letters and the implications of such comments are further considered in Volume 2

The above all suggest that each traveller had, at some time during his life, intended to publish his Grand Tour correspondence and/or journals. It is not clear when Pococke made his own amendments to the three volumes of letters transcribed by his mother (one for each of the three tours), but clearly something put him off the idea of printing his memoirs. The scathing attacks he sustained from rival travel writers on the East (namely Dr. Shaw and Dr. Perry)[57] may possibly have deterred him from publishing anything further on the subject. As noted by the English dramatist Richard Cumberland, who had encountered Bishop Pococke in later life, "That celebrated oriental traveller and author was a man of mild manners and primitive simplicity: having given the world a full detail of his researches in Egypt, he seemed to hold himself excused from saying anything more about it and observed an obdurate simplicity.[58]

The transmission of Pococke's manuscripts can be partially explained. In his Will, dated 10 July, 1763, Pococke stated: "I do leave all my manuscripts to the Ratcliffe Liberary [sic] in Oxford".[59] However, in a Codicil to this Will, of 24 March, 1765 (drawn up just six months before his death), he revoked this bequest, stating, "I do leave all my manuscripts to the British Museum [sic] in London to the Governors and Trustees thereof".[60] No reason is given for this change of mind,[61] but his biographer notes, perhaps with a certain amount of disdain: "Very many volumes of MSS. which ought to have been delivered to the museum were withheld, and for a couple of

---

[57]Discussed in Volume 3 of this edition
[58]Richard Cumberland, *Memoirs of Richard Cumberland written by Himself, containing an Account of his Life and Writings, interspersed with Anecdotes and Characters of several of the most distinguished Persons of his Time, with whom he has had Intercourse and Connexion* (London, 1806-7) 121
[59]NLI, D. 27, 161. Original underscoring
[60]*Ibid.*
[61]Kemp (*op.cit.*, lxviii-lxix) has the following to say on this matter: "Bishop Pococke probably appraised his literary legacy to the nation even at a higher value than his material wealth. It was his own, his life's work - had cost him much time and money, fatigue and hardship - was the product of untold labours and sacrifices. No wonder, then, that he thought the only fitting resting place for his MSS. was alongside similar literary treasures in our greatest national library - in the hope that one day they might be of value, and we are only now waking up to appreciate the gift."

generations remained private property; but subsequently some of them, as they were offered for sale, were purchased by the British Museum Library authorities [and] bought at the sale of Dean Milles' library at Sotheby's so lately as the 15th April, 1843, for £33".[62] It is not known how the material came to be in Milles' possession (especially when was not mentioned in Pococke's Will),[63] but it is conceivable that when appointed as President of the Royal Society of Antiquaries in 1769, at which point he automatically became an official trustee of the British Museum,[64] he appropriated his late cousin's manuscripts for his own use. He then sat on them for the rest of his life and they were eventually sold by his heirs.

In relation to the transcripts of his own travel letters, it must be assumed that Milles either reclaimed these on his return to Waterford, or inherited them on his uncle's death. However, his failure to publish these in the early days could be put down to an increasing lack of leisure time. As soon as he returned from the first tour he was launched straight into a church career in Ireland, and on his return from the second, took on greater responsibilities, including caring for the ailing bishop. Following the latter's death three years later (in 1740), and finding himself now a very rich man, Milles began a new life in England with a more ambitious career, as well as a family. It is possible that he had planned to produce an edition of his travels in later life, but found that his increasing involvement in the Royal Society of Antiquaries and related scholarly activities left him little time to pursue what may eventually have proven to be a lost remnant of his youth.

---

[62]Kemp, *op.cit.*, lxvi. The manuscript volume of copy letters to Mrs. Pococke (Add. 22978), as noted on its cover, "Purchased at Mr Dawson Turner's sale 9th June 1859. Lot 387". In fact, an extensive collection of manuscripts from Add. 22878-23125 is listed, in the British Library Catalogue as having been acquired through this source

[63]Pococke names the Incorporated Society in Dublin as the executors of his Will. However, the catalogue of the British Library describes his executor as Jeremiah Milles, who transmitted the Pococke Collection to the Library on 5 June, 1767

[64]By an act of Parliament, King George V declared that the President of this society should be a temporary trustee of the museum

Scope and Format of this Edition

As already noted, the combined manuscript source material for the Milles/Pococke Grand Tours is extensive, and a full edition of the entire collection (including the journals of both travellers), though a huge undertaking, would be a most welcome addition to this important area of scholarship.[65] The scope of this edition is less ambitious and is based on edited letters from all the collections of correspondence, with supplementary material being provided by the travel journals. Nor does this edition constitute a comparative analysis between the Milles/Pococke travels and those of other Grand Tourists of the period, or between Pococke's travels in Ireland, Scotland and England.[66] Its purpose is to introduce the reader to a series of wonderfully detailed and engaging memoirs of two very interesting and famous individuals who were not only compatible travelling companions but were passionate about their foreign experiences both when abroad (as is evident from their travelogues) and for many years after their return.

Volume 1 of this edition reproduces extracts from forty-six out of the surviving fifty-three letters from the cousins' first tour of the Continent (1733-34),[67] which was cut short after ten months, when Milles was persuaded to hasten to Ireland to take up a preferment in his uncle's diocese; Volume 2 reproduces letters from their second tour of the Continent (1736-37), up to the point at which Milles was again obliged to return to Ireland, this time on account of his uncle's failing health; and Volume 3, reproduces letters from Pococke's continued travels to the East, and begins with his arrival at Leghorn. Chapter 1 of Volume 1 provides biographical accounts of the four main characters in this

---

[65]However, such a study would inevitably involve considerable levels of repetition and overlap, which might prove tedious for the general reader

[66]Such considerations would be a worthy subject for a PhD thesis. Nevertheless, it must be said that there are obvious similarities between all Pococke's letters to his mother, particularly his tendency to "name dropping"

[67]Of the twenty-two copy letters from Pococke to his mother, eighteen are reproduced (or partially reproduced) in the text, with extracts from a further two appearing in footnotes. In addition, two originals (Letters 21A & 22A), which do not appear in the copies, are reproduced in full. Of the twenty-seven letters from Milles to the bishop, twenty-two are reproduced (or partially reproduced) in the text

story, namely the two authors (Richard Pococke and Jeremiah Milles) and the two recipients of the letters (Mrs. Elizabeth Pococke and her older brother, Bishop Thomas Milles). Chapter 2 outlines the course of the first Grand Tour (1733-34) and discusses some of the conventions used by the correspondents in composing their letters.[68] Chapter 3 reproduces letters from the first part of the 1733-34 tour, dispatched from England and France. Chapter 4 reproduces correspondence from their extensive sojourn in Italy, mainly Rome, where they stayed for a period of four months. Chapter 5 reproduces letters from the point at which they left Rome, tracing the final weeks of their tour and return journey; and includes the transcript of a lengthy treatise written by Milles on the general character of the Italians.[69] Finally, there are three Appendices, the first being a transcript of Bishop Milles' Last Will & Testament, the second being transcripts of two family letters; and the third being a list of letters reproduce in this volume. An Index of Selected People & Places appears at the end.[70]

Editing of the Texts

When working on such a large collection of correspondence, the editor must decide which letters to include and which to omit. This is a difficult decision to make, since each letter has its own merits, and the integrity of the collection must be retained. The selection process undertaken in Volume 1 is based on a number of factors. Most importantly, the editor has attempted to give equal voice to each of the correspondents, both of whom wrote assiduously to their relatives. While frequently dispatching letters in the same post, and describing the same places, the two writers generally produced completely different accounts, the difference perhaps being attributable to their relationship with the recipient. Letters from Milles to the bishop,

---

[68]This includes an explanation of the dual system of dating used in letters on account of the new calendar

[69]This appears in his journal entitled "An Account of what I saw Remarkable between Venice & London", Add. 60516, pp 58-80

[70]This relates primarily to the countries, towns and villages mentioned in the text and to the families and associates of Milles & Pococke. It does not include buildings, monuments, mythological or historical figures

for instance, are typically composed of long, scholarly and detailed descriptions of monuments, inscriptions and ecclesiastical buildings (such as would have been appreciated and expected by his uncle) and contain little in the way of informal chat. References to personal or family matters are very rare, except when he is seeking money from the bishop or referring to purchases of books made on his behalf.

By contrast, the letters from Pococke to his mother are full of interesting gossip both about the characters they have met during their travels (especially other Grand Tourists, local nobility and senior members of the Roman Catholic Church), and on family and other matters from home. He dwells on subjects he imagines will entertain his mother, such as food, wine, fashions, plants, gardens and religion, and comments on the more practical aspects of travel such as the quality of the accommodation, the cost of meals and his over-burdening financial problems. At the same time, despite regaling her with snippets of news about the political crisis on the Continent,[71] and the dangers they encounter on their travels, he endeavours to assure her of his safety and his imminent return to England. Though he does give accounts of the various buildings and areas visited, such descriptions are generally far less elaborate than those of his younger cousin who is eager to impress his scholarly uncle and patron, the bishop.

The sequence adopted in Volume for Chapters 3 and 4 in the current volume,[72] is generally (though not always) to reproduce alternately letters from Milles and Pococke, with at least one letter being reproduced from each of the cities visited. However, in centres like Rome, where the travellers stayed for long periods of time, several letters are reproduced, either in whole or in part. In addition, where two letters (one from each writer) describe similar places or events, the editor uses footnotes to draw attention to any interesting details provided in the alternative account. In general, where an exceptionally long letters details a number of different sites or monuments, the editor

---

[71]The War of the Polish Succession, which began in late 1733 and continued until 1735, involved major hostilities in Italy and Rhineland, causing many Grand Tourists to alter their travel plans. See Jeremy Black (*op.cit.*, 1992/2003), Chapter 7 (War, Disputes, Accidents and Crime)
[72]Though a different sequence is adopted in Chapter 5

omits those commonly found in other Grand Tour literature and concentrates on more unusual examples. Since letters from Milles contain very few personal asides, the editor has endeavoured to include as many of these as possible, particularly those which inform the reader of the unfolding relationship between the young man and his patron.

The editor's preference for basing the transcripts on the copies of letters, rather than the originals, is based on necessity as well as on various practical considerations. First of all, there are very few original letters in the collection, with only three out of twenty-seven existing from the Milles correspondence and twelve out of twenty-two from the Pococke correspondence.[73] Secondly, the copies made by Mrs. Pococke and Bishop Milles (or rather his scribe) are infinitely more legible than the originals, which are hastily dashed out in erratic and minute script, with virtually no spaces between the lines and, on top of that, full of subsequent additions, crossings out, holes and blotches of ink.

The originals are of course consulted whenever there is doubt or confusion about the spelling or meaning of words or phrases. In cases where a word is missing or in some way obscured (and cannot be deciphered from the original), the most likely word for the context is included in square brackets. Likewise, the editor occasionally notes, in square brackets, where words or lines have been scored out (a frequent occurrence in the copy letters from Pococke to his mother), and where possible the missing text is reproduced from the original. The deleted passages are generally on personal matters such as Pococke's financial problems, the inadequacies of his bankers, his uncle's failing health, an errant relative and his own sartorial taste; and it is understandable why a man of his standing took the decision in later life to remove such sensitive or embarrassing passages from the pages of these manuscripts. However, he failed to remove them from the originals, which is fortunate for us, since they frequently betray a side to Pococke not evident in the edited texts. We learn, from these deletions, about the cost of a floral silk suit purchased in Rome, his instructions to a wig maker for a new

---

[73]While there are 14 relevant letters in the collection of originals, only 12 correspond with the copies, the remaining two being letters that were never copied out by Mrs Pococke

wig, his fondness for his sister Elizabeth, news from Trinity College Dublin that an earl's son is in prison for shooting a Fellow, and his belief that there is enmity or malice towards him in Ireland. Such details help us to build up a more complete picture a man who has suffered so much throughout history from having been labelled "the dullest man that ever travelled".[74]

In common with the modern edition of Pococke's Irish tours,[75] the editor has retained the original spelling and punctuation throughout, where necessary using footnotes to explain any irregularities or details that might confuse the reader, such as the variety of different spellings used for surnames (whether English, Irish or foreign) and place-names, even within the same piece.[76] Wherever passages from original letters are used to replace missing lines or paragraphs, there is a noticeable change in style. This is because the originals contain numerous abbreviations and variations of small words, which for the most part have been laboriously corrected by Mrs. Pococke. In the case of the journals, the manuscripts are the originals and are therefore full of abbreviations and other irregularities, such as Milles' frequent failure to start sentences with a capital letter. However, unlike the original letters from both travellers, which show evidence of having been written in great haste, the journals, composed at leisure, are neat and a pleasure to read.

Finally, notes are provided where it is thought that the reader may benefit from an explanation of historical, geographical and topographical points arising from the letters, or on the identity of people encountered during the course of the travels.

---

[74] The famous comment of Mrs. Delany, see Chapter 1, below

[75] John McVeagh (1995) *op.cit.*

[76] Examples of words consistently misspelled (or at least written in a style that might be unfamiliar to the modern reader) are: "preist", "peice", "beleive", "cheif", "compleat", "plaister", "bas-releive", "minuit", "chappel", "beautifull", "dutifull", "lye" (for "lie"), "strait", "shew" (for "show"), "heigth", and the frequent use of "then" instead of "than" and "writ" or "wrote" instead of "written". Common abbreviations, found particularly in the original letters and the journals, include, "yt" ("that"), "ye" ("the"), "yn" ("than"), "wch" ("which"), "wt" ("what"), "Bp." ("Bishop"), "K:", (King"), "V" ("Virgin"), "A:B:" ("Archbishop"), "Xtmas" or "Xtian" (for "Christmas" or "Christian") and "Sr" ("Sir"). It should also be noted that Milles, in his journals, very rarely follows a full-stop with a capital letter

CHAPTER 1

Biographical Accounts of the Pococke & Milles Families

Life of Mrs. Elizabeth Pococke (?-1760)

We begin the biographical accounts with a consideration of the life of Mrs. Elizabeth Pococke and her family. She is a central figure in this story, since she was not only the mother of Pococke, but also the sister of Bishop Milles and therefore Jeremiah (the traveller's) aunt. She was, as we shall see, a true matriarch, always involved in the affairs of the Milles/Pococke family, and retaining this role by correspondence even when separated from its members by long distances. At the time of the cousins' first trip to the Continent, she had been widowed for thirty-three years and was living with her unmarried daughter Elizabeth ("Besse") in the parish of Newtown, in the extreme north-west corner of Hampshire, bordering with Berkshire.

The year of her birth is not known but she was certainly an only daughter of Rev. Isaac Milles and Elizabeth Luckin (who were married in 1670) and the youngest in the family. The last of her brothers (Isaac) was born in 1676/77, which places her date of birth somewhere between 1679 and 82, making her between the age of sixteen and nineteen at her own marriage, in 1698. In 1680 her father was nominated by the lord of the manor, Robert Sawyer, as rector to the Highclere Parish,[1] a position which he retained until his death in 1720. In addition, Rev. Milles ran, with his youngest son Isaac, a small private boarding school in the rectory, whose pupils included not only his own sons, but

---

[1] The position became vacant on the death of Rev. Christopher Massey, who was buried on 9 November of that year. See "Extracts from Parish Registers of Highclere", in J. Gough Nichols, *The Topographer and Genealogist*, Volume 1 (London, 1846) 409

those of Thomas Herbert, 8th Earl of Pembroke and 5th Earl of Montgomery.[2]

Sadly, we know virtually nothing about Mrs. Pococke's early life, but on 26 April, 1698, presumably in her late teens, she married Rev. Richard Pococke (1660-1710), the eldest son of yet another Rev. Richard Pococke (Rector of Colmer, in Hampshire) and his wife Constance (née) Newlin. Educated at Magdalen College, Oxford, and ordained as Deacon in 1689 and Priest in 1690, this was his second marriage, his first wife Anne Clutterbuck (daughter of the Archdeacon of Winchester) having lasted only a year (1695-96), owing to her premature death. Since 1690 her husband, Rev. Pococke, had held the position of Headmaster of King Edward VI School (depicted in Plate 1), a free grammar school in Southampton, and in 1694 he was appointed Curate Sequestrator of All Saints' Church, also in Southampton, a curacy he retained until 24 August, 1708.

Plate 1
"Grammar School at Southampton"
Sixty Views of Endowed Schools: From Original Drawings by J.C. Buckler
(London, 1827)

---

[2]One of these sons, the 9th Earl, was to be an important patron of the family, and Pococke dedicated Volume I of his *A Description of the East* to him

The town of Highclere, where the young Elizabeth had grown up, was only about thirty miles from Southampton, and it is likely that she and her future husband had met through her father, since both were clergymen in the same diocese (Winchester) and both were educationalists. Clerical circles within such close proximity would have encouraged such marital opportunities, and judging from the amount of clergymen in both families (together with Rev. Pococke's previous choice of matrimony), theirs would have been considered an ideal match.[3]

In addition to the social implications of such a marriage were the financial benefits, at least for Rev. Pococke, since Elizabeth Milles brought with her a fortune of almost £1,000. It is thought that such an amount could not have come entirely from her father, Rev. Milles, with his relatively small income, but was possibly a joint contribution from his brothers, one of whom was a successful tradesman.[4] This dowry would have greatly enhanced Rev. Pococke's prospects and reputation, since he is described by an anonymous author as: "a Man of great Worth and Integrity, but who was very unsuitably provided for".[5] The authorship of the lengthy biography from which this is cited is problematic.[6] Though traditionally attributed to the subject's eldest son, Bishop Thomas Milles,[7] a copy in the Thorold and Lyttelton Library at Winchester has a hand-written note on the title page: "Said to have been written by Mrs Pococke, daughter of Isaac Milles."[8] While some sources admit that she had some

---

[3] In the same way Rev. Sam Billingsley, who had briefly been "under-master" at King Edward's in Rev. Pococke's time (c. 1696/98), subsequently married the latter's sister, Constance, after taking up a position as under-master of Christ's Hospital, in December, 1698

[4] See Kemp, *op.cit.* xxxi-ii

[5] Quoted in C. F. Russell, *A History of King Edward VI School Southampton* (Privately printed, 1940) 203

[6] *An Account of the Life and Conversation of the Reverend and Worthy Mr. Isaac Milles, late Rector of High Cleer in Hampshire*). This pamphlet, of almost 200 pages, was printed in London, 1721 and will henceforth be abbreviated *Life of Isaac Milles*

[7] Possibly because of its mildly disparagingly references to Mr. Henry Dodwell (pp 52-53), whom Thomas Milles, before becoming bishop, had attacked in print (1707). Other references are made to Dodwell. See, for example, 56ff

[8] See Russell, *op.cit.*, 203, n.1

hand in its authorship, but under the direction of her brother the bishop, the latest edition of the *Dictionary of National Biography* proposes that this pamphlet was in fact the work of a neighbouring clergyman, Joseph Wood, who had also composed the accompanying funeral sermon for the late Rev. Milles.[9] Given that Bishop Milles had been living in Waterford for thirteen years at his father's death, while Mrs. Pococke had nursed him through his last illness; and given that the pamphlet is based partly on his "Diary or Journal, now before me, which he then kept of his life",[10] and towards the end gives a very detailed and full account of this malady, there is no reason to doubt that Mrs. Pococke was the author. After all, she had been continually by her father's side in his last years, had access to his papers, was very pious, respected this virtue in members of her immediate family, and was not only highly literate but well versed in matters of the church.[11] Furthermore, the bishop was not given to modesty and would surely have made it known that he was responsible for this publication had he written it.

Quite apart from the question of its authorship, this is a fascinating publication which, among other matters of personal and family interest, gives details of the parsonage in Highclere and the renovations carried out on this house by Mrs. Pococke's father, "as to render it more commodious for the Reception of Boarders, and the teaching of a larger Number of Scholars." These improvements paid off, since, as mentioned earlier, the "illustrious" Earl of Pembroke "intrusted Mr. *Milles* with the Care of the Education of his sons."[12]

Details of the Pococke family's life are relatively sketchy, though we do know that their two children (Richard, the traveller, and his sister Elizabeth) were born and lived the first few years of their lives at West Hall, Bugle Street (see Plate 1). This was the

---

[9]See D. A. Brunton, *ODNB*. The latter source does not mention the possibility that Elizabeth Pococke may have written her father's biography, and in fact its only reference to this woman (whose name is omitted) is to note that during Rev. Milles' last days he was "tended by his daughter"

[10]*Life of Isaac Milles, op.cit.*, 23. There are other references to his Journal, see for example 43

[11]For evidence of these virtues and qualities, see Letter 2 in Appendix 2

[12]*Life of Isaac Milles, op.cit.*, 75-76

address of King Edward's, which suggests that the family had living quarters in the school. Some sources state that Pococke (the traveller) began his education at King Edward's, though his time there (if at all) would have been very brief, on account of his extreme youth. On 4 January, 1708, Mrs. Pococke's mother (Elizabeth Milles), about whom we know virtually nothing, apart from a few lines recording her female virtues,[13] was buried in Highclere Church. Dying from smallpox ("a Distemper, which she had been always afraid of"),[14] she left Rev. Milles a widow at the age of seventy. Two years later, in 1710, Rev. Pococke also died of smallpox, leaving Mrs. Pococke "a very *disconsolate* Widow",[15] and since they lived in tied accommodation, leaving her young family without a home.[16] She therefore left Southampton and returned to Highclere Rectory, where she was able to look after her elderly father and her brother Isaac, and where her young son could take up his studies at his grandfather's private school. This clearly was a mutually convenient arrangement, which continued to exist for the next ten years, until Rev. Milles himself died in 1720. His death (caused by a series of strokes, which began on 25 November and whose symptoms and course are vividly described in his *Life*)[17] is sentimentally recorded by his eldest son, Bishop Milles, on a monument erected by him in Highclere Church.[18]

---

[13]She is described in the *Life of Isaac Milles, op.cit.*, as "a most frugal, faithful, and diligent Manager of all his Concerns. For Industry, and a prudent Foresight and Care in the providing for, and governing, her Family, she had few Equals. Her Children found the Benefit of her Conduct, and, as I have heard, have ascrib'd the prosperous Condition, in which they now are, chiefly to her Management" (97)

[14]*Ibid.*, 97

[15]*Ibid.*, 147

[16]At this point, Pococke the traveller was six and his sister Elizabeth, who lived until 1774, possibly younger

[17]*Op.cit.*, 151ff

[18]"He was continually resident, and carefully diligent in the cure of this parish of Highclere, for thirty-nine years, two months, and seven days; when, after having contracted a great feebleness by the labours of his life, he sweetly fell asleep in Christ, without struggle, groan, or sigh, on Wednesday, the fifth day of July, 1720, and of his age the 82d year." Bishop Milles was not actually present at his father's death. Though Mrs. Pococke had recalled him from England, "seeing he could no longer be serviceable to him... towards

On her father's death, Mrs. Pococke would again have found herself and her family homeless, with the rectory subsequently being transferred to the next incumbent, Rev. Hastings Lloyd, on 17 April, 1723.[19] However, one child was immediately taken off her hands, since within a week Pococke had matriculated at Christ Church College, Cambridge, at the age of fifteen. It is possible that Bishop Milles contributed towards his university education, extending over the next thirteen years.

Apart from the few lines in her father's *Life*, describing her as dutiful and diligent in nursing her dying father, there are virtually no records which might help us to form an impression of Mrs. Pococke's character or the relationship she had with members of her family. We therefore have to rely on the limited sources available to us which, broadly speaking, are the Milles/Pococke correspondence and the contents of various family Wills. As is evident from the travel correspondence reproduced in the present edition, she and her son were devoted to each other. This mutual devotion took various forms: while Pococke spent long hours abroad composing detailed accounts of his trips, for the purpose both of entertaining his mother and reassuring her that he was safe and well, she was of great assistance to him in the management of his literary output from abroad, taking delivery of the journals which he sent home for safe-keeping and later painstakingly transcribing his letters into neat volumes. Also, as we have seen, she played a vital role in managing his finances while he was away from home.[20]

---

the latter End of this Month of June 1720, took his last leave of him and retired to the *Bath*." *Life of Isaac Milles, op.cit.,* 155-56

[19]The reason for the lengthy delay in appointing Lloyd was that he had not actually taken Holy Orders. He was duly ordained as Deacon on 23 December, 1722 and as Priest, 10 March, 1723. We do not know if Highclere Rectory remained vacant during the intervening three years, or whether it was occupied by a curate, since the records are silent on the matter

[20]It should be noted that Pococke's travel correspondence to his mother was not confined to his two Grand Tours, but was applied just as assiduously to his tours of Scotland and Ireland, right up until her death in 1760, at which point the recipient of his letters became his sister, Elizabeth. His letters from Scotland, for example, address Mrs. Pococke as "Honoured Madam" or "Dear Madam" up until 1760, at which point they are addressed to "Dear Sister"; and the same is true of the letters sent from his Irish tours, where he

Regrettably, though, the correspondence is one-sided, and we do not see the letters she sent in return to each of her son's missives. However, the editor recently came across a number of letters between Mrs. Pococke and the Bishop (including one to her son) which are sufficient to illustrate her literary style, the absolute strength of her religious convictions, her determination to see her son do well in his clerical profession, and her complete devotion to her brother, the Bishop of Waterford & Lismore.[21]

Thirty-seven years after his death, she appears to have still felt a great sense of duty and affection towards her late husband, Rev. Richard Pococke. In her Will, she gives the following instructions to her daughter Elizabeth (or Betse) concerning her burial: "I remmit [sic].... my Body to the ground to be decently and Christianly buried as to my Executrix hereafter to be named shall think fit in or as near my Dear Husbands Grave in Holy Rhood [sic] Church in Southampton as may be."[22] Further details of her character (and of course her financial situation) may be gleaned from the various legacies she received throughout her life, as well as from the contents of her own Will, drawn up thirteen years before her death, in 1747.[23] We know from these sources that by the year 1721, she possessed whatever she had

---

again addresses his mother as "Honoured Madam" or "Dear Madam". However, none in the latter collection are addressed to his sister, as the tours end in mid-May, 1760, presumably just before his mother's death. See J. McVeagh (1995) *op.cit.* On the other hand, Pococke's letters from his tours of England are not addressed to any particular person and it is possible that he simply used the epistolary account as a literary convention. See Cartwright, *op.cit.*

[21]Two of these are reproduced in Appendix 2. They were part of a small Milles/Pococke archive put up for auction on Ebay in February, 2011. For several weeks the supersized scans of these and related manuscripts were available for viewing on the seller's site. Three of these are listed in the Bibliography under "Other Manuscript Sources in Private Collections"

[22]See Elizabeth Pococke's Will, Public Record Office, The National Archives f the UK, Catalogue Reference: Prob.11/858

[23]See Mrs. Pococke's own Will, *op.cit.* See also the bequests made to her in her father, Rev. Isaac Milles' Will, Public Record Office, The National Archives of the UK, Catalogue Reference: Prob 11/578, and likewise the bequests made to her in her brother, Bishop Thomas Milles' Will, Public Record Office, The National Archives of the UK, Catalogue Reference: Prob 11/717

inherited from her husband,[24] plus £100 from her father; in 1740, on the death of her brother Bishop Milles, she inherited a further £500, and at some date between then and 1747, she had received another legacy of £150 together with a house and all its contents. Though the combined amount of £750 may not seem a great fortune, in today's terms it works out at about £105,000 when equated to retail values, or almost £1.25 million, when equated to average wages of the period. Also, this is the minimum we can assume she possessed at that time, since there is the unspecified sum of "all my money" left to her daughter, who at the time of her own death (1774), could afford to be extremely generous to her own relatives and family servants.

Mrs. Pococke died in 1760 and though we do not know her precise age at death, we can assume that she was in her early eighties. Curiously, given his dependence on her while she lived, there is no reference in Pococke's travel correspondence to his mother's decease. At the time of her death he was on a tour of Scotland, and as mentioned in an earlier note, simply switched the addressee of his travel correspondence from his mother to his sister. Mrs. Pococke was presumably buried close to the grave of her husband, as stipulated in her Will, and was joined fourteen years later by her affectionate daughter Elizabeth (by then probably in her seventies), who requested the following very modest funeral arrangements in her own Will: "I resign... my Body to the Ground to be decently buried in Southampton in Holy Roods Church in my most Dear Mothers Grave so as not to disturb her Ashes. And if not already done, to have an Ash turnd just over her Coffin and my Corps laid on it and an Ash turnd just over my Coffin. I desire to have a Coffin rooved in White and everything given in White and all at the least expence consistent with common Decency and no Pall Bearers".[25]

---

[24] Sadly his Will has not been traced so we do not know how well he provided for his wife

[25] Will of Elizabeth Pococke (Spinster), Public Record Office, The National Archives of the UK, Catalogue Reference: Prob.11/999

Life of Bishop Thomas Milles (1671-1740)

We continue the biographical accounts with a consideration of the life of Bishop Milles,[26] since he is the link between the two travellers, and the patron of at least one of his nephews.[27] The bishop was, as we have seen, Mrs. Pococke's eldest brother, born on 19 June 1671, and it is likely that he had attended his father's school in Highclere Rectory. He matriculated at Wadham College, Oxford, on 12 March, 1688-89, aged seventeen, and was admitted as a Goodridge Exhibitioner 1691-92. He obtained a BA on 5 February, 1692, and was ordained as Deacon by Bishop Hough, on 6 June, 1694, in Magdalen Chapel, Oxford. Later that year, on 7 December, he was admitted Chaplain of Christ Church. The following year, 1695, he was awarded an MA from St. Edmund Hall on 28 May, and was appointed vice-principal of St. Edmund Hall. On 16 March, 1701, he was ordained as Priest by the Bishop of Oxford, William Talbot, in Christ Church Cathedral, on 9 May, 1704, obtained a BD from Christ Church, and on 15 July, 1707, gained a DD from Trinity College, Dublin.[28]

There is no record of his having undertaken a Grand Tour,[29] though his critic, Thomas Hearne (see below), notes in a diary entry of 14 September, 1705, "Mr. Milles of Xtchurch tells me he has some design of Travelling into Forreign Countries".[30] No further mention is made of this so we do not know if this design was ever carried out. Nevertheless, the sources considered

---

[26]As in the earlier sections, in order to avoid confusion, Thomas Milles will henceforth be referred to as "Bishop Milles" or "the bishop", though he did not actually succeed to this position until 1708. For a more detailed biographical account of Bishop Milles, see R. Finnegan (*Decies*, forthcoming)

[27]Not only did he finance the education and travels of his favourite nephew, Jeremiah Milles, who was the son of his younger brother, Jeremiah, but he subsequently appointed him as his sole heir

[28]For the various dates, see R.B. Gardiner, *Registers of Wadham College* (1889-1895), Vol. 1, 357, J. Foster, *Alumni Oxonienses* (1887-92), Vol. 3, 1015

[29]No entry exists in Ingamells, *op.cit.*, though this source only begins at 1700

30C. E. Doble and D. W. Rannie (eds.), *Remarks and Collections of Thomas Hearne. Nine Volumes, covering the Years 1705–1714* (Oxford Historical Society, 1885-98) Vol. 1, 44

in this edition suggest that he did visit France. In one of his earliest letters to his uncle, for example, Milles, when describing a Benedictine monastery in St. Dennis', notes: "It is impossible to pretend to give your Ldship any account of this it is so large, and I do not in the least doubt but your Ldship has seen it & viewed it with more accuracy, than I could possibly do."[31]

Bishop Milles succeeded Humphrey Hody[32] as Regius Professor of Greek in 1706, an appointment which incurred the wrath of his most strenuous critic (or "special aversion"), the same Thomas Hearne,[33] whose diary entries contain frequent attacks on his character and his scholarship. The same is true of his subsequent appointment as Greek Professor in the University of Oxford, on 17 February, 1707. However, his colleagues in that University were soon to be relieved of his presence, when, a year later (March 1708) he secured from his patron, Thomas Herbert, 8th Earl of Pembroke,[34] a recommendation to the See of Waterford & Lismore. This honour resulted, in turn, from the Earl's own appointment, the previous year, as Lord Lieutenant of Ireland. From the church records, it appears that Bishop Milles severed all ecclesiastical links with England and took up full duties (though clearly not full residence) in Waterford.

According to a letter he wrote to his sister (Mrs. Pococke), on 12 May, 1708, he was "received with great ceremony, solemnity & kindness both by the Clergy & People" of Waterford, found the town "very agreeable" and claimed, "I shall be very happy if it pleases God to afford me Life and Health".[35] He also referred in this letter to his domestic arrangements,

---

[31]Add: 15773, Paris, 6/17 September, 1733. Other similar comments are made in letters from Milles to the bishop

[32]Hody (1659-1707) was a member of the non-juror movement (whereby six bishops and about 400 lower clergy refused to swear an oath of allegiance to William & Mary, and their successors under the Protestant Succession Act of 1689) and was friendly both with Thomas Hearne & Henry Dodwell

[33]See Joseph Wells, *Wadham College* (1898) 123

[34]The family patron mentioned earlier, who, according to the anonymous life of Rev. Isaac Milles, had such a regard for the integrity and piety of the latter, "as... inclined him to permit his eldest son to attend him into *Ireland* ... and caused him to recommend him to the late Queen for the vacant See of *Waterford* and *Ireland*, which he now enjoys" (*Ibid.*, 89-90)

[35]Manuscript letter in private collection, reproduced as Letter 1, in Appendix 2

noting: "I lodge in my own Palace, but eat generally abroad the Clergy & People of the Town inviting me almost every Day."[36] However, it is not known how long this hospitality was to last, or the extent to which he continued to mix with his flock. His appointment as Bishop of Waterford & Lismore was unpopular in Ireland, especially for his high-church tendencies (he allegedly wore a crucifix as his pectoral cross) and his inclination to give all his important preferments to members of his own family. Though it is well known that nepotism among English-born bishops during this period was rife,[37] it must be said that the number of his younger brothers and nephews appearing in the succession lists for this diocese is quite astonishing.[38]

Furthermore, despite the encouraging welcome afforded him on his arrival, much of his thirty-two year period of office in Waterford was marred by his unhappy relations with Waterford Corporation, with whom he fought for many years (from 1711-1732) over their alleged mismanagement of charitable institutions. In retaliation, they accused him of impropriety, and in particular of entertaining papist servants in his house, which they considered as offensive.[39] It is also clear from the sources that part of their quibble with the bishop was that he did not spend enough time in Ireland,[40] and it is interesting that in a letter to his sister,[41] he mentions the possibility of returning to England at "Whitsuntide", only weeks after arriving in Waterford.

---

[36]*Ibid.*

[37]See Toby Barnard, *op.cit.*, 88 and 98-99

[38]See the entries for Pococke & various members of the Milles family in W. Rennison, *Succession List of the Bishops, Cathedral and Parochial Clergy of the Dioceses of Waterford and Lismore, from the Earliest Times, together with some Hitherto Unpublished Records* (Ardmore, 1921)

[39]See the Minutes of Waterford Corporation, for 26 September, 1712, Waterford City Archives, Ref. LA1/1A/07

[40]As soon as he died, a more spacious palace was built for his successor, in the hope that he "may be incouraged to dwell here". See the Minutes of Waterford Corporation, for 28 March, 1741, Waterford City Archives, Ref. LA1/1/A/10, 105

[41]*Op.cit.*, Appendix 2

Plate 2
Exterior View of Waterford Cathedral, Oil on Canvas, Artist unknown, c. 1730
Courtesy of Waterford Museum of Treasures
Photo Donnchadh Ó Ceallacháin

Plate 3
View of the South Prospect of Lismore Cathedral
The whole Works of Sir James Ware concerning Ireland, revised and improved by
Walter Harris (Dublin, 1764) Vol. 1

When Pococke and Milles set out on their first Grand Tour, Bishop Milles was over sixty years of age and without an heir. We know very little of his relationship with his immediate family, though as we have seen, he showed great admiration and respect for his father on his death in 1720, attributed by some as having written his anonymous biography, and setting up a handsome memorial to him in Highclere Church. Perhaps his most generous and worthy act was that of providing an education for his nephew, Jeremiah Milles, putting him through Eton and Oxford, and then, while on his first Grand Tour (clearly financed by him) offering him a preferment in Waterford.[42] As is shown in the correspondence, the young Milles was astounded at the offer, which he considered to be a great honour that he could hardly live up to, and immediately started home from his travels, making straight for Ireland.

Why Milles felt compelled to write to his uncle every few days is understandable. Since the Bishop was paying for his travels, he felt obliged to keep him informed of his movements, and this also provided an opportunity to prove to him that he was a serious traveller and scholar, and worthy of becoming his heir. However, from the tone and contents of several letters, Milles seems to have had a genuine affection and respect for his uncle. Pococke, who had already benefitted so much from the bishop's patronage in terms of preferments in his diocese, also appears to have felt the same esteem and obligation towards him, and, at least in his later travels, wrote equally lengthy and regular letters from abroad. However, why the bishop took the trouble to copy or have copies made of the voluminous letters from his nephews on their travels is not clear, though perhaps he recognised their literary potential.

Bishop Milles died of gall-stones on 13 May, 1740, from which he had been suffering for at least the previous three years. It is possible that Jeremiah Milles was not actually there at his death, since the British Library holds a manuscript in the Milles collection entitled, "Notes in a journey from London to Holyhead, 6-13 May [1740?]". It is likely, therefore, that he was

---

[42]For the story supposedly behind this act of generosity, see under Life of Jeremiah Milles, below

in England at the time and hurried back to Waterford on hearing of his uncle's deteriorating health. According to some superficial biographies,[43] the bishop was buried in the Christ Church Cathedral, Waterford. However, given that he specifically requested, in his Will that "[his] Body may be conveyed to High Clare near Newbury in Hampshire to be interred in the Chancell of the Parish Church there as near as conveniently may be to the Bodys of [his] ffather and Mother swiftly but with as little ffuneral Pomp as possible and over [his] Grave to be layd a Marble Stone with the following Inscription upon it: subtus jacet Thomas Milles S.J.P. Waterfordiensis & Lismorensis in Hibernia Episcopus...";[44] and since a monument of this description is still to be found in Highclere church-yard, this is highly unlikely. Also, given that Waterford Corporation had been on such bad terms with him for most of his tenure as bishop, and even failed to acknowledge his decease in any of their records; and since there is no plaque to his memory in the present cathedral in Waterford (while a handsome monument to his immediate predecessor, Bishop Foy, takes pride of place in the western corner of the building), it is probably safe to say that his executor and heir, Jeremiah Milles, carried out his funeral arrangements according to his express wishes.[45]

Though the bishop published a number of scholarly works in his early years,[46] and had been engaged in others,[47] it appears

[43]Such as the *ODNB* and the records of the Royal Society

[44]The bishop's Will, *op.cit.*

[45]A transcript of the bishop's Will appears in Appendix 1. This view is corroborated in an article by Commander A.W.B. Messenger, who notes that, "his body was brought to England and buried in his father's church at Highclere, where his nephew the Dean of Exeter erected a tablet to him memory." See "An Eighteenth Century Dean of Exeter and his Family", in *Report and Transactions of the Devonshire Association for the Advancement of Science*, Volume 83 (1951) 29-30

[46]For example, *The Happiness of those that suffer for Righteousness Sake: in a Sermon preached at St. Maries in Oxford, on the XXXth. of January 1700/01* (Oxford, 1701), Του εν αγιοις πατρος ημων Κυριλλου ... τα σωζομενα. *S. patris nostri Cyrilli ... Opera, quæ supersunt, omnia; quorum quædam nunc primum ex Codd. MSS. edidit, reliqua cum Codd. MSS. contulit, plurimis in Locis emendavit, notisque illustravit Tho. Milles* (Oxford, 1703) and *The natural Immortality of the Soul asserted: and proved from the Scriptures,*

that he produced nothing after taking up residence in Waterford. However, as is evident from his Will, he was writing a history: "As for the History of England which I have drawn up as far as the Reign of King Stephen with the Greatest Care ffidelity and Exactness and if God grants me health and Life may sometime hereafter and of which I have two Copys one writ all with mine own hand in which are diverse [Margins?] and Interlineations the other transcribed by several hands and corrected tho but imperfectly by me My Will is that it if be thought proper in time to come to print and publish it that it be printed according to the Copy of my own hand writing and adding the Subjects of the Paragraphs which are to be found in the Margin of the Transcript of this my History but are not in the Original".[48] Sadly, though, the manuscript seems to have disappeared without trace, and it is possible that it remained in the possession of his heir, Jeremiah Milles, to be later disposed of at the sale of the latter's library.

Regrettably, there are few flattering or positive portraits of Bishop Milles in the records, though it is well documented (particularly by him) that he spent a large amount of his own money on restoring churches in the Waterford area.[49] Also, unusually for a man in his elevated position, there is no known portrait of him, though it has been suggested (but not proven) that the large portrait of Bishop Foy hanging in Christchurch Cathedral in Waterford may in fact represent Bishop Milles. One argument against this is that Bishop Milles is reputed to have "possessed a large Roman nose",[50] which is not particularly apparent in this portrait.

---

and first Fathers: in answer to Mr Dodwell's epistolary Discourse, in which he endeavours to prove the Soul to be a Principle naturally Mortal (Oxford, 1707)

[47]Such as an edition of Aristophanes' comedies, which he is said, by Hearne, to have abandoned. See Doble & Rannie, *op.cit.*, Vol. XII, 327

[48]See article 10 of the bishop's Will, *op.cit.*, and the transcript in Appendix 1 of the present volume

[49]For full details of the criticisms of his nepotism, his dispute with the Corporation and his renovations to certain churches in the diocese, see R. Finnegan (*Decies*, forthcoming)

[50]See A.W.B. Messenger, *op.cit.*, 29, who cites an amusing anecdote where Swift humiliated Milles in public on account of his classical learning and his nose

Life of Richard Pococke (1704-65)

Accounts of Pococke's life appear in the editions of his British and Irish travels, in varying degrees of detail. Of his three Victorian editors, Cartwright virtually dismisses the man, with his uncharitable claim: "Apart from his journeying, the life of Pococke presents little to interest the reader, and may be told in very few words",[51] and while Stokes devotes several pages to his life,[52] Kemp provides the reader with a comprehensive "Biographical Sketch".[53] More recently, McVeagh gives a brief account of his life, admitting, "Richard Pococke was a man obsessed with travel [and] no less compulsive was his habit of writing every journey down";[54] and Bartlett gives details of his life in his article on Pococke's visit to Lebanon.[55] Biographical accounts of Pococke also appear in the histories of the various institutions with which he was associated, such as the school his father ran in Southampton,[56] and the Pococke School in Kilkenny,[57] and while deservedly the traveller has his place in the *ODNB*,[58] to date he has never been the subject of a full biography. The present account, in addition to outlining the main points of Pococke's life, also considers matters not previously considered by his biographers, including his domestic arrangements, personal interests, and contribution to learned clubs and societies.

Born in Southampton in 1704, the only son of Rev. Richard Pococke and Elizabeth Pococke (née Milles), Pococke, as we have seen, was educated at his grandfather's school in Highclere Rectory and matriculated at Christ Church College, Oxford in 1720, aged only fifteen. He remained a student of this

---

[51]*Op.cit.*, Preface, i

[52]*Op.cit.*, Introduction, 8-11

[53]*Op.cit.*, xxxi-lxx

[54]John McVeagh (1995) *op.cit.*, 11

[55]See John. R. Bartlett, "Richard Pococke in Lebanon, 1738", in *Archaeology & History in Lebanon*, Issue 16 (Autumn, 2002) 17-18

[56]See Russell, *op.cit.*, 204-9

[57]See Quane, *op.cit.*, 36-43, and Lesley Whiteside with Andrew Whiteside, *Where Swift and Berkley Learnt: A History of Kilkenny College* (Dublin, 2009) 130-33

[58]*Oxford Dictionary of National Biography* (Oxford, 2001-2004)

college for thirteen years, receiving a BA in 1725, a BCL in 1731 and a DCL (Doctor of Laws) in 1733.[59] Though there is no reference in the English records to his actual ordination,[60] on graduating with a BA, he received his first preferment from Bishop Milles with the appointment of Precentor (or Chantor) of Lismore Cathedral (1725-56).[61] As noted earlier, by the time he and Milles embarked on their first Grand Tour in 1733, Pococke had already held this position for eight years, as well as occupying a number of lucrative appointments in the Diocese of Waterford & Lismore.[62] Furthermore, while on his first voyage (or perhaps just after his return) he was appointed to the more senior office of Vicar General of Waterford and Lismore (1734-45),[63] and during his second trip became Vicar of Tullaghorton (1736). As far as can be ascertained, he was an absentee from the whole period 1725-45, though would still have earned a considerable income from the assorted appointments.

Pococke returned to England after his second Grand Tour in 1741, which took him to the East, by which time his uncle and patron, Bishop Milles, from whom he had recently received a bequest of £600, had been dead for a year. On his arrival in England, he was obliged to "wait on" the new Bishop of Waterford in London, presumably to discuss matters relating to the diocese from which he had been absent for the previous five years.[64] On 24 December 1741, he was elected Fellow of the Society of Antiquaries of London and a few weeks later, on 11 February, 1742, became Fellow of the Royal Society on the grounds of being "a Gentleman of Universal Learning, great

---

[59]Foster, *op.cit. 1715-1886 (L-Z)* (1888) 1124
[60]It is likely that he was ordained in Ireland, by his uncle, as was the case with his cousin, Jeremiah Milles
[61]A Precentor was the member of the cathedral body responsible for the direction of the choral services, and the first dignitary in the cathedral after the dean
[62]Vicar of Kiltegan (1729), Rector of Outeragh (1730), Vicar of Cahir (1730), Curate of Lisnakill (1731), Curate of Grangemockler (1731), Rector of Fenoagh (1732), Vicar of Dysert and Kilmoleran (1732), Vicar of Mothel (1732) and Vicar of Stradbally (1732). Dates recorded in Rennison, *op.cit.*
[63]The chief representative of the bishop in the administration of the diocese
[64]This was Bishop Este. See Pococke's letter to his mother from Dover, dated 29 August, 1741, the last in the collection. Add. 22998, Letter LXVI

Curiosity, every way well quallified and likely to be a very usefull and valuable member of the Same".[65] He was also a member and officer of the Egyptian Society and the Divan Club (see below).

For the next few months he worked on Volume I of his celebrated *A Description of the East*, based on his journals and the notes and sketches he had taken while travelling in the Levant.[66] This impressive folio volume, containing 75 etched (and occasionally engraved) plates, was printed for the author by William Bower, London, and the ledgers for this company show that a total of 1,250 copies were printed, of which 1,190 were on demy paper and 60 on royal.[67] Printing of this volume was completed on 31 March, 1743, and it was dedicated to the author's old family patron Henry Herbert, 9th Earl of Pembroke and Montgomery, the so-called "architect earl". The immediate success of this work encouraged Pococke to proceed with Volume II, which was ready for print on 4 February, 1745, and had the same print-run as the earlier work. The two parts of this volume contain a total of 104 etched (and occasionally engraved) plates.

In 1744, Pococke was appointed as Domestic Chaplain to Philip Dormer Stanhope, 4th Earl of Chesterfield (1694–1773). The latter had been appointed Lord Lieutenant of Ireland in November, 1744, but on account of other diplomatic duties,[68] was unable to take up the post immediately. In a letter from sent to his friend Dr. Hartley, on 7 June, 1745, Pococke explained: "I am going again to Ireland, in the month of August, having the

---

[65]RS citation, Ref: EC/1741/15. Among his proposers was Martin Folkes, Inspector of Medals and Coins in the Egyptian Society, of which Pococke was also a founder member (see below). Pococke and Milles met with Folkes on their first Grand Tour

[66]As we shall see from the Milles' Grand Tour correspondence, however, several of the illustrations appearing in the book were actually taken from original drawings by his cousin, though Pococke made no reference to this in his publication

[67]See *Early Printed Books, 1478-1840: Catalogue of the British Architectural Library Early Imprints Collection* (K. G. Saur, 2005) 2745

[68]He was sent to the Hague to persuade the Dutch to enter the war against France

honour to wait on the Lord Lieutenant as his Domestic Chaplain".[69] He and the Earl of Chesterfield eventually arrived in Dublin on 31 August.

It would seem that this was the first occasion on which Pococke actually took up residence in Ireland, even though he had occupied a number of important positions in the Church of Ireland for the previous two decades. He dedicated the second volume of *A Description of the East* to Lord Chesterfield, who reciprocated this public honour by appointing him the same year to the Archdeaconry of Dublin. Chesterfield then returned to England on 11 April, 1746, leaving Pococke in this senior position in Dublin, where he was to remain for the next ten years, and from which he was to be translated to his first bishopric.

His pioneering *A Description of the East*, lavishly illustrated with 179 plates, many of which are dedicated to friends and associates of the author, immediately became a standard work on the Levant, and was translated at the time into French, German and Dutch. Although attracting extensive criticism from contemporary literary and theological rivals such as Dr. Charles Perry, the Rev. Dr. Thomas Shaw and Mr. Warburton,[70] it gained the attention and admiration of academics and architects alike, earning him a place among the *literati* and architectural circles of the day. Its impact lived on well into the next century, when it continued to be held up as authority on the East, and was universally described as a learned, scholarly and desirable work;[71] and of course it is even more collectable today, though surprisingly has never been reprinted in English in its original form. In addition to the book's intellectual and visual appeal was of course its practical value, and it is a good example of a Grand Tourist's views on the benefits of foreign travel - a

---

[69]Quoted in J. Nichols, *Illustrations of the Literary History of the Eighteenth Century, Consisting of Authentic Memoirs and Original Letters of Eminent Persons; and Intended as a Sequel to The Literary Anecdotes* Vol. II (London, 1814) 806

[70]For further details of these criticisms, see Volume 3 of this edition

[71]See, for the example, the comments of the German commentator, F. Ebert, in *A General Bibliographical Dictionary, from the German of Frederic Adolphus Ebert, Librarian to the King of Saxony...* Vol. III (Oxford, 1837) 1443

stock subject with travel writers, particularly as a conclusion to their work.

It is difficult to ascertain precisely where and when Pococke resided throughout the period from his university days until his arrival in Dublin, in 1746, though of course for almost half that time (1733-34 and 1736-41) he was abroad. Also, it is clear from the earlier Grand Tour correspondence that he spent time at his mother's house in Newtown, since this is where Milles collected him when setting out on their second trip. It is unlikely that he owned or even leased a house in London, but clearly he had access to accommodation in the capital at least after his return from his travels, since he is recorded as regularly attending the various clubs and societies to which he belonged.

He was a founder member of the Egyptian Society,[72] whose records contain the "Journal" (kept from 11 December, 1741 to 16 April, 1743), together with poetry, reports of papers delivered by members.[73] This manuscript has had a chequered career. Though Pococke was Reis Effendi (Secretary) for the Society immediately before its demise, and is likely therefore to have held on to the "Journal" throughout his life, it appears to have been subsequently acquired by Milles, since a later owner, Walter Prideaux, a lawyer and clerk to the Goldmith's Company, believed it had come from the former's library. In 1885, Prideaux wrote to the editor of *Notes Queries* (Vol. X, p.427) asking if any of his correspondents could give him information on the Egyptian Society,[74] and four years later, in 1889, the manuscript was sold at Christie's. It then became the property of the Egyptian Exploration Society of London (founded in 1882), where it still

---

[72]The other members are listed as follows: Sandwich, Charles Perry, Frederick Ludewig Norden, Thomas Lisle, Tho. Anson, Ed. Vernon, Wm Lethieullier, C. Stanhope, M. Folkes, Wm Stukeley, T. Dampier, Jeremiah Milles, Montagu, Richmond, Lenox, & Aubigny, Andr Mitchell, Cutts Barton, Smart Lethieullier, Daniel Wray, Roum [Truleman], Solomon Bagrolle, Jo. McKye, H. Legge, Lovell, Thos Hill, Wm Fauquiert, Lincoln, Duncannon, W. Bristow and E. Legge

[73]British Library, Add. 52362

[74]See M. Annis, "The First Egyptian Society in London (1741-1743)", in *Bulletin de L'Institut Francais D'Archaeologie Orientale* 50 (1952) 100, n.9

belonged in 1952 (the date of Annis' article) and in 1964 was given to the British Library.

One of the more spectacular events of this society, which like others of its type was essentially a dining club, was the occasion on which Pococke performed the opening up and dissection of a mummy in the Duke of Richmond's house.[75] The observations were recorded by Mr. Dampier at the following meeting (5 March), after which Pococke communicated to the society some "observations on the manner of embalming bodys amongst the Egyptians". Though the latter account is based largely on Herodotus, it also includes interesting points concerning what he had personally observed in the Catacombs.[76]

We can see from this source that Pococke attended all twenty meetings held between its establishment on 11 December 1741, until its last recorded meeting on 16 April, 1743, during the second year of which (from 3 December, 1742 until the society's demise), as already noted, he acted as its Secretary. It was stated in the "Laws", drawn up during the first session, that meetings should take place every fortnight from the first Friday in November to the first Friday in May. Furthermore (and thus establishing the fact that he spent at least one summer in London) at the meeting of 14 May, 1742, it was resolved that "the further consideration of the Egyptian medals be deferred till next winter, & that in the mean time Dr Pococke, Dr Perry, & Mr Letheilleur, & any other members that shall stay in town this summer be desired to enquire after proper persons to draw & engrave the said medals...".[77]

Pococke was also a founder member of the Divan Club (originally named the Turkish Club), the other nine individuals, who qualified on account of proving "that they have been in the Sultan's Dominions", being Sir Francis Dashwood, Lord Duncannon (future 2nd Earl of Bessborough), Mr. Edgcumbe, Mr. Fanshawe, Sir Everard Fawkener, Mr. Frolich, Lord Granby, Mr.

---

[75]This took place on Monday 24 February, 1742
[76]See Add. 52362, pp 21ff
[77]*Ibid.*, 28

McKye and Lord Sandwich.[78] In a similar vein to the Egyptian Society, the rules of the Divan stipulated that "this Society meet once every fortnight: viz, every other Friday, from the first Friday in December, to the first Friday in May", though this was amended later to every Sunday. Pococke was present at the club's first meeting on 8 January, 1744, and acted as Reis Effendi for its fourth meeting. He then attended the next eleven consecutive sessions, during which he stood Reis Effendi for the second time, as well as Vizir (Chairman). However, he only attended once more, at the last session before the summer recess, on 24 May, 1745, being absent from the last ten recorded meetings. His absence can of course be explained by the fact that on 31 August, as noted above, he had arrived in Dublin with his new patron, the Earl of Chesterfield.

Equally, Pococke must have retained an address in London after taking up residence in Ireland, since he regularly visited the capital, and as can be seen from his Grand Tour correspondence, liked to spend his winters at his family home in Newtown. Two letters in a collection of correspondence between himself and the gothic-revival architect Sanderson Miller (1716-80) regarding some alterations to St. Canice's Cathdral, Kilkenny, give Grosvenor Street as Pococke's address.[79] However, the address of the sender given in such correspondence is not necessarily an indication of a permanent or even regular arrangement. In the letter sent to Dr. Hartley in June 1745 (cited above), for instance, Pococke gives his address as Rawthmell's Coffee House, Henrietta Street, Covent Garden. Since this was one of the more informal meeting places of members of the Royal Society (and was later to be the place of origin of the Society of Arts), we must not assume that he had lodgings there, but rather found it a convenient and convivial place in which to conduct his

---

[78]See "Al-Koran, the Minute Book of the Divan Club", National Maritime Museum, London, Ref. SAN/V/113. Short biographies of all these members, together with some who joined later, are given in Finnegan, *The Divan Club* (*op.cit.*)
[79]See Warwick CR 125B/801 and 2, dated 8 and 17 February, 1757, respectively

daily business.[80] Likewise, a letter dating from January, 1748 gives his address as Adams Court in Broad Street, Behind the Royal Exchange, London.[81]

The question of Pococke's accommodation arrangements for the first few years of his residence in Ireland is uncertain, too, though there is a record of his having taken over a lease of a property belonging to Lord Prendergrasse, in March 1746, which would correspond with his arrival in the country seven months earlier.[82] This is probably Sir Thomas, Prendergast (1702-1760), who had properties in Galway, Tipperary and other Irish counties, as well as a house in Merrion Street, Dublin, where he died. The latter property, however, could not have been where Pococke lived, as that street was not developed until the 1750s. It is possible that Pococke may have resided in the leased house for just a year or two (regrettably the term of the lease is not mentioned in the records) until taking up the Archdeaconship of Dublin, at which point he may have moved into church accommodation (such as the Deanery of St. Patrick's Cathedral), but equally, he may have retained the lease for the duration of his Archdeaconship. There is certainly no mention of the Dublin lease in his Will, even though it was common practice to bequeath the remaining term of a lease to one's heirs.[83]

The See of Ossory became vacant in February 1756, after the death of Bishop Edward Maurice, whereupon Pococke, upon the recommendation of Duke of Devonshire, Lord Lieutenant of Ireland, was nominated as his successor in King's Letter of 5

---

[80]For a discussion of the connection between coffee-houses and gentlemen's clubs, see A.E. Musson and E. Robinson, *Science and Technology in the Industrial Revolution* (Manchester, 1969) 58

[81]Letter to Emanuel M. Da Costa, dated 1 January, 1748, quoted in Kemp, *op.cit.*, xlii

[82]National Archives of Ireland, Pembroke Estate Papers, 2/5/32

[83]Stokes, the nineteenth-century editor of Pococke's Irish tour (*op.cit.*) admits, in his Introduction: "I have tried to find out where Pococke lived when Archdeacon of Dublin and Rector of St. Peter's, but have failed. Perhaps some reader may be able to throw light on this local problem" (11). However, more than a century later the mystery has still not been solved. Neither the archival staff of the RCB, Dublin nor the architectural staff of the RCB Property Department, Dublin, were able to inform the editor of an address for him during this period

March, 1756. He was consecrated in St. Patrick's, Dublin, on 21 March, by the Archbishop of Dublin, assisted by the Bishops of Kildare and Leighlin.[84] Two months later, on 24 March, he was enthroned by proxy, though the exact date at which he actually took up residence in the Bishop's Palace is not known. By late June, however, he described his new circumstances in very glowing terms, claiming, "every one as well as myself thinks I have got the sweetest situation in Ireland, a most exceeding good house, a pleasant garden, wt. we call a noble cathedral, & good neighbourhood, in a fine country, with a good river running through it".[85] It has been held that the Bishop's Palace, erected on the foundations of the medieval palace was actually built by Charles Este, Bishop of Ossory from 1736 to 1745.[86] However, Bishop Este (who as we have seen was Bishop Milles' successor in Waterford) merely enlarged and improved this residence, the error perhaps being attributed to Chetwood's brief description, in 1748, of the palace as being "new built".[87] It is thought that, among his other alterations and additions to this property, Pococke created the palace library, with its characteristic "Pococke pilasters",[88] and other classical ornamentation in oak. This room is now the library of the Heritage Council, and these features have been carefully preserved.

Pococke was to remain as Bishop of Ossory for a decade, during which time he carried out many improvements on other churches in the diocese, as well as establishing and supporting a

---

[84]See J B. Leslie, *Ossory Clergy and Parishes: being an Account of the Clergy of the Church of Ireland in the Diocese of Ossory, from the Earliest Period, with Historical Notices of the several Parishes, Churches, &c.* (Enniskillen, 1933) 30-31

[85]Warwickshire County Record Office, Ref. 125B/798

[86]See, for example, Mark Bence-Jones, *A Guide to Irish Country Houses*, (London, 2nd revised edition, 1990) 167

[87]W.R. Chetwood, *A Tour through Ireland In Several Entertaining Letters Wherein the Present State of that Kingdom is Consider'd and the most noted Cities, Towns, Seats, Rivers, Buildings &c. are described...* (London, 1748) 178. The most comprehensive modern account of this building is 'The Bishop's Palace, Kilkenny', in *Old Kilkenny Review* (2003) 30-53

[88]See R. Finnegan, "Bishop Pococke's Improvements", *op.cit.*

linen-weaving factory at Lintown, just outside Kilkenny.[89] Clearly, he was already a man of independent means, but his promotion to this bishopric greatly increased his income, and, being of a generous disposition, he invested a great deal of his own money in supporting such charitable works.

His transfer to Meath, after ten years in Kilkenny took place as follows: "He was translated, by the King's letter, from Ossory to Elphin, in June 1765, Bishop Gore of Elphin being then promoted to Meath; but Bishop Gore, finding a great sum to be paid to his predecessor's executors for the house at Ardbraccan,[90] declined taking out his patent; and therefore Bishop Pococke, in July, was translated by the Duke of Northumberland, directly to the see of Meath...".[91]

According to an Edwardian history of the diocese, it was Bishop John Evans (1716-24) who "had bequeathed certain funds for the erection of an episcopal palace at Ardbraccan and had obtained plans for the building".[92] However, Evans died before executing the work, and his three immediate successors (Bishops Downes, Lambert and Ellis) allowed the project to remain in abeyance. In 1734 the work was finally taken in hand, when Bishop Arthur Price constructed the two wings of the palace to the design of Richard Castle. However, he was then transferred to Cashel, whereupon the work once again ceased, and it was in this state that Pococke found the palace, with only the wings and no central block. Ardbraccan House was eventually completed by the non-resident Bishop Henry Maxwell between 1772-75, to the combined designs of James Wyatt, Rev. Daniel Augustus Beaufort, and Thomas Cooley. The same Rev. Beaufort some years later praised this episcopal residence, which he described as being "a large and convenient mansion, erected by the present bishop, in a style of superior elegance, and yet with such

---

[89] For detailed accounts of this institution, see M. Quane, *op.cit.*, *passim*, and L. Whiteside, *op.cit.*, especially Chapters 13 & 14

[90] In much the same was as with Bishop Milles, who has to pay £800 to Bishop Foy's heirs

[91] J. Nichols, *Literary Anecdotes of the Eighteenth Century....* Vol. II (London, 1812) 158

[92] See J. Healy, *History of the Diocese of Meath,* Vol. II (Dublin, 1908) 92-3

simplicity as does equal honour to his Lordship's taste and liberality".[93]

While in his short-lived role as Bishop of Meath, Pococke acquired number 13 Henrietta Street, a large and stately town-house in Dublin's fashionable quarter. This cost him the considerable sum of £3,800, but was obviously an episcopal purchase, since not only is there no reference to it in his Will, but the next recorded owner for the following thirty-two years (from 1766-98) was Henry Maxwell, his successor as Bishop of Meath.[94] Many of the other residents of this street from the time it was built until the nineteenth century were members of the clergy, and in particular bishops, who would have needed a respectable residence in the capital city in which to entertain important guests, and where they could stay in relative comfort while attending to their many church and social duties.[95]

With regard to his private residence, as has already been noted, Pococke's mother moved from Southampton to Newtown, near Newbury in Hampshire, after her father's death in 1720, though no further details of her address are given. However, we know from later correspondence that the family subsequently lived in "Newtown House". Whether this house, built in 1740 (the year in which Bishop Milles died), belonged to Pococke or his mother is unclear, though one source maintains that the property was owned by this family for two generations until Bishop Pococke's death.[96] It is likely, however, that it was built by Pococke, on the proceeds of his uncle's recent bequest, and that he allowed his mother and sister to reside there, since in his own Will (drawn up on 10 July, 1763), he states: "First I give

---

[93]Daniel Augustus Beaufort, *Memoir of a Map of Ireland; Illustrating the Topography of that Kingdom, and Containing a Short Account of its Present State, Civil and Ecclesiastical, with a Complete Index to the Map* (London, 1792) 117

[94]Though not his immediate successor, as Arthur Smyth was bishop for a few months before being transferred to Dublin in 1766

[95]For an account of the residents of several houses in Henrietta Street, see *Irish Georgian Society Bulletin*, January, February, March, Vol. II (Dublin 1959) 17-18

[96]See D. Ellis, *Newtown at the Millenium,* (Newtown Parish Council, May, 2000)

and bequeath to my dearly beloved Sister Elizabeth Pococke, Spiner [sic] of Newtown in Hampshire my house and land in Newtown and Hampshire in which she now lives".[97] Had it been the property of Mrs. Pococke, she presumably would have bequeathed it to her son in her own Will, but she makes no reference to it.

As for his personal interests, Pococke continued his membership of clubs and associations after moving to Dublin. He belonged, for example, to the Physio-Historical Society (1744-55), whose purpose was to promote enquiries into the ancient and present state of the counties in Ireland,[98] and the Dublin Florists' Club (1747-66), established for the promotion of ornamental horticulture in Ireland.[99] Pococke was one of the founder members and an officer of the latter organisation, who was charged, at the meeting of 6 March, 1747, with the task of causing "proper receptacles to be made of for the flowers..."[100] Active involvement of such associations, collecting books, antiquities, coins and "curiosities", travelling and travel-writing seem to have been Pococke's major interests outside his actual clerical work, and though obviously close to his immediate family, he did not marry and does not appear to have formed any romantic attachments.

Pococke was very particular about what should happen to his various collections after his death, and in his Will, desires "that all my antiquities and every thing relating to natural history and all my coins and medals be sent to England to London to be sold by Publick auction as likewise all my books which will not sell here According to a just value and I desire that the Revd Mr

---

[97]NLI, D. 27, 161. This manuscript, which is a photocopy of a twentieth-century copy of Pococke's Will and Codicil, has minor typographical differences to that reproduced in Kemp, *op.cit.*, lxiii. In the Codicil (D. 27, 161), he states, "I do leave to my dear sister Elizabeth Pocoke [sic] of Newtown in Hampshire spinster my house and land in said parish of Newtown."

[98]See Royal Irish Academy, MS 24 E 28

[99]The Minute Book for this club is also in the Royal Irish Academy, MS 24 E 37

[100]For an interesting analysis of the club's minute book, see E. Charles Nelson, 'The Dublin Florists' Club in the Mid Eighteenth Century', in *Garden History*, Vol. 10, No. 2 (1982), 142-48

Mervyn Archdall[101] he requested to pack up my natural curiorisities and label them for which I desire that a proper present be made to him Tho he is assigning witness to this Will".[102] In the Codicil to his Will, he further adds: "I do desire that my Chaplain Mr Rev. Mervyn Archdall do pack up carefully my natural collection and direct the packing up of all my antiquities all to be sent to London to be sold in proper lotts at publick auction for which trouble I do bequeath him the sum of Twenty five pounds and it is my will that they be sent by long sea to London as my executors shall direct".[103] This was duly done and (with the exception of his library, which, as already noted, was sold in Dublin rather than in London) his collections were sold by the London auctioneer Mr. Langford and Son at two sales, each of two days' duration, in May and June, 1766.[104] The sale catalogues not only provide detailed information on the nature and extent of his connoisseurship, but also contain references to objects presented for discussion at his clubs. For example, Lot 92 of the first day's sale of his natural history collection is described in the catalogue as "A box with the remains of the mummy (as it seems) of an ibis, a wooden face of a mummy coffin, the scull of a mummy filled with the embalming matter or mumia...",[105] obviously the mummy that had been dissected at the Egyptian Club more twenty years earlier.

Though his British and Irish travels were edited and published long after his death, Pococke did produce several other publications apart from *A Description of the East*. These include

---

[101]His trusted Chaplain in Kilkenny, to whose country vicarage he liked to retire for relaxation

[102]NLI, D. 27, 161

[103]*Ibid.*

[104]See Mr. Langford, *A Catalogue of a Curious Collection of Greek, Roman, and English Coins and Medals, of the Right Reverend Dr. Pococke, Lord Bishop of Meath, Collected by his Lordship, during his Travels* (London, May, 1766) and Mr. Langford, *A Catalogue of a Large and Curious Collection of Ancient Statutes, Urns, Mummies, Fossils, Shells, and other Curiosities, of the Right Reverend Dr. Pococke, Lord Bishop of Meath, Deceased: Collected by his Lordship, during his Travels...* (London, June, 1766)

[105]Mr. Langford, *A Catalogue of a Large and Curious Collection* (*op.cit.*) 7

a volume of ancient Greek and Latin inscriptions (*Inscriptiones Antiquarum Graec. et Latin*) based on his travels and on antiquities, coins and medals in his own collection; a supplement to the latter volume, co-written with Jeremiah Milles (1752); and two sermons (1761 and 762).[106] A further publication appeared posthumously in 1773, in his cousin's newly founded journal. This beautifully illustrated article concerns ornaments and other antiquities found in prehistoric Irish graves.[107]

As for other insights into his character, it is the unfortunate remark of the celebrated letter-writer, Mrs. Delaney (wife of Dean Patrick Delany) that seems to have made the most lasting impression on the world, since it is quoted in every account of Pococke's life. After meeting him while staying in Bulstrode with the Duke of Portland, she wrote, in a letter dated 2 January, 1761: 'The Bishop of Ossory has been here ever since Monday.... We lose not much entertainment, for he is the dullest man that ever travelled: but he is a good man'.[108] This view has been disputed by some critics, such as Maureen Hegarty and Michael McCarthy.[109]

---

[106]For the full and very lengthy titles of these works, see the Bibliography

[107]See "An Account of some Antiquities found in Ireland; communicated by the Right Reverend Richard Pococke, late Lord Bisop of Meath", in *Archaeologia: or Miscellaneous Tracts relating to Antiquity*, Volume II (Royal Society of Antiquaries of London, 1773) 32-41. For modern commentaries on this article, see John Waddell, *Foundation Myths: The Beginnings of Irish Archaeology* (Wordwell Ltd., 2005) 70-71, Aideen Ireland, "A Gentle Luxury: Collectors and Collecting in eighteenth century Ireland", in J.V. Luce et al, *The Lure of Greece: Irish Involvement in Greek Culture Literature History and Politics* (Dublin, 2007) 57, & Aideen Ireland, "Richard Pococke (1704-65), Antiquarian", in *Peritia*, Volume 20 (2008) passim

[108]Mrs. Delany moved to Dublin after her marriage to the Dean in 1743, and much of her correspondence was published in 1861-62 (five volumes). An abridged version appeared in 1900 entitled *Mrs Delany (Mary Granville) a Memoir 1700-1788* (New York and London, 1900. The comment quoted here is stated in a letter dated 2 January, 1761, and is reproduced in many works, including M. Quane, *op.cit.*, 41

[109]See M. Hegarty, "Dr. Richard Pococke's Travels in Ireland, England and Wales", in *Old Kilkenny* Review: Journal of Kilkenny Archaeological *Society* (1987), who states: "Mrs. Delaney, doyen of the Dublin Blue-Stocking Society, dubbed Dr. Pococke a very dull man. Pococke? DULL?

However, the life-size portrait of him by the the Swiss artist Jean-Etiènne Liotard (depicted on the cover of the present volume)[110] shows him in a rather different light, depicting him in a distinctly bohemian manner, with shaven head, and sporting a towering head-dress and beard.[111] It has to be said, too, that he is extremely handsome. The portrait was painted in Constantinople, 1740, and is one of many pictures by this artist of Grand Tourists in oriental costume. This mode of dress seems to have been a popular, if not necessary, part of the experience of visitors to the Levant, though the custom (at least while abroad) was often practiced for considerations quite unrelated to fashion. One such reason was that of disguise to enable easy access into places of interest.[112] A further reason for adopting such dress was for self-protection by blending in with the locals, since it was considered unwise, and even dangerous, for foreign travellers (who were usually quite wealthy) to draw unnecessary and unwelcome attention upon themselves. However, whether such masquerade was an everyday mode of dress rather than one reserved for special occasions, is not so clear and would have varied according to the individual, and both the literary and artistic evidence indicates that this type of costume for visitors was almost the norm.[113]

The only other traceable portrait of Pococke (apart from the many miniature self-portrait sketches or 'cartoons' in his *A Description of the East* and his Scottish journal) is an oil painting representing his head and shoulders (see Plate 4). Formerly in the

---

NEVER!!" (398); and Michael McCarthy, "'The dullest man that ever travelled?' A re-assessment of Richard Pococke and of his Portrait by J.-E. Liotard", in *Apollo*, Vol. 143 (1996)

[110]It is said in some sources (such as Russell, *op.cit.*, 209) that this portrait was at one time in the possession of Jeremiah Milles, which, if true, means he must have inherited it. However, there is no reference to this in Pococke's Will

[111]As described in the catalogue of Liotard's collecton of pictures published in Paris in 1771. See *Jean-Étienne Liotard, 1702-1789, Masterpieces from the Musees d'Art et d'Histoire of Geneva and Swiss Private Collections* (Somogy Editions d'Art, Paris, 2006) 55

[112]See Stanford & Finopoulos, *op.cit.*, 163ff

[113]For an opposite view, see McCarthy, *op.cit.*, 26, who asserts that he "flouted convention by adopting the Turkish dress and wearing hair on his face"

Letters from Abroad, Volume 1

Pococke School, Kilkenny,[114] and now hanging in the new Bishop's Palace, Kilkenny, this portrait depicts the sitter not only as much older, but as more in keeping with Mrs. Delany's unsympathetic view.[115]

Plate 4
Portrait of Bishop Pococke, Artist unknown, 1765
Courtesy of the Episcopal Portrait Collection, RCB
Photo David Kane

---

[114]According to Leslie, *op.cit.*, 31
[115]Since this must be the portrait mentioned in Codicil 1 of his sister's Will, with the sitter in "Parliament Robes", he was sixty-five years of age when it was painted, the year of his death

Exactly two months after his transfer to the see of Meath, Pococke died of "apoplexy", following a visit to Charleville Castle, near Tullamore, where he met a relative of his host, Col. George Stoney, of Greyford [or Greyfort] House, Borrisokane.[116] Fortuitously, his last hours are recorded by Col. Stoney, thus: '1765, 15 Sept. --- He this day confirmed at Tullamore; returned indisposed, went to his chamber, took a Puke, went to bed about 5 o'clock, seemed to rest quietly, but was found dead about 12. He complained of a pain in his stomach, which he could impute to no other cause than a few mushrooms eaten the day before at Ballyboy".[117] Pococke was buried in the churchyard of the parish church of Ardbraccan, in a large vault constructed for his family by an earlier Bishop of Meath, George Montgomery (1569-1621). This vault, known as the Montgomery Monument, has a recessed central panel which contains three half-length figures of Montgomery, his wife and daughter, framed with a border of alternating leaves and flowers.[118]

On the south side of the monument (see Plate 5) is a simple framed plaque, which reads: "HERE LIES INTERED THE BODY OF DOCTER [sic] RICHARD POCOCKE OF MEATH WHO DIED September 15th 1765 in the 63rd year of his age". Considering the extent of Pococke's literary and scholarly reputation, it is not surprising that J.N. Brewer was to refer somewhat disparagingly to this "small slab", which he described as "a humble and ill-executed memorial".[119]

---

[116]At the time, Charleville Castle was let to a Captain Thomas Johnston, the Earl of Charleville having died the previous year and his widow having moved to Dublin

[117]From a Diary published in *Some old Annals of the Stoney Family ... Compiled by Major S. ... Illustrated by C. Stoney of Portland* (London, 1879) 13

[118]For a full description of the structure, see C. Casey and A. Rowan *The Buildings of Ireland: North Leinster* (London, 1993) 115

[119]*The Beauties of Ireland being Original Deliniations, Topographical, Historical, and Biographical, of Each County*, Vol. II (1826) 191

Plate 5
The Montgomery Monument, Ardbraccan, Burial Place of Richard Pococke
Photo Tony Hand

Plate 6
Ardbraccan Church & Tower, with the Montgomery Monument to extreme right
Photo Tony Hand

On his death, as we have seen, Pococke left his house and estate in Newtown to his sister, of the same address. The remainder of his estate was left in trust to the Incorporated Society in Dublin for Promoting English Protestant Schools in Ireland, with the interest being used to support Elizabeth and other members of his family during their lifetime, after which the fortune was to be used for founding "a School for papist boys who shall become protestants and to be bred to linnen weaving". This weaving school, which later became known as the Pococke School, was eventually closed and the endowments were amalgamated with the present Kilkenny College.

Two of the three known portraits of this man have already been noted, and are reproduced above and on the cover and in Plate 4. There is a third, a "fine portrait in oils of the Bishop - representing him three-quarter length seated", which in 1933 still hung in the Board Room of the Incorporated Society in Kildare Street, Dublin.[120] The whereabouts of this, however, is not known, though Leslie also noted two small engravings in the Bishop's Palace, Kilkenny, which were probably taken from this picture.[121]

---

[120]Described by Leslie, *op.cit.* 31

[121]It appears that these two engravings are no longer in the Bishop's Palace

Life of Jeremiah Milles (1714-84)

Jeremiah Milles' connections with Ireland effectively ended with his uncle's death in 1740, when he inherited his estate and returned to England to continue in his church career. His brief time in Waterford, his travels, and his life-long association with Pococke and his family are the focus of the present account, and for further details of Milles' life, the reader is directed to more general descriptions, such as that provided in the *ODNB* and A.W.B. Messenger.[122] However, it should be noted that a full-length biography of Milles is long overdue.

Milles was born on 29 January, 1714, the third son of Rev. Jeremiah Milles (Rector of Riseholme, Lincolnshire and Vicar of Duloe, Cornwall) and his wife Mary. Some sources maintain that he was born in Duloe (where his father had been resident since his appointment as rector in 1704), while others, presumably accepting the following somewhat fanciful story,[123] record his birth place as Highclere. This story claims that the two brothers Thomas (at the time still a professor in Oxford) and Rev. Jeremiah Milles "fell in love with the same lady, but instead of quarrelling over her they agreed to let her state her preference. She according chose Jeremiah, whereupon Thomas... resolved never to marry but promised his brother to adopt and educate the first of his sons who might be born at their father's rectory at Highclere. Jeremiah later became vicar of Duloe, and three times Mrs. Milles set out to journey from Cornwall to Hampshire, but each time, in consequence of the bad state of the roads, she was too late. On the fourth occasion, however, she was more successful, and... Jeremiah Milles the second was born at Highclere."[124]

Whether or not this story is based on fact, it is true that from an early age, Milles was singled out for special attention by his uncle, Bishop Milles, who paid for his education at Eton

---

[122]*Op.cit.*

[123]This tale is first recorded by John Edwin Cussans, *History of Hertfordshire, containing an Account of the Descents of the various Manors; Pedigrees of Families connected with the County; Antiquities, local Customs* ..Volume 1 (London, 1870) and mentioned in subsequent editions of the *ODNB*

[124]See A. W. B. Messenger, *op.cit.*, 22-23

(1725-28) and Christ Church College, Oxford. Having matriculated in 1729 aged fifteen, Milles took a BA in 1733, and within a few months had set off with his older cousin, Richard Pococke, on their first Grand Tour (1733-34). As noted earlier, it is likely that this voyage was entirely financed by his uncle, though by the time he set out on his second he would have had a considerable income from his new and relatively senior position in the Diocese of Waterford & Lismore.

It is clear from the nature of his letters from abroad that Milles had a keen interest in ecclesiastical matters, but his first opening for a career in the Anglican Church presented itself during the course of the earlier tour, and was warmly, though humbly, welcomed by him. Rather than approaching Milles direct, the bishop wrote to Pococke, as described by the latter to his mother, in a letter from Venice, dated 13 June, 1734: "Yesterday [12 June] I received a letter from the Bishop dated April 27th in which is this paragraph: 'I send you this to acquaint you, that Mr Barbon is in such a condition that I think he cannot live a week longer; you know what preferment will be void by his death, & I desire you to let Jerre[125] know, that if he be inclined to the gown, I will bestow it upon him. I think he will stand in his own light if he neglects to embrace this opportunity, if he thinks fit to embrace it, he must without delay make the best of his way to me here."[126] Rev. Hugh Barbon had occupied numerous positions in the diocese since 1702, and was succeeded in several of these (even from as early as 1729) by Pococke and Milles.[127] However, the position being offered to Milles from

---

[125]The family "pet" or nickname for Jeremiah

[126]Add: 22978

[127]He had been Treasurer of Lismore Cathedral since 1729 (succeeded on his death by Milles), Prebend of Donaghmore & Kiltegan since 1716, Lecturer of St Olaves from 1728, appointed Vicar of Cahir in 1730 (but immediately succeeded or replaced by Pococke in the same year), appointed Rector of Outeragh in June, 1730 (and immediately succeeded by Pococke in July of that year), Vicar of Kiltegan since 1716 (succeeded by Pococke in 1729), Curate of Dungarvan from 1702-29, Curate of Kilgobnet from 1705-30, Curate of Ringagonagh from 1705-32, Vicar of Kilrossanty since 1729 (succeeded by Milles in 1736 - there was a delay of two years), and Vicar of Fews since 1705. Dates taken from Rennison, *op.cit.*

abroad was the relatively senior appointment of Treasurer of
Lismore Cathedral - an extraordinary offer given that the young
man had not entirely decided on a church career.

Clearly Milles took a few days to consider this matter, and
in a letter sent direct to the bishop (Verona, 6/17 June, 1734), he
responded to the honour he had done him in offering him this
preferment, "for wch favour with all the others that your Ldship
has continually heap'd upon me I can never return sufficient
thanks."[128] He then promised to make immediate plans to return
to Ireland via the shortest route. In his next (and final) letter,
(Milan, 12/23 June, 1734), Milles agreed to his uncle's request to
make "the expedition...taking the shortest route, not stopping at
any place in the way" and promised to "be in Waterford as soon
as it is possible".[129] The cousins actually arrived in London on 1
July, where they were due to stay "but 2 daies",[130] and from there
made their way to Holyhead, from where they departed for
Waterford on 13 July. In order for this nepotistic appointment to
be secured with the greatest expediency, the bishop, who was
obliged to ensure that his nephew was actually qualified for the
job, ordained him as Deacon two weeks after his arrival in Ireland
(28 July, 1734) and as Priest just two weeks later, on 11 August.
However, the appointment, as far as the records show, was not
actually instituted until the following year, in 1735.[131]

As will be seen in Volume 2 of this book, on 12 April,
1736, after which he had had time to settle into his new role in
the diocese (and presumably engaged a substitute to carry out his
work), Milles left for England to make preparations for his
second Grand Tour. He wrote to his uncle that day, informing
him that he had arrived at Holyhead and was setting out
immediately for "Oxon", where he was to spend a few days,
before departing for Newtown to collect Pococke. After one day,
they would proceed to London, "to get our things in readiness to
be gone".[132] However, their departure from England was

---

[128]See the letter (Add. 15773), reproduced in Chapter 5
[129]Add. 15773
[130]Pococke to his mother, Letter 22, Dover, June 30, 1734, Add. 22978
[131]See Rennison, *op.cit.,* 58
[132]Add. 15773

somewhat delayed owing to news of the bishop's ailing health. In a letter from Calais dated May 24/June 4, 1736, Milles informs his uncle: "Hearing of your Ldships recovery by my Aunt Pococke, and of your desire that we should begin our route we set out on Thursday in the Canterbury stage coach".[133]

Clearly, the two cousins were still at the bishop's command, and once he had given his blessing, they were able to start their travels. They continued their tour of the Continent for approximately fifteen months until further word of the bishop's ill health reached them in Pola, (modern day Pula, in Croatia), in late July, 1737. This news, which arrived in the form of two letters from Mrs. Pococke (the first being a "melancholy account of your Lordships being seized with a fit of the gravel [gallstones]") provoked a concerned response from Milles, who claimed that, though her second letter "gave us the joyfull news of your Lordships recovery.... It was the greatest concern to us that we were not present to have attended on your Lordship during your illness; but now think it my Duty to hasten home as fast as conveniently I can, tho' I have not yet received a letter from your Lordship on that subject".[134] Once again their travel plans had been disrupted, but this time, while Milles proposed to lose no time in returning to Waterford, via England (where he hoped to stay a few days in London, "to settle some affairs"), Pococke was to "follow leisurely, being very desirous now he is abroad to see the most remarkable things in his way".[135] Pococke then reaffirmed this in a letter to the bishop (which has curiously found its way into the Milles correspondence) and respectfully asks his uncle if it will be acceptable for him to delay his return by a few months "in order to see such places as I have the greatest desire to view in a proper manner, and to make some observations which I hope will not be altogether disagreeable to your Lordship..."[136] As it happened, he actually stayed abroad for a further four years, returning more than a year after his uncle's death.

---

[133]Add. 15773
[134]Trieste, 24 July/4 August, 1737, Add. 15774
[135]Ibid.
[136]Treiste, 24 July/4 August, 1737, Add. 15774

Three letters further on, by which time the cousins had reached Venice, a letter had been received from the Bishop, dated 4 June, "which ratified to us the joyfull news of our Lordships recovery". Though the Bishop now did not expect his nephew home "till next summer", Milles still proposed to be in Ireland before the winter.[137] Several more letters were dispatched from Venice during the month of August, and in the last (dated 20/30 August), Milles noted that he would be leaving for England the next day.[138] Since this is the last letter in the collection, we do not know how many further letters (if any) were received by the bishop, or the date at which Milles eventually reached Waterford, though we can assume that he was there to be installed in his new preferment as Precentor of Waterford Cathedral, on 31 December, 1737.

On his return from the Continent, Milles took up a number of further appointments in his uncle's diocese: Vicar of Kilrossanty (1736-45), Precentor of Waterford Cathedral (until 12 November, 1744, after which it passed over to Pococke), and Vicar of Reisk (from an unknown date until 1744). We do not know where he resided during the years he served in these offices, but it is possible that, owing to his close relationship with the bishop, he may have resided with him in the Episcopal House, when in Waterford. Certainly the correspondence from abroad suggests that Milles was genuinely concerned about his uncle's health and regarded it as his role to care for him. Also, by then he must surely have suspected, if not known for a fact, that he was to be nominated as his uncle's heir.

At the bishop's death, Milles, as already observed, was nominated as one of the two sole executors of his Will (the other being Pococke, who, at the time was still on his travels), as well as heir to his estate. It would have been his responsibility, therefore, to conduct the funeral arrangements in accordance with his uncle's wishes (including having his body sent back to be buried in Hampshire), and to put his other affairs in order. Presumably, the latter task would have involved sorting out the late bishop's papers, which is how the transcripts of the Grand

---

[137]Venice, 15/16 August, 1737, Add. 15774
[138]Add. 15774

Tour letters from himself and Pococke may have come into his possession.

Though the termination dates of his appointments in Ireland suggest that Milles retained tentative links with Waterford for some years after the bishop's death, from 1741 he appears to have been fully re-integrated into English society, and in regular attendance at various London clubs. He was elected as a member of the Egyptian Club at its first meeting in 1741, and chosen as its Secretary (or Reis Effendi) at the same time; in the same year he was elected Fellow of the Society of Antiquaries of London, later acting as its President (1769-84); and in 1742 was elected Fellow of the Royal Society, on the grounds of being "a Gentleman of Merit and Learning, Curious in Natural History & Antiquities, well versed in Philosophical knowledge, and qualified to be a useful Member of the Society". The same source also describes him as: "MA Of Corpus Christi College in Oxford, and now in London".[139] Aspiring to be a member of the Divan Club, at the Divan meeting of 17 February, 1744, he was introduced by Lord Sandwich as a person with an intention to go into Turkey. However, this is the last we hear of him in the Divan records, since he failed to make the trip to the East during the short lifespan of the club, and proof of having been there was of course a requirement for membership.

In 1745 Milles married Edith Potter, whose father was John Potter, Archbishop of Canterbury from 1737 until his death in 1747.[140] Milles received several preferments in his father-in-law's diocese, as follows: Rector of Saltwood with Hythe, Kent (1744-46), Rector of Merstham, Surrey (1745 for life), and Domestic Chaplain to the Archbishop of Canterbury (24 October, 1745 until the Archbishop's death).[141] A further preferment was

---

[139]RS citation, Ref: EC/1742/05

[140]The match may well have been encouraged by Bishop Milles, who had been a contemporary of Potter's at Oxford and was even ordained by the same bishop. They had other things in common, too, both being classical scholars and both having fallen victim to the criticism of their Oxford colleague, Thomas Hearne.

[141]Archbishop Potter looked after Jeremiah's relatives, too, in 1746, for example, appointing his cousin, Isaac Milles, as Domestic Chaplain to Rachel, Duchess (Dowager) of Bridgwater

received by Milles a year after Archbishop Potter's death (though still in the jurisdiction of the Archbishop of Canterbury), as Rector of West Tarring, in Sussex, a position he retained until 7 June, 1775 (when he gave it to his son, see below), and another in London, from 1745 until his death.

However, the most important appointments he was to receive, in terms of enhancing his career and elevating his profile (as well as his income), were those of Prebendary and Precentor of Exeter Cathedral. These preferments were bestowed upon him in May, 1747, just months before his father-in-law's sudden death. From there he was to proceed to the more prestigious and lucrative position of Dean of Exeter (1762), where he was to remain for the rest of his life, building on his reputation as a serious and learned antiquarian. As noted above, he published jointly with Pococke a book of inscriptions in 1752 (many of which were collected during their travels), and was elected President of the Society of Antiquaries of London in 1769, a position which he retained until his death, in 1784.

Jeremiah Milles and his wife Edith had a family of two daughters and three sons.[142] All three sons (of whom their father was notoriously indulgent)[143] attended Eton and Oxford. Jeremiah (1751-95) was a Barrister at Law and became Lord of the Parish of Pishobury; Thomas (1753-1830) also pursued a legal career, becoming a Barrister and KC; and Richard (1754-1820), entered the church.[144] After obtaining an MA, the latter received a preferment as Prebend of Exeter (presumably from his father, Dean of Exeter), as well as becoming Rector of West Tarring, one of his father's livings.[145] Edith died in 1761, aged only thirty-five, and was buried in London.

---

[142]Though several more children did not survive to adulthood

[143]See note to correspondence between Frances Burney and Hester Lynch Thrale, in B. Rizzo (ed.), *The Early Journals and Letters of Fanny Burney, Vol. IV,* (Oxford 2003) 527

[144]See J. Foster, *op.cit.,* 1715-1856, Vol. 3 (1888) 957

[145]An obituary notes that, of a number of sinecures he held in England until his death, he resigned one (West Terring in Sussex) "in favour of his son". See "Memoirs of Dean Milles", in *The London Magazine,* Volume 2 (January to June, 1784) 293.

Even after his cousin Richard's death, Jeremiah Milles was to retain links with the Pocockes. An indication of the family's closeness is in the fact that on drawing up her Will on 8 March, 1767, his cousin, Miss Elizabeth Pococke (Richard's unmarried sister), named and appointed him as one of her two executors.[146] For his trouble, she bequeathed him £300. She left generous sums of money (on average £200 a piece) to a number of her cousins, nephews and nieces (including an additional £100 to Milles) and the sum of 3 shillings a week to be paid to her mother's old servant, Martha Ffuller, for the rest of her life. Personal items with important family associations, such as a bible with silver clasps, given to her by her "Grand ffather Pococke",[147] and mourning rings (one of which was issued at the same grandfather's funeral) were also given to family members, and her "wearing apparel" was bequeathed to Mary Shipton, the daughter of her mother's brother, the late Isaac Milles. She desired that "the House and Garden and Premises I now live in at New Town"[148] be sold for as much money as possible, and that, along with her "Household Goods, Household Linnen, Plate China Books...", which were to be "turned into money", the whole amount should be reconstituted as part of her estate. Once all debts, funeral expenses etc. had been paid, the residue of her estate was to be put in trust and the interest paid to Elizabeth Milles (a "spinster" daughter of her mother's brother, Isaac Milles) "during her natural life"; and on the latter's death, the residue of her estate should then be bequeathed "to the School directed to be founded at Kilkenny by my most dear Brother late Bishop of Ossory.... for Papist Boys and to Weaving and to the Protestant Religion...".[149]

Though the terms of Miss Pococke's Will were simple, the seven Codicils, added between 1767 and a month before her death were problematic, since they were written on loose scraps

---

[146]The other executor she appointed was Rev. Dr. Thomas Burton, of St. Canice's Cathedral, Kilkenny, presumably to take care of that part of her Will relating to the boys' school established by her brother in his Will a few years earlier. See Will of Elizabeth Pococke (Spinster), *op.cit.*
[147]Rev. Richard Pococke, Rector of Colmer, in Hamphsire
[148]Pococke's former property, Newtown House
[149]For the above references, see Mrs. Pococke's Will, *op.cit.*

of paper and were not signed by witnesses. The Will was proved
in London, on behalf of the Perogative Court of Canterbury, a
month after her death, on 7 June, 1774. However, five days
earlier Milles, along with a Mrs. Dorothy Box, of Wardrobe
Court, London, was required to appear at a hearing, at which he
testified that he had known her for twenty years and upwards, at
the date of her death. He further outlined how he had been
looking over her papers on 6 May (just four days after her death)
and found her Will, together with the seven Codicils, "locked up
together in the deceaseds Bureau standing in the deceaseds
Drawing Room", and declared that they were "in every respect in
the same Plight and Condition" as when he had found them.
Both he and Dorothy Box also declared that they were "perfectly
well acquainted with her the Deceaseds Manner and Character of
Hand Writing and of counting and subscribing her name", having
often seen her write and sign her name. The additions to the
original Will were relatively minor, concerning family portraits, a
counterpane and chair-covers that she and her mother had
worked, two more legacies worth £200 to be given to her female
cousins, and a sum of £40 to be paid to her servant Mary
[Stokes].

One point of particular interest here is that of the portraits.
In the first Codicil Elizabeth states: "I desire that my Brothers
Picture which was taken the last time he was in England in
Parliament Robes be given to the School that is directed to be
founded by his last Will at Kilkenny and that it may be hung up
there" (10 April, 1767). This must be the portrait of Pococke,
which now hangs in the new Bishop's Palace in Kilkenny,
reproduced in Plate 4. Regrettably we do not know who the artist
was, but since he was in London in March, 1765,[150] and died in
Ireland six months later, we can now date the portrait with some
certainty as having been executed around the first half of that
year. It will be remembered that in the June he was translated to

---

[150]See the Codicil to his Will, where he states: "The above will written with
my own hand on the 24th day of March 1765 I do desire may be lookd on as
a Codicil to the other will signed & sealed as far as it Differs for it not
having here in London convenient witnesses", NLI, D. 27, 161

the See of Elphin and then in July to the See of Meath, at which point he must have been back in Ireland.

In the second Codicil, written four years later, Elizabeth Pococke states, "I desire my fathers picture may be sent to Mr Mant School Master of Southampton to remain to the School for ever as Mr. Pococke was a great Benefactor to that School and my Mothers Picture to go with it that they may not be parted if it may be not thought improper" (July 30, 1771). The reference is of course to Richard Mant, Master of King Edward School, whose grandmother, Dorothea Bingham (née Pococke), was the sister of an earlier Master of this school, Rev. Richard Pococke (Richard the traveller's father). Sadly, the school, which has moved several times since Rev. Pococke was Headmaster, does not have these portraits, and it is thought that they must have been lost.[151] All three portraits were in Elizabeth's possession, those of her parents presumably having been bequeathed to her by her mother, who had died in 1760, and that of her brother probably having been part of the estate which she inherited from him in 1765.

Jeremiah died in London on 13 February 1784, after a serious illness. In his Will, dated three weeks earlier (6 January 1784) he asked that if he died in Exeter, he should be buried in the Cathedral Church, "if possible in the same vault wherein my most beloved son John is interred".[152] In case he died in London, however, he wished to be buried in the Rector's Vault in the Church of St Edmund, King and Martyr, Lombard Street, "near to the remains of my most beloved wife". He desired that all unnecessary expense be avoided and that his "ffuneral [be] as private as is consistent with dignity."[153] He left a fortune of £22,000, bequeathing £6,000 a piece to his sons Thomas and Richard, with smaller sums being left to his daughters, relatives, servants and the poor. His furniture, household goods, books and

---

[151]I am grateful to Di Alexander, Archivist of King Edward VI School, Southampton, for confirming this

[152]As already noted, several of the Milles children did not survive to adulthood

[153]See Will of Jeremiah Milles, Public Record Office, The National Archives of the UK, Catalogue Reference: Prob. 11/1113

plate were left to his youngest son, Richard, and the remainder of his fortune went to his heir, Jeremiah.[154]

The author of "An Eighteenth Century Dean of Exeter and his Family" reproduces a portrait of Milles from 1762,[155] but does not identify the artist. The portrait appearing in Plate 7 (below) depicts Milles seated in front of Exeter Cathedral, of which he was dean from 1762 until his death.

Plate 7
Watercolour Drawing of Dean Jeremiah Milles by John Downman, 1785[156]
Courtesy of the National Portrait Gallery, London

---

[154]See *ibid.*, though the handwriting is difficult to decipher
[155] See Messenger, *op.cit.*, Plate 1
[156]This portrait must have been based on a drawing executed earlier, since Milles died in 1784

CHAPTER 2

Itinerary of the 1733-34 Grand Tour

This chapter outlines the route taken by Pococke and Milles in their first tour of the Continent, and where possible indicates the length of time spent at each place.[1] Firstly, however, it may be useful to look briefly at some of the conventions used by the travellers in documenting this information. Both correspondents are methodical in their approach to dating their letters, and there is only one example from the entire collection without a date or a reference to the place from which it was sent, and another omitting the month.[2] One aspect of eighteenth-century letter writing that can be confusing to the modern reader is the double dating system used in correspondence sent from the Continent, whereby letters are dated according to both the Gregorian and the Julian calendars, with a difference of eleven days.[3] For example, all letters sent from abroad are dated as follows, "Dresden, 20th November O.S.[Old Style] 1st December N.S. [New Style] 1736", or, more usually, "Palma in Friuli, July 28/August 8, 1737". With

---

[1] A very brief summary of the two tours is given in Ingamells, *op.cit.*, under the entry for Pococke (779-80). This is based on an analysis of a limited amount of manuscripts: for instance, the correspondence from Milles to the bishop is not mentioned (apart from three originals), and there is no reference to Milles having joined Pococke on the second tour

[2] However, this may actually have been the fault of the person who made the fair copy. The first example is a letter from Milles to the bishop (Add. 15773) and is located between the letters dated Rome, 14/25 February and 14/25 March, 1733; the second is also from Milles to the bishop (Add. 15773), from Breda, dated 17/28 [June], 1736

[3] The new Gregorian calendar was devised in 1582 and was immediately adopted by a number of countries including Spain, Portugal, Italy, France and the Low Countries. This was eleven days ahead of the old Julian calendar still in use in Britain until 1752. Therefore, when British or Irish travellers before this date wrote back home from the Continent, they included both dates to avoid confusion.

the rare exception when the writer perhaps forgets, the only time this convention does not appear in our correspondence is, of course, when the letter is sent from England, just before embarking from Dover to Calais, for instance, or after returning to English soil.

At the top of each letter is given the place at which the letter was written, though, as is the case with much travel writing of the period, the correspondent generally writes retrospectively, sometimes producing a number of letters from one particular centre, with detailed accounts of places visited in the previous location or on route. It is unusual for an initial letter composed from a city like Rome, Venice or Vienna (where visitors generally based themselves for a considerable length of time) to give any account of this place itself. As noted earlier, when intending to travel to a new place, the writer typically gives a forwarding address to his correspondent, both for mail and for money orders. In fact, the address given is often that of a banker. It should also be noted that the "direction" is generally given in French, regardless of the country in question.[4]

While the correspondence itself is the most obvious source of evidence for the course of their travels, we are also fortunate in that Pococke's *A Description of the East* contains a very precise *Itinerary in Europe*. This takes the form of a

---

[4]Milles notes in a letter from Paris during the first tour, "If you Ldship should have any thing particular to communicate, a letter wrote any time before the 22 of this month N.S. will find me there with this direction A monsieur monsieur Bouer Delore pour render a monsieur Milles a Genes." 25 September/12 October, 1733. Add. 15773. Two consecutive letters sent by him from Rome, however, indicate that he feared his correspondence may sometimes have gone astray. In the first, he notes, "By reason of another gentleman of my name being at Venice, my letters by another mistake are carried thither & I do not know whether I shall ever receive them. I forgot to tell your Ldship in my last, my direction to Rome it is A Monsieur, Monsieur Jean Feissier Banquier pour render a Monsieur Jeremie Milles a Rome"; and in the second he repeats, "For fear my last should any ways miscarry, I will venture to mention my direction again a Monsieur, Monsieur Jean Teissier Banquier pour render a monsieur Jermie Milles a Rome". The difference in spelling is in the original letters, possibly wrongly transcribed by the bishop or his secretary. See letters dated 18/29 December, 1733 and 11/22 January, 1734. Add. 15773

comprehensive list of the places visited, though (unlike itineraries in other literature) does not include details such as distance travelled each day or cumulatively.[5] The account below, though taking into account the published itinerary, has been compiled from an analysis of the letters themselves, and where possible details have been highlighted to illustrate important aspects of the travel itself, such as the various modes of transport used by the correspondents, sailing conditions and threats caused by military activity in particular areas.

Itinerary for the First Tour, from August, 1733 to July, 1734

At midday on Saturday 1 September, 1733, Pococke and Milles set sail from Dover to Calais, on "a rough but very swift passage"[6] that took two hours and fifty minutes, and from which the older cousin was "never so sick in all [his] life".[7] After settling their affairs (with the customs, etc.), they walked about the town, had a dinner of soup, pigeon and duck at the "best Inn", and stayed the night. They departed from Calais at 6.00 or 7.00 the next morning (the two accounts differ on this point) in a hired Post Chaise for Paris, accompanied by "two Hollanders" with whom they had travelled from England. They reached Boulogne at noon and visited some sites, after which they journeyed to Montrevil (modern Montreuil-sur-Mer), where they spent Sunday night (2 September). They stayed Monday night at the picturesque walled city of Abbeville, where they visited several nunneries and other ecclesiastical buildings, and set off from here on the morning of Tuesday 3 September, reaching Amiens, famous for its Gothic cathedral, by noon. They stayed the night in the small village of Wavigny (modern Wavignies) and on Wednesday 4 September, after dining at Chantilly, arrived at St.

---

[5] *A Description of the East*, Vol. II, Part II, Book VI, "Geographical Observations", Chapter II, 272ff. This itinerary is a little confusing, however, since, rather than starting at 1733, when their first trip took place, it begins with Pococke's landing from the East, in November, 1740. Details of the cousins' first tour (1733-34) and the earlier part of their second tour (before they parted ways in Trent) are then inserted afterwards.

[6] Milles to the bishop, Calais, 1/12 September, 1733. Add.15773

[7] Pococke to his mother, Calais, 1/12 September, 1733. Add. 22978

Dennis, where they stayed for two nights, departing at midday on Saturday 6 September. They reached Paris an hour later, after what Milles described as a very agreeable journey. While initially uncertain of how long they were to stay in Paris, and of their accommodation arrangements (the first night was spent at an inn and a Monsieur Dennis was then to recommend them to lodgings), they eventually spent almost a month in the capital, where they visited the sites and took excursions (for which they hired horses) to see the Palaces of St. Cloud, St. Germain, Marly, Versailles and Meudon. On arrival in the capital, Milles informed the bishop that they would be home by Christmas, 1734.[8] This is the first indication in the correspondence of the intended scale of their tour, which was obviously planned to last precisely sixteen months.

They left Paris at 5.00 a.m. on Thursday, 15 October, arriving at Fontainebleau in time for "dinner" (our lunch), where they stayed the night.[9] They next visited Sens and Dijon, where both cousins noted the macabre sight of a criminal's body exposed to the public after execution, and from there to Chalons, where they took a covered boat to Lyons. They were obliged to stay here a week, because their servant had fallen ill with a fever, thus noted by Milles, but euphemistically described by Pococke to his mother, as "some little affair". They left Lyons on Friday 30 October, N.S. (though Pococke gives the date as 31), proposing to travel to Genoa via Nîmes and Marseilles. This route was chosen not only because it contained so many places of interest, but also, "because [they should] not have convenient passage over the Alps the nearest way on account of the army who have employed all the mules & horses they could get, to covey them into Italy".[10]

On Saturday 7 November (N.S.),[11] having travelled through Vienne, Valence, Viviers, St. Esprit (now Pont-Saint-Esprit), Ville Neuve and Avignon (where they spent an evening

---

[8]Letter of 25 September/6 October, 1733, Add. 15773
[9]Milles to the bishop, Lyons, 22/29 October, 1733. Add. 15773
[10]*Ibid.* Milles alludes here to activities taking place during the War of the Polish Succession
[11]Milles sometimes specifies Old or New Style, but in general uses the local date

with an Irishman by the name of Lawless),[12] Pococke and Milles arrived at Nîmes (spelled Nismes in the manuscripts). They remained here for three days, examining the Roman antiquities, and on Monday 9 November made an excursion of twenty-four miles to Montpellier, "in the finest road, & country that I have seen in France."[13] They left Montpellier on Thursday 12 November and, having spent a further two days in Nîmes (13-15 November), went to Arles, which they reached the following day and where they visited some more "curious pieces of antiquity". Later that day they dined in Salon (now Salon-de-Provence), arriving in Aix (now Aix-en-Provence) on Tuesday 17 November.

They departed from Aix-en-Provence the following day (Wednesday), having heard that "20000 Spanish horse, are to pass by here in a week or 10 days time, in order to embark at Toulon for Italy."[14] On their journey to Marseilles, they visited Toulon, which they reached the next day. Having spent a week in this city, they left Thursday 27 November, at noon, and spent the night in the small village of Pignan. The next day (Friday 28) they reached the town of Frejus, where they spent the day examining its antiquities. On the Saturday they travelled to Antibes, at a distance of twenty-four miles, but had to wait there until the following Thursday (4 December) for their Felucca,[15] which failed to turn up. Instead, they hired another vessel, which they embarked that night at 7 o'clock. However, around noon the next day, when they were only fifty miles from Oneglia in Sardinia, "the wind began to be very high, & having been prodigious sick the night before, [they] chose rather to continue [their] journey by land upon mules, tho' in the worst road that

---

[12]"[H]e is brother to Sr Patrick Lawless who is vice roy of Majorca .. [and] seemed to be a very good natur'd affable man". Milles to the bishop, Aix-en-Provence, 18/19 November, 1733. Add. 15773. See Ingamells, *op.cit.,* 590, where he is mentioned as having been in Florence on 26 April, 1732, intending to go on to Rome.

[13]Milles to the bishop, Aix-en-Provence, 18/19 November, 1733. Add. 15773

[14]*Ibid.* Again, a reference to the current war

[15]A small traditional wooden boat holding around 2-3 people

ever was gone, it being nothing but ascending & descending frightfull rocks & precipices".[16]

On Monday 7 December they arrived at Genoa and found their "scheme for [their] travels a little disconcerted by the present war", which made it dangerous to travel to Italy through the Alps. They proposed, instead, to embark on a large English ship that was already in Genoa and was due to sail to Leghorn, "& from thence to Pisa Florence & so strait to Rome".[17] According to plan, the ship ("of 300 tuns") set sail at about noon on Sunday 13 December. As described by Milles, however, "having gone a 4th part of our voyage, we were the next day obliged by contrary winds to return to Genoua, where we waited for a fair wind till Wednesday morning when about 10 of the clock we set sail. After we had been at sea about 30 hours, we met with contrary winds, wch blew us near 30 miles Southward of Leghorn, but however we made a shift to enter the port on Saturday morning" (19 December).[18]

The cousins left Leghorn on 22 December, and travelled fourteen miles to Pisa, which they explored for two days before departing for Lucca, on 24 December. They remained here until they left for Pistoia, on Saturday 26. Early the next morning, they set out for Florence, which they reached later that day. At some stage between Leghorn and Florence they came across a letter from the bishop, with some "commands" relating to a Mr Quinn and marble. They visited a Mr Murphy about this matter, who confirmed that the marble had gone, but sadly no further details of this failed transaction are revealed. Having "sufficiently satisfied [their] curiosity at Florence",[19] they set out on 15 January for Siena, where they remained until 17 of that month. Very little is said about the journey from Florence to Rome, or the dates involved, though Milles informs the bishop that they arrived in the capital city on the day the letter was written (22

---

[16]Milles to the bishop, Genoa, 1/12 December, 1733. Add. 15733
[17]Milles to the bishop, Genoa, 1/12 December, 1733. Add. 15733
[18]*Ibid.* See N. Figgis, *op.cit.*, who cites the *Leghorn Newsletter* for 3 December, 1733 (Richard Brinsley Ford Archive. SP 98/34), which rather prematurely notes: "Mr Mills with Mr Pococke nephews to the Bishop of Waterford in Ireland arrived hre from Marseilles and are going to Rome"
[19]Milles to the bishop, 23 January/3 February, 1734. Add. 15733

January), proposing to stay "some little time until the frost is a little over, & then go to Naples, & so return to Rome afterwards to see it".[20] A further letter to the bishop notes, "We propose to leave Rome about the latter end of May, in order to be at Venice by the Ascension", and on 11/22 April he further notes they will be setting off for Venice in ten days' time and propose to be in England by July.[21]

Though the subject of money rarely arises in Milles' correspondence, the young man informs his patron, in his first letter from Rome that, despite his extreme frugality, he is fast running out of cash. He therefore respectfully asks for a cheque for £80 to be sent to him immediately, at Rome.[22] The very next day, he begins another letter on the same theme fearing that the previous communication, sent by German post, may have gone astray.[23] Similar requests are made from Pococke to his mother,[24] and as mentioned earlier, deleted passages from the copies describe his continuing difficulties in obtaining his rightful money from Ireland.

During the latter part of their stay in Rome, the cousins made a nine-day excersion to Tivoli, visiting many sites and places of interest en-route. Just before dispatching his letter dated 29 April/10 May, 1734, Milles received a letter from the bishop, dated 30 March (which gives an idea of how long it took for correspondence from Ireland to reach the travellers abroad), and assures his uncle, "..& tomorrow we leave Rome for Bologna. We shall make all expedition possible into England". The next letter from the Milles collection is sent from Bologna (dated 13/24 May, 1733), with his subsequent correspondence from their return journey being written from Modena (15/26 May), Padua (21 May/1 June), Venice (30 May/10 June), Verona

---

[20]Milles to the bishop, Rome, 11/22 January, 1734. Add. 15733. However, their plans to visit Naples never materialised during this trip

[21]Letter from Rome, no date given, see note above. Add. 15733

[22]Milles to the bishop, Rome, 11/22 January, 1734. Add. 15733

[23] Milles to the bishop, 23 January/3 February, 1734. Add. 15733

[24]Shortly before they leave for England, for example, he asks for the sum of £15 to be sent to him at Langres, with a further £15 at Cambray, since his original request for £30 to Mr. Hoare, his banker, may have gone astray. Milan, June 12/23, 1734. Add. 22978

Letters from Abroad, Volume 1

(6/17 June), and Milan (12/23 June). It is in the letter from Verona that Milles receives and accepts his uncle's offer (communicated via a letter to Pococke) of a preferment in Waterford,[25] and promises, "we shall make the best of our way to Ireland thro' Lombardy, & France, wch will be by much the nearest way". In his subsequent letter from Milan, since when he has received two more urgent letters from the bishop,[26] Milles assures his uncle that they are hastening to England, taking the shortest route and departing from Milan the next day (13 June).

After leaving Rome, Pococke wrote letters to his mother from Venice (31 May/11 June and 13 June),[27] Milan (12/23 June), Turin (14/26 June), Lyons (20 June/2 July) and finally, Dover (30 June, 1734). In his letter from Venice, he informs his mother that he has received a communication from the bishop concerning his cousin's offer of a preferment, thus explaining why they are hastening their journey home. He also mentions that he had a desire to spend a month seeing Flanders and Holland, spending the rest of the winter with her in England. However, he realises that under the present circumstances the bishop is unlikely to grant him permission to do so, and that he will probably have to return to Ireland sooner. In his letter from Milan (12/23 June), he notes that they hope to be in London in 3 weeks' time, staying in the capital for about two days and then leaving for Ireland (though soon to return to England himself, as he hopes). He asks if she and his sister will meet them in London, and to be sure, in the meantime, to carefully pack and send his gown, cassock and hood (but not his Bachelor of Laws hood). The letter from Dover notes that they will be in London the following day (Monday 1 July), and Pococke asks his mother to find them lodgings at Mrs. Simpson's. As can be seen from Mrs. Pococke's note at the end of this letter,[28] the cousins were indeed met by Mrs. Pococke and Elizabeth, together with a

---

[25] A senior cleric in the diocese is on his deathbed
[26] By now the gentleman in question is actually dead
[27] In the second, he forgets to use the double dating system, or perhaps feels his mother is by now accustomed to the difference
[28] Written when transcribing and editing her son's correspondence, and dated November, 1745

certain Mr. Wood. A touching final comment from Mrs. Pococke is to give praise to God for the safe return of the travellers.

As noted in the Introduction, the last letter in the original collection of letters from Pococke to his mother is written from Holyhead and dated 13 July, 1734. It notes that they (the cousins) arrived at Chester on 9 July, set out for Holyhead on 10, stayed at Aberconway on 11 and visited "Beau Morris" ("a fine situation & pleasant garden"), where they dined with an Irish peer ("Viscount of Cashil"), and were very hospitably entertained. It is not clear how long they remained there, but they were due to "go off in the fastest packet boat about two o clock this afternoon".[29] Though falling slightly outside the period of the first tour, this letter is nevertheless important, as it dates their actual return to Ireland. However, it is a pity that the writer fails to mention which port they were destined for, though it is likely that they took the packet boat from Holyhead to Passage East, which lies conveniently only a few miles from the city of Waterford. This would be consistent with the description in a letter from 1708, where the bishop informed his sister that the clergy "met me in a Body at the Distance of five miles from this place [Waterford]", while the people assembled "in vast numbers to see me land, after I had passed the Ferry upon the Key".[30]

---

[29]Add. 19939
[30]Letter dated 12 May, 1708. See Appendix 2

CHAPTER 3

Letters from England & France

This section traces the steps of Milles and Pococke from the onset of their Grand Tour, starting with their journey from London to Dover and their crossing to Calais, and continuing with their travels through France to Paris. Their sojourn in the capital, where they remained for almost a month, is documented in their manuscripts, and includes the various excursions they took from here to local places of interest, such as the palaces at Versailles, Marly and St. Germain-en-Laye, the latter involving their meeting with the famous writer and librarian, Bernard de Montfaucon. Next follows their journey from Paris to Genoa, with letters being sent from Lyons, Nîmes and Aix-en-Provence until, after a journey fraught with many difficulties, they at last reach the port of Leghorn.

However, since the letters are retrospective, the last in this section, though sent from Genoa, ends with a description of Marseilles, the account of Genoa and the journey to Leghorn appearing in correspondence from Florence, in Chapter 4.

This first part of their journey took just under four months and therefore represented a quarter of their intended continental tour of sixteen months.[1] However, the date of their return was changed several times during their travels, and they finally arrived back in London on 1 July, 1734, therefore precisely ten months after their departure from this city. As a result of various factors (including the political troubles in Italy and Pococke's financial difficulties), they failed to reach Naples, an important centre for Grand Tourists.

---

[1]The first reference to the extent of their travels is in a letter from Milles to the bishop, dated 6/17 September, 1733, where it is stated that they intend to return by next Christmas

Dr Richard Pocockes Letters to his mother in his travels copied Oct 25 1745[2]

LONDON
28 August, 1733
Pococke to his mother
Letter 1[3]

Honoured Madam

I received the favour of your Letter with one included to me.

I am sorry you should be so much troubled upon the account of the journey I am about to take, which as it is undertaken for the improvement of ourselves is a good design & the same providence will I don't doubt, take care of us abroad, that would protect us at home. - - _ [4]

On Monday we walk'd into the city, took places for Thursday to Canterbury.- - - Jerre joyns with me in most kind salutations to you & my Sister.

you may expect to hear from us by next wednesdays post, that is we propose to write on Saturday from Dover, unless we should go off very suddenly for Calais, & then you may not hear from us till Friday.

I am Dear Madam Your most obedient & Dutiful Son Richard Pococke

my direction is A Monsieur, Monsieur Pococke chez Mr Denisprocureur en Parlement dans la Rue D'Anjou pres de la Rue Dauphine A Paris[5]

---

[2] This tiny inscription was inserted by Mrs. Pococke

[3] Add. 22978. There are no corresponding originals for this collection of letters from Pococke to his mother, until Letter 10. When this point is reached, the appropriate references will be made

[4] hese dashes are Mrs. Pococke's, rather than those of the present editor

[5] Monsieur Denis (spelled thus and as "Dennis") is mentioned several times in the Milles/Pococke correspondence for the first tour. He recommends lodgings for them on the cousins' arrival in Paris, arranges the purchase, binding and dispatch of books for Bishop Milles, and, at their request, sends off boxes to London to his brother (Mr. Denis). Reference is also made, in a

DOVER
31 August, 1733
Milles to the bishop[6]

My Lord

We are just got to this place and hope to embark tomorrow for Calais. Jerre is very well and desires his humble duty may be presented to your Lordship. I beg the favour of your Lordship to frank the enclosed letter.

I am with the greatest respect and submission

My Lord

CALAIS
1/12 September, 1733
Milles to the bishop[7]

My Lord,

We set out from London in the Canterbury stage coach last thursday, and arrived there very late at night, at Rochester we took into the coach two Hollanders who are going to Paris, and we go with them,[8] yesterday we hired a coach for Dover, and today, at 12 of the clock at noon, we set sail from Dover, and arrived here eight minuits before three we had a rough, but very swift passage. I was pretty sick but the Dr. was worse.

We walked about the town this afternoon, and saw the fortifications, went to the two monasteries of the Franciscans, of Paula of Minnims, &

---

letter from Pococke to his mother (Letter 13, Rome, 1/12 March, 1734, Add. 22978) to Archdeacon Dennis, see Chapter 4, below, the latter gentleman also being mentioned in article 9 of the bishop's Will (see Appendix 1)

[6]Add. 15773

[7]Add. 15773

[8]These companions left them at Boulogne, but the cousins came across them again on arriving at Paris, where the latter had already been for a day and a half. See Pococke to his mother, Letter 2, Paris, 15/26 September, 1733, Add. 22978

to the Italian Franciscans, or Capuchins, from the last we received great civilitys, they shewed us their library, cells and talked very civilly to us, we went to see the parish church which is very fine, but as it is now late at night, and we shall set out at six of the clock tomorrow morning in a hired post-chaise for Paris, I hope your Ldship will let me defer a particular account till the next convenient opportunity.[9]

I take this opportunity to send my letter to Dover, by a captain of a Pacquet boat,[10] so that the postage will not cost anything.

Dr. Pococke presents his duty to your Ldship, as does my Lord

CALAIS
1/12 September, 1733
Pococke to his mother
Letter 2[11]

[Following a brief outline of their crossing, and a description of Rochester and Dover, Pococke gives an account of their landing at Calais]

We left Dover about twelve o clock & landed at this place in two hours & fifty two minuits; & I never was so sick in all my life. My pupil is very well, for I have been already taken for his preceptor; he desires me to make his compliments to you; [next 3 lines scored out]...

11th. We landed at Calais, we were had to the guard, the Governor, [Admired] the Custom house & are now going to dinner in the best Inn, the Silver [ ] on Soup Migre, pidgeon & a duck; we had our portmanteau's seal[ed at] the Custom house & a permit or else they would have been open'd at [all] places in the way to Paris. The gates are well built a la modern & [the] fortifications strong. I know not whether I shall write any more from [this] place, so desire my kindest

---

[9]He does this in his next very lengthy letter dated Paris, 6/17 September, 1733 (Add. 15773). However, Pococke's account of this town is reproduced here instead (see Letter 2, below, Add. 22978, of the same date)
[10]Spelled variously as "packet" and "paquet"
[11]Add. 22978

love to my Sister -   you will hear from us as soon as we get to Paris;
we set out in a Post chaise to morrow & our Dutch [men with] us in
another, we shall reach it in about three or four days. We have [seen]
only the parish church in this place, in which are eleven altars very
finely adorn'd with columns, statues, pictures; - ...we saw two priests
in the confession chairs; the whole church [is decorated] with tolerable
paintings, on the north side of the great high altar is [a collection] of
relicts, something like those in Winchester C, with the great high altar
with the bones of the Sa[ints]. Mass is said every morning at all those
altars & the people come to say private prayers as well as in the
afternoon. We then went to see the [monastery] of the minims of St
Francis of Poland.... We then went to see the Capuchins, Franciscan
friars, of St Francis the Italian... In the Chappel are [altars] in the same
manner, all adorn'd with statues & pictures as well as the Chappels
themselves, there are Cloysters to them all, we went up into the [...]
which leads to their cells, at the end of which is a small Chappel, built
by Lady Petre, a monk was confessing a young man there, when he
saw us, he left off, & showed it us with great courtesy, & the library &
his cell, the library is a handsome room about 20 feet square with good
books in it, we saw a sort of cross bow to catch mice, at the hole where
the string is fix'd, there is a bait put on a piece of stick under the stock,
the mouse puts his head into the hole to the bait, which lets off the bow,
& catches the mouse. The friars are girded with cords, have no
stockings only sandals on their feet, they live entirely on Charity &
have no lands;   without the gate lives a woman, who is the Mere of the
monks, she receives all charity, they must not take any thing
themselves..... The Governor is Duke de Chalons, his Deputy Governor
Mr Desangle, here is a Mayor 4 [Bailiffs] & two Aldermen, the
President of the parliament of Picardy comes here as judge as oft as
there is occasion, the parliament is held at the chief town Amiens only a
court of justice. There are 1500 soldiers in the garrison, formerly there
were 3000, they are cloth'd in white & look poorly; we give 3 for a
chaise, the horses & horse for our man will cost about 8,[12] we shall be
at Paris in three days, - we set out at six tomorrow morning.

I am dear Madam, your most obedient & Dutiful Son, Richard Pococke

---

[12]The currency is not specified here, though elsewhere he gives the cost of
meals, accommodation, etc., in Livres

PARIS
15/26 September, 1733
Pococke to his mother
Letter 4[13]

[The passage selected from this letter is unusual in that it has been scored out, but with straight lines rather than with wavey ones. Therefore, it is relatively is easy to read. There are however one or two lines which appear to have been rubbed out (rather than scored out with ink), and are very faint. The passage, which Pococke obviously regretted, when later editing his letters, tells of a typical day and an evening's entertainment in Paris]

We rise about 7, go to a coffee house, walk about till one, dine at our lodgings with 7 or 8 gentlemen, some lodgers, some not, one is a very sober German... we go out till 5 or 6. Comedies & the opera... have been at a comedy, a tragedy & an opera, where we saw the Prince... who is a very young man; we always see dancing which is very fine & makes amends for their indifferent musick. [The next two lines have been rubbed out] All the Ladies paint, wear monstrous hoops & [with wigs] not comb'd out, much powder'd, & I think they are very agreeable as to their dress. The men dress as in England, only have much wadding in their shirts or coats to make them stand out, beau's wear red heels, & all their swords con[cealed] under their arms.[14] We were at the Ambassadors on Sunday, office is performed in a parlour, where the better sort sit, the servants &c: in a hall without, & the Ambassadors family & friends in a parlor adjoining, 'tis my Ld Walgrave is Ambassador;[15] we have fine weather & very warm, the summers last long, & the winter [til] may. All that we have seen is mostly on the South of the Scin, we shall finish here in a day or two. [Next line scored out] I would not have you write to me till you hear further from [us] unless about any extraordinary business by the next post after, tho' I should like to hear from you by the very next post. I shall write again in a week. I amYour Most obedient & Dutiful Son, Richard Pococke[16]

---

[13]Add. 22978
[14]From here the text returns to normal
[15]James Waldegrave, 1st Earl Waldegrave (1684-1741), English Ambassador to France from 1730-40. See Ingamells, *op.cit.*, 971
[16]A six-line postscript is entirely scored out

PARIS[17]
6/17 September, 1733
Milles to the bishop[18]

[The journey to Paris is described in this letter, and at the end is an interesting summary]

... We left St. Dennis at noon and arrived here [Paris] at one, we are as yet at an Inn, but tomorrow Mr. Dennis will recommend us to lodgings,[19] our journey has been very pleasant. The country from Calais to Paris is I think very fine, and for fifty miles within Paris, we ride by nothing but vineyards, the roads are for the most paved and strait for several miles together planted with trees on each side, which adds very much to the agreeableness of the journey...

This my Lord is all I have seen at present, we have made but slow journeys on purpose that we might have an opportunity of seeing every thing that is remarkable. Paris will furnish us with abundance of curiosity's and remarkable things, which as soon as ever I have seen, I will write your Ldship an account of

Dr. Pococke presents his duty to your Ldship.

I am my Lord

---

[17]Each cousin wrote three lengthy letters from Paris containing detailed descriptions of places visited in that city and during their excursions outside the capital. Pococke's are dated 15/26 September (the same date as Milles' note reproduced here), 25 September/6 October and 3/14 October; and Milles' are correspondingly dated as 6/17 September (detailing their journey to Paris), 25 September/6 October and 3/14 October. Clearly, for practical and financial reasons, Milles and Pococke arranged their correspondence so that their letters went by the same post
[18]Add. 15773
[19]"[A]t Hotel Imperial dans la rue Dauphin", according to Pococke, Letter 4, Paris, 4/15 September, 1733. Add. 22998. This was very close to the address (albeit the work address) given for Monsieur Denis, in Pococke, Letter 1 (above)

[PARIS]
7/18 September, 1733
Milles to the bishop[20]

I was at Mr. Dennis's this morning where I saw the 9th and 10 vols of St. Chrysostom,[21] for your Lordship, which Mr. Dennis has had these six months but has not had any opportunity of sending them.

My Lord

PARIS
25 September/6 October, 1733
Milles to the bishop[22]

I received the honour of your Ldships last Saturday was se'enight[23] and the letter of credit from Mr. Hoare,[24] the next post afterwards, which I have got exchanged for letters at Lyons, Genoua and Venice. We are now preparing for our journey with the utmost expedition, which we propose to begin next Wednesday se'enight, and hope to be at home by Xtmas next,[25] we propose to be at Genoua about the 7th of next month,

---

[20]Add. 15733. Pococke sent a letter to his mother in the same post detailing their journey to Paris

[21]St John Chrysostom (346-407) was patriarch of Constantinople and one of the four great Eastern Fathers of the Church. Bernard de Montfaucon (whom the cousins were to meet in St Germain-en-Laye, see below) produced a famous edition of his works in 13 volumes (Paris, 1718-38), and this is what the Bishop was hoping to acquire

[22]Add. 15773

[23]Senight means seven nights - i.e. a week last Saturday

[24]Henry Hoare II (1705-85) inherited the family banking business at the age of nineteen. His services were popular with Grand Tourists, and he himself undertook the Grand Tour from 1739-40, aged thirty-four. He spent £3,750 on works of art while abroad (see Ingamells, *op.cit.*, 503), and a year after his return moved into Stourhead, the Palladian mansion completed by his father in 1725. Mr. Hoare appears to have been Mrs. Pococke's banker, too, since she writes to him on another matter in 1737 (Letter reproduced in Volume 2)

[25]He of course means Christmas 1734, which shows that their original plan was to be abroad for sixteen months. However, by April, 1734, their proposed return date has been amended to July, 1734

where we shall stay about a week, and if you Ldship should have any thing particular to communicate, a letter wrote any time before the 22 of this month N.S. will find me there with this direction A monsieur monsieur Bouer Delore pour render a monsieur Milles a Genes.

Mr. Dennis desired me to inform your Ldship that he has pay'd 66 Livres for the three last vol's of Chrysostom viz the 11th 12th and 13 vol's for which I saw the receipt, he has likewise paid 12 Livres for the binding of the 9th and 10th which he will send by way of London, and if your Ldship will have the other three vol's bound here they will cost 18 Livres more, all which sum Mr. Dennis desires the favour of your Ldship to remit to him, and he will send the other three vol's as soon as they are published.

As we were uncertain how long we should stay here, we have made it our business ever since we have been here, to view as many remarkable places as we could. We first of all went to see the Cathedral of Notre Dame, the building of which seems to be very old, tho it has been much beautified and repaired by Card. Noialles the late arch bishop of Paris whose body lyes interred in a chappel on the north side of the choir. Under a round marble stone before you ascend the steps to the great altar, lye the bowels of Louis the 13 and 14th, wth a little inscription on the stone which tells you when they were interre'd there. At the east end of the choir behind the high altar is an image of the V. Mary weeping over our Saviour when dead; on each side of her are the images of Louis the 13, and 14th, on their knees the former holding out his crown and sceptre to the V. Mary, and the other in a suppliant posture looking at her. At the lower end of the church fastened to one of the pillars, is a great colossal image of St. Christopher carrying our Saviour on his back over rivers and mountains, the heigth [sic] of the image is about 20 feet. There are a great many pictures in this Cathedral, both in the nave, and the choir, but I cannot give any judgment of them, because I have no skill that way.[26]

---

[26]In a later letter, dated Venice, 13 June, 1734 (Add. 22978), Pococke informs his mother that they buy books "to give us an account of the pictures... at almost every great city". From his reading of these books, Milles possibly gained more confidence in his descriptions of art, since he does not apologise for his lack of skill in later letters

The second day we went to see the Hospital of the invalids, it was begun to be built in the year 1671 by the late King [Louis XIV], and it was finished in 8 years. The front is broad, in the middle is a large quadrangle consisting of 2 Cloistres one above the other. To communicate to the several chambers, on each side of this large quadrangle are two small ones, each of them half as big as the large one. The west door of the church faces the entrance of the great quadrangle the body of the church is long, at the end of which is a fine altar, 3 fine twisted columns rise on each side of it, and support a crown, which hangs over it. The dome which is very magnificent, is behind the altar, and supported by pillars of the Corinthian order, round the dome are four little chapels equally distant from each other, the cupola is painted and very handsomely adorned on the outside as well as the inside, and I think resembles St. Pauls a little tho it has not that grand look, it takes the eye very agreeably. I think it is reckoned the finest peice of architecture in Paris, the maimed soldiers here seem to be very well provided with all necessarys of life. The hospital they say will hold 3000 persons, but I beleive there are not so many there at present. The hospital itself has no grand appearance, but the church is its cheif embellishment.

The two great Cardinals Richlieu,[27] and Mazarine[28] have left two noble monuments of their magnificence behind them, in the colleges of the Sorbonne and the four nations, the former has a very good library, one of the Drs. shew'd it us, with whom we had an hours discourse, and he was very inquisitive about the state of the Catholick religion in England and Ireland.... The Drs. of this college I think are accounted the most learned men in all Paris, but their disputations did not shew it much for we heard them one afternoon, and they disputed in a random manner without being kept at all to the purpose by the moderator, who sat in his chair and did not speak one word, but was reading some book, the disputants seemed to be very warm, and talked most prodigiously fast, sometimes in Latin then in French, and then in Latin again, and they burst out a laughing.

---

[27] Armand Jean du Plessis de Richelieu, Cardinal-Duc de Richelieu (1585-1642), became a Cardinal in 1622

[28] Jules Mazarin (1602-1661) succeeded Richelieu as Cardinal in 1642. Milles corrects the spelling, of Mazarin's name when editing the text, but only when referring to him on the second occasion

We could not see the library of the college of 4 nations [the Sorbonne] because it was vocation time but the chappel is very handsome. In it is interred its founder Card. Mazarin figured kneeling, and two virtues in bronze big as the life sitting by him. The foundation of this college is for 60 gentlemen of the four nations of Pignerol, Rousillon, Alsace, and French Flanders, who are taught mathematicks, riding fencing &c. gratis. [29]

The best library we have hitherto seen is at the abbey of St. Genevieve. The room is in the shape of a cross, only one end is about 14 years, shorter than the other three, otherwise it would be 100 yards in length each way. Their collection here seems to be very good, they have a Bible of the first edition that was printed in 1482, and a very curious book printed on copper plates of the coronation of Louis XV. Father Courayer was canon and librarian here.[30] Every body gives him the character of a man of great genius...

The observatory is one of the late King's works,[31] the stair case is reckoned a fine peice of architecture built entirely of free stone, as is the whole house, both of an oblong figure, they do not seem to have a good collection of mathematical instruments here, their air pump is one of the worst contrivances I ever saw and not at all in the manner of those that are now in use, under the house there is a subterraneous cavern cut out of the solid rock, tho' some parts of which water distils & soon after petrify's.

---

[29]Thomas Salmon, who published an account of this building twelve years later, describes the Library as a "handsome fabric, extremely well furnished with manuscripts as well as printed books, having the Cardinal's picture at one end of the room, and his bust in brass at the other, the fathers and school-divines are regularly placed one after another, with their respective annotators under them; the college contains apartments for thirty-six doctors, those who are admitted amongst them before they have obtained their doctor's degree are only said to be of the hospitality of Sorbon, and not the society; such is the reputation of this college, that the whole university is sometimes denominated the Sorbon." *Modern History or the Present State of All Nations*, Vol. II (London 1745) 442-43

[30]Rev. Peter Francis Courayer (1681-1776)

[31]King Louis XIV. This observatory was built for the Royal Academy of Sciences, an institution "composed of the most celebrated philosophers, mathematicians, &c.,". See Thomas Salmon, *op.cit*, 443

Near the observatory is the fine convent of Val de Grace, built by Ann of Austria for nuns of the Benedictine order. The chappel is very fine both on the outside and inside. It has a very fine dome likewise esteemed to be a compleat peice of architecture, and finely painted on the inside by Mignard.[32] In this church are the hearts of several of the royal family, and that of Ann of Austria their foundress. They say, that there are a great many persons of quality nuns in this convent, and that they lead a very rigid and devout life...

At the end of the city, out of the town is the hospital general, where there is a very ample provision for poor girls, bastard children, and mad folks. They altogether amount to near 6000 persons, the girls are taught the use of the needle, to make shirts, to embroider &c. There are several women who have the government of the hospital, and who keep every thing exceedingly neat.

Not far from this we saw the Gobelines, a place formerly set apart for arteficers for the King [Louis XV], but is now reduced to tapestry and a little landscape painting.[33] The tapestry which employs almost all this building, is very fine, and it is surprising to see how fast and how sure they work. There are about 20 looms at work upon different peices, but it was all for the King's own use, as to the painting it is not very curious, and there is but one man of the profession there.....

My paper obliges me to finish my letter but in the next, I hope to give your Ldship some account of Versailles, Marly, and all the royal palaces, which we have been to see.[34] Dr. Pococke joins with me in humble duty.

I am my Lord

---

[32]The French painter, Nicolas Mignard (1606-1668), who specialised in works for religious institutions

[33]Though established in the middle of the 15th century, it is most famous as a royal factory supplying upholstery to the court of Louis XIV, the Sun King, who reigned from 1643-1715

[34]This account is not included here, though Pococke's description of their visit to Versailles is reproduced in the next letter. It is interesting to note that Pococke had a copy of *Description de Versailles & de Marly* (Paris, 1701), as listed in *A Catalogue of the Library (op.cit.)* 14

P: S:

Since I finished my letter I have received your Ldships of September the 8th, and shall be very particular in my next letter to your Ldship, which I was not willing to be before, because I thought it would only be troublesome to you.[35] Dr. Pococke thinks it will be unnecessary for him to write any account at present to your Ldship, because I shall do that, but that he writes a full account to Newtown, wch he afterwards intends to copy out into a book when he returns home, wch at present he has not time to do.

PARIS
25 September/6 October, 1733
Pococke to his mother
Letter 5[36]

　　[Both Milles and Pococke give detailed accounts of what they saw at Versailles, but since such accounts are fairly common in Grand Tour literature, more unusual and personal descriptions, such as their sightings of members of the royal family, are reproduced in the following excerpt]

On Monday the 28th we went to Versailles 12 miles,[37] which is said by all to be the finest palace in the world, the description of it, is two Vol.s 8vo. [octavo] to give some general acct.[38]　The grand staircase & apartments which are about twenty rooms are all marble wainscoted [panelled] with marble & where there are hangings 'tis gold & silver & the panels & door cases marble, the Kings apartment[s] consisting of 8 or 9 rooms, are wainscoated with wood carv'd all over & all the carving gilt, the rest is white, the furniture is rich, gold & scarlet damask most of it gold. I think the Queens bed was a rich red damask, she had several things framed, hung together at the head of the frame; & a

---

[35] At this point, the letters from Milles to the bishop (as requested by the latter) become more detailed and descriptive

[36] Add. 22998

[37] Palace of King Louis IV (1710-74) and Queen Maria Leszczyńska (1725-68), daughter of the King of Poland

[38] A book made of sheets of print representing one eighth the size of the original sheet

larger picture of the King over her chimney, there was a gilded rail between the bed & the other part of the room, where we saw the Queen dine in private; we saw her also going & coming twice to Mass & once to Vespers, to wch she was carried in an embroidered armed chair, as they are carried in the Chairs at London: within the rail was a small tent-bed, cover'd with a silver stuff, which I believe was for any of the children when they happen to fall a sleep in her room; she dines alone at an oblong table, 3 dishes or 4 at a time, three courses, a desert, the dishes mostly oblong octagons & the plates scallop, she has a mighty good look, especially when she smiles, seems good naturd, humble & affable; she stood still & talk'd to an ordinary Black as she went to Mass; she had on a black silk flower'd gown in small lozenges, her tail pinn'd after the English manner; cherry colour'd shoes & petticoat under with a border of silver embroider'd in a half lozenge; she had on a blue & silver mantel all of open work, another time a scarlet one with silk fringe, a gauze flower'd black head dress 4 lappels behind, & a hood the same over it, white gloves, ribands at top, & bracelets of pearls about her arms I saw when her gloves were off, an oval black patch from the corner of her eye, as many court Ladies had; & the top dress I see is a laced bodice,[39] the mantua [loose gown] gathered very full about the middle & [...] from the forepart, but no tail pinn'd up, as the Queens, their sleeves [..] inches deep & five rows of short laced ruffles up to them; most of the mantuas [came] but a little more than half way down the back, but the Queens came [down to] the middle, & the Ladies have their shoulders bare behind & before [and those of] quality have very long trains held up by pages...

We saw the King in his chamber dressing & at public Supper with the Queen, the Queen also may be seen at her toilet. After the King was dress'd he went to a chair by his bedside, kneeled down & said his private prayers, the clergy that were there kneeling with him; there is a Crucifix over that chair, & in a frame the last words of Lewis 14 to him, advising him to peace &c: which I have seen in print; he never goes out till he has been at Mass. In two rooms within the bed chamber are many horns of stags lying about, in one, two boxes for small dogs, which the King delights in, - when we saw him go to Fontainbleau they were let loose, & came out to his coach, he had on then a plain light-coloured cloth, but before a rich stuff, the ground [background] yellow,

---

[39]The word "Robe" is inserted above the word "bodice"

but almost all cover'd with small silver flowers which I believe were the [...] de luces [sequins], the sleeve embroidered round, his fine black hair in a bag[40] without a solitaire [black ribbon]. The Queen goes to Fontainbleau a few days after him; they say, the Queen of Poland [her mother] is come to see her soon at Versailles & retires to the Nunnery of St Cyr that is near, till the King is settled in Poland.[41] The King of France delights in hunting, goes out every day at twelve all weathers; I saw him return in the dusk of the evening in an open kind of a coach & eight. He is fresh, but not so handsome as his picture makes him, his face is longer [the next two lines scored out] he is a little yellow I think about the eyes & his eyes a little blood-shed about 5 feet high & well set, looks stedfastly at those he speaks to, talk'd much with Duke Luines[42] at supper & a princess of the blood, who sat at each end of the table on stools at a little distance from it, spoke not once to the Queen;[43] they supp in less state than our Monarch, help themselves, are served by comon [sic] servants, who stand opposite to them at the oblong square table, not by Nobles when they call for drink, the servant calls aloud, a boir pour le roy or la Reine & on a salver is brought a glass a cruit of water & another of wine, they mix it themselves. Two dishes at a course set to the King & two to the Queen, three courses & a desert, among which a sirloyn of beef, & a whole [...] quarter of veal &c: at 9 a clock....

We saw the Dauphin[44] & two princesses at dinner, fine children [with] brown hair, find skins, their complexion on the white, the Princess

---

[40]A type of wig tied up in a bag, usually of black taffeta

[41]This was Catherine Opalińska (1680-1747), wife of Stanislaus I of Poland. It will be remembered that the War of the Polish Succession was underway. Stanislaus (former King of Poland) was supported by most of Poland, France and Spain. He was elected King of Poland that year, but fled because of a Russian threat. Augustus II (supported by Russia and Austria) was elected in his place

[42]Charles Philippe d'Albert de Luynes (1695-1758) held the title of Duke of Luynes from 1712 until his death in 1758. He wrote an important memoir of life at the court of Louis XV and his wife was Lady in Waiting to the Queen of France

[43]The King was notorious for his infidelity and had numerous mistresses throughout his marriage, including Madame de Pompadour (1745-50). In 1732, Marie Anne de Mailly became his mistress

[44]The title given to the heir apparent to the throne of France from 1350-1791. The Dauphin here is Louis Dauphin of France (1729-65)

[about] 5[45] the Dauphin about 4,[46] all are held by leading strings;[47] the Mesdames [wore] white silk embroider'd with gold, red & other colours; the Dauphin [wore] brocade laced with silver; they are very brisk [active]...

I am assured there is no manner of danger in going over the Alps,[48] you know all the top people of England [take] that tour & we never hear of any accidents, the winters here do not begin [until] towards Xtmas, I hope to be safe over before the beginning of November. We set out for Lyons on Wednesday the 14 N.S. I shall desire you to write to me at or before 16th October old stile...

I am Dear Madam

Your most obedient Son

Richard Pococke

---

[45]This must have been Princess Henriette of France (1727-52), aged six at the time. Her younger sister Louise had died in February at the age of five

[46]Pococke is correct, the Dauphin was four at the time

[47]Narrow strings or straps of fabric attached to children's clothes used to support them when learning to walk (hardly applicable in children of this age) or as a restraint

[48]Their original plan was to take this route, but in the end they had to change their plans because of the political situation (see Milles to the bishop, from Lyons, 22/29 October, 1733, reproduced below). However, they travelled over the Alps on their return journey (see Chapter 5)

PARIS
3/14 October, 1733
Pococke to his mother
Letter 6[49]

[This letter contains another amusing account of ladies' fashions, clearly a subject Pococke felt would be of interest to his mother and sister. It is hardly surprising that this topic is not generally a feature of letters from Milles to the bishop, though one or two of the later examples include descriptions of clothing. It also includes an interesting account of their meeting with Bernard de Montfaucon]

I gave you some account of the Ladies dress, they commonly wear slippers, & mind not the showing their under petticoats up to their wasts [sic] when they seat themselves in Coaches or otherwise; the house wives wear no hoops at home in an undress, & have commonly a gown on that comes not ¾ down. As the gentlemen never wear gloves, when they hand a Lady, they put their hand under the foreshirt of their coat or wastcoates, & I believe the Lady rather leans her hand on the gentlemans arm; shoes are very little worn by them; their coaches are not fixed on one beam or perch but hang and balance on each side & are properly Berlins, very easy & the forenhub will turn quite round, so that they can't over set by turning, & can turn short in the street...

On Sunday we went to see Montfaucon[50] at the Abby of St German, & paid him compliments from the Bishop of Waterford,[51] he receiv'd us with much civility, but was going [out] so desired us to come again; since we have been to his room, he show'd us [the] manuscript of some of St Augustines Epistles on Aegyptian paper, a [sort of] stiff linen, thought to be writ 1200 years ago...he [Montfaucon] is now upon

---

[49]Add. 22978

[50]Bernard de Montfaucon (1655-1741), a French Benedictine monk who produced many scholarly works but was most famous for his fifteen volumes of *L'Antiquité Expliquée et Représentée en Figures*, published between 1719 and 1724. Pococke had the complete works (see *A Catalogue of the Library, op.cit.*, 17), though we do not know if he acquired this before or after meeting the author

[51]The bishop may have met him during his travels or alternatively might have corresponded with him on matters of Greek scholarship (while Professor of Greek at Oxford) or when researching for his History of England

Bibliotheca Bibliothec.[52] an [account] of all the manuscripts, in the world, an account of it in print he gave [to us] which when it comes to Newtown I desire you to send to the Bishop: he is to [give] us letters of recommendation to Modena, Rome & Venice;[53] he is a lusty Old [man] clin'd to fat; rises (he told us) at 3, studies 15 hours a day, & shall continue for as long as he lives."[54]

---

[52]*Bibliotheca Bbibliothecarum Manuscriptorum Nova*, Vols 1-2, published in Paris (1739). This enormous work was a catalogue of the Greek manuscripts of the chief libraries of Europe

[53]Letters of recommendation to introduce the two cousins into polite society while in these cities. As described by Milles (Milles to the bishop, Paris, October 4/14, 1733, Add. 15773), the letters were prepared for the following gentlemen: "Signor Muratori, who is publishing a collection of all the Italian Historians at Modena, another to Monseigneur Fontanini, Archbishop of Ancyra in partibus at Rome, and another to his excellence Signor Fiepolo who was formerly the Venetian Ambassador at France, at Venice". As noted by Pococke, the second of these letters was produced on 2 March, when the Archbishop "received us very kindly, with Eloquiums on our Ancesstores Pococke & Milles by whom he understood Mill that published the Testament as well as our relation [the bishop]". See Pococke to his mother, Letter 13, Rome, 1/12 March, 1734. Add. 22978

[54]Milles' account of this visit is similar: "Yesterday we went to wait on father Montfaucon, & made bold to make use of your Ldships name to him. He received us with surprising humanity, & good nature & when we told him we were going to Italy, he promised to give us letters of recommendation. We called upon him to day, when he fulfilled his promise & gave us 3 letters. One to signor Muratori, who is publishing a collection of all the Italian Historians at Modena, another to Monseigneur Fontanini, Archbishop of Ancyta in partibus at Rome, and another to his excellence Signor Fiepolo who was formerly the Venetian Ambassador at France, at Venice; he shewed us a curious manuscript wrote on the Aegyptian papyrus of part of St. Augstins Epistles. It was formerly in the library at Narbonne, and he says was wrote in the 5th or 6th century. There are but 2 more on the Aegypt papyrus extant as he told us; one is at Geneva the other at Milan. He is now at work upon a book intitled Bibliotheca Biblithecarum, which is to be an account of all the manuscripts extant in the learned languages, & will be two Vols in Folio. Dr. Pococke has sent the conspectus operis to my Aunt, in order that it may be transmitted to your Ldship. He says that he now studys 15 hours in a day, rises at three in the morning; & enjoys his health and is as hearty as any man." Milles to the bishop, Paris, 3/14 October, 1733. Add. 15733

LYONS
22/29 October, 1733
Milles to the bishop[55]

[Following a lengthy description of more sites visited in and around Paris, Milles continues with their journey from the capital city to Lyons, which includes an account of an interesting clock they saw in Lyons Cathedral. From this point, Milles' manuscript journal ("An acct of some remarkable places between Paris, & Rome") is used for comparative purposes][56]

...About 5 of the clock in the morning on Thursday the 15th we left Paris, and arrived at Fontainbleau by dinner time, we spent the afternoon in viewing the Palace and gardens...

The next day we set out from Fontainbleau,[57] and arrived at Sens by dinner wch is a poor little ill built city situated on the river Yonne, but however is the see of an Archbiship...

The next morning we arrived at Auxerre, where we staid an hour to see the city wch is little better and larger than Sens, it is situated on the same river the Cathedral is a tolerable good building on one of the pillars at the west end is a colossal image of Christopher with our Saviour on his back wch is 30 feet high in the choir and buried Nicholas Colbert & James Amyst both Bps [Bishops] of this see.

The next place worth observing that we came to was St. Seigne a small village, but in it is a rich Abbey of Benedictines dedicated to the Saint, whose body is in a silver chest over the altar.

The fourth evening we arrived at Dijon the capital city of Burgundy ... As we came out of Dijon at a miles distance we saw lying across the wall, which surrounds the public gallows the body of a criminal who had been broke on the wheel about three weeks before for killing his

---

[55] Add. 15773
[56] 15 October, 1733 to 16 January, 1734. Add. 15762
[57] Here they again saw the Royal Family. According to Pococke's account, the King "appear'd better than at Versailes, he had on a brown cloth, laced with silver in kind of half lozenges; the Queen had the same on, black, as at Versailes & a blue mantile". Letter 7, Lyons, 18/29 October, 1733. Add. 22978

brother, this I find is the manner in France of exposing the bodys of criminals after execution, to lay there till they are rotten.[58] From Dijon we could perceive the high mountains of St. Claude cover'd with snow at about 40 leagues distance.

From Dijon we went 14 leagues south to Chalous, a poor ill built city but very pleasantly situated on the river Saone, wch at this distance from the sea is very broad it is the see of a Bishop, who at present is one Mr. Madon, the cathedral is an old, & a most miserable peice of building, in it is buried John Germann Bp. of this see & chancellor to the Duke of Burgundy, who dyed in 1655 here are likewise buried Cynis Thyadaus & John de Maupeo Bps of this see the chapels of the monks of St. Peter & the Urselines are very neat, being built in the form of a cross, & the inside plaister of Paris, with pilasters of the composite order. The hospital on the other side of the river for the sick, is very large & commodious, and capable of holding 500 persons, about a quarter of a league distant from the hospital is an Abbey of Benedictines called St. Marcel because that saint suffered martyrdome there...

From Chalons we went to Lyons in a cover'd boat, wch goes 3 times a week on purpose to carry passengers, wch come from Paris in the stage

---

[58]Milles mentions this horrific sight, in his journal, too, and notes: "After they have executed them in that most barbarous manner, they lay them across this wall, till they rot to peices, in order to terrify others, from ye like crimes. This manner of their exposing them after their death, seems to me, to be more shocking, than the way that they use in England of hanging in chains. The body was allmost naked, only a rag of a shirt, cover'd int in some places". Add. 15762, p.5. Pococke also describes this incident as follows: "Near Dijon we saw a gallows of 9 peers, 3 in a row, it made [...] & is wall'd round; a man that killed his brother & was broke on the [wheel] three weeks ago, was laid on his back on the wheel, on the wall, his neck broke, hanging towards the road, & his legs broke hung inward, no cover but a shirt, two hours after he was put on the wheel he had the coup de [...] a little further a wolf ran across the road just before our chaise, b[efore] we could get our pistols ready, he was got out of our reach, a [...] black & brown & much like a fox, but as big as a mastiff dog...". Letter 7, Lyons, 18/29 October, 1733. Add. 22978

coach we passed by Macon the see of a Bishop, but a very
inconsiderable town.[59]

Lyons is the capital city of the province call'd Lyonnois, it is situated in
a valley surrounded on every side but the East with very high hills the
cheif part of the city lyes between the rivers of the Rhone, & Saone wch
meet just below the town. It is the see of an A B: [Archbishop] who is a
primate of France, it is reckon'd after Paris to be the greatest city of the
Kingdom, the houses are pretty well built but the windows are for the
most part of paper. There is a great manufacture here of velvet, silk,
Gold and silver stuffs, wch they make very fine. The water of the
Saone is reckoned very good for Dying. The governour of the town is
the Duke of Villeroy, whose family have had this honour for many
years. In his absence the Prevot des Marchands governs the town. The
cathedral dedicated to St. John is on the side of the Saone next to
France, it is built of a brownish stone with four towers at the corners.
The building has no ornaments either without or within, the pillars
next to the wall in the inside of the church are almost all of a reddish
marble, but they are so cover'd with dust that they look no better than
stone. In the choir is buried Clauduis de St. George the late A:B: who
dyed in 1714. The present A:B: is called Charles Francis Chateau neuf
de Rochbonne. In the north isle stands the famous clock a very curious
peice of machinery.[60] It is between 20 and 30 feet high, & was made by
one Nourisson in the year 1660. The vast variety that there is in this
clock is very surprising. On the top is a cock in Grass, who just before
the clock strikes stretches his neck, claps his wings, and crows twice. A
little lower are angels with hammers in their hands, who immediately
afterwards play a tune on the bells.[61] A little lower is the image of the

---

[59]In his note-book, Milles states that they "lay ye night" at Chalons. See Add.
15762, p.7

[60]The famous Astronomical Clock of Lyons was first documented in the
cathedral in 1383 but was reconstructed by master Lyonnais clockmaker
Guillaume Nourrisson in 1660 or 1661. The clock still works and is a great
attraction in the cathedral

[61]The identical wording appears in his journal up to this point, after which he
adds: "in the mean time a door is open'd by an Angel, who comes, gives ye
salutation to the V: Mary, who turns towards her. then a door opens from
above, & the Holy Spirit, in the shape of a Dove hovers over her. God the
Father, who is above moves his hand three times, to give her Benedictions,
then every thing shuts up, & the clock strikes. a little lower are the images
of several saints, & a representation of every day of the week, wch change
every day, & appear in their turns. towards the bottom, is the hand wch

V. Mary on her knees, a door opens and an angel comes out, the V. Mary turns to him, & the Holy Spirit in the shape of a Dove descends & hovers over her head. God Almighty who is over her waves his hand 3 times, to give her his blessing, after this every thing shuts up and the clock strikes. Below this are the images of several saints, & some thing to represent every day in the week, wch change daily and appear in their turns. Towards the bottom is the hand that points the hour. On the same table, one sees the sun his time of rising, and setting, the sign he is in in the Zodiack the length of the days and nights, one sees likewise the age of the moon, and the stars that are above our horizon, and those that are not, with several other things relating to Astronomy. Below this there is a Calendar that last 66 years in wch are marked the golden number epact [?] & the days on wch all the moveable feasts fall. On one side is a minuit hand, wch turns round an oval & is so contrived that it lengthens & shortens so as always to keep close to the oval. ...

In one of the new houses in Belle cour, is a famous cabinet of curiositys belonging to one Mr. Serviere.[62] There are in this cabinet a multitude of curious things cut in ivory; gloves one within another cut out of the same piece of ivory, tobacco boxes within globes of the same peice of ivory, fine carved cups marked after the most exquisite manner with several inventions, models of bridges, engines, & mathematicall instruments, all contrived & made by the grandfather of the gentleman who has the cabinet at present, & who spent forty years in making all these curiositys. The gentleman who has it at present has printed the full account of it, with a representation of all the things in copper

---

points the hour, on the same table one sees in what sign of the Zodiack the sun is, the length of days, & nights, the hour of his setting, & rising. one sees likewise the age of the moon, wch is represented wth its bright side opposite the sun, & ye number of ye days of its wain, or increase. all the fixed stars are represented, so that you may see at any time, what stars are above our horison, & what are not. wth several other things relating to Astronomy. below that there is a Calendar, that lasts 66 years, in wch are marked the golden number, ye epact &c. &c this changes the last day of the year at midnight. round this there is a perpatuall almanack, wth all the feast days marked out for each month. one [sic] one side is a minuit hand, wch turns round an oval, & is so contrived that it never goes without, or within the circle, but always keeps close to it." Add. 15762, p.13

[62]Gaspard II de Servière (1676-1745), grandson of the celebrated inventor, Nicolas Grollier de Servière (1596-1689)

plates.[63] At the corner of Belle cour, is the hospital for the poor, wch is very large, & holds 2000 persons, who are taught to weave stockings, to knit, to work silk and all other employments. Near it is the Hotel Dieu, for the sick, very large and commodious as all the places are of this kind that I have seen in France.

We have been obliged to stay here a week, because our servant fell ill of a fevour[64] but we shall leave this place to morrow,[65] & propose to go by Nismes & Marseilles to Genoua, because there are so many places worth seeing in those parts & because we shall not have convenient passage over the Alps the nearest way on account of the army who have employed all the mules & horses they could get, to convey them into Italy, the remaining acct of Lyons I shall send your Ldship in the next letter, Dr. Pococke presents his duty to your Ldship.

I am my Lord

---

[63]*Recueil d'Ouvrages Curieux de Mathématique et de Mécanique, ou Description du Cabinet de Monsieur Grollier de Serviere* (Lyons, 1719). It was printed by the grandson but written by the inventor's son, Gaspard I, who died in 1716. Milles gives a similar description in his journal, thus: "The cabinet of Mr Grollier de Serviere, is what deserves the Admiration of the curious. it consists of several things curiously carved, & worked one within another in ivory, of several machines, mathematicall, instruments, curious inventions, & models; the gentleman who made this cabinet, was forty years at work upon it, it now belongs to a grandson of his; who has printed a description of it, adorned wth a great number of copper plates, wch represent all ye curiositys that are in it." Add. 15762, p.15

[64] According to Pococke, who presumably does not wish to alarm his mother, "Seeing the town & some little affairs kept us here a week". He also notes that Lyons is very cheap, and that "we had lodging, dinner & supper, about 10 dishes & a desert our wine & all for 3 livres a day". Letter 7, Lyons, 18/29 October, 1733. Add. 22978

[65]No mention is made of this delay in his journal, where he simply states, in a note on the reverse of p.15, "We left Lyons on Friday ye 30th of October, & came to Vienne the same evening." Add. 15762

NISMES
28 October/8 November, 1733
Pococke to his mother
Letter 8[66]

[In this letter Pococke gives a further account of Lyons and then describes the journey from this city to Nîmes .[67] Of interest here is his description of the Papal Legate, whom they saw in Avignon]

Coming to Avignon ye 3[d] we found the sun perfectly warm; Avignon is pleasantly situated on the Rhosne, on the other side is Villeneuf, from which we went n a ferry boat, & cross'd a small island & came over another ferry, there are great remains of a fine bridge built over the two parts of the river & they [consist] of very wide arches 20 of em, but the bridge is very narrow, 'tis all hewn [one] & a quarter of a mile long; the city is finely wall'd round with hewn stone above a league round; it belongs to the Pope[68] & is govern'd by a vice Legate, [who] is sent every three years; the present [vice Legate] is Philip Buon delmonte Knight of Malta Patritius Florentinus & related to the Pope,[69] we saw him, his common habit of cassock button'd down before & a black damask gown, something like the G[... wears][70] when he goes abroad to church, he [wears] a white laced garment, that came half way down & a purple cloth that hangs a little down before & behind, & when he goes to his throne has on a long purple cloth robe with ermin coming about his shoulders: he lives in a large castle where 7 popes resided,[71] no popes

---

[66]Add. 22978

[67]Milles also gives similar accounts of further "curiositys of Lyons" and then describes Vienne, the "small, & nasty city of Valence", the town of St. Esprit, "wch is tolerably large and well built" and the city of Avignon, residence of the Popes. See letter from Nîmes, 10 November, 1733 (the dual dating system is not used in this letter)

[68]Avignon became the residence of the Popes in 1309 when Pope Clement V (in office from 1305 until his death in 1314) moved the Papal Curia to this city, in order to escape the chaos and violence at Rome

[69]Pope Clement XII (1652-1740) and Pope from 1730 until his death in 1740

[70]Perhaps "Governor" - the text is corrupted at this point

[71]This enormous Gothic palace was built on the site of the old Episcopal Palace of the Bishops of Avignon. Its construction took many phases but with the departure of the Popes to Rome in 1377, it began to fall into decline, finally being designated as a national monument in 1909 when it was

were chosen for several years, 'tis mostly furnish'd with scarlet damask velvet; the old chapel of the popes is not now used, but is a large magnificent old room, the stone of the altar is 7 feet broad & long, we saw the large hall where a vice legate invited the nobility of Avignon to dinner & blew em up, upon account of carrying on intrigues against the court of Rome....

We do not pass over the Alpes. This is a great place for manufacturers of silk stockins 8 & 10 s[hillings] a pr the best[72]... here are at Nismes many fine antiquities, as a very perfect amphitheatre which will contain 20,000 people, the temple of Adrian built to his mother Plotina, where she was buried. Diana's temple & a tower on the hill.[73]

I am Dear madam,

your most obedient & Dutiful Son

Richard Pococke

---

restored as a museum. It continued to be the residence of the Pope's Vice Legate and in the 1730s, when our travellers visited the city, it appears to have been in reasonable repair, particularly the interior

[72]This trade was begun in 1658 by English Roman Catholic refugees, who took their silk stocking frames and settled in Avignon, later spreading their manufacture to Nîmes , Lyons and Paris. See the reference to stockings in Milles' next letter from Aix-en-Provence (18/19 November, 1733. Add. 15773)

[73]Milles describes, in his letter from Aix-en-Provence (18/19 November, 1733) the Pont du Garde and other Roman antiquities, details of which can be passed over here, since accounts of them are prolific in Grand Tour literature

AIX
18/19 November, 1733
Milles to the bishop[74]

[As well as providing a full account of the antiquities at Nîmes (omitted here),[75] this letter continues with interesting descriptions of Avignon and Montpellier]

My Lord,

The church of St Peter at Avignon is one of the best in the whole city. It is a Parish & collegiate church, the vice legat hears mass here every day. The other convents wch are the best in the town are the Dominicans, the Augustines, & the nuns of the Visitation. The Jews are tolerated here but upon these conditions, viz, that they shall all live in a small part of the city distinct from every body else, that they shall be locked up there every night, & that men women & children shall be obliged to wear some distinguishing mark about them, the men wear yellow hats and the women a peice of yellow cloath pinn'd to their caps.[76] They are likewise obliged to hear a sermon preach'd to them in Hebrew every Trinity Sunday.[77] All these things they are obliged to under very heavy penaltys. They are for the most part here very poor. & what they get, is by buying & selling again, any little odd things. Their Synagogue is a nasty stinking place and so is that where they live.[78] At the comedy at this city we saw the D: of Ormond who has

---

[74] Add. 15773

[75] This includes the Pont du Gard, the Amphitheatre and the Maison Carrée. These antiquities are described in even greater detail in his journal, which includes inscriptions, annotated diagrams, and numerous prints. See Add. 15762, pp 45ff

[76] The account Milles gives in his journal is very similar, though he adds that the sermon the Jews are obliged to hear is "preached by a Minnim", and reverses the order of his description of the Synagogue and their living quarters by saying: "the place where they live is a little nasty, stinking place, & their Synagogue is as bad". Add. 15762, p.31

[77] The Jewish ghetto was closed off by three doors and the inhabitants were under the protection of the Pope. The piece of cloth referred to was a "badge", imposed on Jews from 1551 until the French Revolution (1791)

[78] The Synagogue was built in 1221 and rebuilt between 1765 and 1767. It was burned down in 1845 and the present structure is of neo-classical design

lived here this year and a half. [79] He looks very old & wrinkled. We saw likewise Lord Inverness one of the Chevalier's Lords,[80] who likewise made him knight of the thistle.[81] The Major of the garrison of this city is an Irishman, his name is Lawless, he is brother to Sr Patrick Lawless who is vice roy of Majorca.[82] We spent an evening together, he seemed to be a very good natur'd affable man...

---

[79]The Irish peer, James Butler, 2nd Duke of Ormonde (1665-1745) went to Avignon in 1715, shortly after fleeing England on being accused of high treason for his part in the Jacobite Rebellion. He later settled there in 1732, and remained in this city until his death. See René Moulinas, "James Butler, 2nd Duke of Ormonde in Avignon", in Toby Barnard and Jane Fenlon (eds), *The Dukes of Ormonde, 1610-1745* (Boydell Press, 2000) Chapter 12

[80]John Hay of Cromlix (1691-1740), styled Duke of Inverness in 1727, also retired to the Jacobite colony in Avignon. The Chevalier is of course James Francis Edward Stuart (1688-1766), the son of the deposed King James II of England, who had been taken to France as an infant, where he was recognised by his cousin, King Louis XIV, and was brought up in St Germain-en-Laye. Under the terms of the Treaty of Utrecht (1713) James (now aged twenty-five) was expelled from France and went to live in Italy. Following his marriage to Maria Clementyna Sobieska (1702-1735), a Polish noblewoman, and the granddaughter of the Polish king John III Sobieski, James accepted the protection of Pope Clement XI and took up his offer of the Palazzo Muti as his residence. The official marriage took place in 1719. A large annuity granted by the church also allowed James to organise a Jacobite court, and he became known severally as the Pretender, the Old Pretender and the Chevalier

[81]Pococke also mentions this to his mother, noting, "There is a Theater lately built, the front is a beautiful Ionick [...]; We saw at the comedy three persons that are called here the Duke of Ormond, Ld & Lady Inverness, the first has been here above a year, he was in scarlet embroider'd with gold, & the second had a star & Riband of St. Andrew, the other that of St George; I saw the old house where he lives; the latter did not please the Lady of the Chevalier, & has lived there for some time & has purchased an Estate". Letter 8, Nîmes, 28 October/8 November, 1733. Add. 22978

[82]Much is known of Sir (or Colonel) Patrick Lawless, second son of Captain Walter Lawless of Talbot's Inch. He was taken prisoner at Aughrim (1691) and in the subsequent inquisition was described as being of Colmanstown in the County of Dublin. He eventually escaped with James II and others and took refuge in Spain, where he later held high rank in the army of his Catholic Majesty, and was known in family history as "The Spaniard". Less is known of his brothers (James, born 1677 died young; Richard, born 1665 was slain in battle, in 1699; and Thomas, born around 1665 died young), so Major Lawless in Avignon could either have been John Lawless or another brother for whom records do not exist

As to the city at present it is pretty large & well built, but the streets are narrow. It is situated at the foot of some pleasant hills toward the north, but has a very extended plain to the East and South. The product of the land is olives wch are exceeding good. There are reckoned to be 18000 Huguonots in the city of Nismes.[83] They have a very great manufacture for silk stockings wch they sell at 9 Livres the best, wch however are nothing comparable to the London stockings.[84]

On Monday we went 24 miles to Montpelier in the finest road, & country that I have seen in France. The city is situated on a rising ground, & the highest part of it commands a fine prospect southward of the Mediterranean sea, westward of the Pyrenean mountains, northward of the mountains of the Sevennes, & eastward of a fine rich country. Your Ldship is well acquainted how serene & healthy a climate it is & we found the heat of the sun troublesome even the 9th of November.[85] The city is well built & the streets capacious, the Cathedral is a plain building - Bosquet Bp of this see who dyed in 1676 is interred here, the present Bp is Charles Joachim Colbertson the famous minister of state of that name. On a small green just out of the town gates is a very fine Equestrian statue in bronze of Lewis XIV, wch was erected by the province. The gate wch faces this is very grand, & adjoined with four bass releieves containing some part of his history. There are a pretty many Englishmen there for their health. The cheif trade of this city is Delph of wch they make a great deal very good, & there are a great number of Perfumers. We went one day to see a very fine seat of one Mr. Bognet at 2 leagues distance.[86] At 4 leagues from Montpelier they have got hot wells, called Balaruck wells wch a great many people make use of. We left Montpelier on Thursday the 12th, in order to go to Arles we were obliged to return by Nismes, where we stayed one day, on Saturday we set out for [Philas?] wch is 5 leagues

---

[83]United to the French crown in 1258, Nîmes later became a stronghold of the Huguenots (French Protestants)

[84]In his journal, Milles states, "they have a great manefacture [sic] for all sort of stockings, but more especially for silk, wch they sell very cheap." Add. 15762, p.57

[85]This is a further indication that the Bishop had once travelled to France. Milles states, in his journal, that this healthy climate is "reckoned very good for consumptive people". See Add. 15762, p.59

[86]According to his journal, this estate is called Mosson and described as "altogether surprisingly grand, & beautifull". See Add. 15762, p.59

distance from Nismes. When we came within six miles of Arles we descended into a flat morassy country, in the middle of wch Arles lyes, & is surrounded by it for several miles. It lyes close to the river Rhosne wch divides a little above the city. Over the great branch is a bridge of boats. The city is tolerably large, but ill built, & very thin of inhabitants but however has several curious peices of antiquity remaining.

The first thing we took notice of, were the ruins of a fine Amphitheater, tho I think in its architecture it is much inferior to that of Nismes.[87] The outward wall is standing almost all round, but not to the top. It is built of prodigious large hewn stone & has 2 rows of arches, there are 60 arches in each row, we took the height of it & found it to be 44 feet high. The lower arches are 10 feet large, & the walls 19 feet thick, the upper arches are a foot less every way, as to the inside there is not so much as a seat remaining: it is all filled up with houses, & they have built houses round it on the outside, so that one can hardly have any view of it. Near the Amphitheatre are the remains of a magnificent Theatre. It consisted of three rows of arches one over another, & the semicircular part had 37 arches in a row, & the diameter eleven. These arches were adorned with dorick pilasters, with a very fine Dorick, & likewise a Corinthian Friese over it & a Corinthian Cornish [cornice]. One of these arches remains entire towards the north, & three one over the other at the south. These arches we found to be 11 feet wide. There are still remaining two very fine Corinthian pillars of Jasper, with a little peice of friese, wch was part of the Proscenium. These pillars are about 24 feet hight 9 feet in circumference, & about 5 foot distant from each other. It is computed that there was in this Theater 150 pillars of fine marble. At the bottom of these pillars about 60 years ago they found a very fine statue of Venus, only she had lost both her arms.[88] The city made a present of it to the late King, who has placed it in his garden at Versailles & has had a copy taken of it, wch he sent to the city, & it is now put up in the Town house, my paper obliges me to conclude my letter, sooner than I could wish. In my next I will give your Ldship the remaining account of Arles.

---

[87]This antiquity is described in his journal as "the remains of a noble Amphitheater". Add. 15762, p.61

[88]The Venus of Arles, uncovered by workmen in 1651, dates from the end of the 1ˢᵗ century BC. It was seized from the Royal Collection at Versailles during the French Revolution, and since this time it has been at the Louvre

We arrived here on Tuesday the 17th & set out tomorrow for Marseilles. We hear of nothing at present, but the war & that 20000 Spanish horse, are to pass by here in a week or 10 days time, in order to embark at Toulon for Italy. Dr. Pococke presents his duty to your Ldship.

I am my Lord

GENOUA
30 November/10 December, 1733
Pococke to his mother
Letter 10[89]

[There appears to be a letter missing from the Milles/Bishop collection, since we find no account of Marseilles, though he does provide a short description of this city in his journal, part of which is reproduced here.[90] Pococke also gives an account of Marseille in a letter to his mother, with an interesting description of the port. This is the first in the collection for which an original letter from Pococke exists, and the footnotes for this short section will serve to illustrate the type and extent of minor differences between the originals and the copies made by Mrs. Pococke, who was at great pains consistently to correct her son's rapid script, in particular eliminating abbreviations peculiar to the period, already noted in the Introduction. Sometimes new words and phrases appear in the copies, presumably the after-thoughts of Pococke himself, on reading his mother's transcripts]

We came through a rocky kind of country on the 20th but covered with olives & a fine sort of pine to Marseilles, the bay stands E&W but comes into the port which is like a river by a narrow straight, on one side (ye south)[91] there is the strong citadel of St Nicolas on a little hill, so that

---

[89] Add. 22978. This is the first letter of the original collection (Add. 19939) and a note next to the English address states that it was received by Mrs. Pococke on 22 December and answered on 23 December 1733

[90] See Add. 15762, pp 77-83

[91] This has been added in the original (Add. 19939)

the fortifications rise in 3 or 4 platforms above each other; on the other
side is the lesser fort of St John & East of it is the old city is a half moon,
to the port the streets which are narrow & the Quay is some thing like
Waterford & much the same length, but not so broad;[92] at this Key ye
Gallies lie 16[93] & along at the edge of the Key the slaves have shops,
which intercept the view of the water; we were aboard a Galley there
were 400 slaves in it & among the slaves we saw an English man for a
chance murder in a [quarrel] & an Irish man for desertion for life,
sometimes they are slaves only 7 or 8 years; they are allowed only
bread water & a little horse [broad] beans; on the other side of the port
is the Dock, the magnificent rope yard, which is supported by a double
Arcade between the arches in the lowest water; there are two over, but
'tis not so long as ours; near it is the Bagne the same length & the same
building except the arcades, where all are [...] wove & made for the
Galleys & slaves, all perform'd by slaves. The buildings are about 900
feet long, they have here 2 wet docks for boats & Tartans, each would
hold a Galley; there are two more for building Gallies these all have
slated covers supported by hewn stone columns, in this & in ye
buildings of the rope yards, they excel[94] our docks; at the east end of
the port is the Hof[...][95] which has a handsome front, here they keep
their canons & arms, the [batter] in the sales d'armes, which is in a
shape of a cross but does not equal the Tower, the arms are disposed
much in the same manner; behind this & East of the Dock & on the
other side of the Old Town is the new town, in which the streets are

---

[92]The magnificence of Waterford's Quay is mentioned in many accounts of the
city, including Charles Smith's *The Ancient and Present State of the County
and City of Waterford. Containing a Natural, Civil, Ecclesiastical, Historical
and Topographical Description thereof* (Dublin, 1746). On this point,
Richard Twiss, in his controversial *A Tour of Ireland in 1775* (*op.cit.*), notes
disparagingly, "He [Smith] probably knew nothing of that of Yarmouth, nor
of the magnificent quay of Rotterdam, both of which are much superior to
that of Waterford" (141).

[93]The previous words are scored out of the copy and here taken from the
original letter (Add. 19939). Milles adds the following information: "The
D: of Tuscany has three galleys here, & about 1200 slaves, 700 of wch are
Turks. We went to the Bagno wch is the place where they are kept. Every
thing is exceeding clean, & well regulated with them. The Turks have a little
Mosque allowed them". Milles to the bishop, Florence, 18/29 December,
1733. Add. 15773

[94]In the original the word "exceed" is used

[95]Indecipherable in both the original and the copy

broad, the buildings very fine[96] & between that & the Old Town is a very fine[97] cours or walk, planted with trees, & there are houses on each side magnificently built. We were at the top of an high hill, where there is a fortification [I think old],[98] 'tis call'd le Gard & [here is][99] the Chapell Notre Dame De Garde [hence][100] we had a fine prospect around especially of a kind of plain round Marseilles, extending about a league in some places more, covered with houses, [insomuch][101] that I believe there may be all over it houses[102] at fifty yards distance, & I imagined it to be like the city of Moscow. This plain [is] environed with high rocky hills; The city of Marseilles is large, I believe not [very] much inferior to Lyons...

[An excerpt from Milles' journal follows][103]

The city of Marseilles is situated round a small bay, wch runs East, & West. at each end of the town is a Cittadel, wch command the mouth of the Harbour, that on the north is called St John, & yt on the south St Nicholas. The Arsenal is a very large, & handsome building, in the sale d'armes, wch is built in form of a T, are ranged all the arms of the Galleys, after a very agreeable manner, but nothing comparable to those in the tower of London. the rope walk, where they twist the ropes for ye service of ye galleys, is to be seen in one part of the Arsenal. they employ 800 slaves to spin cotton, to weave shifts of sacking for to cloath the slaves, & for ye other uses of ye galleys; in another part of the Arsenal they have a dock, where they build, & refitt ye galleys, the number of Galleys here are 16, wch have each of them 3, or 400 slaves in them, some more, some less. about six or seven of them go out to teach the slaves to row every year. in the largest galleys there are 7 slaves to an oar, who when the galleys are in the harbour, are suffer'd to go out about ye town, & to employ themselves in carrying burthens, or in any other handicraft that they can exercise. as this city has a prodigious commerce, one allways sees a great number of

---

[96]In the original the word "handsom" is used
[97]Again, in the original the word "handsom" is used
[98]In the original
[99]In the original
[100]In the original
[101]Added in the copy
[102]"There may be houses every where" in the original
[103]Add. 15762, p.77

merchant ships in the Port, a great number of inhabitants on that part of it wch is call'd the new city is lately built, the houses are all very beautifull, & ye streets broad. the old city is on ye contrary ill built, & the streets excessively narrow...

CHAPTER 4

Letters from Italy

On the reverse of page 46/74 of the manuscript, half way through Letter 11, and marking the beginning of a new volume of copies, is the following note in Pococke's hand: "From this it is only a [line?] journal, The second volume being a account of what I saw beginning with our embarkation at Antibes." It is immediately at this point that Mrs. Pococke begins to order her son's letters in the form of a journal, with the dates appearing at the beginning of each section. This suggests he was not entirely happy with her arrangement of the first volume and asked her order the material differently when beginning the new one. She obliged him this respect for the remaining volumes of this correspondence.

At Genoa, as described by Milles, their travel plans were frustrated: "We here find our scheme for our travels a little disconcerted by the present war: so that we cannot, without great danger of being robb'd pass thro' the Milanese, & there is no other way into Italy by land but that; so that we propose to imbark in a large English ship that is here, & go to Leghorn & from thence to Pisa Florence & so strait to Rome".[1] In this section, Milles and Pococke reach the summit of their first voyage, Italy, where they can spend their days exploring vestiges of classical antiquities and the Renaissance, and count among their other pastimes observing and occasionally fraternising with the gentry and nobility of their own country. All but one of the letters in this section is dispatched from Rome, where they stayed for a period of four months, and from which they took excursions to places of local interest. Here they made many new

---

[1]Milles to the bishop, Aix-en-Provence, 18/19 November, 1733. Add. 15773. He also addes a note about post going astray: "Our Banker here, upon a young shatterd brain'd Englishmans telling him that we were gone to Bologna, has sent our letters there, but we have orderd them to Leghorn, perhaps there may be one from your Ldship"

acquaintances, as well as rekindling those established in Leghorn and Florence, and though spending much of their day sight-seeing, sometimes returning to "review" particular sites, they set aside time for writing their letters and journals, learning Italian, visiting libraries and socialising in the coffee house. Here, in particular, Milles' relatively conservative approach to letter-writing can be compared with Pococke's more familiar and entertaining style.

In this chapter the following three journals by Pococke are used for comparative purposes: "Travels Volume II From Antibes in France To Rome" (covering the period from 3 December, 1733 to 22 January, 1734),[2] a substantial volume on what he had seen in Rome,[3] and a further volume devoted to "remarkable" things he had observed near Rome, or the various excursions out of the city.[4] Milles, on the other hand, produced no journals while at Rome, or at least none are known to have survived.

---

[2]Add. 22979
[3]Add. 22980
[4]Add. 22981

FLORENCE
19 December/2 January, 1733/34
Pococke to his mother
Letter 11[5]

[This is an unusually long but interesting letter. The following excerpts describe the journey from Antibes to Italy (including details about travel, food, accommodation, plants and fashion) and give details of their activities and encounters with Irishmen in Leghorn and Florence][6]

At Antibes we staid [waited] for the felucca we hired at Marseilles, having arrived Saturday at 3,[7] on Sunday morning we walked round the town walls, in the afternoon I walked a mile up a hill, which makes the point of land between Antibes & Golphe Janne [Golphe-Juan], at the top is the church of Notre Dame degard [De la Garde], a monk comes there & saies Mass once a day, in a house adjoining to it an Hermit did live in a little room into which one looked through a grate from his other room is an altar in that & the rooms were adorn'd with little statues, lamps & other trinkets which the hermit has made. He lived there 30 years & has been dead about 3.[8] This hill is covered tho' a rock with shrubs & myrtle...We also saw a milliary in the town.[9] The women hear wear [lace][10] hats of straw much like umbrella's & without crowns, that is the comon people. There was a Theater here, but no sign of it now China oranges are about 7 a peny Sevil 12. We were told as a commendation of the air & climate that they had no rain in 6 months, not since May. The top people of Antibes go with long

---

[5]Add. 22978

[6]Milles' letter to the bishop (Florence, 18/29 December, 1733. Add. 15773) is by comparison quite dull, lacking the informal element included in some of his cousin's correspondence

[7]According to the first page of his journal they departed from Antibes "On the third of December 1733, being Thursday at eight at night". Thus the journey took almost 48 hours. See Add. 22979, p.3

[8]Details of this have not been verified

[9]Possibly related to a measurement of a Roman mile (i.e. a Roman mile stone), rather than a misspelling of milliners, given that the next sentence refers to ladies hats

[10]The word is added later by Pococke but is uncertain

canes of fenel stalk, which are very light, & some of them grow as big
as ones wrist, above half as big they use 'em for staves [staffs]. We
hired the felucca to leave Marseilles on Thursday & having waited a
week from that time at Antibes, we gave a Pistol & quarter each 25 s to
pass in another Felucca to Genoua.[11] On Thursday the 3d in the
evening we embarked with a Spanish Colonel & five Spanish couriers
going to Parma, we pass'd by Nice 3 leagues in Piemont & 5 leagues
farther by Monaco a small sovereign principality under the protection
of France who have 300 soldiers in it; next day about 2 in the
afternoon the wind rising we put into Porto Mauritio in the Genouese,
in the evening we accompanied the couriers to the fellucca who
together with all the company of the town kneeled down & prayed to
themselves on the shoar & embarked, it being too great a wind for so
slender a vessel, about twice as big as a ships boat, tho but a small
wind to a great ship.

We & the Spanish Colonel hired 3 mules; Felucca's are open boats
made narrow for running with 8 or 9 bars, without covering but we
sat all the time in our chaise which was very useful, not without being
sometimes sick. On the 4th we set out passed through Oneglia,
surrounded by the Genouese & belongs to the Duke of Savoy[12]....
[Two days later] we din'd on the road & got to Genoua about 4. From
Utri where we dined we passed all along on the sea shore on the
strand, houses, villages & palaces being all along the shoar almost all
the way, which appeard very delightful many of them being painted
in imitation of stone, marble Pilasters & especially the great houses as
they are at Genoa except those built of hewn stone & marble, most of
this rode to Savana was on ye side of rocky hills & over mountains
which are all terrass'd up, where there is any soil for olives, vines &c:
on one of these terrasses the road is made at the side of the hills
impassable, but by mules, but being all by the sea side made it more
pleasant. In the inns are very indifferent beds in all the road without
curtains:[13] as to plants we say a tree call'd charuba looks like the
strawberry tree, is evergreen bears a sort of bean they give to their
horses & hogs when ripe. They look like beans but are flatter: they

[11]A Pistol or Pistole was the equivalent of an English pound
[12]Charles Emmanuel III of Sardinia (1701-1773)
[13]On the beds, rather than at the windows

had just dropt their flowers, they grow on a stalk four rows round it six in a row & were each about as big as beans when they drop their flowers we saw a sort of pink having 5 or 6 flowers growing together out of one stalk a pale red & an aromatick herb, something in smell & look like marum, call'd stocket, & what they call Folio I take to be Phylerea[14] & myrtle in great abundance. The women & men are black & yellow, the common sort of the former go without caps, their hair plaited & made up in a rope, with a silver Bodkin on high daies; those of a little higher degree have black silk caps with black lace & some with plain scarves without gathering, laced round with black lace, which they put over their heads & so saves a cap & comes half way down their backs. The yellowness of the people is owing to the ref[l]ection of the sun from the mountains which makes it very hot, the more north than France Marseilles is in the same latitude as Constantinople, Toulon is the most southern part of France being in the latitude of 44 & very near 43 that is 8 degrees south of London. On the road in Italy we met with new bad sour wine; sausages & vermicelli soup is brought every where to table, with cheese grated on it & pepper, without that it is very good; we now find good cheese & in most places parmesan 5d a pd [five pence a pound]. tis yellow & made in vast cheeses & something like the most mild cheshire, 'tho I prefer a mild cheshire I have tasted to it, but it is very good.

The first night we came here [Genoa] we lay at the Cross of Malta, were recommended by our banker to St Martha, where the next morning the 8th we moved, we pay about 9d a day each for our lodging & servant, & 18 pence for an exceeding good ordinary: after dinner we visited our Banker & then Mr Bagshaw the English Consul a mighty good sort of man;[15] we went to see the Street of Palaces, called Strada Nova, there are about 8, mostly built of [Pyrenean] marble. We went to St Philips Nereus the church of the fathers of the

---

[14]Possibly Phylarea, mentioned as an example of a tree or shrub that had not outlived the winter from the year 1773, which they had done before that date, in Arthur Young's *Gleanings from Books on Agriculture and Gardening* (London, 1802)
[15]This was John Bagshaw, Consul from 1723-1738. They dined with him the next day

Oratory,[16] in the evening a small fine church to hear an oratorio of Adam & Eve & the Angel, a sermon, a speech made from the pulpit by a youth, it being the conception of the Virgin, a great feast; the musick & voices were very fine...

Our Banker visited us to a private Assembly of French Protestants [Heugenots], they meet at each others houses every night, drink tea, play all cards, Quintill,[17] & dance till 9, the furniture all damask. Yesterday there was as they tell us, about 6 a small shake of an earthquake. Gloves are in fashion here & not muffs... In the afternoon...[we] went to the Jewish Synagogue, from a desk in the middle a man covered with a sort of blanket chanted, I suppose, the Psalms, & the people sometimes joined with him; at one end was a cupboard locked up & a damask curtain before it, which I suppose is the tabernacle for the law. Yesterday at noon we saw the funeral solemnity of Cardinal Grimaldi, a Genoese, who died a board a ship going to Naples & was brought back home about 3 weeks ago,[18] it was performed at Philip Fathers of the Oratory, the coffin was erected about 15 feet high; 1st there was a step about a foot high, & 14 long & 10 broad, on which was placed all round a row of wax candles, in candlesticks appearing to be silver, 4 feet higher was another, with another row of candles in like manner, 3 feet higher another this was all cover'd with black velvet laced with gold, on this about 2 feet higher was placed the coffin, cover'd over with a large crimson Pall, laced & fringed with gold, a velvet Cardinals cap at the West end & a tissue[19] cross upon it, the candles being all lighted, the fathers to the number of 30 took their seats each side the high altar, one attended by two men habited in tissue peformed the funeral service, with which

---

[16]St. Philip Neri was canonised in 1622, and the Oratory of Saint Philip Neri is a congregation of Catholic priests and lay-brothers who live together in a community bound together with the bond of charity. They are commonly referred to as Oratorians. The church is known locally as San Filippo

[17]Possibly some kind of game

[18]Girolamo Grimaldi (1674-1733). He died of an illness while travelling by sea from Naples to Genoa, was taken ashore at Ischia and died there on 18 November 1733. His body was taken to Genoa and buried in the church of San Filippo

[19]Some type of fabric

much fine musick was intermixed; the actual interment was private at night...[20]

12. We visited the English Consul & took leave; we took our bill of health, as we had done in France, our ship being ready to sail to Leghorn first fair wind an English vessel of 300 tuns, & an English Captain Spenser. There are an abundance of English ships come in here with corn, these two days past... This afternoon our servant arrived in the felucca, having been a fortnight in his passage from Marseilles: we were busy all the afternoon about affairs of no consequence.

13. Sunday we embarked about noon, & the wind being contrary, Monday about 4 in the afternoon we came into Genoa again, having been about 10 leagues off, but I was not sick, tho my friend was, but the next voyage I was once sick, my friend oftener & we kept mostly on the bed. Tuesday night the Capn order'd us aboard, but did not sail till the next morning, the 16th about 11 & tho' we could have been at Leghorn in 12 hours 30 leagues, yet we came not to an anchor in the road till the 18th at night & landed the 19th (the King of Spains birthday)[21] at Leghorn, we had a fine ship with a cabin as big as your parlour; we saw Corsica at a distance & the Isles of Elba, Capraia & Gorgona near, & were off the Cape Piombino.... We got our things a shore this day; met Mrs Murpheys son & Captain of a ship who has been 2 months from Waterford,[22] My Ld Bishop told him he would see us here...

Visited Mr Skinner the Consul here & Envoy to Florence at present;[23] the Chaplain is Mr Swinton fellow of Wadham,[24] we knew one

---

[20]He gives an almost identical account of this funeral in his journal, though the place and cause of his death is not given and the description of the crimson velvet pall etc. on the coffin appears earlier. See Add. 22979, p.11

[21]Philip V (1683–1746) was grandson of Louis XIV of Spain, and reigned as King of Spain from 1700-1746

[22]Possibly the Patrick Murphy Waterford Mariner ("Captain") listed in *RootsWeb: Waterford*, for the year 1749

[23]Brinley Skinner (1696-1794), British Consul at Leghorn (Livorno) from 1733-1736

[24]John Swinton (1703-1777), historian and antiquary, matriculated at Wadham College in 1719 and was ordained priest in 1727. He took up the

anothers faces, being of the same standing in the University, the other parts of the day we spent with some English, & the even, with Mr Swinton in company, & a son of the Yorkshire member Mr Shuttleworth,[25] a very pretty young Gentleman,[26] who is here with a merchant & his elder Brother is travelling in Italy, his uncle Nicholas he told me kill'd himself by drinking about 7 years ago, I suppose, the same that was at Highcleer.[27]

21. This morning we waited on the Duke of Liria[28] the Duke of Berwicks son by Lady Vah's sister, who is Lady of Col. Butler of Killcash;[29] he ask'd me how long I had been out of Ireland; I ask'd

---

position of Chaplain to the English Factory at Leghorn around 1729 but claiming that the climate did not suit him, proceeded in 1733 (shortly after meeting Pococke & Milles) to Florence and returning to England in 1734. See Ingamells, *op.cit.*, 921

[25]There is some confusion over the identity of the various Shuttleworths in Italy during this period (see Ingamells, *op.cit.*), which is not surprising given that most of its members were named Thomas, Richard or Nicholas. The "very pretty young Gentleman" mentioned by Pococke could have been any of the sons of Richard Shuttleworth of Gawthorpe Hall (1683-1749), as follows: William (born 1711), Arthur (born 1712), another William (born 1713) or James (born 1714), who would have been aged between eighteen and twenty-one at the time. The "elder Brother" may have been one of these, or alternatively Richard (born 1708)

[26]The word "pretty" is not necessarily a compliment, and often used (when applied to men) to denote looking or sounding pleasant but lacking strength, force or manliness

[27] Highclere being the ancestral home of the Milles/Pococke family

[28]The Duke was James Fitz-James Stuart (1690-1738) and his father, the 1st Duke of Berwick (1670-1734) was the illegitimate son of James II by Arabella Churchill. The latter served in the French army from 1701 until his death and became a French subject in 1703, created Duke of Liria and Xerica, 1707. Pococke records his death, by a canon ball, in Letter 19

[29]The sisters in question are the daughters of William Bourke, 7th Earl of Clanricarde and Lady Helen MacCarthy. The younger of the two, Lady Honora Bourke (the Duke of Liria's mother) first married General Patrick Sarsfield, 1st Earl of Lucan, and subsequently married James FitzJames, 1st Duke of Berwick (son of James II Stuart, King of Great Britain and Arabella Churchill). She died as Countess of Lucan in 1697. The second sister is Margaret Bourke (d. 1744), who married Brian of Iveagh, 5th Viscount of Mogennis, later (in 1689) marrying Colonel Thomas Butler (son of Walter Butler and Mary Plunkett), whose home was Kilcash Castle, near Clonmel in County Tipperary. Though her married name was Butler,

him when he heard out of Ireland,[30] I told him I had the honour to be
known to Lady Vah & Col. Butler of Kilcash; he said he was glad of
this opportunity of being acquainted with me, that he would do us
any service that lay in his power, but that he was but a Cypher
(meaning I suppose that he was only a Lieutenant General, Count
Montemar being Captn. General of the Spanish forces) he sd he was
obliged to go out, [& when] asked was to Mass, & told a gentle man
the next day, who introduced us, that he was sorry he was oblig'd to
go out, that he could have no more talk with us. He is a tall thin man,
speaks good English, about 36, has two sons & a daughter,[31] a Grandee
of Spain, Knight of the Golden Fleece, was Ambassador at Muscovy
[Moscow] & Vienna, & was about 8 years ago at Kilcash, he is Duke of
Vereques by right of his wife,[32] by whom he has got a great estate in
Spain. We spent this day with the English.

22. Visited the Consul & Mr Swinton in the morning, the former not at
home; set out about noon for Pisa, 14 miles, got there in 3 hours,
through a fine level country; I saw little of Captn. Murphy[33] for
Sunday he went to Pisa, & return'd just as we were going from
Leghorn; at Pisa a middling poor city we went to visit Mr Moor of the
Barn in the County of Tipperary,[34] who is travelling these three years
to educate his two sons, one of 12, the other about 17 years of Age,[35] I

---

she was known as Lady Iveagh, sometimes abbreviated to Lady "Veigh", or
in the case of Pococke's spelling, Lady "Vah"

[30]Presumably he asked him when he had last had news from home

[31]They had actually produced six children, though two daughters and a son
died in infancy

[32]Catalina Ventura de Portugal Columbus, 9th Duquesa de Veragua y de La
Vega (1690-1739)

[33]The spelling of this name varies in the sources, even within the same letter

[34]This is possibly Colonel Stephen Moore (1689-1750). He was Mayor of
Clonmel in 1724 and in 1726 killed his opponent, Counsellor Slattery, in a
duel. The two sons he was educating abroad were probably Richard and
Stephen (precise dates of birth unknown). Colonal Moore's brother
(Richard Moore) is said to have built Barne Park, a mansion five kilometres
outside Clonmel on the road to Cahir. See Michael Ahern, *Figures in a
Clonmel Landscape* (Clonmel, 2006), Chapter 8

[35]They attended the military academy atTurin (the Royal Academy of Savoy),
according to a record of payment of their fees in 1733 (see Ingamells,
op.cit., 674)

knew him in Ireland, he has about 3000 pr An... ; we went to a very indifferent opera. The Duke of Tuscanny sent a present to the General Count Montemar, which was carried in form by 40 footmen, who presented each a dish with different kinds of provisions all the way almost to Pisa, we travelled through a pleasant wood of Cork trees, oak & myrtle.

23. We spent the morning in seeing the Cathedral which is a fine old building, the Baptistery which is a Doric by itself of beautiful Gothick Architecture near it is an oblong square cloister called Campo Santo... We spent the evening with Mr Moor. The Spanish General came in this evening & a great number of Spanish Soldiers were drawn up to compliment him; but this is a country of peace being the great Dukes, & we shall pass through no other till we get into the Popes, where we expect to have an audience of him before he dies.

24.... An Irish Physician belonging to the Spaniards came to see me.[36] After dinner we went through a rich soil to Lucca, avoiding the hills, so made it 14 miles...[37]

---

[36] We do not know the identity of this man

[37] Some details are given in this letter about Lucca, but nothing on the remains of a Roman amphitheatre. Curiously, in Pococke's journal, which also ignores this antiquity, appears the following note on an otherwise blank page: "*There are remains here of an amphitheatre two views of which may be seen on the other side" (Add. 22979, p.28). On the subsequent pages marked "p.28.3" and "p.28.1", have been inserted Plates XCV and XCIV from *A Description of the East*, published twelve years later. These engravings are entitled "A VIEW of the other side of the AMPHITHEATRE at LUCCA" and A VIEW of an AMPHITHEATRE at LUCCA, respectively. More curious is the fact that no description is given of this monument, or indeed of Lucca itself. In *A Description of the East*, Volume II, Part II, the plates have been placed in the section on other parts of Europe, which includes places visited on the second tour of the Continent (1736-37). In his journal on places between Paris and Rome (Add. 15762, pp 126-34), Milles devotes more than five pages to an account of Lucca but, like his cousin, fails to mention this monument. This suggests that they did not see the monument but perhaps heard or read about it later, Pococke subsequently obtaining a print which he decided to include in his book. The same is true of another monument,"RUINS of a TEMPLE of HERCULES at MASSA CIUCOLI" (eight miles to the east of Lucca), which appears

27. We arrived [in Florence] at about 3 in the afternoon. I went to a very fine opera here, which I think in every thing exceeds the London opera, fine singing, dancing, scenes & dress & lasted 5 hours. We are recommended to Mr Marten[38] a painter here, an Englishman of French parents, brother to Mrs Andrews the painters wife in Paris, with whom Wests son of Waterford is;[39] he [Mr Marten] has helped us to a Lodging & is very obliging, & was a school fellow at Eton, tho' no remembrance on either side...

I don't find there was any letter for me at Genoua Mr Milles [was] sent from this to Venice to one of his name,[40] we shall stay here a fortnight, as soon as I come to Rome, you shall hear from me, which will come to you about a month after this, & then I will write to you once in six weeks. I shall expect to hear from you soon, & let me know how often you have writ.

I am Dear Madam Your most obedient & Dutiful Son

Richard Pococke

---

both in Pococke's book (Plate CVI) and the same journal (Add. 15762, p. 28.3), but is not described in any of the sources

[38]Charles Martin, painter and dealer, who was in Florence in 1728 and still there in 1752 (see Ingamells, *op.cit.*, 644)

[39]This is the eminent Waterford draughtsman and art teacher, Robert West (d.1770), who went to Paris and studied art under Boucher and Vanloo. On his return to Ireland in the late 1730s, he established a drawing school in Dublin, subsequently being engaged as master of the Dublin Society's school of drawing. West is recognised as being one of the most important figures in the development of Irish art. See W.G. Strickland, *A Dictionary of Irish Artists*, Volume II (Dublin, 1913) 515-16. Pococke must have known West's father, who was an Alderman from Waterford. I am grateful to Dr. Nicola Figgis for identifying him on her reading of this letter

[40]The incident is where post for him was sent to a man of the same name. See Milles to the bishop, Florence, 18/29 December, 1733 and the next letter (Rome, 11/12 January, 1734). Add. 15773

ROME
11/22 January, 1734
Milles to the bishop[41]

[The journals of both Milles and Pococke contain lengthy and very detailed accounts of the churches, monasteries and palaces of Florence. By way of introduction to the city, Pococke notes, "The air here is reckond very good especially in summer is cold in winter, & here, as in other parts of Italy they are liable to Pleurisy, occasiond as they imagine by the cold air they breath, which makes them go with their cloaks & muffs up to their noses. The heat here is so great that from 12 to three they shut up their shops, and go to sleep & nobody appears abroad, as in other parts of Italy."[42] The excerpt chosen from the present letter is a detailed description of the Grand Duke's Gallery, which is likewise described in a letter from Pococke to his mother, as well as in the journals of both travellers][43]

My Lord

The next post after I had sent my last, I received yr Lordships, but from whence it came I know not, it not coming to hand before we left Leghorn; Dr Pococke could not obey your Ldships commands in relation to Mr Quin, but he asked Mr Murphey if the marble was gone,

---

[41]Add. 15773

[42]Add. 22979, pp 53-54

[43]The description in Pococke's letter takes up less than half a page. He notes that their visit "took up the whole day in a word all these things which are most surprising & of vast value are too long to describe in a letter..." See Pococke to his mother, Letter 12, Rome, 4 February/24 January, 1733 (Add. 22978). However, in his journal, he devotes ten pages to describing the building and its contents (Add. 22979, pp 72-82). Likewise, Milles, in his journal, gives an elaborate account of the gallery, the first four pages of which comprise an extended diagram entitled "Part of The left hand side of the G: Dukes gallery at Florence those marked thus †are statues, & thus + are busts" (Add. 15762, pp 106-15). In this he names the statue or bust (if known) and where possible gives its pose, for example, a bust of "Venus sitting wth Cupid in her lap" and a statue of "Aesculapius wth herbs in his hand"

who told him it was, & that Mr Quin had been very much out of order or he would have sent it before.....[44]

I should think my self very much to blame, if I should offer to give your Ldship an account of any trifling things, before that of the gallery of the G: Duke,[45] wch is so deservedly famous all over the world.[46] I hope your Ldship will excuse my entring into a particular description of it, for that would fill several sheets of paper. The form of the gallery is this [inserted is a simple diagram] the form of a greek Π. The entrance is by a little chamber marked (a) [on the diagram] where are placed all the ancient inscriptions, urns, bas-releives, & some busts. The 2 long sides of the gallery are 210 paces long each & 10 broad, & the middle corridor is 70 long. It has glass windows all round on the innermost side, & on both sides. In the middle corridor there is a row of very fine antique statues, & busts on each side all round the gallery wch in all amount to 155. There are a series of the Emperors busts down to Gallienus wch are very valuable. Of the antique statues the most famous are the Hercules & centaur, Leda & the Swan, Mars & Venus, an orator in copper, with characters supposed to be Etruscan on the hem of his garment Ganymede & the eagle, Marsyas Head, the Phrygian commander, Camillus a hunter, a Boar, Bacchus, & Jannus, Narcissus & Cupid & Psyche. Of the busts are those of Pertinax, Geta, Pan Nero, Plautilla, Alexander dying, & Cicero. Of the modern ones are a Laocoon[47] by Bandinelli the famous Bacchus of Michael Angelo, & Cavalier Bernini's mistress a bust.

From the gallery you enter into several apartments where the curiositys are kept. In the first room are 250 heads of the most

---

[44]Probably James Quinn, merchant, listed in Ingamells (*op.cit*, p.792) as being in Leghorn 1727-28, and responsible for shipping monuments to England. Mr. Murphey cannot be the young Captain Murphey of Waterford (mentioned in Pococke to his mother, Letter 11), who had only left Ireland two months previously; but it could be his father. There is no corresponding listing in Ingamells

[45]The Grand Duke who was, at the time, Gian Gastone de Medici (1671-1737)

[46]The modern Uffizi Gallery, founded in 1581 by Grand-Duke Francesco I de Medici, son of Cosimo I

[47]A figure from classical mythology, Laocoön warned his fellow Trojans against the wooden horse presented to the city by the Greeks

eminent painters all done by themselves, amongst wch I observed
those of Sr Peter Lilly [Lely] & Sr Godfrey Kneller,[48] at the upper end
of the room is a statue of Cardinal Leopold de Medicis, who made the
greatest part of this collection. The second chamber is filled with all
sorts of China, & some very fine earthen ware. In the third chamber
are a couple of shelves full of little Idols, sepulchral lamps. Paterae
strigulae, with several instruments used in sacrifice, a Fritillus [Roman
dice box] in wch they threw their dice, a Mural, & a radial crown,
some peices of copper with inscriptions, wch they say were used in
drawing of lots, with several other things. Both above & below the
shelves are great quantitys of very fine original paintings, here is
likewise a fluted pillar of Oriental Alabaster about 8 feet high &
almost transparent. In the middle of the room hangs a sconce
consisting of 2 rows of branches, all cover'd with amber, under wch
are several small heads in bas-releive cut in white amber, wch
represent all the family of Brandenburgh by whom it was made a
present of to the family of Medicis. At the upper end of the room is a
fine cabinet, all inlaid with precious stones, & the choicest marbles. In
the middle of the room is a table done with the same materials, so as
to represent all sorts of flowers. In the fourth chamber is a Glass case
fill'd with all sorts of curious works in amber; 2 more of fine works in
ivory; 2 very fine peices of wax work, the one representing a plaque, &
the other the gradual putrefaction of human corpses, done by one
Zummus a Sicilian. Here is a table of Lapis Lazuli inlaid with marble,
wch represents the plan of the town of Leghorn & another
representing flowers like that in the other room. There are 2 cabinets
in the room one very finely carved & worked in ivory, & the other in
all sorts of fine wood, the rest of the room is adorned with several fine
originals of Titian, Paul Veroneses, Andrea del Sarto, Vandyke, &
several others. In the fifth room is an Ebony cabinet finely carved,
with the history of the old & new Testament in Types & Antitypes
painted on Lapis Lazuli. The inside is four square & turns round, &
on each side is some curious work in amber or precious stones. Here
is a very fine anatomy of a head by Zummus before mentioned,
another cabinet inlaid with precious stones & several originals of

---

[48]Kneller (1646-1723), court painter to the British monarchs from Charles II
to George I

Raphael, Guido, Vandyke, Vanderwearf,[49] & others. Amongst wch we observed a fine picture of Henrietta Maria Queen of England[50] by Vandyke, the Duke of Malborough by Vanderwearf, & on each side of him, Prince Rupert & the Earl of Ossory.[51] The next chamber is fill'd with mathematical instruments, a Celestial, & terrestrial Globe each nine Geometrical feet in diameter, a lead stone yt bears a peice of iron that is near 40 pounds weight, but their pound is but 12 ounces. A branch of aloes near 8 feet long, on the walls of this room are drawn out the dominions of the G: Duke. The sixth chamber wch is the repository of every thing most curious is called the Tribune. It is an octagon crown'd with a cupola. The first thing that we observed at our entrance, were the six fine Graecian statues, at the upper end of the room on the left hand stands the famous Venus of Medicis. Your Ldship no doubt has heard so much of the delicateness of this statue, that I shall not endeavour to describe its beauty. It has been joined in several places. It stands on a pedestal wch is artfully joined to the statue in order that it may appear of one peice, & it is likely the person who did this had a mind to give it an author: for there is this inscription on it Κλεομενης Απολλοδορου Αθηναιος Εποιεσεν.[52] The inscription every body allows to be modern, both on account of its spelling, & its appearing too fresh on the pedestal for an antique inscription. On the right hand of this Venus of Medicis is Venus victrix, six foot high, & a very beautifull statue, as is the Venus Urania on the other side, wch is but five foot high. The next statue to this last is the famous Faun with clappers in his hand, & a wind musick under his feet. This statue taken all together is reckoned near as good as the Venus of Medicis. Its head wch is modern, is by Michael Angelo, & very well done. The next is the slave whetting his knife & listening at the same time (as they say) to the conspiracy of Cataline. It is of a very bright white marble, wch is almost transparent, its beauty is from his shoulders upwards. Opposite to it, is the Groupe of the wrestlers of white marble, & prodigiously fine. Round the room is a shelf fill'd

---

[49] Adriaen van der Werff, Dutch painter (1659-1722)

[50] Henrietta Maria of France (1609-69), a Catholic, was the wife of King Charles I and therefore Queen Consort of England, Scotland & Ireland. She was mother to Charles II and James II

[51] Possibly the portrait of Thomas Butler, by the Dutch portrait painter, Sir Peter Lely (1618-80)

[52] The editor has corrected the original, which contains several errors

with images of Bronze, heads of Emperours in small of Chrystal &
precious stones amongst wch is very valuable a head of Tiberius of a
single Turquoise, under this shelf all round the room are several small
cabinets, all fill'd with medals, & because it would have cost a great
deal of money, & required a great deal of time to see them, besides the
trouble of getting a permission, we did not see the medals, the
cameyaus [cameos], nor intaglio's.[53] These two latter are kept in a
very fine cabinet at the upper end of the room inlaid like the others,
but more rich, & adorned with several costly jewels.[54] On one side of
it is a small closet filled with several rich vases of Amber, Heliotrope
&c. But the most curious is the number of vases, cut in all manner of
shapes our of Rock Chrystal, & so surprisingly formed, that it must
require a prodigious deal of time of art & labour to compleat them.
All about the room are a great number of the choicest originals
amongst wch particularly are the Madonna of Corregio, the St John
Baptist of Raphael, the Crucifixion by Michael Angelo, concerning
wch they tell that story, of his killing a Porter in order to draw his
peice more lively. The rest of the paintings, wch are in great number
are by Tintoret [Tintoretto], P. Veronese, Titian, Hans Holbens,
Andrea del Sarto, Michael Angelo, Caracch [Carracci], Vandyke, &
Rubens. From the tribune we went to another room where is kept the
altar of St Lorenzo before mentioned.[55]

The last room we saw was the armory, wch is very spacious, & fill'd
with all sorts of arms of all inventions, & with several other things,
such as ancient scepters, robes, saddles, swords of various Princes, &
nations, they shewed us the scepter of the Emperour Charlemagne of

---

[53] The extra cost for viewing these collections was possibly associated with
the services of a guide to explain the intricate details of such small items,
and the additional security required to protect them from damage or theft

[54] Pococke mentions these cabinets in his journal (Add. 22979, p.81), but does
not say that they were unable to view the contents: "In this cabinet area
antique Cameaus & intaglios in pretious stones sett in gold, round this room
also are small cabinets of a wood call'd Granatiglia (?) plain, but neat, in
which are kept the medals antient & modern. In a word this room is one of
the most curious & perhaps the richest of the world in the kind."

[55] It will be noted that Milles' powers of description have improved since his
earlier claim that "I cannot give any judgment of [the pictures], because I
have no skill that way" (Milles to the bishop, Paris, 25 September/6
October, 1733. Add. 15773)

Agat,[56] 2 guns one a small one, & the other of a middling size, whose
barrels are of massive Gold, some armour wch by the make of them
were made for women, & like those we saw at Genoua: they said that
they belonged to the Amazons. But the greatest curiosity is the Mane
of a horse above 19 feet long, it was given by a Duke of Lorrain to the
family of the Medicis. Amongst the ancient inscriptions in the
chamber going out of the gallery are two very remarkable ones, one of
wch gives some light into the history of Appius, who made the
Appian way, & the other relating to Q: Fabius Maximus, but they are
too long to transcribe in a letter. I mentioned in my last to your
Ldship the Musaeum Florentinum: I said it was wrote in Italian I
think, but I mistook for I have since seen them, & they are in Latin
very large Folio, fine large letter, & the copper plates exceeding good.
The 2 vols of the Cameyau's, & Intaglios are published, & one vol of
the statues will be published in a very short time.[57]

For fear my last should any ways miscarry, I will venture to mention
my direction again a Monsieur, Monsieur Jean Teissier Banquier pour
render a monsieur Jermie Milles a Rome. I must beg your Ldships
pardon for crouding this letter so much, but I was willing to finish the
account of the Gallery, that your Ldship might have it all together.

We arrived at Rome this afternoon, we propose to stay some little time
here, till the post is a little over, & then to go to Naples, & to return to
Rome afterwards to see it. As to my expences I have been as frugal as
possible, but your Ldship is sensible that it must be a good deal of
expence to travel so many hundred miles. I find now on computation
that in 2 or 3 months time the money I have at present will be near
gone wch will be as soon as I can hear from your Ldship, if therefore
your Ldship would be pleased to order me a bill of 80 pound on
Rome, directed as above with my Xtian name (because there is one

---

[56]Presumably this means the sceptre is made from agate
[57]This work was published by the Florentine antiquary Antonio Francisco
Gori in twelve volumes between 1731 and 1766. The volumes referred to
here are Volume 1, in two parts: *Gemmae Antiquae ex Thesauro Mediceo et
Privatorum Dactyliothecis Florentiae ... Imagines Virorum Illustrium et
Deorum.* (1731-32), covering antique cameos and portraits; and Volume 2:
Statuae Antiquae Deorum et Virorum Illustrium, on Roman statues and
monuments, published shortly afterwards, in 1734

Milles already in Italy) I hope to give your Ldship a good account of my expending it.[58]

Dr Pococke begs leave to present his duty to your Ldship, & so does in a more particular manner, My Lord

Your Lordships

ROME
24 January/4 February, 1734
Pococke to his mother
Letter 12[59]

[This letter gives a further description of Florence, including the Grand Duke's Gallery, and describes their departure from this city and arrival in Rome. We resume the story here with details of the countryside in the environs of Florence, an Apothecary shop, the Carnival and snippets of information about the English and Irish gentlemen they met both in Florence and Rome]

Jan. 1st. We dined early & rid out to see Fiesole the ancient metropolis of Hetruria,[60] it is situated on a high hill 3 miles to the north of Florence, it is now a village but a Bishoprick then. From this place we had a prospect of Florence & the country about it. This city is surrounded by hills at 2 or 3 miles distance, in many parts the country between it & the hills is uneventfull of small hills, but all covered with beautiful villa's & finely improved with rows of vines, olives, Almonds & corn in the same fields: coming back we struck off a mile

---

[58]The reason why Milles may have been running out of money so quickly was because he was having to lend it to his cousin. See Letter 13 (1/12 March, 1734) Add. 22978

[59]Add. 22978. This is the second letter of the original collection (Add. 19939) and a note next to the English address states that it was received by Mrs. Pococke on 16 February and answered the next day

[60]One of the twelve cities of ancient Hetruria, mentioned in Livy and Sallust as Faesulae

to the west of the town to Caseines (you go to it from the Town to a fine avenue, of very large tall pines) to the dairy of the Grand Duke & also the place where his wines are made & kept;[61] here are most delightful meadows along the Arno. Through the woods we returned home, & nothing can be more pleasant than this in summer; & it is the chief ride of the nobility in their coaches.

4.... Sr Thomas Twisden[62] & Mr Brown his companion having paid us a visit,[63] we returned it; I remember the face of the former at University College.[64]

5. We drank coffee in the afternoon with Mr Knight[65] by whom we were visited & also by a Nephew of Sr Paul Methuens,[66] Mr Sherrard[67]...

---

[61]As mentioned above, the Grand Duke at the time of Pococke's visit was Gian Gastone de Medici. He was the seventh and last Medician Grand Duke of Tuscany. This land was first purchased by Alessandro de Medici, 1st Duke of Florence, around 1530 and developed it as a farm (hence the reference to the dairy and vineyards). After his death in 1537, Cosimo I de Medici, 1st Grand Duke of Tuscany, expanded the area and turned it into an extensive park for the private use of the Medici family. In 1737, the park was granted to the city of Florence for the enjoyment of the citizens, and as noted above, is now known as the Cascine Park

[62]Sir Thomas Twisdon, 4th Baronet (1704-1737), eldest son of Thomas Twisden 3rd Baronet of Bradbourne, Kent, spent nearly four years travelling in Italy. For details of his travels, see Ingamells, *op.cit.*, 958-59

[63]Rev. Charles Brown (1693-1748), educated at Trinity College Cambridge (1708); Vicar of West Malling, Kent from 1730-48, and Cheshunt, Herts, 1734-48. See Ingamells, *op.cit.*, 137

[64]Twisden graduated from University College, Cambridge, in 1721

[65]Rudolph Knight (1702-72), was in Italy from 1733-35. See Ingamells, *op.cit.*, 584. Klima (*op.cit.*), however, identifies him as a Robert Knight and his wife, whom Spence met in Paris in 1733 & 1741

[66]Paul Methuen (1672-1757) was the oldest surviving son of John Methuen, Lord Chancellor of Ireland. He was a diplomat, serving as British Envoy and Ambassador to Portugal, Madrid & Turin between 1697 and 1708. The fact that Mr. Sherrard is identified as being the nephew of Sir Paul Methuens (who was not in Italy at the time) suggests that the latter was known to Pococke

[67]Sir Brownlow Sherrard (d. 1748), Baronet of Lepworth Hall, Linconshire, was in Italy from 1733-34. Educated in Leiden University, Sherrard

7.... In the afternoon we went with Mr Marten[68] to see the palace of Girini where are many paintings. We give about 5s 6d to see the palaces of these nobles. Mr Marten came & drank tea with us.

8....We dined by invitation with Sr Thomas Twisden, who is in the same house, he has one Mr Brown with him, he went from Mr Billingsley's School at Horley to Trinity Col. in Cambridge in 1708;[69] he has seen my Grandfather & Father there,[70] he is an Isle of Wight man, & I believe a Clergyman & was Chaplain to a Regiment at Gibraltar, for he was there at the Siege.[71] We went out with Sr Thomas in his coach, to see the people in mask in the square before St Croce, men & women, gentle & others, they mask till night now during the Carnival until Lent, on Sundays & Holy days & for a fortnight before Lent every day, & meet twice a week then in a great room & other nights at the Opera; but there are not many Gentlemen that mask at first they are never allowed to[o] near a mask in the streets by night; they dress vivaciously, some like Harlequins & many more otherwise; this is the second best Carnival after Venice in Italy[72]....

12. In the afternoon we went to the Apothecaries shop in the Convent of the Dominicans,[73] which is very neat, every thing shut up in neat

---

travelled to the East, and was elected Member of the Society of Dilettanti in 1736. See Ingamells, *op.cit.*, 853-4

[68]The same Mr. Marten, painter, to whom they were recommended on 27 December, shortly after their arrival in Florence

[69]Rev. Sam Billingsley

[70]It is not clear whether Rev. Brown had seen Pococke's relatives at the School in Horley, or in Cambridge. However, it should be noted that while his grandfather had attended Cambridge, his father had gone to Oxford. Whatever the case, it is indicative of the close-knit circle of clerical families common in English society of the period

[71]Possibly the 7th Siege of Gibraltar, 1727, in which Spanish forces besieged Gibraltar as part of the Anglo-Spanish War

[72]On English attitudes towards the Carnival, and the commercialism of such festivals in Italy, see Chapter 1 of Terry Castle, *Masquerade and Civilization: the Carnivalesque in Eighteenth-Century English Culture and Fiction* (London, 1986). See also Joseph Spence's account of the "mascarade" in Rome, in the middle of March, 1732 (Klima, *op.cit.*, 94-96)

[73]Herbal remedies were particularly important to such mendicant orders. Fr. Tomasso Pinzocheri (who died in 1346) spent some time as the Senior

cupboards, four or five rooms for the chymistry distilling &c: we bought some essences & lip-salves of jessamini [jasmine], they sell also small boxes for remedies, 12 remedies in each box, very convenient for travelling, & every thing they do, it is looked upon to be the best in Italy; in this Convent of Maria Nouvella, the Spanish Embassador [sic] who is a Dominican resides...

14. We spent the morning in preparing for our journey; visited Sr Thomas Twisden, & Mr Marten, they spent the even with us. Mr Gore Gentleman C.[74] of Xtchurch arrived an acquaintance of my friends...[75]

[On 15 January the two travellers left Florence for Rome,[76] which, as described in all our sources, they reached seven days later, their journey having been prolonged by bad weather.[77] The journal Pococke kept during their four-month sojourn in Rome is divided into thematic chapters according to

---

Infirmarer of this convent, improving the stock of medicinal plants used in the Infirmary

[74]"Gentleman Commoners" were required to pay higher fees than ordinary "commoners" at Oxford and Cambridge

[75]Either Charles Gore of Tring, Hertfordshire (c.1711-68), who graduated from Christ Church Oxford in 1728 and was MP (1739-68) or Charles Gore (born 1712), who graduated Christ Church Oxford a year later, in 1729. At any rate, Gore was in the main Grand Tour centres in 1734 and a gentleman of this name (presumably the same) was elected to the Society of Dilettanti in 1737. See Ingamells, *op.cit.*, 412. Joseph Spence (Klima, *op.cit.*) met Gore in Paris in 1733, and Klima gives the identity as Arthur Gore, who died in 1758

[76]At this point in his journal, Pococke gives a brief account of the manners and customs of the "Florentins" (Add. 22979, p.90), largely concerned with their snobbishness and their mode of dress

[77]He records on 18 January that they were forced to stay at an inn "near two daies by reason of the snow that fell as we were going up & continued to fall incessantly for 24 hours; 19th & when it clear'd up we were oblig'd to hire men to remove the snow in some places, & twas with difficulty we drove 'thro till we got about a mile, and when we came into a lower region, there was not snow..." (22979, p.106). According to Milles, however, who also mentions this episode in his journal, the timing was slightly different: "the next morning we ascended 5 miles to ye top of this mountain [Radicossani], where we were obliged to stay till ye next day at noon, by reason of the great snows that fell there" (Add. 15762, p.122)

the city's regions and buildings.[78] This manuscript differs from
the earlier journals in that it does not contain dates, and consists
wholly of scholarly accounts of what he has seen in this city,
with no material of a personal nature.[79] Another journal from
this period, similarly divided into chapters, describes buildings
and places near Rome which the author visited on day-trips and
as part of longer excursions.[80] However, Chapter III ("Of Tivoli,
Praeneste Frascati, Albano, & places near them") is more
narrative and does include dates and various asides]

22. We came by Bacciano & the wood of that name, formerly call'd
Sylva Moesia, & two or three hundred years ago much frequented by
robbers, but is now almost entirely cut down, & also by la storta to
Rome... we went to a better sort of Inn or rather lodging or dieting
house in Rome, went to our Bankers, had a little sight of the
Pantheon.[81]

23. My Lord Harcourt[82] & Mr Hansted[83] sent word they would come
& see us; his Lordship having company that came in upon him, Mr

---

[78]Pococke, "Travels Vol III Being A Description of Rome", Add. 22980
[79]The first chapter ("Of Antient Rome according to its Regions") occupies
111 pages of the manuscript, with an asterisk appearing on the inside cover
to inform the reader that "This account is taken from Nardini & Donatus, &
from my own view on the informations cheifly which I had from those
books" (Add. 22980, p.1)
[80]Pococke, "Travels Vol. IV Of The Places near Rome", Add. 22981
[81]Pococke's account (both in the letter and in his journal) is disappointingly
dull, compared with that of other travellers, on first entering Rome. Even
Milles allows himself a little excitement, when he says, "We enter'd in at ye
Porta Flammia now call'd del Popolo, to our no small joy, & satisfaction"
(Add. 15762, p. 213). The two last lines of his journal are scored out, but
he signs the bottom of the page with a great flourish and dates it as: "Rome
January ye 11th O:S:, 22nd N:S: 1733/4"
[82]Simon Harcourt (1714-77) succeeded his father as 2nd Viscount Harcourt
(1727) and was created 1st Earl of Harcourt in 1749. He was a Lord of the
Bedchamber to George II (1735-51), Governor to the Prince of Wales
(1751-52), Ambassador to France (1768-82) and Lord Lieutenant of Ireland
(1772-77). He travelled in Italy from 1732-34 with the antiquarian and
traveller Walter Bowmen (see Ingamells, *op.cit.*, 463-64), though the latter
is not mentioned in our sources
[83]It has not been possible to identify this young man

Hansted only came a young Gentleman; Mr R. Bristow[84] I believe Roberts son, Mr Delme,[85] Sr Peters son & Mr Hadsley[86] came to see us, we were not at home; we were busied in the afternoon in moving to private lodgings, we pay about £1 – 10s a piece a month for two rooms a dining room & servants room; & we pay 2s whenever we dine; without wine... My Lord Salisbury is here,[87] Mr Colthrop an Etonian acquaintance,[88] Mr How the rich Esqres son of Gloucestershire, of Pembroke col. & Mr Paul[89] Mr Christmas's Nephew[90]...

24....We were visited by Mr Paul & Mr Colthorpe heir to a great estate,[91] we went to the English coffee house, as usual, for an hour after it is dark, where most of our nation meet there are forty English in Rome. All the remains we see of Ancient Rome are very grand....

---

[84]Robert Bristow (1712-76), eldest son of Robert Bristow of Micheldever, Hampshire. He was elected to the Society of Dilettanti in 1736 and had a political career. See Ingamells, *op.cit.*, 130

[85]John Delme (died 1776), was the second son of Sir Peter Delme of Rowdesford House, Wiltshire, and was elected to the Society of Dilettanti in 1736 (see Ingamells, *op.cit.*, 291)

[86]It has not been possible to identify Mr. Hadsley

[87]James Cecil, 6th Earl of Salisbury (1713-80) was in Italy from 1732-34, visiting the main centres of the Grand Tour (see Ingamells, *op.cit.*, 838). He matriculated at Oxford in 1705 and, being the same age as Milles, would undoubtedly have been known to our travellers

[88]Possibly a misspelling of Calthorpe, in which case it could be Sir Henry Calthorpe (born before 1709 and died 1788), son of Reynolds Calthorpe of Elvetham Park, Hampshire. He was elected to the Society of Dilettanti in 1742, the Divan Club in 1744 and Knighted the same year. For further biographical details of this gentleman. See R. Finnegan, *The Divan Club* (*op.cit.*) 50

[89]Probably Mr. Joshua Paul, son of Jeffrey Paul of Paulville, County Carlow (see Ingamells, *op.cit.*, 749) who was returned to Parliament from 1725 until his death in 1730

[90]The Christmas family lived on the original Whitfield estate in Kilmeaden, close to the city of Waterford. Mr. Christmas would therefore have been known to Pococke and the bishop

[91]Presumably the same gentleman named in the previous entry (Mr. Colthrop), though perhaps Pococke was then unaware of his social standing

26. We went to see Ld Harcourt[92] & several others but none of them at
home; but Mr Paul & Mr Stewart,[93] with whom in the afternoon we
went to the Villa Borghese[94] about a mile out of Town out of the Porta
Pincia or Porta del Popolo, the gardens are large & fine, mostly shady
walks of Evergreens, the house is all covered on the outside with fine
antique as reliefs & statues, among the statues is Curtius leaping on
his horse into the opening of the earth, which statue, they say was
found in the place where the earth opened & where it was raised to his
honour.[95] The house is also full of antique Busts & statues, very
curious.

27. This morning I went & paid some visits without seeing any body, I
was abroad at noon & could hear from Southampton that the new
tower of St Michael was beat down by thunder & lightening on the
16th of December.[96] Here is one Stephens a good mathematician, his

---

[92]It appears that Milles and Pococke never quite succeeded in meeting this
gentleman while in Rome, as he was always out. However, they managed
to track him down in Venice and found his company most congenial

[93]Although this gentleman has not been identified, he is recorded as being in
the company of various Englishmen at Rome, Florence and Padua. See
Ingamells, *op.cit.* 899

[94]Built by Cardinal Scipio Borghesi on the Pincian Hill, just outside the gates
of Rome, to house his famous collections of antiquities, in the early 17th
century

[95]Pococke fails to mention what he feels about this statue, unlike other
writers, such as Nathaniel Hazeltine Carter, who, almost a century later,
notes, "This famous piece of sculpture, did not strike me very forcibly. The
legs of the steed are coiled up in a way that appears unnatural, even while
leaping in the air. There is neither boldness nor freedom in the manner.
The expression of Curtius' face is the strongest in the group. See Carter,
*Letters from Europe, Comprising the Journal of a Tour through Ireland,
England, Scotland, France, Italy, and Switzerland*, Vol II (New York,
1827) 361-62. However, in his journal of the places near Rome, Pococke
further describes this antiquity, noting, "there is a fear & horror in Curtius
face which is not thought proper in his condition [this word has been scored
out and another, illegible, written above it], but wt resolution soever he
might have, when his horse was in the act of precipitation he might have
some natural terror on his mind." Add. 22981, p.37

[96]This church dates from 1070. The steeple was added in 1732 as a landmark
for shipping (see *Southampton City Council - Historic Environment Record
Listed Buildings in Southampton, 2010*) 133. However, the editor has been

father lives near Sr Simeon Stewarts[97] & stood once to be a Parliament man, he lived with Mr Conscade by Newbury,[98] & saies, he is a man of sense & a mathematician, tho' he saies little [I can't tell what he is as yet. Mr.... It seems Stephens's father married & there by displeas'd his son, who comes here & lives retir'd as far as I can find on a little, St Simeon Stewart purchas'd part of his fathers estate.][99]

29. I staid within to examine into the situation of Rome; went out to some booksellers shops, walked on Trinita del monte behind our house, up to which is a very fine noble double pair of marble stairs at least 50 feet high to the monastery del Trinita of the minims, this was Mons Hortulorum & afterwards Pinciana from the Roman Pincii, who had a house on it; on this hill were the gardens of Salust Lucullus & Pompey; we are now examining into the State of this part, & shall thence go to consider the Mons Quirinalis,[100] which is next to it & so round this is the sun shiny walk of the English before dinner, in the afternoon I went to St Peters, walked in it for about two hours admiring its beauties; met Mr Paul & Mr Stewart there, came to the coffee house in their coach: we live at the foot of these above mentioned stairs [the Spanish Steps] in the Piazza d'Espagna, part of the Campus Martius. This placed grows more & more pleasant every day. Sr Thomas Twisden & Mr Brown are come from Florence & Mr Knight & Mr Gore are following. We visited here Mr Codrington[101] & his companion Mr Young:[102] yesterday we were visited by one Mr

---

able to discover no evidence, outside Pococke's letter, to suggest that the new steeple was destroyed by thunder and lightning

[97]His father, Simeon Stewart (1685-1761), was the oldest son of Charles Stewart of Hartley Mauditt, Hampshire. Though there appears to be a gap in the genealogical record (through the various peerages), it is likely that the mathematician in Rome is Sir Simeon Stuart, 3rd Baronet

[98]It will be remembered that Newbury was the parish close to Newtown, the family home of the Pocockes

[99]Scored out in the copy and reproduced from the original, Add. 19939

[100]A description of which is the subject of our next letter, from Milles

[101]A Sir William Codrington, 2nd Baronet (1719-92) of Dodington, Gloucester, is listed in Ingamells as being in Florence in 1742 (*op.cit.*, 223) There is no reason why he could not have undertaken an earlier Grand Tour, making him the same individual travelling with Mr. Young

[102]Young is a common enough name and none of the entries in Ingamells (*op.cit*) are enough to identify this man

Chambers,[103] an Irish convert, as I believe, who has a pension from the Pope. I don't write politicks because our letters are all opened, but we hear the war will be only in the north of Italy, if it is not made up Cardinal Falconier died three days ago,[104] & left a considerable legacy to the Chevalier. You should hear from me once in six weeks pray let me know when you receive this for I do not know how long the German Post is going by which this comes & you must not be in any concern if you hear not in 7 or 8 weeks, because of the uncertainty of the Post, & if once miscarriage happens that makes a Cha[sm] of 12 weeks.

30. Dined with Mr Paul, made some visits, did little else. This after all comes by French [Post] let me know what you pay. I saw the Ch. in his coach & the 2 sons rideing[105] about if you write to Mr Wood[106] he will tell you what to put on the Letters to make them go by Germany, which in case of war will be necessary, or you may write by German Post.

I am Dear Madam, your Most Obedient & Dutiful Son,
Richard Pococke

------

[103] Again, this man has not been identified

[104] Alessandro Falconieri (1657-1734), was born in Rome, the son of Marquis Paolo Francesco Falconieri and Vittoria del Bufalo. He died at Rome, on 26 January, 1734 and his funeral was held on 28 January, the day before Pococke noted his death

[105] The Chevalier's sons were Charles Edward Stuart (1720-88), nick-named "Bonnie Prince Charlie" and Henry Benedict Stewart (1725-1807), who became a Cardinal. At the time, they were aged fourteen and eight respectively.

[106] Not Robert Wood (1717?-71) of Riverstown Castle County Meath, of archaeological fame, whom Pococke was to later meet in Italy in 1737. The Mr. Wood referred to here and in subsequent letters is a friend or business associate of the family living in London at the time, and willing to accept responsibility for receiving various instructions and deliveries from Pococke. He is possibly the "Reverend Montague Wood of the City of London Clerk" assigned by the bishop to conduct a transaction on his behalf with the South Sea Company, as noted on a sealed document dated 6 July, 1717 (see "Other Manuscript Sources in Private Collections" in the Bibliography). The same Mr. Wood also accompanied Mrs. Pococke when she met her son and nephew in London on their return from abroad (see her comments at the end of Letter 22, Dover, 30 June, 1734, Add. 22978)

ROME
14/25 February, 1734
Milles to the bishop[107]

[It should be noted, again, that Milles did not produce any journals for his time in Rome, or at least none have survived]

My Lord

When I wrote my last to your Ldship we were just settled in Rome, & had not then survey'd any of the antiquitys of it.[108] In my following acct to your Ldship I shall make use of the same method that we have done in our search after the antiquitys of this place, wch was, we consider'd Rome according as it was divided into fourteen Regions by Augustus Caesar,[109] & so examin'd one region first & then another, & as we were situated in our lodgings at the foot of the Collis Hortulorum,[110] we first began with the sixth region, wch included the upper part of this hill and valley between it & the Quirinal, with all that hill likewise. But as I shall have occasion hereafter to mention the gates, & walls of the city, I shall consider them as they are mentioned by the Classicks, who wrote in the Augustan age, when the walls of Rome wch were built by Servius Tullius[111] came along the Quirinal hill

---

[107]Add. 15773

[108]One publication that would have been of help to the cousins in trying to understand the antiquities and the layout of ancient Rome was Basil Kennet's *Romae Antiquae Notitia: or The Antiquities of Rome*, a book in two volumes, published in London, 1696. According to *A Catalogue of the Library (op.cit.)*, Pococke had a first edition of this work, which contained a comprehensive examination of the city's regions, hills, buildings and roads (29-56) and was illustrated with engravings of the principal buildings. The popularity of this book is obvious from the numerous editions it went through, still being printed more than a century later

[109]Augusts divided the city into fourteen administrative regions in 7 BC. The sixth region was Alta Semita, whose name means "High Path" and refers to the path passing over the Quirinal Hill, and combines the areas of both this hill and the Virinal Hill

[110]Latin name for the Hill of Gardens, or modern day Pincian Hill

[111]The legendary sixth King of Rome, who reigned from 578-535 BC

& excluded all the with the valley between them as well as that large extent of ground of the Campus Martius.[112]

The walls wch are now standing and are said to have been built by the Emperour Aurelian[113] are computed to be between 13 & 14 miles in circuit. They are built of brick and fortify'd with square towers of the same at about 60 feet distance from each other. On the inside almost all round are little arcades of brick. What use they were for I shall not pretend to determine. The walls of the city shew very various workmanship, being repaired in some places by Belisarius[114] and Fotila, and the several different Popes, to this time, amongst wch Urban the 8 has had a great share,[115] having enclosed a great part of the Regio Transtiberina[116] (and indeed all that we have as yet seen of it) with a new fortification.

The Collis Hortulorum is thought to have been so called from the gardens of Sallust and Lucullus,[117] wch took almost all its space, but as the latter were in the ninth region [the Circus Flaminus] I shall speak of them in their proper place, the former were made by Crispus Sallustius with the money that he got in the Batonship of Africa,[118] and were so delightfull that afterwards they became the residence of several Emperours. These gardens occupy the upper part of the Collis Hortulorum facing the Quirinal, and some part of the valley before those two hills. At the upper end of this valley are still remaining the sides of a Circus[119] wch are built against the opposite hills, there are likewise at the end of it part of the Carceres from whence the chariots started. Towards the upper end is a Temple [of Venus] almost quite

---

[112]The Field of Mars, a publicly owned area of ancient Rome

[113]Roman Emperor from 270-275 AD

[114]Flavius Belisarius (500-565 AD), one of the greatest generals of the Byzantine Empire

[115]Urban VIII (born Maffeo Barberini) was Pope from 1623-44

[116]The fourteenth region, "Across the Tiber", incorporating Tiber Island and all the parts of Rome west beyond the Tiber.

[117]Lucius Licinius Lucullus (c. 117 BC–57/56 BC) was a politician of the Late Roman Republic

[118]Sallust the Roman historian. He served in Julius Caesar's armies in Africa for which he was rewarded with a governorship in North Africa, and in his retirement turned to the writing of history.

[119]A place for horse and chariot races

entire. The whole built of brick, and is thought to have belonged to
Sallust's gardens,[120] and that in this circus it was that they celebrated
the Ludi Apollinares,[121] when by reason of the overflowing of the
Tyber they could not celebrate them in the Circus Flaminius. Livy
mentions these games to have been at a Circus without [outside] the
Porta Collina at a Temple of Venus Ericyna,[122] from whence it is a very
reasonable conjecture that the Temple above mention'd was the
Temple of Venus. The Forum Sallusii[123] is thought to have been on
the Quirinal near it. But as there are so many things, the situation of
which is entirely uncertain I shall only mention to your Ldship such
antiquitys as are either at present remaining or whose situation is
entirely certain.

Some of the greatest remains, that are now extant in Rome, are those
of the Baths of Diocletian,[124] since on the spot where they stood is now
a large monastery and gardens of the Carthusians,[125] a monastery and
a garden of the Bernadines[126] a prodigious large void place, several

---

[120]For details of this temple, see Kim J. Hartswick, *The Gardens of Sallust: A
Changing Landscape* (University of Texas Press, 2004) 73

[121]Games held each year in honour of Apollo

[122]Venus Erycina ("Venus from Eryx"), originated on Mount Eryx in western
Sicily. A temple was also set up to her on the Capitoline Hill. She
embodied "impure" love, and was the patron goddess of prostitutes.

[123]Forum Sallustii, or Forum of Sallust. It is unlikely that a forum (a market
place) would have been part of the original garden complex, but could have
been added by a later emperor. However, it is also possible that the forum
was outide the gardens, and simply acquired the name on account of its
proximity to the gardens

[124]These are the grandest and most extensive of the Roman imperial baths in
Rome. They were commissioned by Maximian in honour of co-Emperor
Diocletian in 298 AD, on the former's return from Africa. However, they
were not completed until 306 AD, the date of the dedication, and then fell
into disrepair after the Gothic invasion of 410 AD

[125]At some point between 1560 and 65 AD, the ruined baths were sold to
Pope Pius IV, who established in one part a monastery of Carthusian
monks. In 1593, these monks sold part of the ruins to Caterina Sforza di
Santafiora, who founded the Cistercian Convent of St Bernardo

[126]This is the San Bernardo alle Terme, a basilica church built in 1598 for a
French Cistercian group of monks called the Feuillants. The building and
adjoining monastery were subsequently given to the Congregation of St.
Bernard of Clairvaux

public grannarys, besides private houses and vineyards. The most entire, and best part of the ruins makes at present a very large and capacious church for the Carthusians, it is much in the form of a cross but all the roof vaulted and large arches on each side, and adorned with 8 large Corinthian pillars or Oriental granite.[127] I met with an account in an author here, that there were 40,000 Xtian slaves employ'd in the building of it, and 30,000 of them dying of hard labour &c.: the rest were barbarously butcher'd.[128] There are other prodigious remains near the church, wch now serve to put hay in. At the four corners of these baths were four round Calidarii,[129] three of wch are still remaining, the two of them are in a ruinous condition, the third is entire, and is a very fine building adorned with a cupola, and is now the church of the Bernardines.[130] Behind these baths the walls of the city project considerably, and form a large square space considerably beyond the other parts of the walls, which most Antiquarys are of opinion was the Castrum Praetorium[131] built by Tiberius[132] at the instance of Aelius Sejanus.[133] Till the time of

---

[127]This church is the Santa Maria degli Angeli e dei Martiri and was built by orders of Pope Pius IV, after a Sicilian priest, Fr. Antonio Lo Duca, had a vision of angels in the ruins in 1541. Work began in 1563, to the design of Michelangelo, after whose death it was continued and completed by Jacopo Lo Duca. In 1749 it underwent major alterations. After the unification of Italy, the Carthusians were evicted from the buildings which were for some time used as a military barracks, until eventually being given to the Fransiscan order of Minims. Therefore, during the time of Pococke and Milles' visit, it was in its original state, as designed by Michelangelo

[128]One source for this information, which may have been available to our travellers, is Cardinal Caesar Baronius (1535-1607), an eminent ecclesiastical historian who published a new edition of the *Roman Martyrology* in 1586. However, his figure for the number of Christian slaves employed in the building of the baths is 40,000

[129]Rooms with a hot plunge bath, used in a Roman bath complex

[130]This church was built in 1598 and was initially given to a French Cistercian group, the Feuillants, through the intercession of Caterina Sforza di Santafiora. After the French Revolution, the building and its adjoining monastery were given to the Congregation of St. Bernard of Clairvaux

[131]A barracks situated just outside the city of Rome, built in 23 AD to house the Praetorian Guard

[132]Tiberius Julius Caesar Augustus, Roman Emperor (14-37 AD)

[133]Lucius Aelius Seianus (20 BC-31 AD), better known as Sejanus, who became Prefect of the Praetorian Guard, exerted a very strong influence

Constantine the great,[134] it remained out of the city enclosed within its own square walls, but that Emperour beating down the partition wall, adjoined it to the city, and removed the soldiers out of it.

On that side of the Viminal, which faces the Quirinal are still some large remains of the baths of Agrippina the mother of Nero,[135] and at a small distance from them are some more small ruins, wch are said to be the baths of Olympias in wch St Laurence sufferd martyrdom.[136]

On the Esquiline hill facing the church of St Maria Maggiore[137] erected on a pedestal stands a fluted Corinthian pillar of white marble wch formerly adorned the Portico of the temple of peace[138] wch was built by Vespasian,[139] it is accounted to be one of the finest pillars that is extant, the workmanship of it is so exquisitely fine...[140] A little further we saw the ruins of the Castellum Aqua Martiae,[141] in wch were two trophys erected in honour of Marius for his victory over Jugurtha,[142]

---

over Tiberius and was eventually executed on suspicion of a conspiracy against him

[134]Flavius Valerius Aurelius Constantinos (272-337 AD), was the first Roman Emperor to convert to Christianity

[135]Julia Agrippina (16-59 AD) was one of the more prominent female members of the Julio-Claudian dynasty and was the sister of Caligula. Her son Nero (Nero Claudius Caesar Augustus Germanicus 37-68 AD) was Emperor from the year 54 AD until his death by suicide, and was the last emperor of this dynasty

[136]Lawrence of Rome (c. 225-258 AD) was broiled on a gridiron; and later a church was erected for him, St Lorenzo in Pane e Perna

[137]A large Basilica believed to be built on the ruins of the Temple of Juno

[138]Also known as the Temple of Vespasian, this antiquity was begun in 75 AD

[139]Titus Flavius Vespasianus (23-79 AD) was founder of the Flavian Dynasty, reigning as emperor from 69-79 AD

[140] It is said that this column was removed by Pope Paul V to this position, where it supported a bronze image of the Virgin

[141]This is a distribution basin for the Aqua Marcia, the longest of the eleven aquaducts supplying the city of Rome. The aquaduct, built from 144-140 BC for Quintus Marcius Rex, terminated in a large tank on the Viminal Hill, no longer extant

[142]Gaius Marius (157-86 BC) was a commander in the Jugurthine War (112-105 BC), in which Rome was victorious over the Numidian King, Jugurtha

and the Cimbrians, and Teutones.[143] They are now removed to the Capitol. A little behind the Castellum, are very large remains of Decagon building, wch seems to have been a Temple. It was arched at the top and has ten niches round the bottom. It was about 72 feet English in diameter. It is commonly called called the Templum Minervae Medicae,[144] but several antiquarys are of opinion that it was the Basilica Caii & Lucii, the place where that stands being called Galluzzo, wch they think is only a corruption from Caius and Lucius.

About a 100 yards from this Temple were discover'd about a 12 month ago 2 ancient sepulchral chambers, at a small distance from each other. One of wch belong'd to a particular family as an inscription found over the door testifyed. Liberti & Familia L: Arunti L: Fr: Ter: this chamber was divided into several small compartments, each of wch belong'd to a particular branch of the family as an inscription over each informed us. In these compartments were earthern vases full of the ashes of the deceased, wch were cover'd with a round earthen top. The vases were of different sizes some deep and narrow, others round and about ½ a foot deep. One of these compartments I observed to be somewhat superior to the rest, wch no doubt was appropriated to the eldest branch of the family. The pavement of this chamber was of Mosaick, the roof arched, and adorned with figures in stucco, wch were all spoilt with the damp. The other chamber did not as I could perceive, belong to any particular. It was full from top to bottom with rows of holes exactly in the form of our Pigeon holes in England; in each of wch was fixed a round earthen vase with a covering over it wch was full of the ashes of the deceased. Under each hole was wrote the name of the dead person. At the upper end of the room was a large niche with two vases full of ashes, wch no doubt were of some persons of distinction. These sepulchres are said to be the most perfect that are remaining; as yet we have not see any others. There were

---

[143]The Cimbrian War (113–101 BC) was fought between the Roman Republic and the tribes of the Cimbri and the Teutons, who migrated from northern Europe into Roman controlled territory, and clashed with Rome and her allies

[144]There was a Temple of Minerva Medica on the Esquiline Hill , which was built in the Republican era, but no remains of it exist

several medals found in these vases wch had been burn't with the bodys.[145]

Adjoining to the walls of the city between the Porta Navia, and Calimontane are the remains of a Circus built of brick, and called Castrense, because in it the ludi Castrenses used to be performed, half of the lower row of arches is only remaining. At a little distance are the ruins of the Temple of Venus and Cupid. Under a church called St Martin,[146] they shew'd us the remains of some baths which they called the baths of Trajan, but Antiquarys are in doubt whether they were baths built by that Emperour, or only some part of Titus's baths wch were repair'd by him, and from thence called by his name; for they are very near the baths of Titus.[147] The remains of wch are called commonly the seven halls, tho' without any reason, for there are nine of them joining to one another; and in each room are 8 doors wch correspond to one another, tho not in a direct line, but slanting so that you may see from one end of them to the other. These chambers are about 135 feet in length 17 in breadth and 12 in heigth. The common opinion is that they were reservoirs of water for the use of the baths.

At a small distance from these are prodigious remains under ground consisting of almost an infinite number of vaulted chambers, wch by their vicinity to the baths, are thought to be the remains of the Palace

---

[145]Pococke's account is as follows: "[I]n the same garden were lately found sepulchral vaults of the Arunti family they look when you go in like pidgeon houses, full of such holes, into which putting your hand deep you find urns built into the wall & cover'd with a lid of earth like a common pipkin, in some were two urns & in some niches 6 or 7, under many of them were pieces of white marble, with the names of them, there were three of them in small rooms together & another by it self a little larger. We saw some [..] & rusty medals found there, the man told us he found several of their heads with a coin in it, the obolus in the mouth to pay Charon". Letter 13, Rome 1/12 March, 1734. Add. 22978

[146] He refers here to the crypt under the church of St Martino

[147]Milles is probably correct on this point. Titus (Titus Flavius Vespasianus) was a member of the Flavian Dynasty and briefly succeeded his father Vespasian as Emperor from 79-81 AD; Trajan (Marcus Ulpius Nerva Traianus) was Emperor from 98 to 117 AD

of Titus:[148] tho several of these rooms are filled up, by the falling in of the earth, yet we went through a prodigious number several of whc had been painted but were spoil'd with the damp. In one of them at the upper end we observ'd a semicircular nich, or concavity, in wch stood the famous groupe of Laocoon, and his sons, so much commended by Pliny, and was the workmanship of Agesander, Polidorus, and Athenedorus, Rhodius.[149] In the same room were found one square peice of painting, wch was not quite spoil'd and seemed to be the history of Coriolanus.[150] Amongst the several rooms we entered into a gallery in wch we could hardly stand upright, it was about 280 feet in length, and 18 in breadth: the roof was arched over and very prettily painted with birds, beasts, flowers, &c. with little square compartments, this must certainly have been a nobleman before it was buried as it is at present.[151] Besides this prodigious number of buildings now under ground, there remains 3 fine peices above ground wch were parts of 3 large Temples, or some very magnificent apartment. They are all round, and have niches all about at bottom, and windows over them the largest of them was above 100 feet in diameter, they were all crown'd with cupolo's, wch were adorn'd with stucco work. It is not well settled what these three great peices of building were. They stand separate from each other, and are certainly members of the Palace [of Nero/.

My paper will not suffer me to mention any thing else, tho' I shall continue regularly in my next, and at present we see nothing but the Antiquitys, and a few churches, because the Palaces are too cold to be

---

[148]These are of course the remains of chambers of the Palace of Nero (Domus Aurea)

[149]This famous statue is now in the Vatican Museums

[150]Gaius Marcius Coriolanus is believed to be a legendary Roman general who lived in the 5th century BC and the subject of Shakespeare's play of that name. The walls of one of these apartments still retain their ancient stucco and beautiful painting, though the theme of Coriolanus is not mentioned in the sources

[151]Though there are many 17th century accounts of these ruins (as well as later ones such as ours), the area was subsequently covered over until 1776, when it was opened up so that the paintings could be published. In 1813 the whole site was cleared to its present condition, and nine years later the Italian architect Antonio de Romanis published his illustrated book, *Le Antiche Camere Esquiline*

visited till the spring approaches a little. Rome continually mends on our hands, and raises our Ideas of its ancient grandeur.

Dr Pococke begs leave to present his humble duty to your Ldship and so does more particularly

My Lord

Your Lordships

ROME
1/12 March, 1734
Pocoke to his mother
Letter 13[152]

[The brief excerpts chosen from this letter (which essentially describes the same buildings and ruins as in the last) are mostly of a personal/social nature. It should be noted that large sections of this letter have been scored out, in two places as much as half a page at a time. These are reproduced here from the original letter. The second is a further example of Pococke's straightened circumstances while abroad, owing to the fact that his income from Ireland has not been forwarded to him]

3. We dined with the 2 Mr Holbechs[153] with Dr Irwin[154] & his son[155] the English Physician & Mr Figgan Eng. young Gentleman.[156] rainy...

---

[152]Add. 22978. This is the third letter of the original collection (Add. 19939) and a note next to the English address states that it was received by Mrs. Pococke on 22-3 March and answered on 24 March, 1734

[153]William Holbech (c. 1699-1771), of Farnborough, Warwickshire, graduated from Trinity College Oxford in 1716 and spent much of his time in Italy between 1730 and 1745. He died unmarried in 1771, and his estate was succeeded by the eldest son of his brother Hugh (also called Hugh). See Ingamells, *op.cit.*, 507

[154]Dr. James Irwin (c.1687-1759) was in Rome from at least 1732, and from 1736 was one of the Chevalier's chief physicians. He is recorded as being present at the first meeting of the Jacobite Lodge in Rome (16 August,

5. Paid some visits to Lutterel an Etonian,[157] come from Naples saw some churches on the Quirinal, visited Dr Irwin...

7. Being rainy staid within all day, & studied the Antiquity of Rome & a little Italian.

8. Went out with Mr Stewart in his coach to Sallusts Gardens,....

10. Went to the Library, at 2 walk'd out to see the walls....This day to my great joy & satisfaction I received your letter of the 23d of Decr & am very glad to find that they you were then all well,[158] [& must return you my hearty thanks & acknowledgements for your very kind offer of giving me credit with Mr Hoare for what I pleas'd. To answer yr letter then I have not recd ye two letters sent to Genoua nor Jerre yt sent to Paris. I shd be glad to know if heads of ye letter opens, you sent a copy of in one of them: as to mentioning my being in Italy to Mr Alington[159] you need not write on purpose but wd you write to let him know .. that you hear I shall be at home soon. My Ld Bp had

---

1735) and then twice afterwards, as an ordinary member. See William James Hugham, *The Jacobite Lodge at Rome, 1735-7* (Leicester, 1910) 15. He died at Rome in 1759. See also Ingamells, *op.cit.*, 545

[155]Dr. Irwin's son was not a physician (Pococke's punctuation is sometimes confusing), and is also James. Like his father, he was involved in the Jacobite Lodge, listed at its first meeting as "JW" (Junior Warden). *Op.cit.*, 15

[156]Mr. Figgan has not been identified

[157]Simon Luttrell (1713-87), 1st Earl of Carhampton was the second son of Major-General Henry Luttrell and Elizabeth Jones. He was elected a member of the Society of Dilettanti in 1736, married Judith Maria Lawes in 1737 and was MP (Whig) for Wigan and Stockbridge. He was created 1st Baron Irnham of Luttrellstown, County Dublin, in 1768 and died in this county in 1787. See Ingamells, *op.cit.*, 617

[158]The following paragraph, up until the word "opera" has been completely scored out of the copy and is reproduced here from the original letter (Add. 19939), though it should be noted that in places it is problematic in terms of the clarity of the script and in the frequent use of abbreviations. Also, the following page of the manuscript has been badly affected by the scoring out, which is in such thick ink that it has leaked through

[159]Probably Rev. Hugh Wallington who, in 1727, succeeded Isaac Milles (Pococke's uncle) in the following positions: Treasurer of Waterford, Prebend of Modeligo and Vicar of Modeligo. See Ryland, *op.cit.* for the various dates

ordered me & Jerre to recommend an Oxon man but it did not take.[160]
I am very much obligd to you & my sister for yr good wishes on ye
19th & in a particular manner for your prayers for ye protection in our
travels which we have so happily enjoyd, & I hope will be continued
to us. I must desire you to write to Archdeacon Denis[161] with my
humble [grace] & thanks & let him know ... of the particulars of the bill
& ....[162] We are as yet in no good way to improve in Italian, we give
ourselves up entirely to seeing things but when the cheif of these is
over I believe we shall take a master to talk to for I look into ye
Grammer now & then & we propose to go to Italian coffee houses &
conversations or assemblies & I intend to read an Italian Terrence, but
ye good memory gets ye better of me in this & in French I just begun
to have some relish for the latter wn I left France, but I believe Italian
is easier: We pass the Carnival here the] opera begins on the 14th,
Sunday, but they mask here only eight days, they are all mad, but we
shall be only barefaced spectators.[163] [The seal of yr letter was so
opend yt it could not be closd so a new seal was put in another place
ye port mark of London was Jan 4th tho' dated Dec 23d on ye back part
in one place was not from Newbury: in another part To The Revd Mr
H. Walkington at Westhatch Newbury to Pay foreign postage. N3. I
can't think how this cd be put on the letter.]

12. We went to the famous Collisaeum or Amphitheatre of Vespasian
which is half entire of the outside, there are as it were four stones
adorned with Dorick, 2d with Ionick, 3d with Corinthian pillars & the

---

[160]Possibly a request from the bishop for them to recommend someone for a
preferment in his diocese

[161]Among many other senior positions in the diocese, William Dennis held
the Archdeaconry of Lismore Cathedral from 1724-49, and was therefore
resident at one of the two church mansions in Lismore. As Pococke had
been Precentor of Lismore Cathedral since 1725 and at some point in 1734
(either during or on return from his tour) was appointed as Vicar General of
Waterford & Lismore, he would have worked very closely with Archdeacon
Dennis. It is likely that the latter was related to the Monsieur Dennis in
Paris and his brother in London, mentioned in other letters. See also the
reference to the archdeacon in the bishop's Will (Appendix 1)

[162]These two lines are illegible line but indicate something about the same
Mr. Wallington

[163]The next five lines are also scored out of the copy and are reproduced here
from the original letter

4th with Corinthian Pillasters, it would hold 8700 spectators, & upon
occasion they could let in water to it & have naval fights. We
measured all the parts of it. In the afternoon we went with on Mr
Chambers (an Irish young Gentleman, a convert & lives here & has a
pension of the Pope, whom we accidentally became acquainted
with)[164] to the Farnese gardens, which occupy almost the whole little
Palatine hill, & where Augustus's palace was, & the ruins of it still
are[165] ..this on festivals, & the Holy week is done by Cardinal[s and
the Pope himself &][166] after they have wash'd each foot & wiped [...]
their feet & wait on them at supper, which they have in plenty [... we]
saw all performed. The Gentlemen spent the Evening with us.
Cos[cia] deprived of all his Preferments, condemned to St Angelo for
10 years [and has his] vote as cardinal taken away for that time;[167] he
is to be tryed for other things so that it is thought he will never be at
liberty; he was guilty of the greatest male administration & of the
vilest debaucheries, in the last Popes time,[168] who minded nothing but
Religion & so his minister did all a Brother monk.....[Pococke's own
punctuation, or his mother's] but I hear since he is certainly to be set at
liberty on Ash Wednesday.

The C---r [Chevalier] demanded guards of the Pope, which he has; the
secret of which is not known, but it is said there was a plot against him
by the English, tho' no such thing: she gives herself up entirely to
devotion, not sleeping about 4 of the 24 hours;[169] & he does not go

---

[164]This is the second time he has mentioned Chambers and the fact that he is a
convert with a pension from the Pope

[165]The next half page is not scored out, but virtually obliterated by the ink that
has seeped through from the previous page, where the passage about
Pococke's banking problems were deleted

[166]Scored out in the copy and reproduced from the original letter, Add. 19939

[167]Cardinal Niccolo Coscia (1681-1755), was appointed to this position by
Benedict XIII in 1725 and held rule in the Papal States during this Pope's
reign. He was accused of financial and venal abuses and on Benedict's
death fled from Rome. He was tried and sentenced in 1731 and so (despite
the fact that sources claim his sentence was reduced to a fine), when our
travellers were at Rome he had already been imprisoned in Castel St
Angelo's for three years

[168]Benedict XIII (1649-1730), Pope from 1724 until his death

[169]The Chevalier's wife, Maria Clementina Sobieska. Their marriage was not
happy and she accused her husband of adultery and of ill treatment,

abroad so often as usual. [Pray let me know what my letters cost for they are sent under cover to Paris wch I hope makes them come early with only the Paris postage.][170]

13. We went again to see the Colisoeum[171] & then Titus's palace of which there are great remains.[172] At 2 walked over at Porta Pia[173] & came in at Porta Magiore,[174] review'd the Amphitheatrum Castrense by St Croce [175]..., met Cardinal Altieri[176] walking thither having got out of his coach a quarter of a mile off to perform some devotion at this church with the greater humility, for that is one of the 7 churches, dress'd in a black coat, a black short cloak, red stockins, a red skull cap, & a black hat with red riband round it for a band; as Bishops wear a green one, & go so in black cloaks ordinarily...

14. We visited Mr Hows son of Gloucestershire, saw a church or two near at 2 went to St Peters which every time appears more beautiful, there are many pictures in it of mosaick done in stone, some of it is marble, but mostly stained glass, so well that if it were not for the shining of 'em you would not know them from painting, pieces of different colour'd small vitrified earth are so put in together.[177] We

---

especially at the hands of Lord and Lady Inverness (John Hay of Cromlix and his wife, see above), in whom he had invested a lot of power. Other sources note that she suffered from depression and spent much of her time in prayer. She died ten months later, in January 1735

[170]Scored out in the copy and reproduced from the original letter, Add. 19939

[171]Spelled differently in the same letter

[172]This was actually Nero's Palace. See above

[173]A gate in the Aurelian Walls, designed by Michelangelo and named after Pope Pius IV

[174]Or Greater Gate, also in the Aurelian Walls, originally built by Aurelian and further modified in 405 AD by the Emperor Honorius

[175]Generally described as the "second" amphitheatre in Rome, after the Colosseum, dated to the first decades of the 3rd century AD, and part of an Imperial villa complex which was built by emperors of the Severan dynasty

[176]Giovanni Battista (1673-1740), installed as Cardinal-Priest of S. Matteo in Merulana, in 1724

[177]The Basilica of St. Peter's, a late Renaissance church in the Vatican City having the largest interior of any church in the world. Many of the mosaics on view at St. Peter's today had not been executed by the time of Milles and Pococke's travels, examples being those in the Alters of Crucifixion of St. Peter, Transiguration, and St. Michael the Archangel

took a walk roud the walls & came in at Porta Janiculensis [Porta San Pancrazio]...We met Cardinal Altieri again walking from his coach.

17. [178] [I receiv'd with a great deal of pleasure your letter of the 13th & an account from Mr Teissier that he had orders from Mr Alexander to give me credit for £60 for which I return you a great many thanks, & am very much obligd to you for your kind offer indeed my stock was just now out, but I borrow on occasion from my companion for a short time, indeed tis very hard yt since I left Ireland I have not receivd one farthing of money from thence, but [that] wch I left in my Bankers hands. Considering my income & yt 500 at least is due to me there so yt I thought I'd have depended on it, & now I have been out of Ireland near three quarters of a year: but I hope soon to have a large remittance to make amends & I have writ from this place to Mr Bagwell.[179] The letter came all the way enclosed. Mr Bentham[180]

---

[178]This whole section has been scored out in thick black in Mrs. Pococke's copy and is reproduced here from the original (Add. 19939). It is hardly surprising that Pococke, on reflection, decided to eradicate this passage, which puts him, as well as the church authorities in Ireland, in a bad light. A paragraph on the same subject is similarly eradicated in Letter 19, from Milan (see below)

[179]This must be John Bagwell, a successful banker in Clonmel, County Tipperary, whose grandfather, a captain in Cromwell's army, was the first member of the family to have come over to Ireland. Mr. Bagwell married the daughter of a Presbyterian clergyman from Dublin (named Shaw) and his success in banking led to his appointment as an agent for the banking houses of La Touche and Keane of Dublin, and for Harper and Armstead of Cork. In addition to buying up thousands of acres in County Tipperary, and being a committed Presbyterian, Mr. Bagwell was instrumental in setting up the Incorporated Society for the Promotion of Protestant Schools in Ireland, in 1733 (an organisation in which, as we have seen, Pococke himself became very involved when later resident in Ireland, and to which he left the majority of his estate). On his death in 1754, Mr. Bagwell left 2,730 acres which gave an income of £20,000 a year, in addition to his lucrative banking business, which passed on to his son-in-law. See Michael Ahern (*op.cit.*), Chapter 14, pp 156-57. It is almost certain that Mr. Bagwell is buried in Old St. Mary's Church, Clonmel, where the remains of other members of his family lie (though later generations are buried in Marlfield Church). Here is a grave stone which records: "Sacred to the memory of John Bagwell Esq., of Clonmel, and Rachel, his wife". However, nothing further is decipherable (see www.clonmelgraveyards.com). Clearly, Pococke needed two bankers, Mr. Hoare to take care of his affairs in

having been laid under an obligation by ... will make him still more careful to do all he can for our relation if hes put under his care:[181] If you should on any occasion write to Ben you may order him to desire Monsr Denis wn he writes to his Brother to enquire of him whether he sent those little bundles or boxes we left with him to be sent to Mr Denis in London to be forwarded to Newtown bid him give it Monsr Denis in writing:[182] & another thing I shd d be glad to know, that is, how Mat:[183] behaves himself, & yt Ben wd sift him cunningly to know whether he designs to stay with me after his term [or time] is ... but not letting him know yt he I ordered so to do. I drink a pint of strong Spanish wine in three daies for th'Italian is not good: I thank you much for all your good advice, & since you seem to desire it in return for your goodness], I shall make all the convenient haste I can home by Loretto, Venice through Germany & Holland, & hope to see you the latter end of the summer...

18. ...[T]he evening we spend in reading of places & writing down what we see; & the first hour of the even at the coffee house commonly. We saw here one Farmer Jefferies of Wedmore near Wells,[184] who brought his son to a sister in law here, & he is gone as

---

England and Mr. Bagwell to look after the income he accrued from his assorted clerical positions in the south-east of Ireland

[180]Mr. Bentham's name appears several times in Pococke's correspondence and possibly refers to Rev. James Bentham, Prebendary of Ely, Rector of Bow-brick-hill in Buckinghamshire and Domestic Chaplain to the Right Hon. Lord Cadogan. After gaining a BA from Trinity College, Cambridge, Bentham was presented to the vicarage of Stapleford in Cambridgeshire in 1733, and became a noted historian of church architecture. A biography of this gentleman appears in J. Nichols & S. Bentley, *Literary Anecdotes of the Eighteenth Century*, Vol. III (London, 1812) 484-94

[181]Possibly Thomas Milles, son of Pococke's uncle, Jeremiah Milles, who is eventually sent to Oriel College. See below

[182]Clearly Mrs. Pococke has reported that the boxes (left with Monsieur Dennis in Paris with instructions to be sent to his brother in London and then to Newtown) have not yet arrived

[183]It is not known who "Mat" is, though it is possible that it is a relative of the Pococke/Milles family

[184]Though the farmer and son have not been identified, records show that a Mr. Jeffreys was travelling in 1733 with a Mr. Hart. See Ingamells, *op.cit.*, 471. Wedmore is a village in Somerset, and Wells, also in that county, is the second-smallest city in England, famous for its cathedral

he came by sea. In the college de propaganda fide[185] they have young men off all nations, to send back into their own country to preach the gospels, when they have instructed them, we saw a Black of about 18 in a students gown, who belongs to them.

19. Staid within, at 2 walked with Mr Chambers a mile from the walls, but 3 from our lodging, to St Pauls a large church adorned with fine pillars that were taken from the moles of Adrian, which is now St Angelo[186]...

21. Saw Barberini's palace,[187] the cardinals & Princes apartments, full of fine pictures, states & Busts, each consisting of two long rows of rooms, one above the other below; visited Mr Paul. At 2 went to see churches in Campus Martius, took a walk out of town, went to the coffee house, Mr Crow who is with Mr Hugh Smithson & was chaplain at Leghorn,[188] Brother to Mr Crow of Brocknus near Lymington[189] knew my father & has been at his house. Stephens [the mathematician] was a month with Mr Conscade of Dennington,[190] he

---

[185]The Sacred Congregation for the Propagation of the Faith was founded by Pope Gregory XV in 1622, and was re-named by Pope John Paul II, in 1982, as the Congregation for the Evangelization of Peoples

[186]The Papal Basilica of St Paul Outside the Walls, founded by Constantine I over the burial place of Saint Paul. The building was destroyed by fire in 1823 and re-opened in 1891. The Moles of Hadrian was a mausoleum built for himself and his family by the Emperor Hadrian (76-138), situated on the right bank of the Tiber, and now called the Castel Saint Angelo

[187]A vast palace begun in 1627 for Maffeo Barberini, Pope Urban VIII and completed by Bernini in 1633

[188]Rev. Benajamin Crowe (c. 1689-1749) was Chaplain for the English Factory at Leghorn from 1716-29 and then visited Italy again from 1733-34 as tutor to Sir Hugh Smithson (1715-86), who had succeeded his father as 4th Baronet of Stanwick in 1733. See Ingamells, *op.cit.*, 256

[189]Christopher Crowe (1682-1749) was a merchant in Leghorn before taking up an appointment as Consul at Leghorn, from 1705-16. In addition to his consular duties he acted as an agent or dealer for British collectors. See Ingamells, *op.*cit, 257-58. Situated between Southampton and Bournemouth, the Georgian market town of Lymington was close to where the Pococke family lived

[190]This gentleman was earlier described as Mr. Conscade of Newbury. There was a ruined medieval castle near Newbury called Donnington (rather than

was of Oxford studied the law, has been here four years is esteem'd,
we spent the even with him, this afternoon we went to the Greek
Church St Athanasius & saw them perform their devotions after the
Greek manner.....

23. I went to the Library, at 2 walk'd out met one Mr Dickson an Irish
Gentleman here,[191] viewed some Antiquities with him; went to a
convent of Irish Dominicans,[192] where the late Pope used to retire, we
saw the room where he lay, the Fryars gave us a glass of wine in their
Refectory....

24. Went to view the Palatine,[193] saw the Church of St Anastasia[194]... at
2 went to see churches in the Campus Martius, we have a book that
gives us an account of all the pictures in the churches....[195]

25. We went to review the churches of Campus Martius, at 2 went to
the Palatino [Palatine Hill] to view the ruins of the Emperors palace,
especially those in the English Jesuits garden, which looks to the
Circus Maximus, we saw the Portico's [...] that way to see the games.

Dennington) Castle, built in 1386 and demolished in 1646, and Mr.
Conscade perhaps lived close to this area

[191]This is probably the John Dixon who was a dealer in antiquities at Rome,
mentioned in Ingamells (*op.cit.*, 303-4), though mis-quoted from this letter
as being "an Irish Gentleman here settled", the word "settled" not being in
the text. If the same man, he later got into trouble for being a Jacobite spy,
when visiting Florence with Sir Thomas Twysden, in 1736

[192]The basilica and convent of San Clemente were handed over to the Irish
Provence of the Dominican Order in 1677, and still operate as the Collegio
San Clemente. These buildings are situated close to the Colloseum and are
famous for their mosaics and other works of art. Pococke records in Letter
16 (Rome, 30 April/11 May, 1734), that he visited the Dominicans again,
on 26 April, where he saw the "'C.....r' & all his family came out"

[193]The centremost of the Seven Hills of Rome and one of the most ancient
parts of the city

[194]The first church on this site dates to the late 4th or early 3rd century, given
by a lady called Anestasia. After going through various stages of
restoration, it was finally restored in the 17th century under Pope Urban
VIII, with minor alterations in 1721

[195]There is no obvious entry for this in *A Catalogue of the Library* (*op.cit.*) so
perhaps this book belonged to Milles, rather than Pococke

We went & measured the Temple of Janus,[196] 'tis 4 feet square with four large gate places, one in each side & is built of very large stone. The spring advances apace, violets blown & wall flowers & I saw Almonds, beans & pease in blossom a fortnight ago, & the sun is perfectly warm in the afternoon...

26... Mr Chamberlain[197] had us to Corneille's Tragedy of Cinna[198] at the Clementines College acted by young Noblemen & scholars , a pretty Theatre & fine scenes & good dresses, which continues during the Carnival.

27. Viewed the churches in Campus Martius. Received a letter from Leghorn from Mr Swinton the Chaplain desiring me to come to Legthorn about 3 months hence to Christen a Gentleman's child then expected during his absence in England; to which I return'd a proper answer. We went to see the Masqueraders parade in the street called the Corso the first time for the Carnival, 'twill be every day; some in coaches, some in Landau's,[199] some in chaises, & the nobility in open Barkella's, made like boats finely gilt & carved without covering, with 4 wheels & seats one over another, when they meet any acquaintance they pelt one another with sugar plums; ladies in mask as well as men, but all over at night fall; & a little before night there are every day here races in this street without riders; they are let loose, have some thing on their backs that pricks 'em as they go, & the first gets a piece of Brocade, a tribute paid by the Jews, who they say formerly run themselves,[200] they are horses of the nobility. We went to the

---

[196]This is in the Roman Forum. Janus is the Roman god of gates, doors, doorways, beginnings, endings and time, generally depicted as having two heads

[197]Probably Thomas Chamberlain (born c. 1710), an Irishman whom the Pretender made a gentleman of the bedchamber in 1731. See Ingamells, *op.cit.*, 193-94

[198]Pierre Corneille, 17th century French tragedian, whose play *Cinna* was first performed in 1639. This play is set in ancient Rome but reflects the age of Louis XIV

[199]A four-wheeled carriage with front and back passenger seats that face each other and a roof in two sections that can be lowered or detached

[200]Jewish races were an established part of the Carnival, but the last occasion on which Jews actually ran was in 1547, when one of them died. In 1668, Pope Clement IX abolished the practice of making the Jews the sport of the

Tragedy of Hircanus son of Tigranes[201] at the Roman Jesuit College, acted by the Noble students there; between the acts something of the nature of an opera, dancing, a fine exercise of vaulting, an appearance of the genius's of all nations, in peculiar dresses paying homage to the Roman Genius the Coronation of Hircanus one of these, with dancing between every act, & the opera between three, all performed in the finest manner imaginable, beyond anything I ever saw.

March 1. ... Went to the Church of Sti Apostoli,[202] saw the Chevalier & Lady come from mass. Mr Chamberlain dined with us. We went to see the Corso & races, to the coffee house, to a sort of farce.

2. Went to see Churches; at 2 to a coffee house to see the Corso & races & my friend [Milles] went mask'd on the Corso & Saluting. Some acquaintance was known & taken into their coach. (The Spaniards are just on the borders of this Kingdom [the Papal States] & will have horses soon if is thought ... – but with the less of some men on the road, there being ...)..[203]

4. Viewed some churches; at 2 took a walk to the Tibur very pleasant to Ponte Milvio,[204] where I saw a few Spanish horse to catch deserters; came home via Flamina.[205] Went to a kind of private Opera, having a ticket presented...

---

populace, and ordered that an annual tax of 300 scudi be collected instead. The elders had to pay this tax to the papal authorities on the first day of the Carnival, with due declarations of loyalty and submission

[201] There appears to be no record of this play

[202] The Basilica dei Santi Apostoli is a 6th-century basilica in Rome, dedicated originally to St. James and St. Philip and later to all Apostles. Today the basilica is under the care of the Conventual Franciscan Order, whose headquarters in Rome is in the adjacent building

[203] This reference to advances in the war has been added afterwards in Pococke's hand and is difficult to read as it inserted between the lines, in brackets

[204] The Milvian or Mulvian Bridge, built in 206 BC

[205] This ancient road leading from Rome over the Apennines to Rimini, was constructed by Gaius Flaminus, during his Censorship of 220 BC. It starts at the Porto del Populo, in the Aurelian Walls

6. Visited Mr Crow at Sr Hugh Smithsons, he went with us to St Peters, at 4 went to the Corso[206] & then to a Comedy a friend giving us some tickets...

8... to the Corso & race, ended the Carnival at a Comedy by the Jesuits, well performed.

10. Ash Wednesday, now sorrow succeeds to mirth & all is repentance in dust & ashes. Went this morning to St Sabine on the Aventine,[207] & saw Cardinal Petra[208] in the Pews, who does not come out, bless the ashes & cross the preheads [foreheads] of the Cardinals & people with ashes; at 2 went to see churches. [I am much surprised that I have no remittance from Ireland & yet I have writ to Bagwell 5 weeks since, & in case I should have none.... but be that as it will on disposing of yt money you have any [addition] I'll take it off you & if I have remittance & you want any for...... my friend tho' if I had it not at command 'twould be very [ ] for me yt you give me [one].....][209]

---

[206]The Via del Corso, the main street running through the historical centre of Rome, originally known as the Via Lata

[207]This is the Basilica of Saint Sabina at the Aventine, a basilica high up on the Aventine Hill, dating from the 5th century. It is the stational church for Ash Wednesday

[208]Cardinal Vincenzo Petra (1662-1747) who, from 1727-1747, was Prefect of the Congregation for the Evangelization of Peoples, established by Pope Gregory XV, in 1622, to regulate ecclesiastical affairs in the so-called "missionary countries"

[209]This whole paragraph is scored out in the copy and is reproduced from the original letter, which in parts is undecipherable

ROME
No date [c. 28 February/11 March, 1734]
Milles to the bishop[210]

My Lord

Your Lships letter dated the 19th of January came to my hands the 13/24th of last month, by wch I find that your Ldship has receiv'd all my letters but one, wch I believe was that wch I wrote to your Ldship from Antibes, being obliged to leave it with the landlord of the house, who I suppose never put it into the post.

I shall punctually obey your Ldships commands in relation to the buying the Bullarium Romanum,[211] but would gladly know whether your Ldship would have them sent to Waterford immediately or else to Newtown with a box which I shall have occasion to send there, & from thence to be forwarded to Waterford, wch last I beleive will be the surest, & most expeditious method, I shall wait for your Ldship['s] determination in this affair.

We propose to leave Rome about the latter end of May, in order to be at Venice by the Ascension;[212] so that whatever commands your Ldship has for me here, if you would be pleased to notify them to me, as soon as possible after the receipt of this letter, I shall have sufficient opportunity to execute them.

It is a prodigious satisfaction to me to find that my accounts of my travels, have any thing in them to merit your Ldships approbation. It shall always be my utmost endeavour, to inform myself in the best manner concerning every thing that I see, but as great part of the antiquitys of this city are so obscure, that even the most learned men cannot agree about them, I hope your Ldship will have the goodness

---

[210]Add. 15773. It will be remembered that this is the only letter in the collection where the date has been omitted by the scribe

[211]A bullarium is a collection of papal bulls or other similar documents, the first of which was published in 1586 by the canonist Laertius Cherobini. The following letter from Milles to the bishop (27 March/7 April, 1734) explains more fully which volumes are available. See below

[212]As commonly planned by Grand Tourists

to excuse any faults that I shall be guilty of in things wch area not entirely evident

I would willingly fill up the rest of my letter but the Post is ready to go out, & I am afraid I shall be too late. Dr Pococke presents his humble duty to your Ldship

I am my Lord

Your Lordships

ROME
27 March/7 April, 1734
Milles to the bishop[213]

[This letter contains lengthy descriptions of famous antiquities such as Trajan's Column, the Antonine Pillar, the Pantheon and the Theatre of Marcellus, which may be omitted here as they are common-place in Grand Tour correspondence. Short excerpts from towards the end of the letter, concerning more practical aspects of his travels, as well as topical matters, are included below]

In my last wch I wrote to your Ldship a fortnight ago[214] I desired a remittance of £80 sterling on Venice not knowing after we have left that place where to appoint to hear from your Ldship, & likewise that if your Ldship has any commands to honour me with them at Venice directed A Messieurs Messieurs Swimmer & Hewett[215] pour render a Monseiur Jermie Milles a Venise, until the middle of may, & if your Ldship should have any thing of importance to communicate to be pleased to direct still to me as above, & we will find a method to have any letters convey'd to us from Venice to any place where we shall be.

The Cardinal Coscia, & his brother the late AB: of Benevento remain still in the castle of St Angelo,[216] the Pope will give him his release upon condition that he pays 20,000 crowns, wch he obstinately refuses. I do not know whether he pleads poverty, or no. The Pope is a little chagrin'd at his not complying with any conditions.

The Spanish army is about the number of 20,000 who lately passed thro' the Popes territorys with Don Carlos at their head are enter'd

---

[213] Add. 15773

[214] 11/12 January, 1734

[215] The same forwarding address is given by Pococke (Letter 15), though the latter uses the correct spelling, Swymmer. A Mr. Swymmer is listed in Ingamells (*op.cit.*) 921, as being in Venice from 1733-37 and it is suggested that he was the English merchant in Venice met by Pococke in August 1737. A Henry Hewitt (c. 1695-1756) is also listed in Ingamells (*ibid.*), again an English merchant in Venice up until his death

[216] See note above, regarding the imprisonment of Cardinal Coscia

into the Kingdome of Naples, the Germans not being potent enough to defend the pass.[217] We hear various news of their exploits, but know nothing for certain as yet, but that they are marched directly to Naples[218] leaving Capua, & Gaetta behind. It is thought they will make themselves masters of Naples, the Germans having not men enough to resist them. We set out tomorrow morning for Tivoli, Frescati, Albano & the parts adjacent. Upon inquiry about the Bullarium Romanum I find 6 vols of the Bullarium wch brings them down to Clement Xth,[219] published here about 90 or 100 years ago,[220] & within two or three years they have publish'd here two more vols viz a 7th, & 8th wch come down to, & include Innocent the XIth[221]. They will continue publishing till they have compleated this work. There is an entire edition printed at Geneva, wch brings them down to the present Pope [Clement XII]. There are likewise two vols of Bulls omitted in the other editions, to be sold separate, I should be glad to know if our Ldship would have those 2 vols of omitted Bulls on supposition that they do not design to print them here. For all Rome is so large a city I found it a difficult matter to meet with these books, & at present I am not certain that those wch I have looked on are compleat. However if they are to be had in Rome our Ldship shall have them.

Dr Pococke presents his humble duty to your Ldship

I am my Lord your Ldships most dutifull

---

[217]Though Don Carlos' army was composed largely of Spaniards, it also included some troops from France and Savoy

[218]Where they were welcomed by the city fathers

[219]Pope Clement X (1590-1676). This volume was published in 1733

[220]These six volumes were published by Girolamo Mainardi, as a supplement to the latest Roman edition of Cherubini's bullarium. See above

[221]Pope from 1676-89

ROME
21 March/1st April, 1734
Pococke to his mother
Letter 14[222]

[The excerpts chosen from this letter include a further account of the Carnival, the Vatican and some matters of family and social interest]

Honoured Madam,

My last to you was of March 11th, that morning I went to Sapienza library,[223] in the afternoon saw some churches near; went & examined Constantines arch;[224] thence to the Church of St Balbina[225] on a heigth of the Aventine, it is one of the finest situations I have seen & commands Rome, Frescati, Tivoli & all the country round: I don't know whether I gave you a very particular account of the Carnival;[226] - they mask about 3 in the afternoon, come to the Corso in Coaches, Chaises, Barkella's the nobility drive their own coaches, some mask'd, some not, servants mostly mask'd behind & walking on each side; they salute their friends gently with sugar plums, which is return'd the same way or by a bow, & they wonder at the English who pelt one another with great ones & the punchinella's &c:[227] there are two rows of Coaches, one going one way , & one another , people in the middle

---

[222] Add. 22978. This is the fourth letter of the original collection (Add. 19939) and a note next to the English address states that it was received by Mrs. Pococke on 13 April and answered on 14 April, 1734. She notes, "& writ again with Bagwells April 30 - to Venice"

[223] A magnificent library added to the Roman University (Sapienza) by Pope Alexander VII (1655-67)

[224] A triumphal arch dedicated in 315 to commemorate Constantine I's victory over Maxentius at the Battle of Milvian Bridge three years earlier

[225] A basilica church built in the 4th century with an adjoining monastery

[226] He cannot have forgotten that he had given his mother a brief account of the Carnival, but the fact that he gives further details shows he knows his mother would be fascinated to hear about such an event

[227] Punchinello is the anglicised version of the theatrical character with a very long nose resembling a beak. This character was called *pullus gallinaceus* in Latin, and in Italian he became *pulcino* or *chick*. The costume for this character (which is the English Punch) was white and the mask black

& one each side & scaffolds against the houses, damask & Tapestry hung out of the windows of most houses, which are full of spectators: a little before night the horses run one length of the street; no masking on Fridays & Sundays, nor after four & twenty hours which is night. In the evening to an opera or the masquerade or to a Fiestin which is a kind of Assembly. Ball & cards at some nobles house, particularly the Popes Niece.[228]

12.... Monseignor Fontanini Archbishop of Ancyra[229] sent to know when we should be at home, & came to see us about 4 a mighty courteous old Gentleman & has all the freedom of a French man & sincerity of an English man, & is particularly civil to our Nation, 'tho he is a native here, is a man of the greatest learning in Rome, & they say in the last Pontificate stood fair for an Hat[230]...

14.... at 2 went to the English college, under the direction of English Jesuits: Father Plowden,[231] brother to Mr Plowden near Sr Thomas Lytteltons whom Mr Milles knows,[232] is Re[ctor] of it; he was going out & left one to show us the college, who entertained us in the Refectory with a glass of wine; there are 5 fathers & 25 Students, Cardinal Howards picture is there, & many of that family[233]...

16. Saw some part of the Vatican, many fine paintings of Raphael; a Gallery 200 paces long, painted in the sides with large descriptions Geographical of the several parts of Italy very fine; from thence we went to the summer apartment called the Belvidere where in the court

---

[228]It is not known which niece Pococke refers to here

[229]One of the three gentlemen recommended by Montfaucon, see above. Juste or Giusto Fontanini (1666-1736) wrote many scholarly works, especially on the antiquities of Rome

[230]Presumably this means it was thought he might be appointed a cardinal

[231]Thomas Percy Plowden (1672-1745), of Plowden Hall, Salop, studied in Rome from 1701-4 and was the English College of Rome from 1728-34. He was appointed Rector in 1731. See Ingamells, *op.cit.*, 777

[232]Probably 4th Baronet (1686-1751). Milles must be one of Mrs. Pococke's brothers. Jeremiah became very friendly with Lyttleton's second son, the antiquary Charles Lyttleton, who was Dean of Exeter from 1748 until 1762

[233]Hon. Philip Howard (1629-94), son of Henry Frederick Howard (later Earls of Arundel), joined the Dominican order at sixteen and was appointed a cardinal by Pope Clement X in 1675. He died in Rome and is buried there

are the most famous statues in the world, of Laocoon, Apollo &
Antinous[234] in white marble & several others, together with a large
bason of Porphiry for a fountain 21 palmes (9 inches) diameter &
about 4 deep, a palm is 8 inches & ¾ all one stone. In the afternoon we
went a mile out of Town in Via Tiburtina[235] to St Lorenzo, where that
saint is buried & as they say St Stephen the Proto martyr.[236] We saw
the stone stain'd with blood &c: on which St Laurences body was laid
after it was broiled. We went into the Catacombs which go a mile
towards Tivoli cut out of the rock just high enough to walk in, both
sides are cut out in holes 1 foot deep from 2 to 6 long, when bodies
were put in they were clothed with tiles or marble plaister'd round as
we saw: & in some that were broke down we saw bones lie, in their
proper order very rotten, & remains of vials [bottles] set in mortar
within 'em, in which they say they put the blood of the martyrs; in a
vineyard near we saw a passage into Catacombs which communicated
with these; & the Gentleman shewed us his pleasant villa & a heathen
Temple under ground, which from altars we saw in the garden
concluded to be the temple of Sylvanus.[237]

17. We went to see the other apartments of the Vatican, Sixtus's
chapel, where is Michael Angelo's famous piece of the day of
judgment, & where they choose the Pope in the Ducal Hall near some
of the Cardinals cells are made, in the time of the Conclave,[238] others in
rooms near & the Gallery over the portico of St Peters is full.[239] We
saw the Popes apartment which is hung with scarlet velvet, the seams
all covered with Gold lace, his bed is scarlet damask laced in the same
manner; the last Pope Benedict 13th did not like such a stately bed, &

---

[234]Antinous was a member of the entourage of the Roman Emperor Hadrian,
who was deified after his death and of whom many portrait statues were
made. For accounts of these three statues, see the various entries in Francis
Haskell & Nicholas Penny, *Taste and the Antique*: *The Lure of Classical
Sculpture 1500-1900* (Yale University Press, 1982)

[235]The ancient road from Rome to Tivoli, built by the Roman consul Marcus
Valerius Maximus around 286 BC

[236]This martyr was stoned to death around 34-35 AD and is usually depicted
in art with three stones

[237]The travellers are perhaps confused with the tomb of Sylvanus. A similar
description of this church and the Catacombs is given by Milles, see below

[238]The Papal Conclave is the meeting at which the new pope is elected

[239]The syntax, and therefore the sense of this sentence is difficult to follow

lay over in a plain white room; they say there are more rooms in the
Vatican & 23 courts, tho' I could make out not above 10....

18. Visited Dr Irwin not at home; went to view & measure the
remains of buildings about the Via Sacra & Forum; at 3 went to hear
some Divinity disputations, by the Dominicans & others, an Irish man
answered, it was in the Church of Maria dell Minerva, here are
abundance of Irish monks, Franciscans & Dominicans. Went to the
Pantheon musick & coffee house... The Duke of Liria is at the
Chevaliers, Lord Derwentwater[240] (who is married to the Irish Lady
Newburgh widow of Clifton)[241] goes with him as aid de camp, or as I
have heard since volunteer, his family lives here, 'tis thought Don
Carlos will shortly be King of Naples without opposition. Mr Moore
& 2 sons we saw at Pisa,[242] passed here without seeing any body & are
at Naples...

22. Went to see some antiquities about the Capitol; dined with Mr
Knight & Mr Gore by invitation; - went to see a Ladies Collection of
Medals & curiosities.

23. In the morning went to the Minerva[243] & Sapieza libraryes to look

into the Geography of Old Italy in Cluver[244]...When I came home I
receiv'd your letter of the 17th of February with great pleasure, only

---

[240]Charles Radclyffe (1693-1746), 3rd son of 2nd Earl of Derwentwater, was an
ardent Jacobite who escaped to France after the 1715 rising and then to Italy
after his marriage in 1724. He was executed as a Jacobite in 1745. See
Ingamells (*op.cit.*, 793-94)

[241]Charlotte Maria Livingston, Countess of Newburgh, widow of Hon.
Thomas Clifford by whom she already had two daughters, see Ingamells,
op.cit..793-94. Pococke claims she was Irish but the sources suggest that
the title Earl of Newburgh was created for the 1st Earl in the Peerage of
Scotland, 1660

[242]Of Barn Court, Clonmel, County Tipperary

[243]The Minerva Library, now known as the Biblioteca Casanatensa, was
established in 1701 by the Dominicans of the Monastery of Santa Maria
Sopra Minerva. It was opened to the public according to the Will of
Cardinal Casantata (1620-1700)

[244]Philipp Cluver (1580-1623) was a Dutch cartographer and publisher who
produced not only maps of Italy but books on the antiquities of Sicily,
Sardinia & Corsica, and Italy

wish it had been something fuller, as I informed you in my last I had
the satisfaction to receive two from you here before I received only one
from you at Paris, & neither of those sent to Genoua. [I must repeat
my acknowledgements for the credit you have given me on Mr Hoare
which I have not made use of yet, & will forebear as long as I can. My
Irish affairs do some wt surprise me: you may be sure that I shall not
make any use of this or any other money contrary to your indications,
I did indeed think to gratify my inclination in design of a few books
was to be had in England, & some other things in the Virtuoso way,
but am resolv'd to confine my expences to wt is absolutely necessary
unless I shd have a large remittance from Ireland to supply all, wch I
think I have a good deal of reason to expect, but I fear that malice
towards me so far, & in reality designs to distress me, tho' I find 'tis
not in their power],[245] I am sorry my uncle has not his health as well
as usual,[246] exercise, & making experiments what kind of food, diet
best agrees with him may contribute very much to his health, as
abstaining from gross sorts of meats to see what that will do,
abstaining from greens, vegetables, trying the mild diet; & so the like
with regard to liquors, to see what agrees best with the constitution, I
take to be much better than Physick, till necessity forces to it. I am
glad he has fixed his son at Oriel[247] which I believe is the best he could
do.[248] Most of the news, votes &c. come constantly here to the
Chevaliers, which go to all the lodgings of the English, from the
English doctors; - but we have none of the diverting news you
mention. The young Gentleman is much to be pitied who lost his
mistress but much more the widow of unfortunate Stanley who I

---

[245]Scored out in the copy and reproduced from the original letter, Add. 19939.
Without the mention of any names, we do not know the identity of those
whom he accuses of malice, though perhaps one of the suspects is Rev.
Hugh Wallington, Treasurer of Waterford, mentioned in other letters

[246]The uncle in question is Isaac Milles (1675/6-1741), brother of Mrs.
Pococke, who it will be remembered ran his father's school in Highclere
until taking up a position as Rector of Litchfield, Hampshire, in 1727. He
survived this illness, though died seven years later

[247]There is a record of his son Thomas Milles matriculating at Oriel College,
Oxford, in 1733-34, aged seventeen, see Foster, *Alumni* Oxoniens (*op.cit.*)
957

[248]This may be the "relation" referred to in an earlier letter, whose behaviour
was a matter of concern for the family

should have thought to have been a different sort].[249] We have given over our Naples expedition, & design for Venice by Loretto, & purpose to avoid the sea, we did design to come down the Rhine; but if we should be hinder'd, I hope we shall be able to come by Geneva [Jerre has his health very well & takes so much pleasure in travelling that he is not over desirous of returning home, at least has not so great an inclination for it as I, nor I think such in ... months; as to Language, I make very little progress he talks pretty well & wd soon be master of it, but we are entirely taken up with antiquities & converse with few except english].[250] As to diet, soup or broth, a small piece of boyled beef, a fricassee & roast fowl is the general way; I have order'd once wild boar which is good; kid here is exceeding good & plenty since we have been here, their pork is incomparable, & pidgeons very fine, their veal called vitello is a year old & looks like roast beef, & there being no salt to it, eats not well, mutton is coming in not very good; provisions of meat are scarce in Lent & we have nothing but meat & there must be a license for it. Spanish officers come here every day, 'tis talked the Duke of Liria will be Vice roy of Naples if the Spaniards succeed & Don Carlos does not reside there. The letter you mention I opened having forgot to put the date. I don't know the persons whose morals & principles are objected to, in regard to preferment. I see the Duke of Chandois is talk'd of for Ld Lieutentant of Ireland.[251] 'Tis much Dr Bland should oppose his own creature. I have drank what they think the Falernian wine, it is called Lacrymae [...] it is a very strong wine, almost as strong as cherry brandy & is not to be drunk under two or 3 years & keeps a great while...

24. Went to see some of the great collection of antique statues & trophies that area placed about the area of the Capitol...

25... The Spaniards are all encamped at Truinone [Frusinone] forty miles off, from thence, to march in a body to the Kingdom of Naples: - since I hear they did not en camp but enter'd the Kingdom of Naples

---

[249]Obviously a piece of local gossip from Mrs. Pococke, scored out in the copy and reproduced from the original letter, 19939

[250]Scored out in the copy and reproduced from the original letter, 19939

[251]James Brydges, 3rd Duke of Chandos (1673-1789). Lionel Cranfield Sackville, 1st Duke of Dorset was Lord Lieutenant of Ireland from 1731-37

directly, & so must en camp every night, I believe there are about 20,000

26. Went to see the busts, statues & paintings in the Capitol which consists of three palaces; one of which is for the Residence of the City Magistrates Conservatori, the other is for the Senator & a large hall for a court of justice, & the other is entirely for Antiquities.[252] At 2 went to view & measure the Pantheon; went to see Nero's tomb & baths at Porto del Boralo, & Damitians naumachia near; walk'd in the Medici gardens on the hill by us very pleasant, many statues in 'em a grove & a mount of 60 steps, on which they say, was a Temple of the sun. Sr Thomas Deerham an English gentleman of small estate lives here, he hearing we designed him a visit, came to see us, but we were not at home.[253]

27. Went to the Popes palace on Monte Cavallo or the Quirinal, to see the ceremony of putting the hat on the new Cardinals, in a publick consillory, in which the Pope was at the upper end in a chair cover'd with purple & gold Brocade, under a Canopy of Scarlet damask, with which the long loom [?] was hung, the seams covered with gold lace & all round the same; the cardinals sat on seats down each side of the room; each of the new Cardinals was introduced by two others, & kissed first the Popes foot, then his hand, & after this the new cardinals salute & compliment all the old ones, then the new one by one, kneel down at the Popes footstool, & the Pope puts the red hat on their heads, making use of a form of words, not very short: then the

---

[252]Given his interest in antiquities, it is surprising that Pococke did not give further particulars of what they viewed at this museum. However, a full account is given by Milles, in a letter to the bishop from Rome, dated 17/28 April, 1734 (see below). The Capitoline had only just opened to the public, having been inaugurated by Pope Clement XII in 1734, which means the two cousins must have been among the first tourists to have entered its doors in its official capacity as a public museum

[253]Sir Thomas Dereham (not Deerham), 4th Baronet (1679-1739), of Dereham Abbey, Norfolk. On account of his Roman Catholic faith (he was proscribed in England), he was educated in Tuscany and lived in Italy from 1701 until his death in Rome. A handsome monument with Latin inscription was set up for him in the Venerable English College, Rome. Living in Italy for so many years, Sir Thomas was noted in the accounts of several Grand Tourists (see Ingamells, *op.cit.*, 292-93)

first of the new created makes a speech to the Pope, & the Pope answers it. The Pope is clothed in white it seemed not to be silk, over his shoulders a scarlet cloth mantle coming almost down to his wrists sown up before, lined with plain ermin, a stiff collar over which a camerick covering, a scarlet embroider'd sort of broad ribbon with a gold fringe at the end he had over all, as we wear, a scarfe hanging down almost to the feet: a white scull cap, & when performing any office a red cap lin'd with ermin standing up about half a foot higher than the head, little short laced ruffles, red shoes, round [lap'd],[254] rings on both the ring fingers, a cross headed cane with an Ivory top stood by his chair; his throne was advanced two steps, he walked out very stiffly & slowly, being 84,[255] is blind they say, but looks well, of a pale complexion, & white thin hairs...

28... [W]ere visited by Mr Dingley,[256] who took leave of us, his father a jeweller in London, afterwards by Mr Chamberlain... The Spaniards are marched to besiege Capua, the Germans that were to defend a pass ran a way. Three loads of money were brought with a guard to the gates of Rome for the Spaniards, but they were denyed entrance...

30. We propose to set out the beginning of May for Venice, by Loretto, Bologna & Modena. Afore I leave Rome you shall hear from me which will be in about a month [I expect to have money from Ireland every week, but lest I shd not receive it I must beg ye favour of you to order Mr Hoare to send me credit on Venice for forty pounds directed a Messrs Swymmer & Hewett pour render a Monsr Richard Pococke gentilhomme Anglois a Venice, you'll put Italie large at top of your letters].[257] I desire you to put this into your letter to Mr Hoare:[258] My son writ to me to let you know, that he desires you to send any money you shall receive on his account by letter of credit to him to Venice any

---

[254]The spelling of this word and therefore the sense is unclear, but perhaps it means taped or overlapped/overlapping

[255]Born in April 1652, Pope Clement XII would infact have been eighty-two years of age at the time

[256]Robert Dingley (1710-81) was a merchant of the Russia Company and was in Italy from 1733-34 where he commissioned Rosalba Carriera to exectute some paintings. See Ingamells, *op.cit.*, 302

[257]Scored out in the copy and reproduced from the original letter, Add. 19939

[258] Underlined in the original, Add. 19939

time till the tenth of May, & if you receive any afterwards, he desires
you to keep it by you till he writes to you. If you should have any
thing of great importance to impart pray write to Rome & to Venice
too: if after the 10th of May you have any thing of moment to write
before I let you know where to direct, be pleased to direct still to
Venice; your last letter to Venice had best be sent about the 13th or 14th
of May, unless any thing particular to write & you'll besides send me a
letter to Venice, on the receipt of this if it be a fortnight before the 4th of
May. We have heard once from the Bishop & expect a letter every
week. Rome agrees very well with Jerre[259] [Pray my most kind
affection to my sister. I have now taken part of the money for which
you gave me creditt, wn I mention any thing to be done in England I
however intend old stile as the 4th (?) & 10th of May, my motions here
are according to new stile][260]

ROME
11/22 April, 1734
Milles to the bishop[261]

My Lord,

We arrived last Friday evening at this place, having spent 9 days very
agreeably in our tour.

I wrote my last to your Lordship last Wednesday was seenight [a
week ago] & the next day we set out for Tivoli, at about 4 miles
distant from this city. We passed the small river formerly called
Albula, now Solferata, wch issues out of a very small lake about a mile
higher,[262] & is one of the greatest natural curiositys I ever saw. The
little lake is of a figure pretty near round, & about 200 yards in

---

[259]Mr. Milles, in the copy

[260]Scored out in the copy and reproduced from the original letter, 19939. This
is the first time Pococke has spelled out to his mother the old/new style
system of dating, and this is because he is anxious that she follows his
instructions properly regarding arrangements for his money

[261]Add. 15773

[262]Lake Solfatara, formerly called Lacus Albulus

diameter. The water of it as well as of the river is of a light blew colour, & luke warm & withal smells so prodigiously of sulphur, that we could hardly bear it. The water in several places is perpetually boiling up, & at the same time comes up from the bottom a sort of dark thick scum, very much resembling the spawn of a frog. The top of the water has likewise a very thin scum, wch swims about on it wch is parity colour'd, & exactly like what one sees at all mineral waters. The floating Islands are from 16 increased to 20, wch continually increase in bulk.[263] They are of very different sizes. The largest I believe was near 50 feet long, their thickness is in proportion to their size, some 3, & others 5 feet. They are almost all cover'd with rushes, & are on one side of the lake all together where the wind drives them in several holes in the Islands. The water ooses up & leaves a great deal of sulphur behind it. In other parts there is a sort of salt or hard cake left in wch probably is that part that petrifys, & becomes stone. Most of these Islands we could push from the shore, some were not large enough to bear our weight & others I observed were almost grown to the bank, so that in a short time they will become firm ground. It is said that the depth of the lake is not to be sounded. We flung in several stones, & observed that the water boil'd up afterwards for about two minuits wch I suppose was the time of its descent. The water has a prodigious taste of sulphur. The little river that comes out of this lake is about 12 feet over, & runs rapidly into the Tyber. The sides of the bank have a white scurf upon them, wch as far as I could judge, hardens, & grows into stone, & so have the tops of rushes wch hang in the water. At a place where the water made a little cascade & dashed against a stone, that stone was covered with moist sulphur about half an inch thick. I took some off & when it was dry it burn't just as sulphur, and is yellow exactly like it. All about this river is a prodigious bed of Tybertine stone wch supply Rome, & all the country. It is supposed that this river adds to it continually. I thought when I felt the water of the river that it was considerably warmer than that of the lake. It boils up like it. At the sides of the lake are some antique walls, wch some say were the baths of Agrippa,[264] & others the

---

[263]This islands are formed by bunches of bull-rushes
[264]The Roman statesman Marcus Vipsanius Agrippa (c. 63-12 BC)

villa of Queen Zenobia.[265] A mile further we crossed the Anio over a bridge called Pons Lucanus, & at the foot of it saw a large round sepulcher cased with hewn stone belonging to the family of the Plautii as two long inscriptions on it informed me.

The city of Tivoli is small, & very ill built situated on the side of a hill, & from whence you have a good prospect of the Campania di Roma. The cascade of the Anio, wch passed on the outside of the town is very large, after wch the river runs in a narrow channel between very deep rocks, so that for some space you loose [sic] the sight of it for wch reason the people call it Bocca dell' inferno, or the mouth of hell. Besides this cascade there are several other smaller, before it comes into the valley & the water is distributed into several parts of the town to turn mills, from whence likewise it falls in several cascades more high, but not so large. Just below the cascade on the side of the rock stands the remains of a very beautifull round Temple built of brick & surrounded by a Portico of 18 fluted Corinthian Pillar.[266] All the walls of the Temple & half of the portico remain, the Temple had 2 square windows on each side of the door. On part of the portico, is remaining the following part of an inscription L: Calio; L: F. The Temple on the inside is 24 feet in Diameter, & the portico 4 feet 4 inches wide. Some call it the Temple of the Sibella, others of Hercules, others of Vesta. In a little square before the Cathedral stand two large statues of an Aegyptian God of red Granite. From hence we walked to the descent of the hill to see the remains of the Villa of Macenas.[267] The foundations of the house lay in rubbish. On each side it had a double portico. Between them in the middle were several chambers...[268] A little below this villa is a Temple of brick quite entire, & round with a

---

[265]Zenobia was a third-century queen of Palmyra (in present day Syria), married to King Odenathus. In 270 AD she ordered the Palymyrene army to invade the Roman province of Arabia. The Emperor Aurelian's forces defeated her army and granted the queen a villa in Italy (probably Tivoli, where she lived out her days. For a full account of this elusive character, see Pat Southern, *Empress Zenobia: Palmyra's Rebel Queen* (2009)

[266]Temple of Vesta, dating to the early 1st century BC

[267]Gaius Cilnius Maecenas (70 BC-8 BC), political advisor to Octavian & important patron of the arts

[268]Milles explains the form of the building by means of a simple diagram. It is thought that the building was actually the foundations of an ancient temple complex, named after Maecenas.

foramen at top resembling the Pantheon. It consisted of 7 niches, &
was 40 feet 6 inches in diameter. I can not meet with any account of it
in any author, it seems to have been built in the latter times. From
hence we took a walk to the other side of the river to see the remains
of Horace's villa, situated on the other side of the Anio on wch his
gardens descended, Hortus ubi & tecto vicinus jugis aquae fons,[269]
quite to the river. I think a poet could not have had a more agreeable
scene to work on than this spot. On one side he sees the cascade with
the water pouring down into Praeceps Anio that prodigious depth
Tibur supinum & over it the city of Tiber situated on a prodigious
craggy, & preceptious rock. Southward of him he has a full view of
Rome & the fine plain of the Campania. On the North & West he is
shelter'd with hills rising gradually, above him, wch no doubt &
paulum silvae super his foret[270] were planted with olives or other
trees. There are some remains all down the hill but very obscure.
Where the Convent of the Franciscans stands are 2 pretty large arched
rooms. The monk who shew'd us told us he did not doubt but that
there was a treasure in the garden, for that is an universal notion with
the Italians, where ever there are antique ruins. He likewise very
seriously asked us who this Horace was.

As for the modern state of Tivoli there is nothing to be seen of it, but
the gardens, & Palace of the D: of Modena's family.[271] The former are
large & have several good water works.[272] Some of wch are out of
order. They have water here prodigiously at command. At one of the
fountains I observed the statue of the Sibylla Tiburtina with a little boy
standing by her. The Palace is very spacious, there are some good
paintings al Fresco by Raphael, Muziano, Zuccari and Annibal

---

[269]"This is what I prayed for - a piece of land not so very large, where there
would be a garden, and near the house a spring of ever-flowing water...",
lines 1-2 of Horace, *Satires* 2.6 (only line 2 cited in original)

[270] "[A]nd up above these a bit of woodland", continuation of Horace's satire,
line 3

[271]Villa d'Este, at the time owned by Rinaldo d'Este, Duke of Modena (1655-
1737), who the previous year had sided secretly with Austria in the War of
Polish Succession. The villa is considered to be one of the most outstanding
examples of renaissance culture and the gardens in particular influenced
garden design throughout Europe

[272]Water works is the term for ornamental water features found in gardens

Carrach.[273] There are several good antique statues in the Palaces most of wch were found at Hadrians Villa. In the garden is an antique statue of an Unicorn of yellow marble.

We left Tivoli the next morning, & in our way spent two or three hours in seeing the remains of the villa of Hadrian situated at 2 miles distance under the hill. The ruins are the largest & most extended, & withal some of the most magnificent that I ever saw. I beleive verily they are 4 miles in circumference: but there [are] so many Portico's, Halls, Temples, & other buildings that it would be endless to describe them. On the side of the hill we saw the remains of Cassius's villa. We arrived at Palestrina Ol[d]: Praeneste at mid day, this city is small & situated likewise on the side of a hill. At the top of the city is the Palace of the Barberini family,[274] wch stands upon the same ground, & is allmost exactly in the same form with the upper part of the Temple of Fortune.[275] The famous peice of pavement in this Palace stood where the altar of fortune was, & is surprisingly well put together, so that I think it is as good as any modern mosaick I have seen, notwithstanding they are now come to a great perfection in that art.[276] The whole Temple stood upon the same ground that the city does now, & the ascent to the several parts of it was by stairs. There are some walls & capitals of pillars, here & there remaining of it, but nothing at all entire.

From Palestrina, we went the same night to Frescati, this is likewise a small but very pretty town situated on the ascent of a hill about 14 miles from Rome, of wch you have a fine prospect. It is surrounded about with several very agreeable villa's of wch at present the only remarkable are Mondragone of the Borghese, & Belvedere of the

---

[273]Girolamo Muziano (1532-92), Federico Zuccari (1542/3-1609) & Annibal Carrach (1560-1609), three Italian painters, the first two being of the mannerist style

[274]The town was purchased by this family in 1630

[275]The Temple of Fortuna Primigenia was redeveloped after 82 BC as a spectacular series of terraces, exedras and porticos on four levels down the hillside, linked by monumental stairs and ramps

[276]Though surprisingly he does not give a description of this famous piece, clearly he refers to the Nile mosaic of Palestrina, a late Hellenistic floor mosaic depicting the Nile in its passage from Ethiopia to the Mediterranean, still on exhibit in the Palazzo Barberini

Pamphilia.[277] The villa Ludovisia had formerly very good water works, but at present none of them play.[278] The Mondragone a mile above Frescati, is a large Palace, but is very sorrily furnished on the inside & has nothing worth speaking of.[279] The water-works likewise are not extraordinary. The gardens are large shady & pleasant. The villa Belvedere has a prodigious large extent of ground for it reaches from Frescati to the top of the hill to old Tusculum, wch is above a mile.[280] The water works here are pretty good & indeed the best we have seen in Italy. The hill of Parnassus with Apollo & the nine muses who play upon instruments is the best thing.[281] From the top of the gardens you have a very extended prospect....

---

[277]Pococke in his journal, states, "But the most famous villa for prospect & waterworks is the Belvedere of the Pamphily family just above Frascati. There is a fine terras under the house, another at the entrance, & then going up severall steps to the back part of the palace you come to the waterworks" (Add. 22981, p.58)

[278]This villa was built by Cardinal Ludovico Ludovisi in the 1620s. The water works here refer to a cascade. Pococke also refers to this garden in his journal: "The Gardens of this villa are very pleasant & there were fine waterforks in them, but they are out of repair" (Add. 22981, p.57)

[279]This villa was built in 1573 by Cardinal Marco Sitico Altemps and takes its name from the heraldic dragon of Pope Gregory XIII (1502-85) who frequently visited it as the cardinal's guest. The villa was at its height during the period of the Borghese family. Thomas Salmon, *op.cit.*, notes (from his visit in 1688), "The furniture of all the three houses was mean, and every thing about them appeared neglected when I was there..." (367)

[280]This is also known as the Villa Aldobrandini. It was it was rebuilt for Cardinal Pietro Aldobrandini and is famous for its "Water Theatre"

[281]Pococke continues, in his journal: "The whole building is in this shape [diagram shaped like a bridge with a single opening] there are 3 arches on each side the semicircle adornd with Ionick pillars & is the fall of water, on each side are statues in niches, at one end is the statue of Pan playing on pipes & opposite a Centaur on a horn, wch mov'd their instruments, & a sound was heard of those instruments on an organ behind wch being wound up & set to tune with proper stops appears to the ignorant as ye musick of the statues, as like wise in the stanza call'd mound Parnassus where Apollo & the muses are on a sort of mount in small statues painted, & ye organ plays with ye stops of the several instruments they have in their hands, in the middle of the room is a pipe wch sends forth air that raises up a brass van & theres one on each side the door wch by ye sudden gush of air surprises those yt goe out, the room is painted in fresco by Dominicheni &

My paper will not allow me to finish my account of this journey in this letter, so must defer the rest till my next to your Ldship. Since I came home I had the honour of your Ldships bearing date March the 2d, & return your Ldship my most humble thanks for the remittance, for wch I received a bill from Leghorn last Saturday on two Bankers here. I do not know, whether I mentioned in my last to your Ldship that three weeks ago, I begged the favour of your Ldship to remit me a bill of 80 on Venice, & the reason why I desire so much is, that I cannot fix my place between that & England, where we shall stay long enough to receive a letter from your Ldship. I only mention it again for fear of any miscarriage in my former letter.

In about ten days time we propose to set out for Venice.

I have lately according to your Ldship commands bought the Bullarium Romanum, the Roman edition, wch with the volume published the other day includes Innocent the IIth the 8 volumes cost me as exchange is at present of English money 5£: 18 pence. They tell me that there will be 5 more volumes to bring them down to the present times, one of wch will be published every four months. Dr Pococke presents his humble Duty to your Ldship I am my Lord

Your Ldships most Dutifull

We propose to be England in July & Dr. Pococke has wrote by this post to your Ldship on that subject.[282]

---

ye rest is mosaic work....In ye semicircle mention'd were 3 or 4 basons with groups in them & waterworks, as likewise all round & on each [ ] in rooms waterworks that play every way to surprize the spectators. There are up the hill steps to several stories of temples that are over the semicircle, at the first is a sheet & on each side are two spiral columns down wch spires or twists water us'd to run & from them all down ye sides of the stairs in little basons, & there are statues all round on the balustrade wch is at the top of the lower building; Ascending higher there is another cascade falling in to a bason above that, higher still another in Grotesque work falling in three streams; At the top one with Grotesque work are one & two over it [the text is corrupted here]. Through this there is an ascent by pleasant walks to the top of the high hill which is Mons Puscularus..." Add. 22981, pp 58-59
[282]This letter from Pococke is not part of Add. 22978

ROME
11/22 April, 1734
Pococke to his mother
Letter 15[283]

[This letter provides further details of Pococke's financial difficulties and, among other details scored out of the copy, gives instructions to his mother on ordering a wig]

Honoured Madam,

My last to you was sent April 1st. That day went to see Sr Thomas Dereham he was not at home, saw Ruspoli palace in the Croso,[284] the best furnished I have seen in Rome, there is one room with a fine silver table with bas reliefs & ornaments of silver valued at 4000, a looking glass & a vase for coals, 4 large candle sticks standing & 4 sconces against the wall all of silver: the lower apartments painted in fresco countries, battles &c: & marble door cases. At 2 went to St Clements to hear the disputations of the Irish Dominicans, others being opponents, to which we were invited & afterwards regaled with a glass of wine. Visited Monseignior Fontanini Archbishop of Ancyra, he always talks much of Dr Pococke grande home literato nella lingua Arabica,[285] he gave us tea & was very courteous & civil. [Mr Paul tells me Captn Alcocks Eldest son is to be married to Col. Loftus daughter I purpose about £4000 fortune, & Miss Argyle become £5,000 fortune by ye death by her uncle Eton married to her old lover Mich. Head equally belov'd by her Mr Heads eldest son].[286]

---

[283] Add. 22978. This is the fifth letter of the original collection (Add. 19939) and a note next to the English address states that it was received by Mrs. Pococke on 9 May and answered on 12 May, 1734

[284] A palace bought by Prince Francesco Maria Marescotti Ruspoli in 1713, and regarded as one of the four wonders of Rome

[285] The famous English orientalist, Edward Pococke (1604-91), author of several scholarly works, including: *Specimen Historiae Arabum* (1636) and *Historia Compendiosa Dynastiarum* (1663). He and Richard Pococke were distantly related

[286] This very obscure piece of gossip, which hardly becomes a person in his position, is not surprisingly scored out in the copy. It is reproduced here from the original letter, Add. 19939

2. Went to see the Villa Medici.[287] On the hill near there is only a gallery of curious antique statues & busts worth mentioning. We saw in a garden [a fine collection of double white with a reddish casthyacinths very sweet &][288] a small flower like the blue bells but yet low & very small & smell call'd muschi greci. At 2 went to Minerva Library, then to the disputations of the Irish Dominicans again; were very civilly regaled afterwards [& many handsom speeches in relation to a parent of ours][289] heard some musick at a church.

3. Went to see some palaces, but did not succeed; spent the afternoon at the Library; walk'd in the Medici garden on the hill by us.

4. A German we met at the Archbishop of Ancyra's came to see us, a great virtuoso, & two Irish Franciscans, one Welsh of the Country of Waterford, some of whose relations I know at 2 went to see the palace of the Duke of Parma alla Lungara,[290] where are the famous paintings of Raphael, the marriage of Cupid & Psyche, a Council of the Gods Galatea in fresco & some others; Went to see some churches, reviewed St Peters; walk'd in the gardens Barberini on a very high ground near the arca of St Peters, it commands the country to the north, all the city, & is a wonderful pleasant situation: The gardens & country near Rome, the Pines the Cypress, Bays, ever green oak &c are very beautiful....

[From 11 April, Pococke goes on to document the excursion to Tivoli, Frascati, providing his mother with accounts of the sulphuric lake, Cassius' villa, Hadrian's Villa and the mosaic at Palestrina ("all of the natural colour of several stones so set in, tht the men, brids, beasts &c: look as if they were painted"), noting that at Frascati, "we met with tolerable accommodation but should have fared badly before, if we had

---

[287]Situated on the Pincian Hill, this villa was acquired by Cardinal Ferdinando de Medici in 1756

[288] Scored out in the copy and reproduced from the original letter, Add. 19939

[289]Scored out in the copy and reproduced from the original letter, Add. 19939, and is an allusion perhaps to their relation, Edward Pocock

[290]The Villa Farnesina, situated on the Via della Lunghi, built for Agostino Chigi in the early 1500s and later re-named Farnesina when purchased by the Farnese family in 1581

not carried our own provisions", and that the situation around the area is "something like Highcleer palace". After arriving back at Rome, on 16 April, he spent a day "at home" writing then visited the Pope's Chapel, which is described as follows]

16...Came to Rome [& found a letter from Mr Bagwell informing me he had receiv'd an acknowledgment from Mr Hoare of ye receipt of £50 bill he sent ye 17th of Novr last, wch tho' I was to .. Hoare... & desire his son (?) to remit to me wt ever money came to his hands ...I desire you to ask whether or no he did send me a letter of credit for yt bill wn he receiv'd it as I desired, & yt if he did if it ever came to my hands, by that time this comes to you, I shall have 50 more in his hands & as I am certain yt further remittances I shall have, If I have need I shall write to you to write to him to send to me wt I want, in my last I desir'd you to write to him to send me £40 to Venice to Messrs & Hewett & Hewett wch if you have not done I desire it may be 50 but otherwise you need not mention on any greater sum, this want of punctuality in Mr Hoare has caused in me some uneasiness & I have there by lost sight of Naples wch ye Spaniards have enter'd & taken not for Don Carlos but ye King of Spain, Caprea & Gaeta are to be besieg'd, ye Castle of Naples 'tis thought soon will be surrender'd & Sicily is for ye Spaniards & will follow of course. I hope you let no money...in Hoares hands on my account for I have as yet drawn for but £30 & I have had £80 in his hands ever since November & you need not for your stock will give me creditt if I should want tho I believe I shall not][291]

17. Staid at home writ all day.

18. Went to the Popes Chapel at his palace in Monte Cavallo to see Palm branches distributed, the cardinals were dressed in Priests habits embroidered with Gold, the Cardinal Bishops the same, but came over their arms with buttons before as big as eggs; as he came, every one went up to the altar & received a palm branch on his knees; as likewise Bishops, Generals of orders of monks & confessors, the inferiors had olive branches with crosses tied to them, the Palm

---

[291]Scored out in the copy and reproduced from the original letter, Add. 19939. Some parts are impossible to decipher

branches 7 feet high, 'tis a sort of white bark twisted in a knotty manner, & there is a branch of palm comes out at top: this done they went out in Procession out, the doors were shut & returning they made use of Aperite portas, lift up the Everlasting doors, & then the passion was sung or chanted, a kind of Dialogue of our Saviours passion, a very uncouth performance.

Thence we went to hear the Maronites[292] say solemn high mass, with a very odd tone & at certain devotions two persons held two sticks with flags to 'em & a silver thin plate round at the end, with small round bells about it, over the Priests head & shook 'em to make musick, at other times was jingling of bells & a noise with other odd instruments; we saw a Prince of Morrocco there turn'd Christian, but was in a sort of rebellion against the present Emperor of Morocco.[293] The Panis Benedictus was distributed here at the Greek Church. Went to see the Ghigi palace at 2,[294] the Rospigliosi where is the famous Aurora of Guido,[295] & in both many fine statues; walked in the large gardens of Montalto made by Sixtus V.[296]

19. Went to see Vigna di Papa Julia,[297] pleasant water works & as to the vegetable race in our tour we saw Jerusalem cowslips, & I think

---

[292]Members of one of the Lebanese or Syriac Eastern Catholic Churches

[293]The identity of the Christian prince is not known, but the Emperor was Abu Abdallah (1678-1757), who was Sultan of Morocco several times, this being the first occasion. Six months later, in the October of 1734, he was "deposed by his black army", according to *The Gentleman's Magazine: or Monthly Intelligencer for the Year 1734*, Vol. IV (London) 572

[294]The Palazzo Chigi, completed in 1580 for the Aldobrandini family and now the residence of Italy's Prime Minister

[295]This famous fresco is painted on the roof of the summer-house of the Rospigliosi

[296]Felice Peretti di Montalto (1520-90), who was pope from 1585 until his death

[297]Milles explains the form of the building by means of a simple diagram. It is thought that the building was actually the foundations of an ancient temple complex, named after Maecenas.he complex built by Pope Julius III (1487-1555) which includes the Casino della Vigna (di Papa Giulio III), now known as Palazzina di Pio IV, and Villa Giula. A fountain and and ornate wall originally stood opposite the Casino, and it is possible that this is the fountain admired by Pococke

Honesty & Solomons Seal & much of it: at 2 walk'd to Ponte
Lamentana above Ponte Salaria[298] on the [Tevergne].

20. Went to see the Pamphily palace,[299] a great number of the finest
pictures in Rome, & the famous 7 sacraments of Nicolas Poussin;[300]
went to the Chancellary belonging to Cardinal Ottoboni,[301] reviewed
it. Dined with Mr Gore & Mr Knight by invitation. Saw the famous
Statue of Meleager in the Picchini Palace,[302] visited a person or two [I
desire you to send to Ben the underwritten powers to send to the
persons to whom directed, the instructions & memorandums are to
goe with them - pray desire him to speak to Leatherbarrow to make
me just such a wig as my last against next September coming full to
the lower part of the face as that (?) & long that way as that was: Ben
is not to fail to distrain ye people of Mr Wallington's house if they do
not pay soon after ye rent is due, & is to speak to Sr Matthew[303] to spur
up the tenant of his house at Lismore if he's behind hand: desire him
to let you know when my Lord talks of coming to England & to write

---

[298]The Ponte Salario or Salaro is a road bridge just outside Rome, where the
Via Salaria crosses the Aniene. It dates back to the second half of the 1st
century BC, and in Pococke's day would have looked very much as it was
depicted by Pirenesi (an arch bridge with an 8th century tower), though is
now virtually unrecognisable
[299]The Palazzo Pamphilij or Pamphili, in the Piazza Nerona, was built for
Cardinal Giambattista Pamphilj (who became Pope Innocent X), in 1644
[300]The French artist Poussin (1594-1665), is known to have painted the Seven
Sacraments at least twice. One series was commissioned by Cassiano dal
Pozzo, in the 1630s and subsequently purchased by the 4th Duke of Rutland
(Belvoir Castle, Leicestershire) in 1785. Of these, one was lost in a fire at
the castle, another was sold to the National Gallery in Washington in 1946,
and a third was sold at auction in 2010. Another set (admired by the artist
Bernini who saw it in Paris in the 1660s) is in the National Gallery of
Scotland, forming part of the Bridgewater Loan, 1945
[301]The Chancellery Palace was built 1483-1517, and Cardinal Pietro Ottoboni
(1667-1740) held the position of Vice-Chancellor of the Holy Roman
Church from 1689 until his death
[302]This famous life-size statue, believed to be the work of Scopas, was in the
house of the doctor to three popes, Francesco Fusconi. It remained in the
Palazzo Pichini or Pighini (named after his heirs) until 1770, when it was
bought by Pope Clement XIV for his collection at the Vatican
[303]Possibly Sir Matthew Deane, 3rd Baronet (1680-1746/7) of Dromore,
County Cork

immediately by every ship as usual and not to speak of any affairs I write to him about. I don't know but I may be oblig'd to be Ireland by winter so yt if you have order'd nothing in relation to the boy you may forbear. 21st we went out in summer clothes of silk for the youth flower'd I think of a light colour & bought Bullarum Romanum for the Bishop].[304]

22. We are going today to see the Popes Deputy wash the feet of 12 poor preists who represent the Apostles, if the Pope was well he would do it himself as Xr[ist's] vicar: you shall have an account of all in my next a month from this, on Wednesday the fifth of May we propose to set out for Venice; where I should be glad to hear from you at Messrs Swymmer & Hewett, the next post after this if you have any thing at all to impart, & the more the more acceptable. If any think of importance write afterwards.

[Pray my most kind love to my Sister. My humble service at White Oak. My friend is very well & desires his best respects][305]

I am Dear Madam
Your most Obedient & Dutifull son

Richard Pococke

ROME
17/28 April, 1734
Milles to the bishop[306]

[In this letter, Milles completes his description of their recent excursion out of Rome, giving a brief account of Albano and a more detailed description of the Capitoline Museum. The

---

[304]Scored out in the copy and reproduced from the original letter, Add. 19939. Parts of the manuscript are obliterated by tears and holes in the paper

[305]It is not clear why Pococke should have scored out this reference to his sister, though it is not the only occasion on which he did this. The identity of White Oak is not known, though he is also mentioned in Letters 17 & 18

[306]Add. 15773

text of the latter section is reproduced here, being of interest since the museum had only just officially opened to the public]

The next thing that I shall give an account of to your Ldship shall be the modern Capitol wch is built on the remains of the Fortress of the ancient Capitol, wch appear in several places. It consists of a front, & 2 side buildings all done by the design of Michael Angelo. On the bottom of the stairs as you ascend are two lyons, made of Aegyptian marble, & taken from the Pantheon, & the statue of Rome Triumphant of Porphry, but without a head, the drapery is excessively fine. On the top of the stairs you enter into a square court on the Ballustrade on each side is the statue of a man holding a horse in his hand, both of white marble, & supposed to represent Castor, & Pollux. Beyond them on each side is a Trophy erected to Marius for his victory over the Cymbrians, & Teutonichs, & placed at the Castellum aquae Martiae from whence they were removed hither. Beyond these at one end is a Miltiary of white marble round, & the figure of I marked on it to represent the first mile from the heart of the City... On the other side corresponding to it is another column with a globe of brass on it, in wch formerly were the ashes of the Emperour Trajan. In the middle of the court stands that fine Equestrian statue of M: Aurelius of bronze gilt, wch was found near St John Lateran, where the house of L: Venus stood. At the upper end of the court under the stairs that lead to the middle building is the statue of Rome Triumphant of Porphry represented sitting, & armed with a spear & helmet. On one side is a fine colossal statue of white marble, representing the Nile, & on the other another representing the Tyber. In the court of the right hand building is another fine statue of Rome triumphant of white marble, on the pedestal a woman lamenting supposed to be Dacia, on each side of her stands a statue of a slave in black marble all finely done. On each side of these is an Aegyptian Idol of red Granite. On one side of the court is a Colossal head of bronze, as some say of the Emperour Commodus,[307] but others say of Apollo wch stood before his temple on the Palatine; next is a hand of the same Colossus. It stands on the monumental stone of Agrippina the wife of Germanicus, who upon his being poisoned, starved herself to death. ... Next to this are the

---

[307]Marcus Aurelius Commodus Antoninus Augustus (161-192 AD) was Roman Emperor from 180 AD until his death in 192 AD

standard measures viz the length, breadth, & thickness, of which the people of Rome are obliged to make their bricks. Next is a Colossal head of white marble supposed to have been of Domitian. On the opposite side are 2 Colossal feet of white marble, belonging to the above mentioned head, & next the ancient measures viz: the Greek and Roman feet, with the modern measures of Rome as the Can, & Braccio &c. On each side of the door as you enter the court are the statues of Julius, & Augustus. At the foot of the stairs is the famous Columna Restrata of Duilius. This pillar is of the Dorick order, & about 9 feet high with six Rostrums of vessels projecting from it, three on each side. On the front of the Pillar are three anchors on the pedestal is part of an inscription, but it is so imperfect that it will be a difficult matter to make it out, I shall not therefore trouble your Ldship with it. After you have ascended one flight of stairs you come into a small square court, in wch are 4 fine peices of bas-releive representing part of the history of M: Aurelius. In the first he is represented in the habit of a preist sacrificing before the Temple of Jupiter Capitolinus for his victory over the Parthians. In the second the Emperour is going on horse back on his expedition against them who fling themselves suppliantly before his horses feet. In the third the Emperour is drawn in a Triumphal chariot after his victory, & in the fourth he receives the globe of Empire from Rome, who stands in armour by him. On the stairs painted al Fresco by Ca Valier D'Arpino with several parts of the Roman history, as the rape of the Sabines, the battle of the Horatii, & Curalii, with several others. On one side of the room is the bust of Mary Casimir Queen of Poland,[308] & opposite to it that of Christina Queen of Sweden[309] both in Profile with inscriptions under them, signifying that both those Queens were received in state at the Capital, by the consuls, & Senators. At the upper end of the room is a statue of white marble of Leo Xth.[310] On one side that of Urban VIII[311] done by Bernini, & at the lower end that of Sixtus V in bronze done by Domenico Fontana.[312] The next room is painted al

---

[308]Maria Kazimiera (1641-1716) was consort to King Jan III Sobieski from 1674 to 1696

[309]Either Queen Christina of Holstein-Gottorp (1573-1625) or Christina Augusta (1626-89), Regnant Queen from 1632-54

[310]1475-1521, pope from 1513 to his death in 1521

[311]1588-1644, pope from 1623 to his death in 1644

[312]1520-1590, pope from 1585 to his death in 1590

Fresco by Pierino del Vaga, with other parts of the Roman history. The busts of Julius Caesar, & Hadrian are remarkable in this room, & so are the modern statues of Carlo Barberini, Alexander Farnese, Fransesco Aldobrandini, Thomas Rospigliosi, Arc Antonio Colonna, & the bust of Virgilio Cesarini, with the wolf suckling Romulus & Remus, [313] of marble antique, likewise two fine pillars of Verd antique.[314] In the next room the freise is painted with the history of Marius's triumph. There is the wolf suckling Romulus, & Remus in bronze, & wch is thought to have stood near the ficus Ruminalis.[315] The left hinder leg of the wolf is partly melted by thunder. The statue in bronze of the shepherd pulling a thorn out of his foot, after he had brought the good news to the senate. Another statue in bronze I believe a Camillus, with the rare, & very fine bust of L: Junius Brutus[316] in bronze likewise. In the 4th chamber are several fragments of the Fasti Consulares.[317] Over the door is the head of Mithridates in bas-releive, & a memorial of Marc Antonio Colanna's naval victory at the Lepanto adorned with Columnae rostratae [triumphal columns]. The freise of the sixth chamber is all painted by Annibal Carrach. There are the statues of Virgil, & Cicero with his Cicer, that of Hercules with his club of bronze, & found near the Bocea della Verita, where the Ara Maxima stood. The four ancient measures, made in form of pedestals, & about 4 feet high, 2 for grain, one for wine, & one for oil. Over one of the doors is the head of Alexander the great and over another, that of the famous Appius Caecus,[318] the former of white marble & the latter of a red Aegyptian marble. In the next chamber is the bust of Rhea, of Sappho, of Medusa, of Scipio Africanus. The next chamber is painted al Fresco by Peter Perugin, in wch are represented Rome triumphant, Hannibal passing the Alps, Hannibal in a council of war, & the fleet of the Carthaginians. There are three fine statues, the Goddess of silence, Cybele, & Ceres. In the middle of the building is

---

[313]Rome's twin founders in its traditional foundation myth who, when left exposed, were rescued by a she-wolf who suckled them

[314]Ancient green, a term usually denoting a marbled effect

[315]The ficus Ruminalis was a wild fig tree on the Palatine, where, according to tradition, Romulus & Remus were found in a trough

[316]Founder of the Roman Republic and one of the first consuls in 509 BC

[317]The official annals or chronicles drawn up by the consuls each year, generally listing the major events that took place during the year

[318]The blind Roman statesman, Appius Claudius Caecus (c. 340-273 BC)

nothing to be seen but some pictures in Chairo Oscuro, & the statues
of Paul 3d, & Gregory the 13th, & of Charles D'Anjou, K: of Naples,
Senator of Rome, Count of Provence, & Brother to St Louis. In the
other side building are several things to be seen. In the court opposite
to the door is the Colossal statue commonly called Marforio. In this
court at present stand several statues, & busts wch the Pope has lately
bought of Cardinal Alexander Albani.[319] At the foot of the stairs is a
colossal foot probably belonging to that of Nero. It stands on a stone
wch has an inscription relating to Caestius's monument. Near it is a
beatifull tomb of the Emperour Alexander Severus, & his mother Julia
Mammoea with a bas-releive on it, representing funeral games. On
the stairs are two square bas relieves taken from a triumphal arch wch
stood in the via 'Flaminia', one peice represents L: Verus publishing
the laws to the people, & the other the apotheosis of the elder
Fasustina, who is carried up to heaven by a winged Deity. Antoninus
is represented sitting & beholding her. On each side of these bas-
releives is a statue one representing the eldest Faustina, & under it is
wrote Pudicitia, the other is of Juno Lanumvina. The upper apartment
consists of 3 chambers, wch are all beautifying so that the statues,[320] &
busts are removed out of them, & placed in a lodge together. In the
great room are the statues of Paul the 4th [321] & Innocent the Xth,[322] the
former of marble & the latter of bronze. In one of the chambers is the
statue of the Aventine Hero the son of Hercules of black marble.
Among the other statues [that] are remarkable [are] that of Agrippina
the mother of Nero, the nurse with Nero when he was an infant, the
old Sybyl contemplating the heavenly signs, the Ceres, the statue of
Marius of Flora & Adonis, the busts of Trajan, & Antoninus Pius,[323] of
Plato, Hiero, Diogenes, Socrates, & Alcibiades, with a fine bas relief of

---

[319]Alessandro Albani (1692-1779) was a nephew of Pope Clement XII and a
cardinal. He is best known for his connoisseurship and patronage of the
arts, and the fact that he befriended wealthy English and Irish Grand
Tourists (such as William Ponsonby, 2nd Earl of Bessborough), continuing
to correspond with them for years on matters related to their collection of
antiquities

[320]He means they were being decorated at the time

[321]1476-1559, pope from 1555 until his death in 1559

[322]1574-1655, pope from 1644 until his death in 1655

[323]Aelius Hadrianus Antoninus Augustus Pius (86-161), Roman Emperor
from 138-161AD

hunting the boar. In the court lay several old inscriptions &c not fixed up as yet, amongst wch I took notice of two round altars about 2 feet high, towards the top projected 2 Rostrums of a ship. On one of the altars was wrote Ara tranquillitatis. On it was represented a ship with sails extended to the wind, on the other was wrote Ara ventorum, & on it was a God of the winds blowing. In all probability these altars were placed by the Romans on the sea shore, & they sacrificed on either as they found occasion...[324]

---

[324]The description of the museum ends abruptly here

ROME
25 April/6 May, 1734
Milles to the bishop[325]

[In this letter, Milles he gives a lengthy account of the interior of St Peter's: "I shall now begin with the so much renowned church of St Peters. As for entring into a description of it, it would be too tedious, as well as useless, your Lordship no doubt having several plans, cuts, & prospects of the entire building". The account includes details of its statues, paintings, frescoes and monuments, as well as the Vatican Library, the latter of which is reproduced here]

From hence we went into the other gallery opposite to that we were in before, in the middle of wch is the door of the famous Vatican Library.[326] It is exactly in the form of a great T before you enter the Library, is a little room with the pictures of the Librarians all round. The Pontifical Library properly so called is the first room wch is 231 feet in length, & 41 in breadth. In the middle of it are large square pilasters. It is all painted by several hands. On the left hand side are painted all the Library's, that were ever collected. It begins with Moses delivering the law to the Levites to be kept by them. Next are the Hebrew, Babylonick, Athenian, Alexandrine, Roman, Jerusalem, the Caesarean, & the Apostolical one made by St Peter. On the right hand are all the Councils, that of Nice, the 1st of Constantinople, that of Ephesus, of Calchedon, the 2 of Constantinople, the 3d Do [ditto]; the 2d of Nice, the 4th of Constantinople, a convention under Alexander the 3d, & Frederic for the regulating of the clergy &c the Lateran Council, that of Lyons, the 2d Do, that of Vienne, of Florence, the 2d Lateran Council, & that of Trent. On the pilasters in the middle of the room are painted all the inventors of Letters. The ceiling is painted with the history of Sextus V.[327] At the lower end of the room on the

---

[325] Add. 15773
[326] Curiously, though Pococke mentions other libraries visited in Rome, he does not refer to the Vatican Library when noting the various places viewed in the capital
[327] It was he who commissioned the architect Domenico Fontana to construct a new building for the library, which is still in use

left hand is the statue of Hippolitus Bp of Porto, on the chair is wrote in small Greek characters the Cyclo-Pasqualis wch he made. Opposite to him is the statue of Aristides. Towards the upper end of the room stands a prodigious fine twisted column of Oriental alabaster transparent about ten feet high. Near it is a large sarcophagus. In it they preserve a peice of linen, made of the Asbestos stone, in wch the body of the deceased had been burnt. It was found in the time of Clement the 11th,[328] who gave it to the Library. At the upper end of this room on the left hand are 2 rooms full of armorys in wch are printed books, wch were given by Sixtus V. Beyond whc is a very long room. The armorys on the left hand contain the library of the Elector Palatine & those of the right that of the Duke D'Urbin.[329] Returning into the first room on the right hand are two rooms full of books, whc were given by Paul the V.[330] The next room is that part of Queen Xtinas library, wch was bought, & given by Alexander the 8th. The third room is a very long one, the armorys only on one side are full with the addition made by the present Pope, & Cardinal Querina the present Librarian.[331] On the armorys all round are ancient Hetrurian vases given by the present Pope.

The books wch were shew'd us as curiostys are the following, an ancient Mass book with exceeding fine painting in miniature, done by one Julio Clovio a Canon regular, a Greek Bible wrote in square characters, the little tablets called Pugillaria in Samaritan, or Malvaric characters, a fine manuscript of Plinys natural history, with all the beasts, birds, & fishes finely painted, an ancient martyrology with very antique miniature, the acts of the Apostles wrote in letters of gold, & given Innocent the 8th[332] by Carlotta 2: of Cyprus, the letters of St Charles Borromeo, & some of Thomas Aquiinas in his own hand writing, two very ancient Virgils both in square characters, the one a large Quarto, the letters very large supposed to be near a 1000 years old, it has some paintings in it, it has not the four first lines Ille Ego &c: the other is not unlike it but less, there are two Terences near about the

---

[328] 1649-1721, and pope from 1700 until his death in 1721
[329] The manuscripts of the Dukes of Urbino were acquired by the library in 1657
[330] 1552-1621, and pope from 1605 until his death in 1621
[331] Angelo Maria Quirini or Querini (1680-1755)
[332] 1432-92, and pope from 1484 until his death in 1492

same age, with all the comick masks painted, & a peice of painting before every scene. It is large thin Quarto. The Manuscript of K: Henry the 8ths book against Luther, sent by him to the Pope, at the end of it are these two lines wrote in the Kings own hand. Anglorum Rex Henricus, Leoni Decimo mittit hoc opus, & fide testem & amicitiae. Under it was signed Henricus in his own hand. In the same book was a manuscript letter of the Ks writing to the Cardinal Vice chancellor recommending Cuthbert Tunstall to be made A.B. of Canterbury. It was dated 1521. They shew'd us likewise a thin Folio book of his love letters to Anne Bolen some in French, & some in English. Besides these are the 12 vols of Cardinal Baronius's Annals wrote by his own hand. An original Code of Theodosius wrote in his time. Among the books of the Duke D'Urbin is a large Hebrew Bible with Thassonile commentarys. It is as large as a man can carry. The lives of Fredreic da Monte Feltro, & Francis the 1st della Rovere with very fine miniatures. In the library of the elector Palatin they shew'd us a bible wch they say was wrote by Luthers own hand. There is likewise the hand writing of Melancthon.[333] Among the books of Queen Xtine is a very fine Manuscript giving account of all the medals wch were in the Queens collection.[334] Descending from the library you go into the armory made by Urban the 8th & they say sufficient for 20,000 men. They are but in a very poor condition, & do not believe are sufficient for above half the number...

---

[333]Philipp Melanchton (1497-1560) was a German theologian of the Protestant Reformation and a founder of Lutheranism

[334]The library of Queen Christina of Sweden was bought by Pope Alexander VIII on her death in 1689

ROME
29 April/10 May, 1734
Milles to the bishop[335]

[The third letter in this group involves detailed descriptions of colleges and churches, including the Roman College, founded by Pope Gregory XIII, the College of the English Jesuits (with its "very dirty slovenly chappel") and the Church of St Lorenzo. The account includes a short description of the Catacombs, reproduced below]

We went to view the Catacombs under this church [St Lorenzo],[336] wch I think are the most perfect of any. The passages are from 2 foot to 2 & ½ wide, & on each side are 5 or 6 rows of niches made in the shape of coffins of all sizes, to inter the dead, wch afterwards were stopped up close either with tiles or marble several of wch I saw stopp'd & entire still. I likewise saw some remains of glass viols fasten'd with mortar to the rock wch they call Ampulla, & say that they contain'd the blood of the martyrs. I think at St Lorenzo there are 2 or 3 storys one over another. [337] About a mile and a half out of the Porta Capena is the

---

[335] Add. 15773

[336] Pococke recorded a visit to this church and to the Catacombs on 16 March, so either they "reviewed" this site in April or Milles is including here details that he had forgotten to include in earlier letters

[337] The same Catacombs are described by Pococke in his journal of places near Rome, who notes, "From the church you ascend the Catacombs wch extend about a mile underground towards Tivoli. They are about two feet & a half wide & 6 feet high, & on both sides of them are holes cut about a foot deep from [ ] feet to six feet long, for the different sizes of the dead, & narrow at each end & broader in the middle coffins, they were shut up with tiles or peices of marble ty'ld with plaister [next line scored out] several of which we saw remain'd untouched, & in some that were broke down we saw the human bones lying in their [proper] order very near consumd or very rotten, at the corners of some we saw the remains of glass viols set into mortar, wch they say was for the bloud of the martyrs wch the Sts Gather'd up; I saw one in a hole but two feet long [next line scored out]. Tis thought by some that these were the burial places of Christians in the time of persecution, but I rather think these were made after this religion was countermined by the Emperors, as they are works too considerable for a persecuted people. In a vineyard near we saw an opening into Catacombs which we were told communicated with these". Add. 22981, pp 18-19

church of St Sebastian, they keep the body of that saint there.[338] The Catacumbs [sic] here are by much the largest of any about Rome, they say they reach 12 or 14 miles. I observed nothing particular in them.[339] In these Catacumbs they say were found the bodys of St Peter & Paul, of 46 Popes, & 17400 martyrs. At the church of St Pietro in Montoria situated on the top of the Janiculum on the other side of the water is the famous Transfiguration of Raphael the last & best work of that great Painter...[340]

Since I wrote this I received your Ldships of March the 30th, we have taken the manner of sending the Bullarium as your Ldship appoints, & tomorrow we leave Rome for Bologna. We shall make all expedition possible into England. Dr Pococke joins with me in humble respects to your Ldship...

ROME
Pococketo his mother
30 April/11 May, 1734
Letter 16[341]

[The excerpts reproduced below are interesting since they are Pococke's observations on the religious ceremonies performed in the Vatican and the Pope's Chapel at Monte Cavallo during the Easter period. The letter also contains a description of ordinations, a curious "disciplining" scene and brief notes on the cousins' final days in Rome and preparations for their departure to Venice. Also included, in a deleted

---

[338] A basilica church dating to the 4th century and dedicated to the popular martyr St Sebastian

[339] This is probably a result of the fact that they have always been the most accessible Catacombs in Rome and therefore difficult to preserve

[340] An altar-piece commissioned by Cardinal Giulio de Medici, later Pope Clement VII. It was removed from St Pietro in Montorio in 1797 and taken to Paris, but returned to the Vatican Museum in 1815

[341] Add. 22978. This is the sixth letter of the original collection (Add. 19939) and a note next to the English address states that it was received by Mrs. Pococke on 24 May and answered on 26 May, 1734

passage, is news of "a strange thing" that happened in Dublin, involving the shooting of a Fellow at Trinity College]

This day the 22d of April, [I put a letter for you into the post &][342] went to the Vatican, where in the chapel of Sixtus IV Cardinal Barberini[343] Dean of the Sacred College said mass, musick being performed all the time vocal only; & the Cardinals present, thence the Sacrament was carried & exposed in the Capella Paulina[344] near which was all illuminate with candles, especially about the altar. Then we went to the Ducal hall & saw Cardinal Barberini wash the feet of 13 poor priests, cloathed in white serge, among which three Irish; he washes only one foot, just puts his hand on it with the water in the bason, & a kind of a muslin towel finely plaited, being put into his hand, he wiped it, kissed the foot or leg, & gave the towel to the person washed, together with a large nose gay; this done a silver & gold medal of the Pope was given to everyone of the Popes; [ ] that was at the upper end kissed the Cardinal, as he went away as betraying our Saviour. This ought to be done by the Pope if he were well & able.[345] We went then to see these 13 priests dine, served by Canons & dignitaries of the Church, a very elegant dinner, desert, the best wines, &c. We saw the Cardinals dine in publick, a long table finely set out; in the middle a tree of painted paper or such like, one in a triumphal carr with Angels over, three persons by, over vocavit salvatorem meum, I know not what it signified; at equal distances on each side five statues of saints about 16 inches high of the same make with a Label of a piece of scripture, four dishes of sweetmeats round each, & a large one between with a stone & a bunch of Artificial flowers rising out of it; there was a plate opposite to every saint with a nose gay on a handsome stone, & to every plate were ten plates of sweetmeats etc; Lobster, Flummery [stewed fruit] Strawberries & other things all cover'd with glass covers, which they came & took away in baskets, then took off the artificial flowers from the plates, they put oyl vinegar & a liquid greenish liquor in a cruit in some things where it was proper: after that there were two large dishes of fish set at each end of

---

[342]Scored out in the copy and reproduced from the original letter, Add. 19939
[343]Francesco Barberini (1662-1738)
[344]The Pope's private chapel in the Vatican
[345]He was totally blind from 1732 and suffered from ill health

the table, at the corners on silver chafindishes [warming dishes] which done the Cardinals came the Dean sat at the upper end, some of 'em had laced bits over their heads & hung down before to catch their driblins. We only staid to see 'em settled at dinner, not being willing to make ours on the smell of it. Paid a visit, went to the Vatican, the Misereremei[346] was sung there again & a sermon to the Cardinals; one of the Cardinals viz Petra went to St Peters sat in a chair, & blessed all the people that came to him, by touching 'em with a long white rod, he being the Cardinal Penitentiary.[347] The canons went all with white wands at the top of wch was a large tuft to the High Altar & spunges full of vinegar being squeezed on it they all rubbed their tufts on it, I need not tell you what that alludes to. I went to see the cardinals wash the feet of pilgrims & wait on them at table & put their broth out of a large kettle, each pilgrim had 5 dishes viz two of fish, soup, salad, Apples & Almonds & raisins on long tables. The Cardinals put on the red glaz'd linnen frock that comes all over them, & a towel or white apron about their middles as all the rest of the society, & give money to the poor pilgrims, when a Pope goes abroad he does the same. Before at St Peters we saw several companies of tradesmen go in procession to St Peters with a cross & candles before them.

23. Good Friday. Went to the Vatican, saw Cardinal Petra perform the office there, they say, the Priest receives the mass only in one kind the wafer, on this day they made a procession from Sixtus's chapel to Pauls & took down the Host & went in procession with it to Sixtus's chapel & put it up in the Pyx;[348] [several words inserted in Pococke's hand, which is illegible] then the cardinals had a publick dinner as yesterday: I think feasting at this time is very improper. We went & dined at a house near, an ordinary, [not being... very well of late at our Lodgings],[349] & we are at 1s 6d a meal. There were of five nations at the table. We went to a Greek Church, a statue of our Saviour dead in wood painted laid along on a stage 3 feet high, with a canopy over, supported by Pillars at the corners, it was laid on a lace sheet, a red cloth cover under that [cushions] of flowers round, the Bishops & the

---

[346]From the opening words of Psalm 51, "Have mercy on me..."
[347]He was appointed to this position by Pope Clement XII in 1730 and held it until his death in 1747
[348]The cup in which the Holy Eucharist was carried
[349]Scored out in the copy and reproduced from the original letter, Add. 19939

college to the number of 20 came in, his usual habit was taken off, a habit of scarlet velvet was put on, with Brocade down before, then a habit of red & gold Brocade was put over that a piece of white damask made stiff came over like a scarf, & one end going on to the ground, the other turned back behind, it had on it 2 or 3 large crosses in red, he had a square thing hanging by his side, stiff with a cross on it, such as they put over their chalices, & a gold cross hung down his breast; the mitre is like a flat globe, only turning out at bottom to fit the head, a small silver cross gilt at top, embroidered round at bottom, & by embroidery divided into 4 parts, it was of Gold stuff with a cherubim on each quarter, with several wings finely embroidered; they chanted like the reading Psalms, stanza's or verses relating to the passion, in several parts, between the several parts the Bishop twice in [ ] the body, at the four sides of the stage, threw flowers on it at the four parts. Then they all kissed the feet, making reverences & crossing themselves thrice, & [again] after; then the Bishop came & sat at the feet of it, as he had come before & returned to his usual chair & made a motion towards it, with a branch of [ ] afterwards with a branch in each hand, putting his arms a cross & before this he went with his college in procession round the inside of the church with an handkerchief printed with Mount Calvary & the Crucifixion; above the stage there was a large crucifix set up in the ground; the Bishop kissed every garment & the mitre before it was put on him & I observed the Maronite kissed them when they were taken off; whenever they give the Bishop his Crosier or any thing else, they kiss his hand....

24. We went to see the ordinations of St John Lateran[350] by Cardinal Guadiagni[351] Vicar General of Clerks, subdeacons & deacons & priests, which was perform'd among many other ceremonies, by putting on a sort of a white thing with crosses on it as a scarfe, then the garment, giving a chalice, oyling them, giving the Bible, laying one hand on the inferior orders, & two on the priests, as likewise did the priests after the cup, the priest's hands being oyl'd, the Bp in his seat holding out his hand all the while, they then put 'em together, & one

---

[350]The Papal Archbasilica of St. John Lateran, official ecclesiastical seat of the Pope
[351]Giovanni Antonio Guadagni (1674-1759) was elevated to Cardinal in 1731

tied 'em together with a white handkerchief, & then all kneeled down, & going to the Bishop they put a chalice & patten to their hands, which done, their hands were untied & cleaned with bread first & then water. There is a ceremony I don't understand, at the outside of the church door there is a pan of coals, a table with a priests habit on it, & a plate with some sort of pulse, they go in procession with a cross a large candle 3 inches diameter painted over & a staff 6 or 7 feet high cover'd with flowers, 4 or 5 gilt pine apples that are after wards stuck in the candle, which I believe stay by the altar till Whitsontide, one saies some prayers, incenses those things & sprinkles them with Holy water, which done they go in procession into church & one of the three candles on the top of the staff cover'd with flowers is lighted, a short devotion performed, at the middle a 2d [2nd] lighted in the same manner, & near the altar a third, then one return'd to a pulpit these things before him & read the Gospel, this candle & flowers were fix'd near the Altar at St Johns during The ordination, some of the persons ordained as the clerks, & after others carried a wax candle, not upright nor lighted, to the Bishop in both hands the Bishop lays his hand on it, they kiss the candle & his hand, this is the form of confirmation, they say together with oyling; we were too late for a ceremony; - This Bishop's baptizing a woman Jew & her Daughter in the Baptistery, they went a procession with the candle & flowers, he breathing on the water, pour'd in oyl & Balsam, & the Jews being questioned, their heads were made bare & he poured the water on them, this done every years on this day you must know their ordinations are always on a Saturday; the Candidates are all clothed in white surplices tied round the middle with a white cowl, which the Bishop put over the head of the subdeacons & 'twas put back again: Mass was said aloud after all by the Bishop, the Priests being obliged to repeat it themselves, & all receive. On Good Friday none but the priest elevates the host & [   ] having been consecrated the day before. At baptizing the Bishop crossed the water, & when he put in oyl & balsam, he cross'd the water again.

At 2 went to St Peters, saw nothing, look'd on some statues at Palazzo Al[   ] where Cardinal Aquaviva lives.[352] Went to see here what they call disciplining themselves, 'tis at a church of the Jesuits; - at first

---

[352]Troiano Aquaviva d'Aragona (1695-1747)

there is only a dim light of 3 or 4 candles, then the candles are lighted up, some devotion performed & discipline or cat or nine tails dispensed about, the candles put out, a Jesuit preaches warmly & raises 'em up to a pitch of enthusiasm, about the [ ] our Saviours sufferings &c: then they fall to beating themselves, some being in chains & others make a terrible noise of beating with chains cords & groans, the doors being shut, this lasts for about half a quarter of an hour, the priest sometimes putting in a sentence to keep up their passions; while the candles are lighted they joyn in devotions; the priest with the cross in his hand spoke some thing more & concluded with a Blessing. This done three times a week, & every night this week; when women go, all the Avenues are guarded that no men may enter; 'twas a very moving thing how strange soever it appeared at first hearing of it.

25. Easter Sunday, Went to the Popes chapel at Monte Cavallo where Mass was celebrated 33 Cardinals being present, afterwards the Pope [made] his Benediction from a Balcony towards the square before the Palace, the Cavalegieri[353] & Corasti[354] two companies of horse answering to the Kings horse guard, & the foot soldiers were drawn up in the square, trumpets & kettledrums beating & a flag from the tower was displayed, & the large Piazza full of people many thousands; the Balcony over the gate was hung with Tapestry & damask a canopy over it within; a speaking cloth was spread from the top of the window some small distance out, & then over that from the Eves was a vast large one coming out a great way & drawn tight by ropes going over at a great distance to the opposite houses, this was to convey the voice & it was wonderful to hear the Popes voice tho' 84 years old, I believe all over the square, I heard it in the middle plain. The Cardinals filled the Balcony & a gold cross or gilt being brought forward some time before the Pope appear'd, he was wheel'd forward in a scarlet velvet chair to the sight of all the people, with his triple crown on & in his robes, two kind of large screens being held of each side of him in this shape [insert diagram] the upper part being long feathers of white Peacocks, a book was held to him for form, being blind, & he said two prayers, then raised himself up majestically on

---

[353]Pococke inserts the word "Troopers" above this word
[354]He inserts the word "Dragoons" above this word

his feet & gave his Blessing, first to all the world waving his hand out as they always do, then sits down, & after a while raised himself up again, & blessed all the people present, they being on their knees all the time, they say he spoke something; & when he was drawn back he made the benediction motion with his hand, the guns fired, the Bells rung & it was a noble sight indeed, well contrived to move the people. At 2 went to St Isidore the Irish Franciscans,[355] Father Flemin [Flemming] the Guardian entertained us very diverting[ly][356] for two or three hours in the Library, we having seen him before, tho' I went to see one Welch of the County of Waterford.[357] Saw the Aldobrandi gardens[358] fine statues & reliefs & in the Summerhouse the famous painting of a heathen marriage in fresco the walls were brought hither from Vespasians baths where twas found.[359] Went to St Peters in vinculo[360] to see again the famous colossal statue of Moses by Michael Angelo;[361] met some Spanish officers there to whom I told what I knew concerning it, & some discourse about the war; one told me I talk'd Italian well, I told him, as I tell you, I did not.[362] I heard some musick at Madonna de Morti, came to the coffee house...

27....This day I received with a great deal of pleasure your letter of the 2[4] of March. [My Ld sends bills as they are requir'd 160 at first 80 since & 80 to come to Venice but that concerns not me][363] My Lord in

---

[355] The Irish College of St. Isidore was founded by Friar Luke Wadding of Waterford (1588-1657)

[356] In the original, Add. 19939

[357] He spells it "Welsh" in his previous reference to his friar (Letter 16)

[358] The Villa Aldobrandini was built at the beginning of the 17th century by Cardinal Pietro Aldobrandi. This patron of the arts built up a famous collection of art and antiquities, many of which were displayed in the grounds of his villa

[359] The "Aldobrandini Wedding", from the 1st century BC, now in the Biblioteca Apostolica Vaticana

[360] Chuch of San Pietro in Vincoli

[361] Commissioned by Pope Julius II, in 1505, for his tomb

[362] Further on in the letter (on 27 April), he informs his mother, "We make a shift to be understood in Italian, our common talk at table is in French, most being Germans"

[363] Scored out in the copy and reproduced from the original letter, Add. 19939. Clearly, this refers to the amounts of money being sent to Milles by his uncle

his last letter says he thinks it will be necessary I should be in Ireland by Michaelmus[364] but I am in some hopes of a reprieve, which if so, I shall hear of it at Venice, but I shall only make use of it to stay the longer in England unless that restraint should oblige me to cut short my journey very much & not come through Germany, which yet we must of necessity do if England declares war: in exchange besides provision money &c: [   ] at present 6d in the pd as near as we can compute, it was 1s & 1s 6d [a while] ago In my last I inform'd you yt Mr Bagwell had an acknowledgement of Mr Hoare of ye receipt of a £50 bill sent t him for me on the 17th of Novr and yt he never as I can find remitted to me as I desir'd: ... I hope you have not told on my account... strange never ... and it is to you, but I am very much obligd to you upon this account more than I can express:][365] I thank you for your copy of Horace's verses very proper for us... The Vice Queen of Naples is the Vice roys wife,[366] who was of the name Viteo [   ] came off with about 4000 men to the East of Italy & its thought all will suffer. - but since I hear they are like to make a good resistance; they say 2 of the three castles of Naples have surrender'd prisoners of war; - but it was writ the castle of Baia. We did not see the Great Duke he constantly keeping his bed. We have had a fortnight or 3 weeks ago as hot weather as the hottest in England, this day some rain. Straw berries & every thing that you have in June are here now. I shall be obliged to yourself if you fill your letters with all little affairs which are agreeable. [Mr Matthews[367] is like Cardinal Pico Mirandola... St C Casio, Cardinal Borghese a young man is ye very picture of Signor Morgan but wears his hair:[368] a strange thing happend at Dublin .... lads went to break a fellows windows he fir'd at em but went & fought their arms, he fird again & they returnd it & shot him dead, 3 among 'em a Barons son in jayl, 5 young men have left the college on it, the

---

[364] A feast day celebrated today on 29 September, but latterly on 10 October

[365] Scored out in the copy and reproduced from the original letter (Add. 19939), which in places is difficult to decipher

[366] The last Viceroy of the Kingdom of Naples (1733-34) was Giulio Visconti Borromeo Arese, Conte di Brebbia

[367] An unidentified friend or associate of the Pococke family

[368] This appears to be a reference to another acquaintance of the Pococke family (a clergyman) who did not wear a wig

cause was he being but a Junior punishd them for punching a porter yt had affronted 'em: one letter only came enclosed they are not..][369]

28. Went to see the Cloacae which are arched over with hewn stone, about 12 feet wide & 10 deep, their chief use to carry off the rain water & overflowing of the Tiber. [At 2 went to a merchant... is absolutely necessary & ... a summer suit of silk; all but a coat I must have bought my black is pretty much wore & being so [hot] in ye shirts grows too heavy my grey indeed is tolerable, & I thought to have worn it with a new silk waiscoat & velvet... I considerd a ... suit of silk wd not cost above 40 more than that, I resolvd to buy one wch is black........ something smaller yard wide & 7s a yard lind with black Taffeta 4s a yard & same width. 9 yds of each are coming to a little more than 8 or rather 9 making ... & in yr country any one is almost pointed at that wears both in summer: both ye silks are the manufacture of this place. I went to the Minerva Library to read in Kirchers Latium[370] about Ostia &c where we are to go]fl

29....Went to see curiosities at ye Roman College again; 200 scholars there 25 masters & a school for every class, I believe not less than 30,

---

[369]Scored out of the copy and reproduced from the original, Add. 19939. This incident is verified in the Trinity College Dublin "Board Register" for the period (TCD/MUN/V/5/2) which records the following entry for 27 April, 1734: "Several aspersions being cast upon the government of the College on occasion of the late riot and the unfortunate murder of Mr Ford one of our fellows, it was this day ordered that an humble application be made to the Visitors of the College that they will please to visit and make such publick inquiry into the state of the College as will give us an opportunity of justifying our conduct to the world and freeing our selves from those imputations And the Provost [Richard Baldwin] and Dr Elwood are deputed to make an humble representation of this to the Visitors in ye name and behalf of the Provost and Senr fellows" (p.608). A later entry, from 10 June, 1734, notes that a citation was ordered to be posted on the college gates, "appointing Sr Davis to appear before the Provost and fellows on the 30th of June" (p.610) and on 13 July, 1734, it was recorded that the following five culprits were expelled for their part in this murder: Mr. Jacob Cotter, Mr. William Crosby, Charles Boyle, Jacob Scholes and Mr. Rowlands Davis (p.613)

[370]Regrettably, this passage, taken from the original (the copy having been scored out) is very difficult to read owing to the poor condition of the manuscript. Kirscher's book was published in Amsterdam, 1671

as they come in they go to the Church & say their private devotions, & a short prayer to themselves at going into the schools which are kept shut, & you hear nothing; they punish not as we do but with a whip on the hands & legs, they seem to love & esteem their masters, & they treat them with much kindness & little distance; when they pas by 'em going to school, they kiss their masters hand if they meet 'em...

30....Went in the road to Marino & dined at a small Inn call'd Posticiciola 5 miles from Rome; the woman told me none but jews eat meat on Fridays, I told her travellers might, she said it was excommunication to eat it I had a dish of fascoli [fagioli] dryed, kidney bean broth, all beans allmost, eggs & a good sallade & a pint of wine for 6d 2.[371]

May 1. Went to see the Barberini Library,[372] could not see the fine vase,[373] but saw a serpent stuff'd 13 f long, with a head like a shark 4 rows of teeth, found near Rome; saw the famous bas relief in marble of Homers Apotheosis, & the twisted pillars of Julius Caesar sacrificing in relief of Egypt Rosso, in the Collonna Palace...

2. [We were] obliged to dine with the Irish Franciscans at St Isidore, we dined in the Refectory, but by mistake not at the time that all the monks dine, but we saw some at dinner, we were civilly entertained by the Guardian[374]... Visited Monseigneur Fontanini Archbishop of Ancyra; he said he would get ready some letters for recommendation of his own motion.

---

[371]It is not clear what the "2" stands for, but perhaps it denotes ½ or the price for 2 people

[372]In the Barberini, Palace, already noted. The library was acquired and made part of the Vatican Library by Leo XIII in 1902

[373]This is the famous "Portland" Vase, dating from the 1st century BC. The antiquity was acquired by Cardinal Francesco Maria del Monte, at the end of the 16th century, whose heirs sold it to the Barberini family, who displayed it in the Barberini Palace. It was eventually purchased by Sir William Hamilton, who sold it to Margaret, Dowager Duchess of Portland, in 1784; and it is now in the British Museum

[374]Father Fleming. Pococke notes, on 4 May, a return visit by the Irish Franciscans of St Isidore

3. Went to see Mr Fowkes [sic] a very ingenious fellow of the Royal Society,[375] he & his family were here; were visited by the Irish Dominicans; at 3 went to see some medals, visited Mr Wills an English painter;[376] went to see the Villa Ghigi near St Mary major, where are many curiosities of all sorts [in] the Musaeum...

5.... prepared for our journey. Went to St Peter's [bought some brocoli seed, lettuce, sweet fennel, chicory (?) & onion, & French beans...][377]

6. Staid within to write what we had seen... Took our leave of Monseigneur Fontamini [sic] who had sent us Letters to Fierrara, Bologna & Venice.

7. Mon Seigneur sent a compliment to us, Segnior Giovanni & one of the Greys[378] came to see us... at 2 visited Dr Irwin.

8. Packed up - went with a box to the boat which is to go to Leghorn, & from thence to Mr Wood in London to be forwarded to Newtown, which I desire you to advise him to send it to Newtown. You may let him know that in the box are books, maps, some old clothes Linnen &c: ..

9. Went a mile up Fiamicina [sic] to the Tiber where it divides & makes this Island, cross'd over in a boat to the Continent & went a mile & half to Ostia:[379] I should have told you Porto is a Bishoprick,

---

[375]Martin Folkes (1690-1754), who later became a member of the Egyptian Society (appointed Inspector of Medals and Coins) and the Divan Club. Pococke, Milles & Folkes were also Fellows of the Royal Society, and the latter was President of the Royal Society of Antiquaries from 1750-54. Folkes was in Italy from 1733-35, see Ingamells (*op.cit*) 363-64

[376]This is possibly Rev. James Wills (*fl.* 1740-77), painter and priest, who was Director of St Martin's Lane Academy from 1743-6. See Ingamells, *op.cit.*, 1006

[377]Scored out in the copy and reproduced from the original letter, Add. 19939. The latter part of the passage is impossible to decipher but relates to the price paid for these vegetables

[378]No further details are given of any of the Greys referred to here, and there are no relevant entries for this period in Ingamells

[379]Also described by Milles in his letter of 9/20 May, 1734 (Add. 15773). See Chapter 5

the city wall'd round a very small cathedral like a chapel more; in the city is only the Bishops sorry palace & the Inn & no houses for suburbs. Ostia is likewise a Bishoprick & wall'd city, may have 30 houses in it, & the Bps castle & palace, the cathedral small, in a chapel of it is St Monaca died, it being then a bedchamber, she was waiting to embark for Africa, her son Austin being with her, her body was moved some years ago to St Austins here..[380]

10. Spent the morning in writing, 'tho we have been here 4 months we have much to do to get away, & have not had a day to spare. I caught a tortoise in the way, & saw the first grass cut: this day was very hot. Went at 3 to the Minerva Library visited by Messrs Paul, Stewart, Chamberlain, Hartford the last an Irish student here in Divinity pack'd up.[381]

11. And this morning about 8 or 9 we set out [Jerre is very well love to my sister][382] (you will hear from me in a month, we go to Bologna by Loretto)

I am Dear Madam

Your Most obedient & Dutiful Son

Richard Pococke

---

[380]In Chapter IV of his journal on places near Rome (entitled "Of Porto, Ostia & the Places in the way to Them"), Pococke includes a note that gives us some idea of his mode of writing: "On The 9th of May I set out for Porto & having diverted myself by taking down every minute particular even to the description of the road I here transcribed it from my notes as I put it down." Add. 22981, p.72. He also makes similar comments about the size of the town and the fact that the cathedral "is no better than a chapel". *Ibid.*, p.74

[381]There is no record of Hartford at the Irish College at Rome, nor is there a record of his ordination

[382]Scored out in the copy and reproduced from the original letter, Add. 19939

CHAPTER 5

Letters from the Return Journey

The next four letters dispatched by Milles to the bishop were from Bologna (9/20 May & 13/24 May), Modena (15/26 May) and Padua (21 May/1 June), with his first and only from Venice dated 30 May/10 June. His final two communications from the first tour were sent from Verona (6/17 June) and Milan (12/23 June). After leaving Rome, Pococke did not write to his mother until he reached Venice, his first from this city (Letter 17) dated 31 May/11 June (a lengthy manuscript covering the period 11 May to 4 June) and his second (Letter 18) dated 13 June.[1] His final letters from this collection (Letters 19-22) were sent from Milan (12/23 June), Turin (15/26 June), Lyons (June 20/2 July) and Dover (30 June), with a further letter from another collection sent from Holyhead (13 July).

The correspondence reproduced in this chapter represents their homeward journey, and though the cousins had originally informed the bishop they would be back by Michaelmas (late September), on reaching Venice they had to suddenly change their plans. In order for Milles to take up the unexpected offer of a preferment in his uncle's diocese, and on account of the Dean of Lismore being "dangerously ill", they had to depart early, reaching London on 1 July and embarking on a packet boat at Holyhead, destined for Waterford, on 13 July, 1734.

In this section the sequence of letters adopted for the earlier sections has been slightly altered: instead of those of Pococke and Milles being reproduced alternately, excerpts from their letters are reproduced in order of date. Therefore, we begin with five consecutive letters from Milles, followed by seven from Pococke and ending with two more from Milles. Several of

---

[1] In the original letter (Add. 19939), Pococke has omitted to use the dual dating system, though clearly the date of this letter (13 June) is in Old Style. His mother has faithfully reproduced this omission in her copy

their journals exist for this part of their travels, two composed by Milles[2] and two by Pococke.[3]

Included in this chapter is the essay which appears towards the end of Milles' journal, on Italy & Savoy and the Italian people. This is placed exactly where it appears in the manuscript, namely on their arrival at Le Pont de Beauvoisin, the border between Italy and France, and is thought to be a fitting conclusion to their first Italian journey.

---

[2]"An Acct of My journey from Rome to Venice" (11 May, 1734 to 13 June, 1734) and "An Account of what I saw Remarkable between Venice & London". The former manuscript was purchased by the British Library from Thomas Thorpe, on 25 April, 1846

[3]"Travels Vol. V. From Rome To Milan" (11-21 June, 1734) and "Travels: Vol. VI Milan & from Milan to France" (21 June, 1734 to 1 July, 1734)

BOLOGNA
9/20 May, 1734
Milles to the bishop[4]

[It will be remembered that Milles, at the end of his last letter, informed his uncle that they were leaving Rome for Bologna the next day (30 April). At the end of the present letter, he states that they have just arrived at Bologna, which means the journey took them almost a week]

My Lord

In my last weeks letter to your Ldship I finished an account of all the churches, & a great many of the Palaces. I shall begin the present letter with an account of the Villa Borghese, by much the finest & most agreeable about Rome.[5] It is reckoned 7 miles in circuit, & is situated just on the outside of the walls between the Porta Flaminia, & Pincia. All the outside of the walls of the Palace are incrusted with antique bas relieves. On one side is the statue of the famous Curtius on horse back praecipitating himself into the gulph. It was found about the middle of the Forum Romanum, about the spot, where it is supposed that the Lacus Curtius formerly was.[6]

The most remarkable things in this villa are the statues of the famous Gladiator, a copy of wch I remember to have seen in Mr Herberts garden.[7] On it is the sculptors name Αγασιασ δωσιθεου εφεσιοσ εποιει.[8] The wolf suckling Romulus & Remus, of a red Aegyptian

---

[4]Add. 15773

[5]Pococke briefly refers to this villa in Letter 12 (entry for 26 January) and again in Letter 16, where he notes (entry for 4 May): "[A]t 2 saw the Villa Burghese [sic] again, half a mile out of the end of town, where as I told you before are a great number of fine old statues, busts & reliefs & some excellent modern groups of statues of Bernini"

[6]Also noted by Pococke in Letter 12 and in the corresponding journal (see Chapter 4)

[7]Probably an acquaintance from Highclere, as a Mrs. Herbert is mentioned in a family letter from the private collection viewed on Ebay, dated 31 August, 1721 (not included in this edition)

[8]The Borghese Gladiator, by Agasias of Ephesus, son of Dositheus, now in the Louvre

marble, & thought to have stood in the Temple dedicated to them.
The statue of Seneca expiring in a bath of Pietra Paragone,[9] a young
Nero with the Bulla aurea.[10] And here I cannot but take notice of Mr
Addisons mistake who says that this is different from that wch is in
Prince Chigis cabinet; whereas there is not the least difference in the
bulla itself, & very little or none in the part by wch it hangs
[illustration]. The former is the Bulla in the Chigi cabinet & the later
that in Borghese, your Ldship may perceive what a small difference
there is between them.[11] There are three fine peices of sculpture by
Bernini in this Palace, viz: Apollo pursuing Daphne who is turning
into a Laurel, David going to fling the stone at Goliah, & Aeneas
carrying his father Anchises on his shoulders.[12]

The P: Chigis villa is between the Quirinal, & Viminal, here is a very
great repository of all sorts of curiositys. Amongst wch the most
remarkable are an Aegyptian Mummy,[13] a Tripod, & vase on it for
sacrifice, the Idol of the God Canopus, in shape of a jug bottle, the
Bulla aurea mentioned above. It is about the size of a small watch, &
of the same make tho a little flatter. It is of very fine gold, but thin, &
hollow on the inside. On the upper part of it is marked in gold studs

---

[9]Lucius Annaeus Seneca (c. 1 BC-AD 65), the stoic statesman and
philosopher who committed suicide in a bath for his part in a plot to
assassinate Nero

[10]The bulla aurea was the amulet or locket of gold given to the infant Nero
(future Roman Emperor) by Pompeia

[11]This is presumably the poet, playwright and politician, Joseph Addison
(1672-1719). While the precise context of this reference is not clear, the
criticism is indicative of the sort of argument Milles was later to indulge in,
as for example in his scholarly discourses printed in *Archaeologia*

[12]Three famous statues which are still to be seen in the Borghese Villa

[13]Further described by Pococke, in his journal on places near Rome, "an
Egyptian mummy wrapt up in many swathes with a painted covering over
it, there is a hole in it by wch I saw ye mummy, a bone, it smelt like murk,
but they say stinks in the summer". Add. 22981, p.35. It is worth noting
that Pococke's collection of antiquities and curiosities, as can be seen from
the sale after his death, included several mummies or parts of mummies. As
mentioned in Chapter 1, he conducted a dissection of a mummy for the
Egyptian Society, and wrote a scholarly piece on this topic in the society's
"Journal"

CATVLVS.[14] Here is likewise a Jewish shekel, at the Verospi Palace is a famous Gallery painted by Albano representing the sun, the 6 Planets 4 seasons, night & day &c.[15] Here is a very good statue of the Goddess Nania.[16] Here is likewise a very curious peice of machinery it consists of 3 Spinnets, Harpsichord, & Organ, placed separately & at a considerable distance from each other, yet there is a secret communication between them so them so that the person who plays on the Harpsichord only, may at the same time sound the 3 Spinnets, & Organ or on any one of them singly, but this is done by an art wch only one man in Rome is master of. It was done by one Albana a Roman.[17]

At the Palace of Maximi are several old peices of painting, & Mosaick. Amongst wch of the latter are two, representing the figures of gladiators. But they are so ill done, & so damaged by time, that one can see little of them. In the courtyard is a very fine & large statue of white marble of Pyrrhus K: of Epirus. In the courtyard & on the stairs of the Palace Mattei are several good bas-releeves statues, & four or five antique marble chairs. Amongst the bas-releeves is a remarkable one called Pompa Isidis.[18] It represents 4 persons preists of Isis with all the instruments of sacrifice &c.

On Sunday we set out for Porto, & Ostia.[19] Three miles out of the Porta Ostiensis I turn'd aside a little to see a church called the Three Fountains. It is said to be the place where St Paul was beheaded, & at the corner of the church is a column of white marble about 3 feet high, on wch they say he was beheaded, & that his head afterwards made three leaps, & at each leap sprung up a fountain, wch all remain still.

---

[14]This object is also described by Pococke, in his journal on places near Rome, where he notes, "In the villa Chigi... are many curiosities...among the antiquities a bulla aurea it is round about an inch & a half diameter rather longer the cross way with a loop made of gold... it is hollow and the name of Catulus is round the loop." (Add. 22981, p.35)

[15]This is not mentioned in Pococke's journal account

[16]A goddess worshipped in ancient Mesopotamia and Persia

[17]Also noted by Pococke, in Letter 16, in his entry for 4 May, 1734

[18]The Procession of Isis, an engraving of which was printed by Pietro Santi Bartoli, in 1693

[19]According to Pococke's account, this trip took place on 8 & 9 May, 1734 (Letter 16)

People drink the water for devotion, the nearest his head, they pretend is the warmest, the middlemost colder then [sic] the first, & the third colder than the other two. I drunk of all the three waters, but could not perceive any difference because I did not taste them immediately one after another. At one of the altars, is a very fine peice by Guido Reni representing the martyrdom of St Peter. Near this church are two more one called St Vincenzio & Anastasia, & the other Sta Maria in Scala Cali, wch title was given to it because of the number of Xtians that were martyr'd there under Diocletians reign. It was likewise called the Macellum Xtianorum [Christian Market]. A great part of the via ostiensis is remaining, I measured it in one part, & found it to be 14 feet wide. Porto so called from the ancient Portus is situated about 13 miles from Rome, & two from the sea. Just above it the Tyber divides into 2 branches, & so runs into the sea. Porto is of the righthand of it, tho very near the right hand branch, of the famous Ports of Claudius, & Trajan - little or nothing of the former is left, & whereas when the latter was made, the former was an outer port or a bay to it, now the former is allmost all dry ground over run with rushes & bushes. The form of the latter is remaining wch is sexangular [hexagonal], & likewise some arches of the Port & near it the remains of a round Temple, wch is called the temple of Portumnus. One may likewise trace where the walls of the city stood. The present city of Porto one of the Cardinal Bishopricks, consists only of the Bps Palace a church, one Inn, with some out houses, & is surrounded with a wall.[20] It is situated on the East side of the ancient town. The present city of Ostia is about 2 miles distant on the other side of the river. It is some what larger then [sic] Porto, & joined with sexangular is one of the Cardinal Bishopricks. There is a little castle in the town belonging to the Cardinal. About a mile South of it are very large ruins of old Ostia scattered here & there about the feilds [sic]. I cannot by the remains say positively what any thing was, but one peice of building wch I took for an Amphitheatre or a Theatre.[21] It is about a mile & a half from the sea. On the North side of Ostia is a very large Lake or Pool,

---

[20]In Pococke's words, "in the city is only the Bishops sorry palace & the Inn & no houses for suburbs" (entry for 9 May, Letter 16)

[21]The theatre at Ostia was built by Agrippa between 12 and 9 BC. It was excavated several in 1880/81, 1890 and the early 20th century and has been restored very extensively

besides wch the country is so flat, & has so much water, that it is prodigiously unhealthy to live there in the summer, nay all most impossible.

I returned from Ostia on Monday [10 May], & on Tuesday [11 May] noon we left Rome, & took the road to Loretto passing over the Pons Milvius, & going along the Via Flaminia....[22]

My paper obliges me to conclude by informing your Ldship that this day [20 May] we arrived safe at Bologna, I would not send this from any little town for fear of miscarriage...

I hear that the Germans have pass'd the Po at a place called St Benedetto near Mirondola & that they have demanded one 10000 carriages of the Duke of Modena

---

[22]His journal for this period begins, "On Tuesday ye 11th of may N:S: at about half hour after twelve, we left Rome, & took ye road for Loretto..." Add. 15763, p.2. This journal is kept very methodically, with every bridge, village and pass duly described, and with reference to the days on which they arrived and departed from each place. It contains numerous inscriptions in Latin

BOLOGNA
13/24 May, 1734
Milles to the bishop[23]

[The excerpt taken from this letter is an interesting description of Loretto, which is also described fully in his journal]

From this city [Recanate][24] we had the first 208isq of Loretto , & we had 20, or 30 people following us to show us the Cupola of the Madonna. We were very much molested all along this road with thousands of beggars, who make a livelihood of begging from those who go out of devotion to the holy house, & who at such times are very charitable.

We arrived about Saturday noon at Loretto. We spent the afternoon in viewing the curiosities of the place. This city is very small, tho surrounded with water to defend themselves from the Turks who have attacked them. I need not enter into a long dissertation concerning the travels of the holy house miracles &c.[25] but shall only give your Ldship some description of the house itself.[26] As it is

---

[23] Add. 15773. The original letter has survived (Gloucestershire Archives, Ref. D2663/Z8), bearing signs of minor editing, mainly in the addition of brackets and corrections to punctuation, particularly the incorrect use of capital letters

[24] The surrounding countryside of which is described in Milles' journal as being "one of ye most delightfull I ever saw" (Add. 15763, p.19)

[25] The Christian Emperor Constantine built a basilica over the house where Jesus was believed to have been born, in Nazareth. In 1291, under threat during the Crusades, this "Holy House" was, according to Roman Catholic tradition, miraculously translated by angels to a site in Croatia. Three years later, the house was again moved by angels because of the Muslim invasion of Albania, and it landed first in Recanti, and shortly afterwards to its present location in Loreto

[26] In his journal, Milles notes, somewhat contemptuously, "the famous Madonna of Loretto, wth ye holy house is what most people have heard of. to give as breif an acct of this as possible, & not to fill my paper with ye idle storys of Legends yt ye Roman Catholicks tell of it. this house is supposed to be..." (Add. 15763, p.19)

impossible to take any measure of the holy house by reason of the croud always there I shall set down the measures taken from a printed book sold there, & wrote by one of the officers of it. The holy house is oblong, & is 32 feet long & 13 feet one inch wide & 13 feet ten inches high. The whole house is built of brick, of a greyish red. The people of Loretto say it is of stone. It is cemented with mortar, & does not appear to be very nice workmanship.[27] The walls are about two feet thick. In several parts of the holy house appear remains of ancient painting of the Madonna &c but it is so very dark that one can hardly see them. When the holy house first came it had but one door wch was in the middle of the North side, but it being too small for the concourse of people it was shut up, & two opened on the South side, & one on the North with another door on the outside casing only, to go up to the top. With part of the old materials they stopped the old door, & buried the rest under ground. The old ceiling was of wood, wch for fear of having it burnt with lamps, they took away & placed one of brick over, but did not let it rest on the holy house.[28] The famous image of the Madonna with our Saviour in her hands made of Cedar, & as they say by St Luke is two feet eleven inches high. Her face is black, & her hair flowing over her shoulders, she is placed just over the chimney, just as she stood when the house was brought. They shew'd us a peice of a sort of silk Grogram,[29] with wch the statue was cloathed, when she came to Loretto, & make a miracle of its being so preserved. The rest of the furniture wch came with the house are 4 porringers of delph, exactly like those wch we now use.[30] Here devoutpeople touch their beads, & crucifixes. There are likewise as I

---

[27] In his journal, Milles notes further, "the whole house is built as ye people of Loretto say of stone, but they are made exactly in ye form of brick, & pretty much ye colour, only are rather grayer, & indeed so exactly resemble ym yt it may be doubted. they are cemented with mortar, but not in a very regular manner, nor are ye bricks of a regular size". *Ibid.*, p.20

[28] In his journal, Milles notes, "they shew part of ye roof of ye house, wch when first it came was of wood, but for fear of catching fire by ye lamps it was taken away & a stone one put in its stead, ye preservation of this likewise is a miracle." Add. 15763, p.21

[29] A stiff fabric once used for clothing

[30] As Milles further explains in his journal, "out of wch they say our Saviour, Joseph, & ye V: Mary used to eat. They are all of earthen ware glazed over in ye manner of ye plates used now a days. one of them is broke but peiced together again, & all set in gold." Add. 15763, p.21

have been told two bells, the altar made by the Apostles, the stone on wch St Peter said Mass. But these we did not see. On one side of the statue is a little cupboard, with a wooden shelf across it, wch they say the blessed virgin used to put her houshold [sic] utensils in; another miracle of the preservation of the shelf! At the lower end of the room is a small square window, larger then it was at first. Thro' this they say the Angel Gabriel came when he gave the annunciation. Over it is the Crucifixion painted on a wooden cross supposed to be done by St Luke, & St John.

As to the present state of the holy house it is all cased on the outside wth very fine white marble, adorn'd with Corinthian pillars Bas-releives &c: by the best hands. On each side are 6 Corinthian fluted pillars 2 at each end & 2 in the middle. Over each of the side doors is a large Bas-releive representing some part of the V: Marys life, the 4 over the 4 doors are, her birth, her marriage, the birth of Xt, & the adoration of the Magi. At each end are 4 Corinthian pillars & between them 2 bas relieves. At the last end the death of the blessed V: & the translation of the holy house. At the West the annunciation. Above the square window on one side of it the visitation, on the other their going to be taxed. Between every two pillars are two niches one over another, in the lower are 10 Prophets, & above them the 10 Sibyls. The entablement over is very rich, & crown'd with a balustrade. The four doors are of bronze. They say the casing dos [sic] not touch the holy walls, because it was repulsed when endeavour'd to be joined to them.

But now how to enter into a description of the immense riches wch are within this place I do not know; They are in so great number that I hope your Ldship will be satisfied with some general account.[31] As for the vest of the Madonna, it is stuck as full of crosses, hearts &c: all adorned with the richest jewels that it is possible to imagine, & all the gifts of Princes, Cardinals, or Dukes. Particularly ye crown of the Madonna, & our Saviour are particularly rich, & set with prodigious fine Jewels, the present of Louis the 13th. On the right hand of the Madonna is an Angel in gold holding out a heart of the same with a

---

[31]Again, in his journal, Milles, after giving a lengthy account of the gifts, notes, "it would be endless for me to name all ye rich presents, yt appear in this little house. they are allmost innumerable & inestimable." *Ibid.*, p.22

flame coming out at top all adorned with rubys, & precious stones, wch was the gift of K. James the IIds Queen. Opposite to it one of silver given by her mother the Dutchess of Modena, in order for the Queen to obtain a male heir. Besides these there are near 20 little Angels of gold, & silver, & images of babes of gold, presented at the birth of princes; all wch I cannot pretend to name particularly. Besides these jewels, there are 12 lamps of solid gold always burning before the Madonna the largest of wch weighing 37 Pd was given by the State of Venice. But the most beautifull is one given by the Duke of Urbin, & made by this own hands. Another of 37 Pd made, & presented by Sigismond K: of Poland. Besides these are 28 silver lamps within the holy house, & 29 without & about it. With regard to the situation, the holy house bears to the Cathedral the latter is built with its Octangular Dome directly over it. It is painted by Roncalli.[32] The high altar of the church is against the West end of the holy house, I forgot to mention that the upper end of the holy house is divided from the rest by an iron grate cased with silver. It is called the sanctuary, just without the iron grate is an altar at wch they say Mass every day. The Cathedral is a handsome church. There are 7 very good gates of bronze to it adorn'd with bas relieves, with historys of the old Testament. Just before the door is the statue in bronze of Sixtus V exceedingly well done. From the Cathedral we went to the Treasury where we saw 17 Lockers full of the finest presents of gold precious stones, that one can conceive. Amongst wch I remember a very large peice of rock Emarald [sic], with prodigious large Emaralds in it. The crown, & Scepter of Q: Xtina, a golden heart studded with jewels presented by Catherina Maria K: Charles the 1sts Queen, with numberless other jewels, wch for brevity I pass over likewise very rich 211isqué211211 habits, & others for the Madonna. In the room stands a silver statue as big as the life of Adelaide the Electress of Bavaria.[33] It weighs 153 Pd. The roof of this chamber is all very finely painted by Pomorancio. From hence we went to view the Apothecarys shop, & the 366 vases all painted by Raphael with sacred & profane history. It is said that Q: Xtina would have given them, for [ ] them vases of their weight in silver, all finely adorned with bas-releives taken from the

---

[32] The mannerist painter Cristoforo Roncalli (1552-1626)
[33] Henriette Adelaide of Savoy (1636-1676), wife of the Elector of Bavaria, Ferdinand Maria

paintings, & they shew'd us one Pot with the history of Job, for wch they say the Emperour offer'd 6000 crowns. Lastly we 212isqué the cellar consisting of 12 large vaulted rooms full of prodigious large vessels one of wch they say holds 420 Barrels. Out of another they draw three sorts of wine, out of the same barrel, & only by turning the same cock. They reckon 132 vessels in this cellar. What they call the Pontilicial Palace is in the square before the Cathedral. The Jesuists, Poenitentiarys of the place, the Bp, & Governour live there.

Having satisfied our curiosity at Loretto on Sunday morning we set forward for Ancona, wch is 15 miles distant....

MODENA
15/26 May, 1734
Milles to the bishop[34]

[The excerpts chosen from this letter include a lengthy description of Ravenna and a brief account of Bologna, to be continued in the next letter of 21 May/1 June, 1734]

My Lord,

My last that I wrote to your Ldship, I wrote on the 24th of this month & sent it by the German post. Because this part of our journey has furnished abundant matter, & curiositys to us, I have therefore been obliged to be pretty long in my account, & because I would not be behind I have sent these letters so soon one after another....

The city of Ravenna is very much changed as to its former situation of pools being dry in wch it stood, so that it now stands on dry land. The sea likewise has forsook it, & is at three miles distance from it.[35]

---

[34]Add. 15773. This is the second letter in the collection for which an original exists (Gloucestershire Archives, Ref. D2663/Z8)

[35]Milles describes this further in his journal: "The city of Ravenna boasts of a very great antiquity to have been built 480 years after ye flood. it is still call'd Ravenna La Antica. this city was formerly of a very remarkable situation, particular to only ye city of Alexandria in Aegypt. viz: it was

Ravenna is at present a pretty large city, & tolerably well built, but not well inhabited. The Cardinal Legat residing here is not doubt of great advantage to the city. The Cathedral called the Basilica Urbiana is an old dark, & disagreeable building. The 4 Isles, & nave are supported by 56 marble pillars. The Tribune is all mosaic. Under the altar lye all the A:Bs (St Severus only excepted) who were elected by the holy Ghost. The doors of this church are made of large branches of vine of about a foot wide, & 2 inches thick. They are at present repairing this church, & digging up the pavement. They shewed me a skull that they found lately, wch by an inscription appears to be the skull of Cardinal Francis Alidosius Legat of Bolonia in the time of Julius the IId who was killed at Ravenna by Fransesco Maria Duke of Urban, & nephew to the Pope. The skull had three great wounds in it; one on the right side with a great peice of the skull cut out; another in the pole; & another on the top of the head. Meeting with a very exact account of so particular an action, in one Jeremy Rossi a very good writer of the history of Ravenna, I beg leave to relate it to our Ldship in a few words. In the troublesome times in Italy, the above said Cardinal complained to the Pope that he suspected his nephew to have some intelligence with the French King, upon wch the Pope was in a great rage. The Duke coming to Ravenna the next day to audience, the Pope would not receive him. The Duke in indignation goes towards the Cardinals lodgings, who was going to dine with the Pope. The D: meets him, goes up to him as to speak with him, with his left hand takes hold of his mules bridle, & with his right thrust his sword into his breast, tumbling him from his mule. One Mondulfus with a broad sword cut off his cheek, & car, wch was I beleive the same wound in the side of the skull. Philippus Auria wounded him in several places, & at last the Duke run him thro' & then got upon his mule, & rode quietly into Urbin. The Cardinal had a guard of sixty archers on horseback who never moved to his assistance. Being carried into a house he dyed soon after. This happened about 12 of

---

built in ye middle of pools, & marshes so yt ye whole city was built on piles, drove into ye water, & stood in ye middle of ye pools, with no passage to it by water... in some time these pools drying up, left ye twon on dry land as it is at present, & ye sea wch came close to it is now retir'd three miles from it..." Add. 15763, pp 43-44

the clock on the 24th of May in the year 1511. There is a sign of a cross on a peice of marble on the very spot where he was killed.[36]

The church of St Vitalis is by much the most beautifull in the city. It is an Octogon [sic] with a Portico all round. On the inside, above & below, the roof is very exalted, the whole cased with marble, & the pavement likewise formerly of beatifull mosaic. This church is supposed to have been built in Justinians time. It belongs to the Benedictines who have a very spacious, & handsome college here. In their garden we were shew'd a little church dedicated to St Nazarius & Celsus, built by Galla Placidia daughter of the Emperour Theodosius.[37] At the upper end of the church is a marble sarcophagus, very large in wch they say her body lyes. At the end of the cross Isles are 2 more of the same size, in one of wch is the body of Honorius her brother, & of Constantius her husband,[38] & in the other that of Valentinian, the third her son. At the entrance of the church are two more marble sarcophagus's in wch they say are the foster father, & nurse of the Queens children. The church of St Apotlinare [sic] is remarkable for the mosaic all along each side of the nave above the pillars. It is supposed to have been done by Theodorick & for that reason called aureu lecturm Theodorice. The pavement before the high altar is of very fine marbles. On the outside of the church, I copied the following inscription: Propagatori Romani nominis, fundatori Quielis publicae D:F:C: Constantini maximo victor, Semper Aug: Divi Claudi Nepoti, Divi Constanti filio Sertorius Silanus V: P: Praepositus Fabricae Devotu: N: M: Q: E: At the church of the Theatins called Spirito Santo in a window over the great altar is the figure of a Dove, & lighting on the persons head, who was to be chose A: B. After the death of St Apollinare, & so continued to do for 11

---

[36]Milles gives a more detailed account of this incident in his journal (*Ibid.*, pp 45-46) and notes that the remains had been found during renovations and improvements to the church ("they are about repairing ye church now & making it more beautifull. In their digging, they found ye skull, & bones..."). He also notes that another skull was found, "of another person kill'd by him, but I find no acct of it in history at ye place" (p.46)

[37]Aelia Galla Placidia (392-450 AD), daughter of the Roman Emperor Theodosius I

[38]Flavius Constantius (d. 421 AD), or Constantius III, was Western Roman Emperor for seven months in the year 421 AD

times. They shew'd us a stone on wch the dove rested, & the corner in wch Severus who was the last chosen in that manner, stood, & who was a very plain & simple man. Among the pictures of the great men of their order I observed one Thomas Gouldwell Anglus Eps C:R: in Tridentio Concilio contra haereticos & Anglia contra Elizabetham fidei Confesse conspicuous. Opposite to the church is the bed chamber of St Severus turned into a chappel. The church of St John the Evangelist, they pretend was miraculously consecrated by St John who appeared himself, & did it. In the court is a prodigious beautifull well done by Michael Angelo. The monks of St Romuald, besides a hansome convent have a most beautifull Library for the size of it. It has a little arch facing the street, & adjoining to the monastery of St Francis, is the monument of the famous Italian Poet Dantes, there is a bas-releive representing the Poet leaning on a desk, & reading, with his head crown'd with Laurel...

In the Piazza at Ravenna is a very good statue of bronze of Alexander the VII: & at one end, 2 granite composite pillars, on whc the arms & Patron of Venice stood, when they were masters of the place, now these are the statues of St Victor, & St Apollinaris. About half a mile out of Ravenna is the mausoleum erected by Ama[lasuntha][39] for the tomb of her father Theodoric. It is built of large hewn stone, is about 31 feet, but the most amazing part of this barrack is a stupendous large stone made concave, & which covers the whole top of the mausoleum. I measur'd it on the outside as well as the convexity of the stone would permit me & found it to be about 35 feet in diameter. It is a dark greyish stone. It is cut all round the extremitys into 12 pedestals, on wch stood the statues of the 12 Apostles, wch are now transported to Venice. There are the names of them wrote on the pedestals. In the middle the stone rises up a little on wch stood the Porphry Sarcophagus of Theodoric wch was beat off by a bomb, & is now fixed up in the wall of the convent of St Apollinaris. It is of that sort wch are

---

[39]The bishop or scribe obviously could not work out this word, as in the copy it is "Ama" followed by a gap, and the original has been amended with the result that it is difficult to read. Amalasuntha was the daughter of Theodoric by his wife Audofleda

much wider, & longer at top than at the bottom. The only thing that I
could measure was its length at bottom wch I found to be 9 feet.[40]

We left Ravenna on Wednesday noon, & travelled 20 miles to Faenza
thro' a very pleasant & fertile country. The city of Faenza is famous
for making very fine earthen ware,[41] Faenza is about the size of the
other middling city's. The cathedral, & great square are both very
beautifull. Before the former is a very fine fountain of bronze. There
is a very handsome stone bridge over the river now called Amone
formerly Anemo. The women of this city, & all about the country
instead of going bare headed, as many of the other women in Italy do,
cover their heads with very small straw hats, wch are not near so big
as a small pewter plate.[42] On Thursday morning we pursued our
journey to Bologna, 10 miles from Faventia. We pass'd thro' Forum
Cornelii now called Imola a middling city, with a very pretty Piazza or
square, & nothing else remarkable. It is situated on the Sanerno
formerly called Vatronus. Twenty miles further, in a flat pleasant
country brought us to Bologna, where we arrived about noon.

The city of Bologna is situated in a plain fertile country having the
Apennine mountains on the South, & the wide extended plain of
Lombardy on the East & West sides. After Rome I think it is the
largest city I have seen in Italy, & the most agreable. Allmost all the
streets have large & very handsome Portico's on each side, wch is a
manner of building we have not seen before in any part of Italy. They
are mighty convenient both in winter & summer being a very good
shelter both from the rain, as well as sun. Besides these the streets are

---

[40]On an otherwise blank page (between pages 50 and 51) in his journal,
Milles makes the following note: "I observed whilst I was at Ravenna
several towers of churches &c: most, or all of wch leant on one side, &
thee being two remarkable ones at Pisa, & Bologna, I am apt to beleive yt it
was a taste, wch ye architects got into at ye time, as a very particular thing."
Add. 15763

[41]This description is continued in his journal, where he notes, "call'd Delph,
in English, but Fayence from ye name of this place in French. *Ibid.*, on the
blank page between 51 and 52

[42]A strange analogy, and the first instance, throughout the whole of the
collection, where Milles comments on the costumes of the locals. In his
journal, he makes the same comparison, noting also that, "in other parts
they go quite bare-headed". *Ibid.*, p.55

very large; the houses well built of brick, & plaister'd over. The walls
of the city are computed to be five miles in circumference. Their
longest diameter a mile, & three quarters the number of souls 90,000. I
must defer a more particular account of Bologna to my next. We set
out from Bologna this morning for this place [Modena] wch is only at
20 miles distance. The country is flat as before, & towards this place
very marshy. About 6 or 7 miles from this place we pass'd by a strong
fort built by Urban the VIII, & called after his name. Within 3 or 4
miles of Modena we crossd the river Panaro in a boat, wch is a pretty
large river. Close to it are the limits of the Bolognese & the dutchy of
Modena.

Dr Pococke joins with me in humble Duty to your Lordship

I am my Lord your most Dutifull –

I hear that the Germans to the number of 30,000 are approaching near
Parma, with an intent as I suppose to besiege it, if the Germans had
not pass'd the Po, the French would have made themselves masters of
the D: of Modena's territorys by force, they were enter'd into
Mirandola

PADUA
21 May/1 June, 1734
Milles to the bishop[43]

[This letter continues the description of Bologna, with
the first two pages devoted to churches and monasteries.[44] An
interesting account of the Academy of the Institute for Sciences
is reproduced here, with a description of their meeting with a
famous female professor, together with an account of a religious
ceremony at Montagna della Guardia]

The Academy appointed for all sciences call'd the Institute, is one of
the best things in its kind that we have seen since we have been
abroad.[45] It was richly endowed, & one may say in a manner founded
by General Marsili. For it is to him that it owes all its splendour. As to
the building it is a very handsome Palace, built round a square court.
In one corner of it are places several old inscriptions, & a very fine
Greek trunk in armour. The apartments of the Academy are laid out
in the following manner.[46] The first room is appointed for the scholars
of painting to learn to draw &c. In the second are the models of
several of the finest statues in Rome done in Gess.[47] The third room is
appointed for the study of Architecture, in the fourth are the models of
all the obelisks, large pillars &c. that are in Rome. In the 5th chamber
are placed all the peices of drawing that have gained the yearly prize,
wch is six medals of gold. In the 6th are those drawings of Architecture
that have gained the prize, with the names of the authors. The 7th is
set apart for operations in Chimistry. The 8th for the art of Navigation.
The room is adorned with models & pictures of vessels & a little
cabinet of books relating to that science. The 9th is to be made a
Library. In the 10th are several machines for turning &c. The 11th is the
chamber where they give the prize every year. The 12th is where the

---

[43]Add. 15773. There is no original for this letter

[44]A similar account is given in Milles' journal (Add. 15763, pp 55-69)

[45]The account of the Institute in Milles' journal (*ibid.*) extends from pp 69-72
and in Pococke's journal (Add. 22982) from pp 73-78

[46]Pococke, in his journal, gives a similar account of the rooms and their uses,
though not in quite such an orderly manner. See Add. 22928, pp 62-64

[47]Gesso, a mix of an animal glue binder, usually rabbit-skin glue, chalk, and
white pigment, used to coat hard surfaces such as wooden painting panels

Academy of sciences meet. The 13th at present serves for a Library till
the other is finished. The 14th is full of all sorts of antiquitys, amongst
wch I observed a collection of all sorts of Hetrurian & Roman weights,
some of the latter were stamped on money, all sorts of
Lacrymatoires,[48] sepulchral urns, & lamps. Idols of all sorts,
instruments of sacrifice &c. The 15th is fill'd with instruments for
experimental Philosophy, wch seemed for the most part to be inferior
to ours. The 16th with loadstones & other things of the like nature.
The 17th is for the study of fortification, & is fill'd with models of
Bastions mines & all things belonging to that art. In the 18th are all the
different sorts of marbles, & stones, as well Pellucid as not. All round
the 19th are glass cases filled with all sorts of earths, fossils, minerals,
sulphurs, alums, vitriols, & all things of the country. They find it three
or four miles off, it has no particular virtue as I was inform'd till it has
been prepared; wch is done by baking it, after wch if you put it in the
sun for a small time, or even if the sun dos not shine, & afterwards
look at it in the dark, it will have so imbibed the rays of light, that it
will appear, just like a burning peice of charcoal. It loses this light by
degrees. It will not imbibe any light from a candle. They have 2 in a
box together, wch they sell for half a crown. The 20th chamber is filled
with all sorts of sea corals, & all products of the sea in the vegetable
kind - spunges &c. The 21st has all sorts of exotick seeds, & fruits,
leaves, gums, woods, barks of trees, fungi, & Tubera. The 22 is full of
all extraordinary sorts of animals, serpents of all kinds, one of wch
was 20 feet long, of that sort called the hooded serpent [cobra] from
where they take that famous stone;[49] the back part of its hood, exactly
resembles the face of an owl. There are likewise all sorts of shell fish,
& other fish, birds flying insects & butterflys. From hence we ascended
a square brick tower, built for their Astronomical observations. At the
top is a square room with windows all round, & full of instruments for
observation. I observed that they have even dared to have a model of

---

[48]Lachrymatories were bottles in which tears were collected and placed at the
    tombs or graves of loved ones. While they were first used in antiquity, there
    was a revival of these objects in the Victorian period
[49]That sold in boxes, as described above

Copernicus's system in brass wch in Rome would be a very high crime nay even to speak of it, as of a true system.[50]

The fabric of the public schools was raised in 1562. They are built round a square court, & are a handsome building. The schools are in number 54. Just at the entrance of the gate I saw an inscription erected in memory of the famous Talicotius Theorist in ordinary; famous for his great skill in anatomy. Besides this, there are the memorials of all the great men that have been of the university, with the arms of all the strangers, who have had their Doctors degree here. In the anatomy school the chair is supported by 2 human figures of wood representing all the muscles, & nerves of the human body. Round the room in niches are the statues of some of the greatest anatomists, amongst whc is that of Talicotius with a nose in his right hand. In another school we saw another inscription to the same Talicotius....

Whilst we have been here, we have had the pleasure of conversing for 3 or 4 hours with Laura Catherina Bassi the noted lady who was made a Doctor of this University, & performed all her exercises.[51] I cannot but say, that we found an uncommon spirit, & genius in all her conversation, & tho' we changed the subject three, or four times, yet she appeared to have a very good understanding of every thing. She was prodigiously obliging, & shew'd us the habit in wch she appears in at the schools. For she is obliged to read 3 or 4 public lectures every year; for wch she has 25 P a year allowed to her. At those times she goes habited with a short cloak of black, & white fur lined with red. When she took her degree she wore a silver crown in imitation of

---

[50]The heliocentric system proposed by the Polish astronomer Nicolai Copernicus (1473-1543) in his book *On the Revolutions of the Heavenly Bodies*, in which it was proposed that the Sun (rather than the Earth) was the centre of the Solar System.

[51]Laura Maria Caterina Bassi (1711-1778) would have been only 23 years of age when Milles & Pococke met her. She had been appointed as Professor of Anatomy in 1731 at the University of Bologna, elected to the Academy of the Institute for Sciences in 1732 and in 1733 was given the Chair of Philosophy. She was described in similar terms by other visitors to Bologna. In his journal, Milles refers to three other women from the 14th century who took their degrees in this university; and adds, "& Laura Maria Caterina Bassi, who at present enjoys yt dignity" (Add. 15763, p.73). See also Pococke's description of this lady (Letter 17 & journal entry) below

Laurel. She told us that what she studied at first, was only for her pleasure, wch grew upon her prodigiously, till by continual application she arrived to the knowledge she at present is mistress off [sic]. I have a medal of brass, wch was struck for her, on it her head & round the fore part is this inscription - soc: anno 20 1732. On the reverse is Minerva, holding away her Gorgons shield from, & with her right hand holding a lamp to this Lady, who has a book open in her hand. Between them is a globe on wch is perch'd an owl; round it is this inscription Soli cui fas fidesse Minervam.

Plate 8
Medal commemorating Laura Maria Caterina Bassi Italy, 1732
Courtesy of the Science Museum, London

At three miles distance from Bologna on a mountain called Montagna della Guardia, they keep a Madonna painted by St Luke, wch they have a custom every year on the Saturday before Ascension Sunday to bring in state to Bologna, where there are great processions &c. till Thursday following, when she is carried back again, & in order to carry her with more grandeur, & conveniency they have built a Portico from the gate of the town, quite up to the church wch are above three miles. We took a walk up there on Saturday morning. The Portico is built of brick, cover'd at the top, & supported by square pilasters of brick, either one side or the other all the way is walled up, so the Portico is only left open on one side. It is from 12, to 10 feet wide well paved, & indeed a very grand, & surprising thing, & what is yet more that, as it is all done by different persons, there are several parts of it built at the collective expence of servants, & day labourers. It is finished all to a small part at the church, wch likewise they are going to build anew, & very handsome. On Saturday afternoon about two hours before night we saw the procession enter. It was preceeded [sic] by Torches, Lamps, Crosses, trumpets & drums &c. After wch came the preists singing the Litany; then came the Madonna prodigious richly adorned with Gold & jewels, & with flowers of silver all round her, but nothing of the picture itself to be seen. Over it is carried a Canopy, & because it was fair weather they made no use of the Portico. The people as it passed by were all on their knees & express'd as much veneration for it as if the Virgin Mary in person was present. As soon as ever it enter'd the gates of the city the canon were fired & all the bells of the city rung to give notice of its arrival. It was carried to the nuns of St Mathias, where it remains till Sunday, when they carry it to a different church, & on Thursday carry it back again. All the four intermediale days they make great processions thro' the city & carry her each day to a different church.

This I think is all that is worth communicating to your Ldship concerning Bologna. I believe I must be obliged to defer my account of Modena till the next letter.[52] We left Bologna on Sunday morning,

---

[52]They visited Modena on a short excursion. According to Milles' journal, they departed from Modena on Thursday 27 May "about 4 of ye clock in ye morning", returning to Bologna, from which city they then departed "on Sunday ye 30th at ye same hour" they left Bologna taking the road for Ferrara, about 35 miles distant. Add. 15763, p.83

go to Ferrara by noon staid till the next day, & on Monday morning left it, & arrived here at Padoua about 6 or 7 of the clock at night.[53] To morrow we propose to leave this place, & go to Venice when your Ldship shall hear from me by the first opportunity. Dr Pococke joins with me in humble Duty, & respects to your Ldship

I am my Lord your Ldships most Dutifull

VENICE
30 May/10 June, 1734
Milles to the bishop[54]

[In this letter Milles gives an account of Modena and Padua. The excerpts reproduced here relate to their visit to the Duke's Library at Modena, the Duke's family, the fountains at Abano, the city of Padua and an update on the war]

My Lord,

My last I sent to your Ldship immediately after our arrival at Padoua. In it I finished an account of Bologna. I shall now begin that of Modena. On Wednesday the 26th we set out for that place, wch is 20 good miles distant from it. The city is but small, & the fortifications are but weak.[55] It is tolerably well built, has double Portico's like Bologna, & does not seem to want for inhabitants. The Palace of the Duke, wch is but half finished, will be the most beautifull one in Italy. It has a large square turret in the middle, & one at each end. It is built with brick, the doors & window cases of stone. Within is to be a large

---

[53]Neither traveller described Ferrara in their correspondence, but both wrote a substantial account of its history and principal buildings in their journals

[54]Add. 15773. The original letter exists (Gloucestershire Archives, Ref. D2663/Z8)

[55]According to Pococke's journal, "The city of Modena is fortified a la moderne the fortification extending beyond the city almost a mile to the west so that there are no suburbs; Two or three streets of the town are tolerably well built with Portcos as at Bologna, the rest but indifferent & looks poorly." Add. 22982, p.89

Quadrangle, with a double Portico all round. It is not finished. The apartments we could not see, because the Duke had pack'd up his pictures & other valuable goods ready to be sent away, whenever the French should enter the city.56

We were recommended here by father Mountfaucon57 to one Muratori a very learned man & Library keeper to the Duke.58 He shew'd us the Library which consists of five rooms59 all full of printed books, & another of manuscripts; amongst wch he shew'd us one of St Matthews gospel thought to be about a thousand years old. This Muratori has published 22 vols. of a body of all the Italian historians who have wrote on Italy.60 The cathedral is an old dark building & has nothing remarkable in it. In a room by it they shew'd us the famous bucket stole from the Bolognese so much celebrated by the name of La Secchia rapita.61 The church of the Dominicans is the most beatifull in Modena. It being the feast of St Philip Nerius, whilst we were there, we saw the Duke62 his two unmarried daughters, & the son & two daughters of the Prince who married the D: of Orleans's

---

[56]A fact noted by both travellers, in their letters and journals

[57]Thus spelled both in the copy and the original, though the correct version appears in all previous references to this man

[58]Ludovico Antonio Muratori (1672-1750) held the position of Archivist and Librarian in Modena's Ducal library, from 1700 until his death. See Pococke's brief account of this meeting, below (Letter 17, Add. 22978)

[59]According to Pococke's journal, there were four rooms plus one for manuscripts. *Ibid.*, p.73

[60]His Rerum *Italicarum Scriptores ab Anno aerae Christianae 500 ad Annum 1500* was published in Milan from 1723. The number of volumes differs according to the various accounts. In a letter, Pococke notes that there are 28 volumes; in his journal he notes, "there are or are to be 25 volumes in folio", and, as we have seen, Milles (both in the original and in the copy letter) gives 22 as the number

[61]Milles explains this further in his journal: "They shew'd us in a room adjoining to it, wch was firmly bar'd, & bolted a bucket of wood, wch when ye Modenese, had war with ye Bolognese they stole from them, & ever since have hung it up on triumph, & they say moreover yt ye Bolognese would give any money to have ye bucket again so inconsiderable a thing as this had made a great deal of noise in ye world, so yt that there has been an Italian Poem worte on it, call'd La Secchia rapita". Add. 15763, p.82

[62]Rinaldo d'Este (1655-1737)

daughter63 come to the church to the exposition & benediction.64 The Duke is about 80 years of age, of a middling stature very thin, pale, & feeble. He wore a great black tye wig the curls standing up a foot above his head, according to the old fashion; he had a white cravat round his neck, & as well as I could perceive in the dark a black coat on.65 Seeing us there & strangers, he was mighty inquisitive of the persons who were about him to know who we were. The two princesses his daughters are about 20, & 22 years of age, & are handsome enough. The Princes son, is a fine boy about 5, or 6 years old. He was dress'd like a hussar having sort of boots half way up his legs. His two sisters about the same age are fine plump children...66

We arrived at Padua that evening & early the next morning walked seven miles to see the fountains of Abano, one of the greatest curiositys we have seen in Italy.67 It even exceeds the Solferata. It is situated amongst the Euganean Mountains. The springs rise on an

---

[63]In 1721, the Prince, Francesco Maria (1698-1780) married Charlotte Aglaé d'Orléans (1700-1761)

[64]Their three children were: Ercole d'Este (1727-1803) and his sisters, Maria Teresa Felicitas d'Este (1726-1754) & Matilde d'Este (1729-1803)

[65]Milles is less than charitable in his journal account of the Duke: "Ye day we were at Modena we had ye good luck to see ye Duke & all ye family. He is about 80 & a very ugly face, he wears a great black tye wigg, wch frises up in ye forehead about half a foot according to ye old fashion. He wears a cravat about his neck, & goes in black cloaths plain". Note the difference of six inches between his two accounts of the ducal wig. Add. 15763, p.82

[66]In Letter 17 (Add. 22978), Pococke describes the Duke's family as follows: "[H]e is 80 years old, Brother to a late Queen of England, father of the Dowager of Parma. Very thin, wears a high black wig in deep red trim'd with black, a stiffness in his neck & a very odd figure. We were told he asked who we were; the eldest daughter is very handsom; the Prince his only son married the Duke of Orleans's sister, they lived at Reggio but on the war retired to Genoa, their son & 2 daughters we saw, the eldest 6, the son [seemed to be cloth'd in a ... but wn he came out of ye coach was dress'd like a hussar or highlander] close up the legs & thighs with no shirts, fine children." The line in square brackets is supplied by the original letter (Add. 19939), that from the copy having been scored out. In his journal Pococke makes no mention of the family's dress

[67]This place, and the experiments he conducted with eggs, are described in greater detail in his journal, and include ancient references to its medicinal qualities. See Add. 15763, pp 90-92

elevated ground. The soil is so impregnated with sulphur, that the water boils up continually, & that with just as much heat as water boiling over a fire. One cannot bear ones finger a moment in the water. I made an experiment there by boiling some eggs, wch I did in different springs, & I found in four minuits that they were well done, & even in three minuits sufficient for some peoples taste. The water is of the same colour with other water, tasts68 a little of sulphur, but nothing near so much as that of Solferata; & hardly smells of it at all. The prodigious steam that arises from these 3, or 4 springs is very great, & made me sweat terribly. The ground also under my feet was so hot that I could hardly bear it. From the water there arises a white scurf wch hardens into stone. But the greatest curiosity of these waters is, that between & allmost close to these very hot sulphurreous waters, there arise four other sorts of waters coming from minerals all of a different nature, viz from Vitriol, Lead, & Salt. That of iron I think is the hottest after the sulphureous water. The colour of the water is inclined to red, it is more than warm. The scurf at bottom is of several sorts of red, & consists of several coats one over another. The water tasts strong of the mineral. That of Vitriol is of a greenish colour, tasts very strong of the Vitriol & is warm only, a green scum arises from it. That of Lead is close to it, it is of the same warmth, & strength, a leadish colour'd scum arises from it. That of salt does not taste very saltish, & is only luke warm a yellowish scum settles at bottom & the water flings up a small quantity of prodigious fine salts. These waters are conveyed into houses wherein are baths, wch they can easily make hotter, or colder according to the occasions of the person that bathes. The Italian Physicians are so ignorant, that I beleive they have searched very little into the virtues of these waters, wch must be very great. There is no great use made of them I think. These fountains were called fonts Aponi by the ancients.

We returned to Padoua about noon.[69] The city is really very large, & I beleive the walls may be between 5, or 6 miles in circuit. The fortifications seem to be pretty strong, tho the walls are low, & the

---

[68]Thus in both the original and the copy

[69]For the journal descriptions of Padua, see Milles (Add. 15763, pp 92-101) & Pococke (Add. 22982, pp 99-108)

fosses shallow.[70] There is a great deal of space within the walls, wch is waste ground, & not built upon. The houses for the generality are ill built & the streets narrow, & have double Porticos. The cathedral is building anew, & not yet finished. In it is the monument of Cardinal Barbadicus the Bp of this city....

The town house of Padoua is a very fine Gothick building adorned with 2 Porticos one over the other. The Hall is a prodigious large room, but withal dark, & disagreable. It has in it several notarys & other shops. At one end is the monument of Livy the famous historian, whose bones likewise they pretend to have found. I could not find that they had good reason for their suppositions. They found in the same place, or near it the following antique inscription, wch they have put up as part of his monument V:F/ TITVS: LIVIVS/ LIVIAE T: F:/ QVARTAE: L:/ HALYS/ CONCORDIALIS/ PATAVI/ SIBI ET SVIS/ OMNIBVS/ I made these marks[71] to distinguish the lines in order that the inscription might take up less room...

The famous university of Padoua is reduced to one single College called the public schools. It is a very beautifull building, built round a square court with a double Portico. There are 11, or 12 publick schools, & a good theatre for Anatomy. I observed arms & names of severall Englishmen, who had taken their degrees here. There is still remaining some part of the Amphitheater of Padua. It is of an oval figure 139 paces long, & 85 wide. The arches are 6 feet 10 inches wide, & the peers 3 feet. It is built of square white hewn stone cemented with mortar. It now serves for a court to a palace. The garden of simples [medicinal garden] in this city is the best we have seen in Italy. It is of a circular form, has a tolerable number of plants & is well kept. The garden of Papa fava a noble Venetian is likewise remarkable on the same account.[72]

---

[70]In his journal, Milles has the following footnote about the fortifications: "Padoua besides ye fortifications yt surround ye whole city, part of it surrounded by a simple wall, some are so ignorant as to think to be ye walls built by Antenor". Add. 15763, p.92

[71]The marks he refers to are, in the original, straight lines, indicated here with a slash

[72]This is further described by Pococke in Letter 17 below (Add. 22978).

We left Padua on Wednesday morning...[73] We made all the haste we possibly could in order to arrive in Venice on the Ascension to see the famous ceremony of the Doge marrying the sea;[74] wch we accomplished, but as I shall not have room to speak of it in this letter, I must defer it to my next.[75]

Last Friday I had the honour of the bill from Mr. Hoare wch your Ldship was so good as to send me, & two or three days after your Ldships came to hand. We do not purpose to stay here any longer then we can see the famous things of the city wch we shall dispatch soon.

We have an account here that the Germans have taken possession of Parma & that the French abandoned it to them; & that the prince Eugene has been forced to make a retreat on the Rhine, & to lose his lines. The Emperour has set a price on the K: of Sardinia whoever brings him dead or alive, nay it is even said that the German forces in Italy propose to march to Turin. But this last is not certain. General Mercy who commands the Emperours forces in Italy has allmost lost his eye sight, for wch he has bathed at Albano.[76] It is doubted whether he will return to the Army.

These my Lord are some little intelligences that we receive here concerning the present posture of affairs.

Dr Pococke desires his humble Duty to your Ldship

I am my Lord Your Lordships most

---

[73] According to his journal, the date was Wednesday, 2 June
[74] A traditional ceremony performed in Venice on Ascension Day
[75] Pococke's detailed version of this ceremony is reproduced in the next letter (Letter 17, Add. 22978)
[76] The hot springs described above

VENICE
31 May/11 June, 1734
Pococke to his mother
Letter 17[77]

[As mentioned in the introduction to this section, this letter covers a period of more than three weeks, from 11 May to 4 June, 1734. Since part of Milles' account of the journey from Rome to Venice (via Bologna, Modena and Padua) has already been reproduced, the excerpts from this letter, which begins at their arrival in Bologna, have been chosen for their more general and personal interest. Included here are transcripts from the journals, the first being Pococke's description of the Bolognese people and a further two giving the travellers' first impressions of Venice]

20. Passed though Immola Forum Cornelii 10 miles,[78] & 20 miles further at noon arrived a Bologna... I lay below at the Borgo, demanded what I was to pay over night before I eat, - they told me a penny my bed, I might have a pennyworth of soup, 1d & salad, to which at supper I added a 1d fricassee & 1d cheese, & a large quart of wine 1d more; I had the best vermicelli soup I ever eat all served very well, I paid 9d in the morning, 2d more than my reckoning came to [I made no words].[79] There are two monasteries one in the town, the other in the country, & one nunnery in the town...

21....[When ye box we have sent from Rome arrives I shall beg the favour of you t open it & I beleive you may examine into evry thing that is in it so yt the things yt are in the small boxes together be kept by them selves without being mixd because of different properties, likewise the maps; ye two small boxes incl are mine; the two large ones my friends; it is one comfort to see if I were ever to be able to send you or my sister any thing, ..cd not be sent by reason of ye strict

---

[77]Add. 22978. This is the seventh letter of the original collection (Add. 19939) and a note next to the English address states that it was received by Mrs. Pococke on 21 June and answered on 27 June, 1734, to Langres
[78]Imola is a town in the province of Bologna, known in ancient times as Forum Cornelii, after L. Cornelius Sulla, who founded it around 82 BC
[79]Scored out of the copy

searches are every where made; ye 8 vol fol of Bullarium Romanum are to remain at Newtown till ye Bp orders about them][80]

22. Went to see churches & monasteries, which are very fine & spacious here & beautiful libraries & good paintings, staid within the afternoon by reason of rain. The common price of wine on the road was 1d a quart & once I had it for ½ & good enough some of it; at Tolentino 4 pd of cherries for ½ the common price every where is a ½ penny a pd the best sorts. We pay here 1s 6d for dinner each, eat very well, five dishes & a desert by our selves, 6 each for beds, we went out towards the evening. Gratian the great Lawyer who compiled the Decretate is buried in St Petronius...[81]

24. Saw St Dominicks Sepulchre at an altar in a fine chapel at the Dominicans, & at Corpus Domini St Catherine of Bologna[82] dressed up very fine, sitting, we saw her through a grate over an altar, she looks black in face & hands which is all one sees & an ugly sight it is, I could not see that her nails & hair grew, as it said; they gave us a piece of her garment & cotten & some powder for fervours. ...

26. We had a letter from Muratori the Dukes Library Keeper who has published 28 vols of the Italian Historians in fol.[83] Is writing against Burnet de statu mortuorum, & an account of the Learning & Antiquities of the middle dark ages:[84] We had much discourse with him in the Dukes Library. The Dukes palace is a very noble beautiful building, one side not finished; we saw the Duke & 2 daughters going to church...[85] Before the Germans came, the French sent to desire him to put the town & fort into their hands, to protect him, which he

---

[80]It is not clear why this passage was deleted from Mrs. Pococke's copy, since there is nothing of any particular sensitivity in it

[81]Gratian wrote and compiled the *Decretum Gratiani* or *Concordia Discordantium Canonum* (a collection of Canon law) in the 12th century

[82]A native of Bologna (1413-63), and founder of the Order of Poor Clares, she was canonised in 1712. She is still to be seen in the same fashion as described by Pococke, seated on a gold throne surrounded by gilt cherubs and angels

[83]See Milles' account, above

[84]Probably his *Antiquitates Italicæ Medii Oevi*, published in six volumes (Milan, 1738–42)

[85]See the full text of his description reproduced above

refused: ordered all his pictures &c to be packed up & was ready for a march to some retirement, so that he could see nothing in the palace but that is however...

27. In the evening at Bologna.

28. Saw Palazzo del Monte, the publick palace where we saw a Ladies picture with along beard & Aldrovandi's 200 large volumes writ with his own hand,[86] & the palace Sampieri.[87] We went to see Madam Laura, Maria Caterina Bassa,[88] to whom they gave a Doctors degree here in Philosophy, & she is now a Lecturer in Philosophy & reads 4 times a year in the Schools, in a cloak of skin lined with red silk, as other Doctors, she wears black at that time turned a little back with Diamond loops, as I saw by her picture there in wax-work her watch hung before in the middle, at her creation they gave her a crown of silver in imitation of laurel, which she wore then only, under her picture were these lines:

Ingenium Specta Pallade major erit
Si faciem Spectes, Veneris illa lepores.

& on the reverse being a large medal struck is.... Soli cui fas vidisse Minervam.[89]

We had much talk with her about the methods of the university, the Institute for which she is fellow, & answers to the Royal Society, about systems of Philosophy, Hypotheses &c: she talks exceedingly well on all Learned Subjects, has a good address & is in all respects a very accomplished woman, agreeable but not handsome.[90]

---

[86]The famous naturalist, Ulisse Aldrovandi (1522-1605), born in Bologna and author of hundreds of scholarly works
[87]Famous for its frescoes by Annibale Carracci (1560-1609)
[88]See the account given by Milles in his letter from Modena (21 May/1 June, 1734), reproduced above
[89]See Plate 8 for an image of this coin, acquired by Milles at the Institute
[90]See the description by Milles, above. Pococke also mentions Professor Bassi in his journal, as follows: "Among the lecturers is a Lady of the name of Laura Maria Caterina Bassi whom they gave the degree of a doctress in Philosophy" (Add. 22982, p.73). He notes the three other ladies who took

29. Walked 3 miles, half of it up a high hill to a church where is kept a Madonna painted by St Luke...[91] & they say formerly the picture used to come itself, & the people go up frequently to this church on the hill to pay their devotions... Windows of all the streets it passes through are hung with silk & damask, the piers of the Portico of the street where it passes are hung in like manner, & strings being carried from one window to another & silk hung along on them, the procession begins; first, there come men in surplices with silver top'd staves, then two crosses are carried, drums beating, then 4 glass Lanthorns [lanterns] with candles, trumpets, several persons with candles, Priests before it, in & the Image is carried on two silver staves under a canopy supported by 8 persons 2 Lanthorns after, it is adorned with made flowers all about, behind is a sort of covering of flowered velvet, red, & yellow, coming from the top & stretching out like a hoop petticoat, & about are chains of Gold, at top a crown, they go along singing with intermezzos of trumpets & drums, when it comes into the gate the canons are fired, all the bells jangle, for they never ring in these countries, the people throw flowers out of the windows, all go out to meet it & the road & streets are lin'd with coaches, the Ladies in their coaches, coachmen in their boxes, all fall on their knees as it passes by, the windows are crowded & the women throw out flowers on it as it passes along; it is carried into a church & set up over the altar & musick is performed for a short time. The churches it passes by are all open & the altars illuminated, the four days it staies in town there are great processions made to it by the magistrates & companies, & every day it is moved to another church.

---

their degrees there, and the years, and in an asterisk, on the reverse of this page, has a footnote which is difficult to decipher, though largely commenting on the medal struck in Professor Bassi's honour, and on her dress

[91] See the less elaborate account of this procession in the letter from Milles to the bishop (21 May/1 June, 1734) above

[On 30 May, the cousins depart from Bologna]

Milles' Journal Account of the People of Bologna[92]

The people of Bologna are very learned, their university is famous, & the institute is a great advantage in studying all the liberal arts & science... They are a very polite obliging people, especially to strangers & seem to take a particular pleasure in being civil to them. [Footnote 4: They are withal very religious & devout & spare no cost in what they think may be for the honour of Religion] Those middling sort of people that value themselves on being citizens, dress in black jackets as at Florence tho' one sees but few of them. The dress of the women is very modest, a black petticoat, their bodice commonly colourd wch you do not see as they have a black scarfe wch comes over their heads brought across their arms, & comes almost down to the ground, & is gatherd about their faces, is only a peice of plain black silk. This is the universal dress except of Ladies of quality who dress after the French manner. [Footnote 1: I observd in the country round about, many poor children with a sort of Bulla either round or in shape of a Lozenge coverd over with cloth, which doubtless is a custom come down from the Romans] [Footnote 2: The Patrons or Protectors of this city are St Petronius, St Florianus, St Proculus, & St Dominique. They permit no Jews to live in there & those that pass through the town are obligd to go to one certain inn"] Add. 22982, pp 86-87. Milles, in his journal, has a footnote on the women's dress in Modena and Bologna: "The women of Modena for ye most part wear a sort of black silk scarf, wch covers all their heads, & flyes behind them, ye women of Bologna wear ye same but bring it over their arms before ym as they wear scarfs in England".

---

[92]Pococke, Add. 15763, p.82

30. I travelled 30 miles by 11 a clock to Fierrara..

31. We passed over the Po, went through Rovigo where the Bishop of Adra resides & then over the Adige by Monsalice [Monselice] near 40 miles to Padoua, we were told as we were going over that they had seen several naked bodies swim down, which probably were dispatch'd in some slight skirmishes,[93] when the Germans passed the Po tho' we hear none for they all ran away & the germans are in Parma & march directly to Turin, but 'tis said P. Eugene has lost 1200 men on the Rhine since, whc I hear, it was only a good retreat. From Monsalice we turned aside to Arqua to see Petrarch' house & tomb.[94]

June 1. [In Padua] The schools are a good building exactly like Bologna. About 1000 students mostly for Physic, the Physick garden is [round],[95] a balustrade on the top of the wall, 'tis the best I ever saw; has all curious thing in it Fountains &c: saw another garden for pleasure called Papafava belonging to a noble Venetian of that name, it is laid out in parterres & grass-plats[96] enclosed with high cut Elm hedges, very pleasant, & an intricate Labyrinth of box, small but difficult to find, the garden is not above a quarter of a mile round; they pretend to show Antenors tomb their founder. The City is 7 miles round, with new fortifications, but many gardens & meadows within, not many houses empty, & about 60,000 people they say in it.

2. Saw the gardens mentioned & St Justina.[97] at 10 went 18 miles by Dolo to Fusina, where we got into a Gondola & went 5 miles to Venice, a city you know as it were in the sea, an odd place & which does not please me; the Piazza at St Mark the only pleasing thing that's

---

[93]This horrific detail is also noted by Milles: "The boatmen told us that they had seen great numbers of dead bodys carried down the river the effect of some skirmish & suppose when the Germans passed this river". See his letter from Venice, May 20/June 10 (Add. 15773)

[94]This is where the celebrated Italian poet, scholar & renaissance humanist died, in 1374

[95]Thus in the original, though "of circular..." in the copy. Subsequent editing of both versions has made the sentence difficult to decipher

[96]A parterre is a formal garden with beds and paths arranged to form a pattern; and a grass-plat denotes an area of grass in a formal garden often surrounded by flower borders

[97]The Basilica of St. Justine, at Padua

obvious;[98] we dress'd went with Father Montfaucon's letter to his Excellence Signor Tiepolo a noble Venetian Procurator of St Mark & formerly Embassador in France, & they say, stands fair for next Doge,[99] he received us very civilly, was dress'd, in a brown damask night gown, slippers the same, no cravat, a tye wig, lives in a fine Palace.

3. Saw the great ceremony of the marriage of the Doge with the sea, of which in my next. [100] I found your letter here of April 14th [101] [& credit for £40 for which I thank you, Mr Bagwell you see has sent £100 to Mr Hoare wch is just the sum Mr Hoare has sent, but I never heard of ye 1st £50 any way till I had a letter from Bagwell 2 months ago as I mention'd to you I desire you to know of Mr Hoare whether he has sent any bill for ye money as he promised me if twas sent to Genoa as it ought I had left directions to have it forwarded to Rome & not receiving it has been a great disappointment & by wch I lost ye sight of xxx.[102] Mr Bagwell had a letter from Mr Hoare of ye receipt of the first as he wrote me word: I am very glad my cozen Tommy has a tutor that keeps him close to his business wch is the way to avoid evil & learn what is good & I don't doubt but my uncle returns his thanks for it].[103] I am sorry to hear Mr M. Is so near his end as he must be, if he goes so much out of his way, as to go to church.[104] At Bologna we had excellent cherries 2 inches round near 1 inch long white hearts ½ a pd. 4d. I cant well liken the Pope, his face is pale [some thing like R. Cummins but not so big any way].[105] The Doge is like an old

---

[98] See Pococke's journal entry about Venice, below

[99] He did not make it to this position, the next Doge being Alvise Pisani (1664-1741), elected to this office the following year, in January 1735

[100] This ceremony was established around the year 1000, symbolising the maritime dominion of Venice

[101] The following passage in scored out in Mrs. Pococke's copy. As in earlier letters, Pococke was anxious to delete any reference to his financial problems

[102] This word is obliterated from the original, but perhaps "Naples", as mentioned in an earlier letter

[103] Thomas Milles, the errant son of Pococke's uncle, Jeremiah Milles

[104] Pococke's uncle, who as mentioned earlier, was ill

[105] This spiteful comment was deleted from the copy, but the identity of Mr. Cummins is not known

woman,[106] has a camerick coif with long ends coming down like old fashioned night caps, a cassock & gown of silver, flowered with gold, an ermin mantle, the length of 3 ermins, the black tails of which hang down, his cap is in this form [sketch] the high part behind; [he's some thing like Goody Long but a large face & plumper][107] fair & red, pretty old of no power, none of 'em [I thank you for yr good thanks & advices][108]

4. This day I received your letter of April 30th & Bagwell's inclosed [in wch I am much oblig'd to your for your kind offers. I heard not of ye Princesses going to bath][109]. Ld Harcourt,[110] Ld Rockingham an Etonian,[111] Duke of Leeds,[112] Mr Crow,[113] Mr Colthrop Etonian[114] &c: are here [It will be a satisfaction to me if Ben lets me know by you whether Mr Barbon received the spirit & a small box].[115] We shall set out Sunday afternoon with Mr Crow up the river to Padua, Monday night we shall hear an opera at Vicenza, at which Faranelli sings,[116] & on Tuesday go to Verona & then make the best of our way home

---

[106]The Doge at the time of their visit was Carlo Ruzzini (1653-1735), who by then was almost 80 years of age

[107]Another comment which Pococke, in later life, thought may be better to omit from his memoirs

[108]Deleted in the copy

[109]This lines is scored out in the the the copy

[110]The elusive 2nd Viscount Harcourt (1714-77) noted in Letter 12 (Rome), whom Pococke failed to meet until 13 June, 1734, at Venice, where he gave a glowing account of the young man (see Letter 19)

[111]Lewis Watson, 2nd Earl Rockingham (c. 1714-45) travelled in Italy from 1733-34 with his tutor, E. Clarke. See Ingamells, *op.cit.*, 819-20

[112]Thomas Osborne, 4th Duke of Leeds (1713-89) was travelling in Italy in 1734 with his cousin, Robert Hay. See Ingamells, *op.cit.*, 592

[113]The same Rev. Benjamin Crowe (c. 1689-1749) noted by Pococke in Letter 13 (Rome), who was Chaplain for the English Factory at Leghorn from 1716-29 and then visited Italy again from 1733-34 as tutor to Sir Hugh Smithson

[114]Already noted by Pococke in Letter 12 (Rome)

[115]It is not clear why this sentence was deleted from the copy. Mr. Barbon was the senior clergyman in Waterford whose death was to provide Milles with a preferment (see below)

[116]The celebrated castrato singer, whose real name was Carlo Maria Broschi (1705-82). Later that year (1734) he went to London, where he joined the Opera of Nobility company

through Germany, at some distance from the Rhine north wards, but in my next you will hear more. [Pray my very kind affections to my sister]. Lingue vill a young General of the Emperour riding round Colorna after they had taken it, not far from Parma, was shot by two priests out of a window, he was a Lorrainer & so beloved, that the soldiers would have torn the priest to pieces, but they are reserved for justice, not without some suspicion that they were soldiers drest in priests habit, & the Germans gave the soldiers leave to plunder the Town.[117] [My best respects to White oak]

I am Dear Madam

Your Most obedient & Dutifull Son

Richard Pococke.

---

[117]It has been impossible to verify this account

Pococke's Journal Account of Venice[118]

The extra ordinary situation of Venice is, so every one has heard much of, at the nearest part four miles from the Continent, was at first built on an Island or a few Islands & finding it for their advantage surrounded by the sea they begun to build in the water by piling & laying the foundation on the piles it is sd there are 72 Islands, if every part that is surrounded by water be an Island there are they say a great many more. All this bay of Venice is very shallow & is call'd the Lacuna, & is thought to be overflowed land. [Next four lines scored out] There are very narrow keys before the houses wch [are] on the canals: [next line scored out] tis very difficult to walk to any place as there are a great number of narrow little streets or rather lanes, & some times you come to the end of a street where there is no bridge. Indeed tis possible to walk every where, there being 900 bridges at least in the city. Upon this account tis no agreeable city no walks, but the piazza no stirring into the country, no walk or ride without going to sea; & then the difficulty that attends all this makes it a very unpleasant place for those that delight in the variety of a country walk or ride.

Milles' Journal Account of Venice[119]

We left Padouaon Wednesday ye 2d of June for Venice wch is about 28 miles distance we kept all along ye left hand bank of ye river Bacchiglione... at Fuscino 5 miles distant from Venice we took a Gondola in wch we put our Baggage, & left our chaise behind on ye shore. in a little more yn an hour we arrived at Venice.

The situation of ye city of Venice is so singular, yt it ought not to be pass'd over in silence, & tho' every body knows yt it is situated in ye waters, yet perhaps there are few yt know in what manner they lay the foundations of their building. Venice therefore may be said to be situated in ye sea because it is all surrounded wth waters, & is 5 miles distant from ye main land. but these waters all about here are very

---

[118]Add. 22982, p.111
[119]Add. 15763, pp 101-3

shallow, & are what they call ye Lagune's, these Lagune, are pretty long & about 10 miles wide. They are allmost separated from ye sea by a long string of Islands, wch have only small passages between them, wch give a great deal of shelter to Venice agst ye winds, & roughness of ye sea. As all the Lagune are said to be only overflowed land, & ye water has no great depth ye most part of ye houses of Venice are built 5 or 6 foot under water, & in order to strengthen ye foundation in order yt it may not give way, by ye moistness of ye ground, they drive in great numbers of piles, wch make ye foundation firm, tho' notwithstanding this ye foundations very often in particular places sink, as is plainly to be seen in ye church of St Mark, where ye pavement is very uneven it is true some houses no doubt are built upon Islands in ye city. Venice therefore thus situated in ye middle of ye waters cannot but be a very agreable & uncommon sight to any body who beholds it.[120] most of ye streets are fill'd with water, there are some indeed yt you pass thro' on land, but then they are very narrow. There are very few keys along any of ye streets, so that ye water runs up to ye very thresholds of ye doors, but there are allys, & back ways wch communicate wth one another, wch by ye help of bridges over ye streets make it possible to go all over ye city on foot, tho' ye streets are very intricate, & you must make a prodigious number of turnings, & go a great way about before you can arrive at ye place design'd. ye foundations of ye houses as high as they are wash'd by ye water are all of stone. Ye Grand Canal, wch is really a very fine, & broad channel, adorn'd with ye best Palaces of ye city on each side, runs thro' ye uppermost, & largest part of ye city in ye shape of an S over it is one bridge only wch is placed about ye middle of ye canal, & is ye famous Rialto. The whole city of Venice is pretty much in ye shape of an egg. Ye large end lying North West, & ye small one South East. Having thus given a short description of ye situation of Venice, I shall begin to speak of its buildings....

---

[120] As can be seen from his letter and his journal, however, Pococke certainly did not find Venice agreeable or pleasing

VENICE
13 June, 1734
Pococke to his mother
Letter 18[121]

[This letter marks the beginning of their journey home, with the news of a preferment being offered to Milles by his uncle, the bishop. Pococke's account of the ceremony of the Doge marrying the Sea, which took place on 3 June, is reproduced in full, together with shorter excerpts of interest][122]

Honoured Madam,

My last to you was of June 11th from Venice the account of my self ending on Holy Thursday here the 3d. when we saw the ceremony of the Doges marrying the Sea, one of the finest sights in the world: about 9 I saw the Doge at Mass in the chapel of the Palace with the nobles, then they went in Procession to the Bucentaur or fine galley[123] with flags display'd the sword of state going after the Doge before the Procurators & head nobles, the Popes Nuncio on the right of the Doge & the Emperors Ambassador a Neapolitan on the left dress'd in black with flower'd damask cloak, the Nuncio in purple; the canons fireing, drums beating & trumpets sounding, all the nobles that are Procurators, in office or have been Embassadors followed, in red , a gown of Padua say almost like a Surplice, but not gather'd at top, a piece of red flower'd velvet coming before & behind over their shoulder, large wigs, such as judges wear, as they always wear & long loose black caps, which they never put on but carry in their hands at all times; under they have a black silk waistcoat, & under that over the culot a sort of short black silk gather'd petticoat, coming but very little lower than the knees, which is the habit of citizens in most parts

---

[121] Add. 22978. This is the eighth letter of the original collection (Add. 19939) and a note next to the English address states that it was received by Mrs. Pococke on 26 June and answered on 27 June, 1734

[122] This famous ceremony is not described in the journal of either traveller

[123] This was the last of the four major Bucentaurs or state galleys used for this ceremony, from 1729 until 1798, when it was destroyed by Napoleon; and is immortalised in the paintings of Caneletto. The earlier three were made in 1311, 1526 & 1606

of Italy, & the citizens go drest as the nobles here; these distinguished
persons of the nobles, as mentioned above, wear red only on these
days, at other times go habited in purple the sleeve not so large as the
red with stiff collars to both, no cravats or necks, but mostly a pair of
buttons to the neck of some colour'd stone; both the red & black
gowns open before, but commonly kept close, especially the red: the
nobles in all are 2000 some say 1200 only. This part of them who
attended the Doge went into the Bucentaur with him; this Vesesel is
built like a Galley, & without doubt is the finest ship in the world, it is
about 150 f long & 25 f broad, it has two decks, one below where the
rowers are & an opening for every oar, about 22 of aside; over is the
upper deck, which is covered with wood, the top of which is covered
with scarlet velvet, & this covering of wood is supported by 10 pillars
in the middle & as many on each side, with a bench along on each side
of the middle partition which is about 3 f & on each side it being all
open between these 3 feet from the floor: the floor is of wood inlaid
with handsome figures, every thing else you see inside & out, the
Pillars the ceiling & every part finely carved & gilt all over in the most
beautiful manner, so that every thing but the benches & floor are
cover'd with gold; & besides this the stern & head adorn'd with
carvings & a great number of statues gilt in like manner, especially at
the head is Venice in the figure of a woman, the Sun & Zodiack & with
the statue of a man in armour & on his breast sanguine partum at the
helm is the Doges gilt throne; the nobles being ranged all down this
vessel has no mast, only a pretty large staff with a flag; being set off
she is rowed by 44 oars, two fine large galleys of the state row at some
distance after the boats of Ambassadors keep near the stern & many
thousand Gondolas all about; musick in several boats, the bells all
ringing, the ships firing as it passed by, & the canons discharged from
the town: we went in a Gondola near, thus they went above a mile to
the Isle of St Nicolas, where the army of the state were drawn up, &
fired several times as it passed, the horse wheeling about the Island
gave several discharges; within this Island is the port of Venice; &
when got without it the Vessel turned, & the back of the Doges throne
being let down he got up turned round & threw the Ring into the sea,
making use of words to this purpose, By this Ring I marry the sea in
testomonium perpetui domini. On which all the Guns fired, & they
returned to St Nicolas, & landing went in procession to the church,
where Mass was celebrated solemnly by the Bishop called the

Patriarch of Venice: returning to the Bucentaur they returned to
Venice; the great number of fine Gondola's added much to the beauty,
of this function; the Emperor had three with curious carvings, nothing
but gilding appearing; the Patriarch three, built in a different manner,
carv'd & gilt, & the Gondola men dressed, some in satin some in
Brocades & silver stuffs, 8 or 10 to a Gondola: in a word all agree it is
the finest sight they ever saw; at 4 they went to the Murano Isles a
mile off, where they make the glass;[124] in the large channel which
divides the Isles, all the company met in their Gondola's, & it is called
the Corso, & rowed backward & forward under the bridge, many
having musick, some boats trying which could run fastest: we had a
very fine day or the vessel would not have gone out, being high built
& not bearing much wind, & if she is Shipwreck'd the Admiral loses
his head.

4. Staid within to write an account of what we had seen in our journey
Letters &c: ...

5. Spent the whole day in seeing churches, the Patriarchal church or
cathedral of St Mark; several nunneries, the nuns have great liberties
here, have large grates in the churches near the doors where they
converse as much as they can; in one they called to us, asked us what
book it was we had to give us an account of the pictures, for we buy
such an one at almost every great city, told us what pictures we were
to observe, and the History of them; it shock'd me at first, we parted
soon; but recovering the surprise went & talked to them about their
nunnery; no harm in all this, if it proceeds no further as I believe it
can't easily, except that it is not very decent in the church but this is
only to get company to talk to; the grate at the entrance of the
nunnery not being so publick, some we saw at work, & in one
monastery their Quire is behind the high altar, the room on each side

---

[124]In his journal, Pococke notes, "the Murano which like Venice consists of
several Islands is a city & Bishoprick about a mile from Venice tho' divided
by a large canal over which is an wooden bridge... here they make the glass,
for which Venice is so famous which art they preserve in the same
perfection tho' other nations especially the English now Excell them, but
they make it very curiously of all sorts of Colours, & compositions to
imitate Lapis lazuli, chalcedony & other stones, & glass like tortoise shell."
Add. 22982, p.131

of it entirely open with large grate all up to the top, but no man can
lawfully go within & all is lock'd & it is excommunication for a man t
enter at Rome, & I believe here. The Piazza of St Mark is filled with
wooden shops of all sorts of goods, a kind of fair for 17 dais.[125]

6. Saw churches. We went at first to the White Lyon, moved
yesterday to Kennets a very good English publick house, but more like
a lodging, paid 1s 6d each night, 3s each for a dinner, but eat very well
in the English way have 6 or 7 dishes, in company with Mr Colthrop
7000 pr An. This is a very dear place; but our stay is short, there is no
possibility of doing without a Gondola & we pay 13 each a week for
one & two men you know the shape of them they are all by law black,
strangers may have 'em coloured. At 3 we saw some churches, went
to the Pieta Church to hear musick vocal & instrumental perform'd by
girls, whose fathers are not known, 'tis a Hospital for foundlings, who
are left there; those that leave legitimate children are excommunicated
ipso facto there are 1000 boys & girls; the women are kept there till
they are disposed of in matrimony or otherwise, boys put early to
business.[126] Thence to the coffee house, had much discourse with Ld
Harcourt who is going to Vienna five days journey.

7. Saw a church or two. Visited Signor Apostolo Zeno, who is or was
Historian & poet to the Emperor & Nobilis Venetus Cretensis;[127] - as I

---

[125]Pococke describes St. Mark's Square in greater detail in his journal,
admitting, "The Piazza of St Mark may truly be sd to be the Glory of
Venice." Add. 22982, p.136. It is described by Milles, too, who in addition
includes in his journal account a rough sketch of the square (Add. 15763, pp
124ff)

[126]Milles, in his journal, gives the following description of this institution:
"The two hospitals of ye Pieta, & incurabili have a concert of vocal, &
instrumental musick every Sunday, & holiday. the former is set apart for
Bastards, wch when ye mother has a mind to put in she lays it in a certain
place, & rings a bell, upon wch it is immediately taken in. There is an
excommunication agst any one who puts in legitimate children. there are as
I am told about a thousand in this monastery. they put out ye boys to
apprentiship [sic], & ye girls they keep in ye hospital till they get them
married, or provided for in some manner, or other." Add. 15763, p.113

[127]Apostolo Zeno (1669-1750) was born in Venice of Cretan descent and was
a librettist as well as a literary journalist. He was Poet Laureate to the
Imperial Court of Vienna in 1718, where he remained until 1729

...cture, but he dresses as other gentlemen, so
...le Cretan of Venice: he has a most choice &
... Medals & Curiosities, compleat series of the
...e different sorts of Copper & also consular
...we saw his 400 Gold medals & his large
...to see us I find he has a pension from the Emperor,
...ing desired to retire. We went at 3 to see churches. To the coffee
house & opera, which no where comes up to London but good
dancing by a girl of 10 or 11: Faranelli the top voice in Italy, we shall
hear at Vicenza, he is to go to England; Caristini[128] who went least
season to London sings well, but is saucy & so comes back. Hendal is
laid on his back by Heydegger,[129] & goes over with the Princess or
Orange.

8. Went & took a pass of the French Ambassador; saw churches,
especially St George a fine building of Palladio's; saw a marriage
there of a noble Venetian, many nobles came, in an Isle from the town;
the Bride dressed after the Spanish manner was led up to the rails of
the altar without any veil of signs of Confussion [sic], & made very
decent Curtsies, to the no[bles] as she passed along, she had a light
coloured silk on, a long train, her hair curl'd & turned towards the
face, & two long straight tresses hung down below which she had
waving curls at the end, no cap, flowers on one side of her head &
down her breast, a deep border of lace came up high on her breast ...
tho' her shoulders were bare all round; & a lace turn 9 down from the
tucker about 3 inches down on the garment, the sleeves very short,
they... kneeled, & a very short ceremony of putting on a ring by the
father &c: this performed, Mass was said, & all went home. We saw
her & another at the Opera last night; there was a sort of publick
espousals before matrimony; the Ladies seem not ashamed of these
affairs, when they blush, not at evil...

---

[128]Giovanni Carestini (1704-c.1760), another famous castrati who sang in
music composed by Handel
[129]In 1728 Handel was hired to produce operas at the Kings Theatre, London,
with Heydegger (or Heidegger) as manager. He left this company after the
unsuccessful 1733-4 season (the one alluded to by Pococke) and joined
Covent Garden, where he was to have greater success. In the same year,
Handel's student, Princess Anne, married Prince William of Orange and in
her honour he produced *Parnasso in Festa*

9. I spent the morn in the Booksellers Shop [I laid out about 11 in books chiefly history/Italian as Davia &c: very cheap I had for yt money 11 books].[130] At 2 went a mile to the Islands of St Christopher & St Michel both inhabited by monks only Augustinians & Camaldoli, about ¼ of a mile round, thence to the Murano Islands a bishoprick all joined by bridges 14 churches, at a Nunnery, talked the nuns to us, one happened to be of the name of Porter, she said her father was an Englishman, Sr Thomas Porter Governatore di Londra, if any truth in it, he must be Lord Mayor; she said he was knighted by a King of England & died 6 years ago, she was born in the Isle of Zanth, we first saw her at the grate at the entrance & when we told her we were going to see the church, she said she would meet us at the grate, which she did, 2 or 3 women on their knees joyn'd in the discourse which was chiefly of the pictures & monastery; she said she hoped we would come & see her again, before we went away we promised her we would [She was a natural daughter of Sr Thomas Porter a rich merchant or ... & formerly of London but I don't find he way Ld Mayor][131] they are dress'd in white, & what is particular had a sort of yellow net going over their heads as a cross, so that it covers not all the head.

11....Went to see the Islands of Le gratie & St Clemen near, in the later [sic] is a very beautiful church, & the pattern of the Holy house at Loretto, exactly the same inside, built like it, & outside cased with marble & just the same except the relicks, which are only in the front, this Isle belongs to the Camaldoli hermits about 18, they have their gardens & houses separate; one with his long beard showed us all his, the garden was full of exotic herbs, tho' small, & they have a large comon garden & all is very pleasant. The resident here is Col. Burgess.[132]

---

[130]It appears from this scored out sentence, that his books cost on average £1 each

[131]Scored out of the copy and written in Pococke's hand on the reverse of the previous page

[132]Colonal Elizeus Burges (d. 1736) was resident in Venice from 1719-22 and again from 1727-36. His diplomatic correspondence was concerned greatly with Jacobites and the Wars of the Polish Succession, see Ingamells, *op.cit.*, 157-8. Pococke describes him in Letter 19

12.... We went to visit my Ld Harcourt & Mr Crow [bought a few more books prodigiously cheap].[133] Visited Signor Apostolo Zeno but did not see him. Settled our affairs with our Banker. Yesterday the Resident we went to see when he was not at home, sent to invite us to dine today, Whit-Sunday, as with you, & we are to dine with him; intend to visit Ld Rockingham, Signor Apostolo Zeno & at 6 or 7 shall set out with Mr Crow for Padoua.

Yesterday I received a letter from the Bishop dated April 27th in which is this paragraph. "I send you this to acquaint you, that Mr Barbon is in such a condition that I think he cannot live a week longer; you know what preferment will be void by his death, & I desire you to let Jerre know, that if he be inclined to the gown, I will bestow it upon him. I think he will stand in his own light if he neglects to embrace this opportunity, if he thinks fit to embrace it, he must without delay make the best of his way to me here."[134] So this hastens our journey by Geneva, & I desire to hear from you first at Langres in France; put France at top direct to me as Gentilhomme Anglois, & I shall find it at the Post house & I desire the favour of you to order Mr Hoare to send me a bill of 15 on Langres & a bill of 15 on Cambray, & to direct to me as above, if he thinks it more proper, he may only let me know where I may receive the money in these two cities, & desire him if he can to let you know also, & you to write to me; I would not have him send both letters of advice to me to Langres, but the second to Cambray where I am to receive it, & there also I shall hear from you, a week after your letter to Langres, but if any thing relateing to my bills, you'll write immediately to both, & afterwards to Cambray; I must give you this trouble because I have laid a scheme to spend the winter with you. I thought it a better request to desire the Bishop to permit me now I am on this side the water to see Flanders & Holland, which will not take up above a month & so spend the rest of the winter in England, than to stay behind, only to stay in England: but if it be necessary I should come soon into Ireland & not have time to see Holland, I have desired to stay a month in England & that Jerre may go on, who had been writ

---

[133] Again, it is hard to see why he should have deleted this from the copy letters

[134] Milles' response to the bishop is reproduced below, in his letter from Verona, 6/17 June, 1734 (Add. 15773)

to not long before to come into Ireland [& not have time to see Holland].[135] You will hear from me about 3 weeks, or according as affairs happen. Pray my very kind love to my Sister & respects to White oak.

I am Dear Madam, your most obedient & dutiful Son Richard Pococke

P.S. this letter will not leave this place till the 19th. I have writ to Mr Hoare to place all money [that he has or shall receive for me to your account].[136] We have sent 2 boxes from this place to be left with Mr Wood, the least he is to keep with him, & the large one is to be sent to Newtown, but we shall see him...

VERONA
6/17 June, 1734
Milles to the bishop[137]

[The only section reproduced from this letter is that relating to the bishop's offer to his nephew of a preferment in his diocese. For descriptions of Venice, see Pococke's accounts in Letter 18]

My Lord,

Dr Pococke had the honour of receiving your Ldships letter last Saturday, whc he immediately communicated to me, in whch I find that on the approaching death of Mr. Barbone,[138] Your Ldship does me

---

[135] As he had said he wished to do, in an earlier letter.

[136] Unfortunately the last word of this deleted sentence cannot be read with certainty

[137] Add. 15773. No original exists for this letter

[138] As noted in Chapter 1, Rev. Hugh Barbon occupied numerous positions in the diocese, several of which were carved up between Pococke (four years before his death, suggesting perhaps that he was already ill) and Milles. However, the position being offered to Milles here was the senior appointment of Treasurer of Lismore Cathedral, an extraordinary offer given that he had not taken Holy Orders. Rev. Barbon had succeeded to this position on the death of Rev. Richard Moore, who had died at the age of 36,

the honour to offer me the preferment, that that gentleman had in the church; for wch favour with all the others that your Ldship has continually heap'd upon me, I can never return sufficient thanks. Tho' your Ldship is so kind as to put it to my choice whether I will accept of it, or no, yet my duty, & obedience to all your Ldships commands, & withal the inward inclination, that I always had for the gown preferable to any thing else, makes me embrace with joy the opportunity yt your Ldship lays before me. The only objection that I can make against my taking upon me so great an office, is my own unworthiness & inability to exectute it as I ought, & withal my youth, wch is not capable of that judgment, and learning wch ought to appear in a Minister. Never the less if your Ldship out of your great goodness, will be pleased to dispense with these failings, wch I will use my utmost endeavours to remove, I shall with pleasure accept the honour that your Ldship promises to confer upon me trusting in God, that he will strengthen my weak endeavours, to perform the office that I am going to take upon me. The opinion your Ldship has of me, to think me capable of undertaking so great an office is, I am very sensible, much greater, then either I do, or ever, shall deserve; the only return therefore that I can make to your Ldship for this honour designed me, is cheerfully to accept of it, & tho' with an entire sense of my own unworthiness, yet at the same time, with a stedfast resolution at least to endeavour to make my self more worth. In obedience therefore to yr Ldships commands we shall make the best of our way to Ireland, thro' Lombardy, & France, wch will be by much the nearest way. The most proper place that we can pitch upon to hear from our Ldship will be Cambray, where if your Ldship has any commands for us, a letter will find us with the following direction A: Monseiur Monsieur Milles Gentilhome Anglois a Cambray, & the sooner your Ldship writes that will be the better. With relations to what your Ldship says concerning the Geneva edition, as I have bought for your Ldship that of Rome, which is present brought down to Alexander the 8th, & will in a short time be compleated, so I suppose your Ldship does not mean that I should compleat the set with the rest of the Geneva edition, but only with the omitted bulls in the other editions,

---

on 18 October, 1729 and is buried in Old St. Mary's Church, Clonmel. The latter was of the Clonmel Moore family whom Milles & Pococke encountered in Italy (see above)

wch two volumes If I can get them separate from the others, I will buy for your Ldship, & now to come to some description of Venice.

The day after we arrived being Ascension Day, they performed the usual ceremonies of the Doges espousing the sea....[139]

I shall not pretend to speak to your Ldship concerning its situation &c your Ldship being informed in every particular in that point, better a great deal then I can be who had not time to consider its circuit, the number of souls &c: being wholy employed in seeing the churches Palaces &c: In order that we might make all possible hast to England. They talk of there being 400,000 souls in Venice. It is certainly very populous...

My paper obliges me to conclude. We left Venice on Sunday evening, & arrived at Padoua on Monday morning. We went to Vicenza on Tuesday morning, left it on Wednesday morning, & came here [Verona] this morning, Dr Pococke begs leave to present his humble duty to your Ldship

I am my Lord your Ldships most Dutifull

---

[139]See Pococke's account in Letter 17 (Add. 22978), above

MILAN
12/23 June, 1734
Milles to the bishop[140]

[This is the last letter in the collection of correspondence from Milles to the bishop on the first tour, though we are fortunate in that we have his journal for the last stages of his tour. This manuscript begins on 13 June, the day they departed from Venice and ends with their arrival in London, on 1 July, 1734.[141]

The excerpts reproduced in this letter are Milles' final observations on Venice and include brief descriptions of churches, palaces, the Rialto Bridge, the Arsenal, the island of Murano and the amphitheatre at Verona]

I sent my last to your Ldship last Friday the 7/18th from Verona,[142] in which I could not finish my account of the churches of Venise, on which I shall proceed in this.

The church of St Maro Zobenigo has a beautifull facade adorn'd with statues, and monuments of the Bargerigo family. The facade of saint Zachary and St Fransesco della vigna likewise are very beautifull, the latter by Pallado. In it are the monuments of the Doges March: Antonio Justiniani, Andrea Gutto, and Francis Contareni. At the church of the Conventual Franciscans, is by much the finest monument in all Venice and I may almost say the finest I ever saw. It is erected to the Doge John Pesaro, besides which there are the monuments of the Doges Francis Foscari, and Nicolas Juronus, that of one Hieronymus Gazzoni Admiral & of Almeric D'Este sent by Lovis the 14th with auxiliary troops to the Cretan war, Titian is said to be buried in this church but without any memorial.

---

[140]"An Account of what I saw Remarkable between Venice & London", Add. 15773

[141]The manuscript is Add. 60516

[142]This letter has not survived and is therefore not part of the collection

The islands about Venice are prodigiously agreeable. The smallest of them are taken up by single convents, that of St Michal di Murano and St Clemente are the most agreeable, of those which we saw. Murano is a large town and the see of a Bp. about a mile from Venice. This place is the magazine of the Venice glass, and where they make it all, I think it is by much inferior to our English glass; tho' they have a thousand ways of colouring it & transforming it into a great many pretty things. I shall have the honour to shew your Ldship a specimen of their ingenuity when I come to Ireland.[143]

The Arsenal at Venice gave us great satisfaction, for it is really what one may properly term a well provided Arsenal.[144] It is surrounded with walls whch they say have about 2 miles in circumference, it has 3 canals, they carried us, to shew us 14 or 15 apartments all filled with their particular commoditys as cordage timber, oars, gun powder, and in short all things necessary for the rigging out of a fleet. The armory for the Galleys is well furnish'd tho' they pretend to have a greater number of arms then they really have. Amongst them they shew'd us the arms of Scanderberg, of the famous Marc Antonio, who was fleed by the Turks, and the cask of Attila K: of the Hunns. They have a place appointed for the building of their vessels, with a canal in the middle for the launching them. All round are lodges, where they stand in the dry. They had about 9 new ships on the stocks when we were there; some of which, had been begun for a dozen years. Besides these they have their lodges for their Galleys, Galeassess, and Galeotta's. The second are a larger sort of Galley, with what they call

---

[143]Milles further notes, in his journal, "the town of Murano is famous for making all ye glass, wch is commonly calld Venice glass. allmost all ye town are full of these houses, & they drive a vast trade their glass is not near so good as ye English, but they have mere whimseys in making them of different colours, painting them wth flowers wth [   ] and other inventions, wch make them very curious." Add. 15763, pp 120-21

[144]This is further described in both journals. See Milles (Add. 15736, pp 130-31) and Pococke (Add. 22982, pp 141-46). Pococke considers that the English Docks are inferior to the Venetian ones only in one respect, in that the latter have covered docks for building their ships and galleys (p.141). He is also comments on the fact that "the people of the dock are allowed as much wine & water as they can drink, in the cellar is a large cistern which they keep full of wine... this cellar they say costs 'em 63400 ducats a year... which is about 1500 pd." (p.142)

a Torre in the prow as well as in the stern. The Galeotta's are vessels much less then the Galleys. The orders of the Galeasses are to combat with 24 Turkish galleys, and are obliged not to turn tail except a 25th comes up. Comprehending these 3 sorts of vessels they have a 100. The Bucentaur[145] is likewise kept here. They shew'd us amongst a great number of brass canon, 2 very fine ones, one of which was cast while K the 3 was to see the Arsenal, and the other in the time whilst Frederic the IV K: of Denmark was here.[146] Before the gate of the Arsenal are 3 Lyons of white marble brought from Athens by the Venetian fleet and a Leopard from Corcyra.[147]

The Palaces in Venice for the most part of an old Gothick architecture, some indeed upon the grand canal about 5 or 6 are of a very beautifull Architecture. The famous bridge of the Rialto is built over the grand canal about the middle of it. We took the measure of this so much renown'd arch, but have not had time since to measure the string. It is built of the beautifull white stone that they have here. The top is divided into 3 streets a row of shops on each side making the division, between the middle, and side streets. The middle street is 7 paces wide, and the 2 side ones about 4 paces each. By an inscription on this bridge I find it was built in the year 1590, and in the Dukedom of Paschales Ciconia. This my Lord is I think all that is worth acquainting yr Ldship with in regard to Venice.

We left that city at 8 of the clock on Sunday evening [13 June], and went with an English Gentleman[148] in a boat quite [all the way] to Padua, where we arrived at about 7 in the morning. We staid there that day, and on Tuesday morning set forward 20 miles for Vicenza; where we arrived about noon.... The town house very much resembles that of Padoua in every respect only it is surrounded with a very beautifull modern Portico, whereas that of Padova is Gothick. In the whole it is a very fine thing. The Theater of the Academy here call'd

---

[145]The galley used for the ceremony of the Doge marrying the sea

[146] Frederick IV (1671-1730) was King of Denmark & Norway from 1699 until his death

[147]One of these, the Piraeus Lion, was plundered from Greece in 1687 by the Venetian naval commander Francesco Morosini. It is famous for the runic inscriptions found on it

[148]Mr. Crowe, see Pococke, Letter 19, below (Add. 22978)

the Olympicks is a piece of Palladio's very much esteem'd; that is the inside of it, and particularly the scene part which is adorn'd with very good statues of Stucco.[149] There are a great many of Palladio's houses in this city.[150] Just out at the gate that goes to Verona is a prodigiously beautifull field call'd the Campus Martius where the coaches of the quality [gentry] assemble every evening. All the entrance is a very beautifull arch built by Palladio, and is a great ornament. The quality likewise walk in an agreeable garden of the Count de Valmarana's[151] which is opposite to this arch

We left Vicenza on Wednesday a little before noon, and 253isqué'd about 20 miles that evening, thro' a most delightfull country. About 12 miles more the next morning brought us to Verona.[152] The walls of Verona are said to be near 7 miles in circuit, I beleive it is pretty near as large as Padova and like that too has a vast deal of waste ground within its walls. The fortifications are pretty strong. The city is commanded by 2 Castles on a hill on the North side of the town call'd St Peter, and St Felix; besides which it has an old Cittadel in the plain within the city, called the castel-vecchio which is of no use at all. The Addige [sic] a very large and rapid river winds thro' the middle of town, over which are 4 handsome bridges: the uppermost of which consists of 3 arches, the largest of which as far as we could judge by the eye, is much higher and larger, then that of the Rialto. The Cathedral church is a handsome Gothick building. On the pavement before the high altar is the monument of Pope Lucius the III[153]... Besides these are the monuments of the Cardinals Augustinus

---

[149]This edifice is further described by Pococke in his journal (Add. 22982, pp157-60)

[150]In his journal he notes, about the Palladian architecture, "there is one thing wch makes their Palaces after they have stood some years appear very indifferent, wch is they are almost all built with brick, & plaister'd over with white plaister, & rusticated, in order to make them look like stone, the pillars also the same, so yt in a short time ye plaister drops off, & ye house appears very shabby." Add. 60516, p. 2

[151]According to Sir Philip Skippon, who visited this place in 1646, the garden had a "labrynth of myrtle hedges". See W.H. Matthews, *Mazes and Labyrinths: Their History and Development* (New York, 1970) 127

[152]According to Milles' journal, they arrived there at "about 9 of ye clock in ye morning" (Add. 60516, p.7)

[153]C. 1100-1185, and pope from 1181 until his death in 1185

Valerius, and Bernard Navageri, both Bps. of this see, with 2
memorials erected one to Cardinal Norris, and the other to Monsigner
Bianchini a very learned Antiquary who dyed lately, both natives of
this city. Adjoining to the church of St Zeno, a very old Gothick
church, is a very fine vase of porphyry, which is about 10 feet
diameter, all of one peice....

The famous and perfect Amphitheatre of Verona gave us an infinite
deal of satisfaction.[154] It is all built of 2 sorts of marble which they find
here abouts viz: a red, and a white. The outer circumference consists
of 3 storys with some small remains of the fourth. The 3 storys are all
adorn'd with pillars of the Tuscan order. The fourth they suppose had
windows like the Collisoeum. There are 72 arches in every row all
round. The whole is rusticated. On the outwards circumference there
are only four arches remaining. Each of these arches is about 12 feet
wide, the peers about 7 feet wide, there is only one Portico on the
outside of this Amphitheater, whereas there are 4 in the Colisoeum.
The whole second circumference is entire and consists of 2 rows of
arches. In them are placed the stairs, and passages into the Area,
none of which are now entire. The 4 arches at the largest Diameter of
the oval, are bigger then the others. Entring in at these doors, when
you are about half way within the Amphitheater you come into a
second Portico which communicates all round, and leads to the stairs
of the second row of vomitorio's[155] from the bottom as from the
outermost you go to these of the 3d & 4th. This Portico is 10 feet 6
inches wide. Beyond this after a passage you come into a third
portico, which communicates all round to the vomitorio's of the
lowest degree, and to the strait passages that lead from the outer

---

[154]According to Milles, who gives a further description of this antiquity in his
journal, "ye Amphitheater of Verona is famous all over Europe, for being as
perfect on ye inside as ever it was, whereas there are few others yt have any
of ye inside left." Add. 60516, p.9. Likewise, Pococke, in his journal, gives
a lengthy account of this, and notes, "As to the antiquities of Verona that
which is extraordinary & exceeds any in the world for the inside is the
Amphitheatre" (Add. 22982, p.163)

[155]A vomitorium is the passage behind or below a row of seats in
amphitheatres, designed to allow the spectators to exit after the performance

Portico's into the Arena. The cavea[156] of the Amphitheater, by
continual repairing is kept perfect, and indeed there are but very few
of the old degrees remaining. They are 45 in number one of which is
buried. They are for the generality 1 foot 6 inches deep, and 2 foot 6
inches wide. There are 4 degrees of vomitorio's all round, 16 in each
round on the each side. The 3d row is placed perpendiulalry under
the 1st and the fourth under the second, at the 2 principal entrances are
2 large door cases of stone, with a sort of a small terrass at top, and on
the front & sides of the door case a balustrade of stone, but all this is
modern work. For it appears plainly that at first the great passage did
not enter into the arena, but went no further then the 3d portico,
where people dispersed to their several vomitorio's. What is very
particular in this Amphitheater, is, that under all the 3 portoco's, and
across the longest and shortest Diameters of the Amphitheater, under
the pavement are channels of water about 3 feet wide and 6 feet deep.
People are not agreed about the use that this water was put to. The
arena in its longest Diameter is 96 paces; and in its shortest 57.[157]

The Academy of the Philarmonici is a very beautifull building. They
have a very fine theatre for the acting of Operas. Round the court are
a prodigious number of old inscriptions fixed in the wall. On the
north side of the town on a hill lyes the castle of St Peter, built upon
the ruins of the ancient theatre part of which we saw in a convent just
under it. Under the theater was the Naumachia in a pretty feild call'd
the Campus Martius. They have a large square building consisting of
a great number of pretty shops, divided by streets, and enclos'd with a
wall, which is the place appointed for the keeping of their fairs.

On Friday the 18th about noon we left Verona, and 255isqué'd 10 or 12
miles over a very barren and stony plain call'd La Campagna di

---

[156]Subterranean cells in amphitheatres or arenas, where the beasts were
enclosed before going into combat

[157]Pococke includes a curious footnote in his journal account, as follows:
"Since I left Verona I saw in Lord Burlingtons possession in some old book
an engraved plate of a Theatre at Verona, the small remains of which he
saw & two people have heard of it." (Add. 22982, note 2 on p.166). This is
the Richard Boyle, 3rd Earl of Burlington (1694-1753), commonly known as
"the Architect Earl", though not to be confused with Pococke's old patron,
Henry Herbert, 9th Earl of Pembroke, also an architect

Verona. At 15 miles we pass'd by a very strong fort belonging to the Venetians call'd Peschiera. It is situated at the south corner of the Lake de Garda ol[d]: Benacus about 30 miles long and 10, or 12 wide.[158] The river Mincio runs out of this lake, thro' the fort. We lay that night a mile or two beyond Peschier [Peschiera], and the next day at noon arriv'd at Brescia...[159]

We arriv'd at this city [Milan] on Monday the 27th NS about noon.

Since I wrote this I had the honour of receiving both your Ldships letters one bearing date May the 4th, & the other May the 8th with the news of Mr Barbon's death, [160] concerning the honour your Ldship did me in your last, to offer me Mr Barbon's preferment, I have inform'd your Ldship in my last from Verona, and as soon as we found that your Ldship desired us to hasten to England we left Venice with all expedition, and now your Ldship repeats it again in these letters, we shall make the expedition that is possible, taking the shortest route, & not stopping at any place in the way. Your Ldship may depend upon our utmost endeavours to be in Waterford as soon as it is possible. We shall leave Milan tomorrow morning early.

I am my Lord

---

[158]The first lines of this passage are absolutely identical to the description given in Milles' journal, though in the latter the lake is 25 miles long and 9 or 10 broad. See Add. 60516, p.22. It is clear from such similarities (found in the writing of both travellers) that they based their letters on their journal accounts. Incidentally, in a footnote to Pococke's journal account, the lake is described as being 40 miles long (See Add. 22982, note to p.172

[159]See Pococke's Letter 19, Milan, 12/23 June, 1734 (Add. 22978), below, for a brief description of this town

[160]Though the facts have already been reported (and reproduced here) in two separate letters, one from Pococke (Letter 18) and the other from Milles (Verona, 6/17 June, 1734), they were based on a letter from the bishop to Pococke. This time, the bishop has directed two letters to Milles himself

MILAN
12/23 June, 1734
Pococke to his mother
Letter 19[161]

Honoured Madam,

My last I writ was of the 13th Instant from Venice, I dined that day
with the Resident of England Col. Burgess a most facetious merry old
Gentleman, but a little prophane, in company with Lord Harcourt, the
Early of Rockingham, Mr Crow, Mr Colthrop &c. Col. Burgess was a
Lieutenant Colonel, has been here many years, with an intermission of
some years when he was in England, is much troubled with the
gout,[162] [an English dinner, except kidney beans with a ... fried... we
had two courses or 6 or 7 each & a desert].[163] Apricots are come in &
are 20 a peny [sic]. We visited in the morning Signor Apostole Zeno &
Ld Rockingham, who was of Eton & is very young. My Ld Harcourt
sailed after dinner for Trieste in order to go for Vienna & we set out
about 8 in the evening, in a large cover'd boat called a Builo (?)[164] for
Padua with Mr Crow, taking in our Chaise at Fusina; we arrived at
Padoua about 7 in the morning; walk'd about the City to show Mr
Crow what was to be seen,[165] dined, & spent the afternoon mostly in
writing. My Lord Harcourt is a most amiable serious fine gentleman,
of good nature & good sense & without any vice, is much inclined to
the sword & will I am perswaded make a great figure in the world, &
dare say understand as much of the art of war as any man in England
that has had no experience of it, tho' but 2 or 3 & twenty, in his own
hair:[166] we returned his trip to us, as I believe I told you in my last; Ld
Rockingham is the only English traveller left at Venice, who will soon

---

[161]Add. 22978. This is the ninth letter of the original collection (Add. 19939)
and unusually, there is no note of receipt

[162]He died, in 1736, having suffered "violent apoplectick Convulsions,
occasioned by the Gout in his Stomack" (Ingamells, *op.cit.*, 158)

[163]Some of the detail of this dinner is lost, on account of Pococke's terrible
handwriting

[164]This word is lost in both the copy and the original

[165]Pococke and Milles of course had already visited Padua on their way to
Venice, and so were familiar with the places of interest

[166]By this we may comprehend that Lord Harcourt did not wear a wig

leave it for Florence &c: to spend the winter at Rome. Mr Wynne[167] elder brother of Wynne Gent.n comonor [sic] of C.C.C.[168] in my time, who took his brother to travel with him, has been 2 or 3 years at Venice, enchanted with a mistress. I send you this riddle

> Filia sum solis, Genuit me ferrea Mater.
> Stat Genetrix terra, stat meus axe Pater.

Our route is, Turin, Lyon, Chalon, Dijon, Langres, Rheims, St Omer, Calais. Not Geneva.

14. We got to Padua up the river Brenta by 7 in the morning as above; the evening of that day, we walked to the pleasant small garden of Papafava mentioned in my last. Went to see the great fair at Prato della Valle a very large kind of square or meadow built round mostly for Cattle & Shows; about 8 there was a Corse or promenade of Coaches very fine, & in which we saw some of the most beautiful Ladies in the world, dressed a la mode de Paris.

15. Set out for Vicenza & got there by 11. Dined in company with Mr Colthrop who arrived the day before, here is the Duke of Leeds who is going to Florence, Sr Harry Lyddal[169] & Sr Hugh Smithson, to hear the Opera of the famous Faranelli who is to come into England against next winter, has 1400 guineas & a Benefit night.[170] We saw a Theatre of Palladio's, some churches. A kind of Triumphal Arch by the same, at the entrance of a pleasant field called Campo Martio, & the fine

---

[167]Richard Wynne (born c. 1704), son of Richard Wynne of Aldersgate, Middlesex, matriculated at Worcester College, Oxford in 1719. He was in Italy with his younger brother William (see next note) between 1729 and 1734, along with their governor, Dr James Hay. See Ingamells (*op.cit.*) 1031

[168]William Wynne (born c. 1705), second son of Richard Wynne of Aldersgate, Middlesex, was at Corpus Christi College, Oxford

[169]Sir Henry Liddell (1708-84), 4th Baronet of Ravensworth Castle, Durham, eldest son of Thomas Liddell was in Italy from 1733-34. See Ingamells, *op.cit.*, 601

[170]This is the last we hear of the Farinelli opera, which suggests that Pococke and Milles did not actually manage to attend the performance mentioned in Pococke's Letter 18

Town house, by him also, with a Portico above & below all round; this place is 20 miles from Padua.

16. Set out for Verona, lay at Tavernelle 19 miles from Vicenza, dining by the way, because we set out late.

17. Came by 10 to Verona 11 miles further; here are all the Company, except the Duke of Leeds, that were at Vicenza...

18. At 3 set out passed through Peschieri, a strong Venetian fort 14 miles out, we waited for leave to pass, after having given in our names & country it stands on a large Lake called Lago di Gardi, 'tis towards 20 miles north of Mantoua; we ascended up hill gently from Verona, the road & Country covered with loose stones, but fertile, especially in trees. The 15th we first saw corn cutting down, as since every where, 'tis ploughed before the corn is carried quite off, for a crop of Indian wheat for this year, the much flowering oak growing against walls as Laurel &c: we lay at a county inn a mile on this side Peschiera. The Post being as dear again in the Popes Country; we hired horses & a man, a Postilion, at Padoua to carry us to Turin, 2 horses for the Chaise, one for the servant...

19. Brescia for the most part is indifferently built, where the chief places of trade are if tolerably built & a good Town house; a fine Cathedral building. A nunnery called St Julia of 150 Nuns Benedictines founded by King Desiderius,[171] in which several Queens & Princesses have ended their days, the Nuns in black dressed like Queen Mary 1st with a white plain ruff, a black crape standing up stiff & pointed over the head, very neat; we talked to them at the grate, & when we went to see the beautiful church they came to the grate which is over the High Altar, 2 or 3 young & old talked to us, we standing at the altar & had a step to stand on to see into their Quire; they told us 3 Queens had retired to their Monastery, had much the air of Gentlewomen, but I did not think it decent to talk thus over the high altar; a grate at another part of the Church for that purpose would have been better.[172] At 4 we set out & travelled 12 miles

---

[171]Last of the kings of the Lombards, who died in 786
[172]Pococke makes this complaint, as he did in an earlier letter from Venice, but it did not stop him chatting with the nuns

through a strait level road, but a little rough & the road this day has
been a little dirty, which is rare, but finely 260isqué260'd on each side,
we lay at a village call'd Cocatio.

20. at Palazolla [Paazzolo] we passed near the Lake Iseo, we travelled
15 miles to Fornaci passing over the river Adda at Canonica,[173] a small
town, where the Custom house officers demanded what we had in our
trunks in the name of his Majesty of Sardinia,[174] but were content with
a piece [a coin], it seems, he, as Generalissimo has this country, & 'tis
declared to be taken from him. From the Adda a canal is cut 20 miles
to Milan, by the contrivance of the great Leonardo da Vinci, the Adda
not being navigable by reason of shallow water.[175]

21. We travelled 12 miles mostly by the Canal to Milan,[176] we entered
with less trouble than at the little fort Peschiera in the Venetian State;
they demanded our Pass & that was all, the same fine country we
passed through as before: we are here at an excellent Inn, pay 2s for
lodging & 3s each for dinner, the city is very quiet, only a battalion of
French in the castle... we staid within till 4, & went to buy some maps
& a book of the city... Sir Hugh Smithson & Sr Harry Lyddal went to
the French army near Mantua - their Companions & Mr Colthrop
came here this afternoon. Marshal Villars died at Turin in his way to
France when he was returning on account of his infirmities:[177] It is

---

[173] According to Pococke's journal account, this is "a town pleasantly situated
on a height over the river, tis a poor place but a Milanese Prince has a very
fine Palace there with hanging gardens towards the river." Add. 22982, p.
174

[174] Charles Emmanuel III (1701-73), King of the House of Savoy from 1730
until his death in 1773

[175] Pococke further describes this in his journal: "What is most extraordinary
here is a canal made by art for four or five miles along close by the Adda, &
in some places 15 or 16 feet higher & then cut twenty miles to Milan almost
in a straight line, & near as right angles with the river, twas cut near the
river because the Adda is not navigable... tis like what has been attempted at
the river Liffy at Dublin." (Add. 22982, p.174). The canal is also described
by Milles in his journal (Add. 60516, pp 23-34) in similar terms

[176] Arriving at the city on Monday 21 June, 1734

[177] The full name of Marshal Villars was Claude Louis Hector de Villars,
Prince de Martigues, Marquis & later Duc de Villars (1653-1734). More
than eighty years of age, and with the title Marshal General of the Kings

reported Duke of Berwick was killed with a ball, as he was riding to survey the works at Philipsburgh.[178] All sorts of trades are carried on here: At Brescia their chief manufacture is fire arms & Iron ware, their being iron mines near, & also Course linnen; we saw lines tyed over the Principal street which look'd very odd, & 2 or 3 breadths of linnen laid along on them, for almost ½ a mile over the street, & 'tis the same here in some narrow streets.

22. We went on a fine walk planted with trees level with the top of the low city walls, where they walk & some in coaches, & they also come in their coaches to the square before the Cathedral, & the coaches stand mostly still, & the gentlemen stand by them & talk to the Ladies; almost all the people here, are good looking, handsome people, & fine women, only some have swell'd necks, we saw abundance within 40 miles vastly large especially the women, almost all the people of Bergamo are so & near the mountains, occasioned by snow water.[179] This day I received your Letter of May 12th sent to Venice. [Mr Hoare gave me a letter of credit only for the money I had in his hands & I'd none for no more nor wd any body give me money for my bills any further if I had desir'd it, but that we shall settle, I hope you have not told & if he requires it you may put if off till I come, I have not had one portion of more yet than what I had in his hands. I am never the less highly oblig'd to you for your credit & you may be sure nobody should suffer on account of it nor could indeed for I am ow'd a great

---

Armies, he opened the campaign in the Wars of the Polish Succession, but died at Turin on 17 June, 1734

[178]He was killed by a cannon ball at the siege of Philipsburg, on 12 June, 1734

[179]Pococke further describes this in his journal as follows: "For 40 miles through the country we observed the people especially the women many of 'em have swelld necks some of 'm very large as likewise some at Milan, this is a General disorder about Bergamo occasiond at M[ilan] by drinking the snow water that comes from the mountains. But it has been of late considered that it is rather owing to the mineral qualities with which the waters are chang'd." Add. 22982, pp 174-75. The high incidence of goitres (a disorder causing the swelling of the thyroid gland) in the Alpine regions is recorded by writers from antiquity (such as Vitruvius, Pliny, Juvenal and Pliny the Younger) and is a phenomenon frequently observed and noted in Grand Tour literature. See for example Joseph Spence's letter to his mother from Turin (24 October, 1731), in Klima, *op.cit.*, 71

deal of money you now, I don't usually talk of more then I'd not always of what I intend].[180] Jerre rec'd two letters to day from my Lord, one that Mr Barbon was dead, the other that Dean Alcock was taken dangerously ill,[181] & therefore desired us to hasten home with the utmost speed; in my last I acquainted you that my Lord had writ to me of Mr Barbons illness, & that he would give his preferment to Jerre, & desired us to hasten home. I had desired you to order me £15 at Langres in France, & £15 at Cambray, & had mentioned it to Mr Hoare to write for your order, if he did not receive it soon by reason of any miscarriage, now I would not have this done, only desire you to send him up order to answer your bill of £30 which you shall draw on in my favour, which bill of £30 I desire you to send to me directed at Mrs Rowlers; & to write to Mr Wood to receive any letter we order to be left with him. I desire you to request Hoare when he writes to Mr Alexander at Paris, to desire him to send any letters to Mr Hoare that are sent to him for us. We set out this evening or tomorrow for Turin, & hope to be in London in 3 weeks time; we shall stay in London about 2 daies, & so for Ireland, but I hope to be back in England again before the winter, but I can't tell how that will be; if it would not be too much trouble & it would be agreeable to you, I should be glad to see you & my Sister[182] in London [and in the end the charges of the journey should be disbursd to you];[183] you see what a hurry I am in [I

---

[180]This whole of the following passage is scored out in the copy

[181]Rev. Alexander Alcock (1665-1747) graduated from Trinity College, Dublin, in 1692 with an MA. He held the following offices in the diocese: Precentor of Lismore (1692-1725, when succeeded by Richard Pococke), Vicar of Dunhill (1694-98), Vicar of Guilcash (1694-98), Chancellor of the Waterford diocese (1699-1740, when succeeded by his son), Curate of Kilbarry (1699 until his death), Vicar Choral of Lismore Cathedral (1734-41), and the Dean of Lismore (from 1725 until his death). See Rennison, *op.cit.* for these dates. The dean was married to Jane Mason, daughter of Sir John Mason, Waterford and clearly recovered from his dangerous illness, since he lived a further thirteen years, until the age of eighty-two

[182]In the original he reverses this order, saying: "I should be glad to see my sister & you in London."

[183]By this he means the cost of his mother and sister's trip to London will be covered by him

am.., & you will see to what purpose][184], you need not mention any
thing further than than Mr Barbons affair. I thank you for the abridg'd
letters full of important informations. I just desire you to send my
gown & cassock & hood to London directed to me at Mrs Fowlers: my
other things I desire you to send in a box to Mrs Thomas in the Horse
fair near St James's Church Bristol, let her know we are sorry for her
loss, & that I will pay her with many thanks this charge & the others
by the first ship; & desire her to forward it by the first ship that goes to
Waterford.[185] The drawer I would have broke open,[186] & what relates
to Mr Wallingtons Accs &c. put up very carefully with my gown &
sent to London, & all the care taken to guard against any miscarriage
by the carrier because things of great importance.[187] If the box comes
from Paris, I would have what is in mine, sent in the box to Bristol, my
portmanteau must go to Bristol, perhaps it will hold all if not put my
papers & things of most consequence in the box;[188] my cloth coat need
not be sent nor the very worst of my shirts, my scarfe you'll send to
London & my wig; & my old beaver hat I wish it cd be taken a little
lower in the crown & made a very small matter less in ye crown & I
beleive paird round: this quick work will embarrass me I fear as to
money affairs for I must pay my debt wt ever I owe to my fellow
traveller at London & I know not how that will be, so perhaps may
want 10 more or so but do refuse you that thing which I now desire is
the only sum in which I have exceeded by credit Bagwell having sent
100 wch is ye sum you have already given me credit for, & ye rest I
had in Mr Hoares hands when I left London, that is all I drew before I
came to Rome, & had his letter for it but say nothing of it to Mr
Hoare, twill be a proper thing for me to talk of my accounts with him
in London.] The Batchelor of Laws hood need not be sent. I would
have the things for Bristol sent by the first opportunity without fail, &

---

[184]The meaning here is a little obscure. The next fourteen lines of text were
probably never intended for publication. Though entirely legible, they are
marked with a large cross

[185]Presumably this would be to Passage East, in County Waterford

[186]He must have remembered that he locked the drawer and went away with
the key

[187]Pococke needs these documents in London, so that he can sort out his
finances with his banker, as described below

[188]Possibly the journals he has been compiling during the course of his travels

desire Mrs Thomas to write to you that she has rec'd them [& if they are not brought to her to enquire for them at the ware house:]

They say Berwick is certainly dead. [Pray my most kind love to my sister]. I hope to be in London in a week after this comes to you, possibly sooner. [Pray let Mr Wallington know by a letter as soon as conveniently you can, that I shall be at Waterford in so short a time yt he may immediately honour me with his commands...][189] I am Dear Madam

Your most obedient & Dutyfull Son

Richard Pococke

P.S.

you will after this send every Post to the Post house, for I shall write I know not how often, tho' probably you may have one the two next Posts & after I believe we shall go as fast as the Post, so it will be to no purpose to write, [but I may write withstánding]

TURIN
15/26 June, 1734
Pococke to his mother
Letter 20[190]

[The opening lines of the copy letter are: "I wrote to you the 23d from Milan, that we had receiv'd an Account from my Lord &c: & Jerre was to hasten home &c: ". However, this is only a fraction of what actually appears in the original. The passage is unusual in that Mrs. Pococke herself has deleted virtually a whole passage, omitting it when making the copy, presumably because it repeats much of what was said in the

---

[189]Now that his return is imminent, it is safe to inform the Treasurer of Waterford that he is on his way home

[190]Add. 22978. This is the tenth letter of the original collection (Add. 19939) and there is no receipt.

previous letter. The full text is reproduced below. Pococke's penultimate journal ("Travels Vol. V. From Rome to Milan") has now come to an end, and his final journal is entitled "Travels Vol. VI Milan & From Milan to France".[191] Though this numbers 56 pages, more than half the volume is taken up with engravings of views and drawings of buildings, etc.]

Honoured Madam,

[I writ to you the 22d from Milan that we had receiv'd an account of Mr Barbones death that Jerre is to hasten to take his preferment & to still hasten our return that Dean Alcocke was dangerously ill, & that we are oblig'd to go in all haste to Ireland. I desird you to send my Gown & Cassock, my hat died taken down in the crown & a little lessen'd, my hood & scarfe what they are in my drawer, & a sermon on, Make full proof of thy minds, & another on, The Glory of their latter house shall be greater than of the former if to be found in the drawer wch you will break open. I am certain whether I brought 'em over, all these things I desird might be sent to London together with my wig & with whatever papers relate to any accounts, all the other things to be sent to Bristol to Mrs Thomas in Horse Fair near St James, Bristol who will forward them tho' her husband is dead & let her know I'll pay her wth thanks wt ever I have disbursd on my acct. We shall stay two daies at London where I should be very glad to see you & my sister if the journey will not be too troublesome to you, & if you set out it must be in two or three daies after the receipt of this letter in wch time I hope to be in London & shall travel so fast that no other letter will come to you before we land in England, I shall not withstanding write to you from Lyons to Newtown & to Mr Woodto be left with him, ye place we go to will be Mr Simpson. My black coat & some of the worst of my shirts need not be sent to Bristol and have my leather portmanteau go to Bristol. I desir'd you also to give me credit on Mr Hoare for £30 wn I am in London wth whom I have not exceeded my credit one farthing as youll see, & wn I come to London wt ever credit you have given before it £30 will be immediately disburs'd, I am notwithstanding equally oblig'd to you as if I had no money on his hands.]

---

[191] Add. 22983

23. We saw some churches and where T Charles Boromoeus lies in the Cathedral uncorrupted but could not see the body. at 3 went to the Lazaretto a building with a portico about a court a good mile round & without the gates, for the plaque; it is now the Magazine of the french; went to the Castle was all over it saw the execution done by Bombs &c: & the new works they are making; Lord Rock of Ireland is Major of the castle,[192] they are making it still stronger. Saw some churches; packed up.[193]

---

[192] It has not been possible to identify Lord Rock

[193] This is the extent of Pococke's description of Milan. In his journal, however, he devotes 28 pages to a description of its situation, churches, cathedral, libraries, squares, hospitals and palaces, concluding: "The people of Milan are mostly good looking & many handsom; They are very civil & polite: & the city is in every respect a most agreeable place", p.28. Likewise, Milles devotes 11 pages to an account of this city, an interesting part of which is his description of the Ambrosian Library, which is: "one of ye greatest curiositys of Milan. ye outer room wch contains all ye printed books to ye number of 42,000 as the Librarian inform'd me, is a very handsome chamber: another is allotted for ye manuscripts, wch amount as they say to 15,000. a third room is fill'd with several designs of fine painters, amongst wch is yt of ye school of Atheneus by Raphael, & likewise several moulds of ye most famous statues in jess, of particular limbs, &c: the fourth room is fill'd wth a great quantity of very choice peices, amongst wch are particularly fine, even beyond expression ye four seasons of ye year by Bruguel a Fleming, with several other remarkable peices. they have here 12 vol's of an unequall size, all full of designs of fortification, mechanicks &c: by Leonardo da Vinci. one is a very large volume in Folio over wch they have put an inscription, yt a certain King of England would have given 3000 Pistoles for ye book wch amounts to about 3000 Pd English. all ye writing in it instead of being wrote in ye common manner is wrote from right to left, so yt you cannot read it, without ye help of a looking-glass. it is thought he wrote it so yt other people might not easily understand it. ye other eleven vol's are very small. they shew'd us likewise a very ancient manuscript of Josephus's history of ye Jews in Latin, wch they say is 100 years old. it is wrote on ye ancient papyrus. they have likewise here a manuscript of St Carlo wch contains heads of discourses. they keep here a handchercheif [sic], & a shirt of ye saint by way of memorial. they have a book likewise full of all sorts of beasts, & birds, very finely painted. there is likewise a very fine collection of antique & modern medals. there is a room in this apartment set aside for ye study of painting, where bodys are exposed &c:". Add. 60516, pp 32-33

24. Set out in a Post Chaise for Turin, passed through Novara the last place in the Milanese, & din'd at Verceil the first in Piemont, the fortifications were destroyed I believe by Lewis XIV. Cardinal Ferionio the Bishop resides here. We travelled 65 miles to Chivauz, a small town 10 miles from Turin, having passed the Dutchy of Monserat, which belongs to the Duke of Savoy. We were 6 or 8 hours, after the King of Sardinia, who always rides post between the army at Mantoua & Turin, he goes it in one day 3 chaises & 4 saddle horses: as our time is much taken up you will excuse my Attick [abbreviated] Style.... I should be glad if you write by the first post to Dover to me to be left at the post house.

25. We came to Turin about 10. Mr Bristow & Mr Delme are here,[194] great part of this small city is exceedingly well built, wide strait streets,[195] fine Palaces, the Kings, the Dukes his eldest sons exceeding beautiful, the Prince of Carignois,[196] the Seminary & Academy & the most beautiful Square of St Carlo, a chapel n the Cathedral wainscoted with black marble where is the St Sudaire, are all the things worth seeing, which may be seen in half a day. We went to see the Citadel but raining were forced to return, it is a very strong one, Dignel an Irish man is major if it[197].... Mr Bristow came to see us in the morning, & he & Mr Delme in the afternoon, & we walked together in fine walks planted with trees near the Citadel, went to the coffee house & came home. The Germans it seems never had Parma, & have lost Colorna; Longuevill lost his life there, in entering some castle & not as in my former. Many of the English have been to see both armies. The Alps now [have] no snow where we are to pass, but it is all a very temperate climate. We hope to be in London in a fortnights time from this day, or at furthest by the 1st of July. Upon considering matters I

---

[194]Gentlemen whom they had met the previous January, in Rome

[195]In his journal, Milles describes the city, on entering it, as "a small, but prodigiously beautifull city...The old part of ye town is not very well built; but ye new is quite Beautifull; the houses are all built of brick but ye misfortune is yt most of them want to be plaister'd on ye outside; so yt they look quite rough & unfinishe'd" (Add. 60516, p.36)

[196]Louis Victor of Savoy (1721-1778) was a Savoyard Prince and the Prince of Carignan from 1741 until his death

[197]The editor has been unable to identify him. Pococke notes, in his journal, "Dignel an Irish Gentleman is major of the Citadel." (Add. 22983, p.44)

believe I shall want no more than the£30 [& that I hope to send you very soon after I am in Ireland. I am very sorry I can bring home no small thing for you & my sister, I should have run some risque if my circumstances would have admitted].

26.... We went to the Cathedral saw the King & his eldest son the Duke of Savoy at Mass; all dressed in black for the Marshal Villars, the King had his star higher than with us, his cravat twisted & put into his button hole; the Prince thin & small of 18, on his breast a star & also [a] chain about his neck: the King has a large underlip.[198] We part this afternoon.[199] [My very kind respects & love to my sister]

I am dear Madam your most obedient & Dutiful Son, Richard Pococke

Berwicks head was taken off by a canon ball

---

[198]Milles records this in his journal, as follows: "The Cathedral wch is dedicated to St John adjoines to the Ducal Palace, so yt when ye Duke or Royall family go to Mass they go immediately from ye Palace into ye church; we saw ye Duke & his son ye Prince at mass. they were in a little closet on ye north side of ye church." (Add. 60516, pp 37-38)

[199]On Saturday 26 June at about 5.00 in the afternoon. Pococke's last comment on the city in his journal is, "The city of Turin is very Antical", noting some inscriptions relating to the fact that its ancient name was August Taurinorum. *Ibid.*, 48. Milles' last words about Turin, however, are in relation to its people: "The Turinese are a very polite & civil people; but I am apt to think they are a little enclin'd to roguery. there is great abundance of every thing there. ye country about it being prodigiously plentifull. the people for ye most part talk French & follow ye French customs, & fashions. ye court of Turin is reckon'd one of ye politest in Europe they drive a great trade at Turin in silk stockings, wth wch they furnish allmost all Italy. they are very thin, & not half so good as ye English stockings, & indeed they cost but 6 shillings a pair. besides this they are remarkable for mill'd gloves, Rosasolis [cordial water] & Tobacco" (Add. 60516, pp 40-41)

LYONS
20 June/2 July, 1734
Pococke to his mother
Letter 21A [200]

Honoured Madam,

This I send with a particular account of my journey to Newtown, we may possibly be in London the 29th of June Old Style, I believe at furthest will be the 1st of July, we propose to come by Canterbury Coach but know not yet how it will be. We are here arriv'd this day & part this afternoon.

My most kind affections to my sister.

I am Dear Madam

Your Most obedient & dutifull son

Richard Pococke

---

[200] Add. 19939. This letter does not appear in the collection of copy letters (Add. 22978), as it was sent (according to the address) to Mrs. Pococke at Mrs. Fowler's in Rice Lane, London, where he had arranged to meet her. He refers to this note at the end of Letter 21 (see below)

LYONS
20 June/2 July, 1734
Pococke to his mother
Letter 21[201]

[This letter, which is reproduced here in full, gives a detailed account of their crossing of the Alps]

We left Turin Saturday the 26th about 5 in the afternoon & travelled 12 miles or 6 leagues to Aveliana there is a fine wide road, planted with trees on each side like an avenue & strait for 6 miles from Turin to Rivoli at the end of it one sees a palace of the Kings there, & at the other end you see Turin, & 5 miles beyond it on a hill the Cupola of the monastery of Superba where the late king lies & where I believe he returned & was confined. The country on each side fine, tho' few vines here abouts, but a most pleasant road as can be imagined; being a little in the night, we saw the fiery or glowing flyes, they are about a quarter of an inch long, narrow the tip of the head black, next part yellow the rest of the body on the back black, has wings, like chafers, the belly black except about ¼ from the tail which is yellow; this yellow part when they make any motion shoots out light & appears pellucid; when they fly it appears as they move their wings & is like a small flash; we saw hundreds of 'em appearing & disappearing in flashes, & catching them, as they make motions they flash continually, as they crawl every step or progression causes a flash, & tho' the light be from the belly, yet when you do not see the belly, you see the flash, which extends about a quarter of an inch round, in the dark it appears like fire, with a candle the light is like a gloe worm.[202]

We give 6 guineas for 2 horses for the Chaise, one for the man, all to be carried over the Alps on Mules to Pont Beauvosin [Le Pont de

---

[201]Add. 22978. This is the twelfth letter of the original collection (Add. 19939) and there is no note of receipt
[202]So struck were the two travellers by this sight that they both recorded it in their journals, Milles claiming to have seen "millions of these little flys for about half a mile together all along ye road, & they appeared like so many sparks of fire flying about" (Add. 60516, p.42), and Pococke maintaining (as in his letter) that they saw "hundreds of 'em appearing like sparks of a fire & disappearing like flames." (Add. 22983, p.49)

Beauvoisin] the first place in France, about 120 miles, the road pretty plain hitherto, but we shall go all day tomorrow in Valleys between the Alps & next day over Mount Cenis.[203]

27. We passed between the Alps by the river Doire or Dori[204] by soleil Busolino where we dined, just under Mount Roch me [Mount Rockmelon] top, which is higher than Mount Cenis they say to go to the top from the bottom is six miles, there is a church on ye top of it to which the people go to at our Ladies feast in August, by the help of grappling irons. We saw no snow on this mountain but a great deal in Mt Cenis, which I believe has great hollows in it, into which the snow drives & is not melted all the summer, we see the clouds lying half way down the mountain & moving about: at this place we found a march wind & perfect hurricanes like winter which they have often even in summer; we passed along the narrow valley by Susa, where are fortifications not to be passed by an enemy, & hinder any coming this way into Italy; we saw a fine triumphal arch there, but the occasion of [building] it I know not:[205] we lay at the foot of petit

---

[203] The ordinary pass for those travelling from France to Italy, or vice versa, was that leading over Mount Cenis, and as such, this mountain features very much in accounts of Grand Tourists

[204] The valley of which, as noted by Milles, "by ye melting of ye snows upon ye hills is often so much swell'd, & so very impetuous, & withal ye valley in wch it runs is so very narrow yt it sometimes carries away allmost whole villages, cattel, men, & women, nothing can resist it." (Add. 60516, pp 43-44)

[205] One detail Pococke spared his mother is recorded by Milles, as follows: "As we return'd from this Arch to ye Town, we were surprised to hear some soldiers tell us, yc we must go before ye governour. tho we were conscious of having done nothing yt we should not do, yet it being time of war, we did not know what ye governours reasons might be in sending for us. we went up to his house wch is an old castle, standing almost close to this arch. after having staid there a little time out comes the gentleman. drest indeed in a silk coat, but one yt was worn quite into threads; & wth a great air of importance ask'd us who we were, whence we came, & whither we went? having satisfy'd him of this; he next asked us, what was ye reason yt now in ye time of war, we came into a fortify'd town wall'd all round ye walls, & took memorandums down in writing. without ever asking ye goverrnours leave; as for a fortiyd town says we, it is none, & we did not perceive even yt it had any walls; ye notes we took were about an old Roman Arch, wch was ye only thing yt we wanted to see in ye city. well says he in order to

Mount Cenis;[206] we are to ascend in the morning from a village called Novalese the road was very rough.

28. At ¼ before 5 we set out to cross over the Alps[207] they call it 2 leagues up but this way is not near so bad as that we passed to Genoua nor so dangerous; at top of the mountain at the grand cross is the division of Italy & Savoy,[208] & an Inne, we eat very good butter there, & near it are two lakes out of which the river Dora rises; we passed by an Hospital for pilgrims where I bought a salted Marmot [a large ground squirrel], which they say eats like Ham & cost 1s 6d; here the mountains rise still higher on each side, perhaps 3 lines the heigth of Beacon hill,[209] & the tops are cover'd with snow, but none where we pass'd; but a cold wind like March with you, both above & below; they have not always such winds but very frequently, & always cold, except in the middle of the day, & in August they have something of a summer, below they see not the sun till 7 or 6 a clock & not after 4 or 5 in the middle of summer: the corn is green in ear, the

---

see this you should have asked my leave. we did not know replyd I where ye Arch stood; I thought it was in ye middle of ye town; yt does not signify says he, if it had, you should have asked my leave & for such a thing as this you are liable to be imprisoned. I saw he had a mind to domineer; & as we had French passports in our pockets we would not humble ourselves, or yield in ye least to him. vex'd yt we did not ask his pardon, & express our sorrow at doing so impudent an act he say'd I hope Gentlemen you will not do any such thing any more. we told him we were English gentlemen yt travell'd to satisfy our Curiosity, & we should go wheever yt led us. he then seeing yt he could prevail nothing turn'd ye discourse, & asked us about ye army. & after a little talk took our leaves. your pretty fellows yt are in office very often take it in their heads to be impertinent in this way. they fancy themselves very considerable persons just such anaffair happen'd to us at Antibes a little town in France; but ye Govenour, there had a great deal more good manners yt this Piedmontese. as soon as we had taken leave of ye Governour we left Susa..." Add. 60516, pp 45-47

[206] At the village of Novalese

[207] After having "pull'd our Chaise to peices & lodged one mile wth ye wheels, another wth ye body, & a third wth ye shafts, a fourth with our baggage", Add. 60516, p.48

[208] As further explained by Milles, "when you pass this cross you are out of Italy." *Ibid.*, p.49

[209] There are many Beacon Hills in England, but Pococke is perhaps referring to Warnford, Hampshire, since this is the county where his mother lives

fruit not ripe & much the same all along the mountains we are to go between for 3 days we came to the brow on this side, where the hill is steep, & but a league down, we were carried down in a chair without legs, with poles to the sides carried by two men,[210] one chair for each & came to Laniburgh at the foot of the mountains; near are some villages & an estate of Prince Eugenes who was born at Chamberry:[211] we rid over the Alps on mules, our wheels were carried on one mule, the head of the Chaise on another & the shafts on another & our baggage on a fourth, we waited 2 or 3 hours for the coming up of those things, having got to our Inn ¼ after 10,[212] so that we were 5 hours & ½ passing & allowing an hour we might linger by the way that brings it to 4 & ½ in passing, & indeed it is nothing at all; in winter it is very cold, but the French army passed about the time we were to have pass'd & the passage may be easier then, for you are carried or slide down on a machine most of the way; we travelled in the afternoon 12 miles through to Savoy high mountains in valleys, there is one next the Alps covered with snow, higher than any part of the Alps except Roch melon. Bad Inns here & dear & roads rough.

---

[210]A type of sedan chair, as further described by Milles, in his journal, and depicted in a sketch reproduced in Plate 8 (Add. 60516, pp 51-52): "here each of us got into a little arm'd chair without any feet but a sort of stirrup to put your feet into to keep you firm in ye chair: a pole is fix'd on each side, & two men carry you down. ye descent is pretty steep, but not in ye least rocky. it is almost all cover'd with grass. it is about a league or 2 Savoy miles from ye Ramassa to Lasnebourgh at ye foot of ye hill & porters carried extremely quick, & tho' tye descent was steep yet they trode as sure as if it had been even around...." Add. 60516, pp 50-51

[211]Chambery, corrected by Pococke on his mother's copy, in the second reference, below

[212]Milles further describes this place, as follows: "ye people seem to be very poor, & wretched. we arrived there about a quarter before ten; so yt we were but 5 hours & a half in passing, & we staid near an hour by ye way. we dined here, & waited 2 or three hours for ye coming of our baggage. the women here are very shorty & ye uglyiest creatures yt I ever beheld. their dress is very comical their gowns plaited all round, & their stays made so yt they all look as if they were big-belly'd. their caps have a peice of blue cloath in them." Add. 60516, p.51

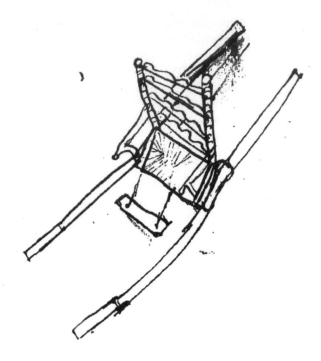

Plate 9
Sketch of "a little arm'd chair", by Jeremiah Milles,
from "An Account of what I saw Remarkable between Venice &
London", Courtesy of the British Library, Add. 60516, p.49

29. Travelled 8 miles mostly on Terraces on the sides of the hill to St
Michel. The hills are covered with firr, little worth because no
convenience of sending any where, only just for use of these places
they are near; our journey has been all along by the river Arca: here
are many Goosberry bushes with fruit as big as a pea, Barberries,
Campanula, a reddish Lilly with the head downward, I think call'd
the Crump or Crown Lilly, many walnut trees.[213] The villages & little
towns are very thick here, & it is wonderfull to see the worst country
in the world so improved with corn, any where that the plow or spade
can work: 'tis cultivated even to the top of the mountains: the woods

---

[213]The same observations are made in his journal, Add. 22983, p.52

here are inhabited by wolves, bears chamois, wild deer &c: Marshal Villars heart is sent into France his body as yet remains at Turin, where I saw his son the Duke de Villars.

We met yesterday on the road Mr Goff & Mr Crawley English Gentlemen going into Italy:[214] at this place there lives a Gentleman which is the first I have seen any sign of in Savoy, the mountains from this become lower, no snow on them & the valleys wider to St John de Morien, so that we found it warm & saw something of harvest, from that, 4 miles, the valleys narrow to Chambery where we lay, so called because they have much flax thereabouts. In Piedmont almost every body talks French as well as Italian, the former is used entirely among the better sort. In Savoy all is French among the vulgar corrupted with a little mixture of Italian. The most wonderful thing is to see how the poor creatures improve the mountains; many small spots wherever they can stand to dig all up, but distant from another, by reason a twentieth part is too steep to work on. This is sown with corn, there are also some few vines, you may be sure no part of the vale is untilled, & this they are obliged to, the country being populous, & they must have within themselves the necessaries of life, which would be brought hither with great difficulty, & I believe they would not have money to purchase it, and so little land they have improveable, that it can only suffice for themselves, so that I can't see they can have any trade, the little money that comes in is chiefly by travellers; & suppose they deal much with one another by trucking. We came but 8 leagues to day which they call but 14 miles. The people here are small & of very indifferent countenances tho' not many with swell'd necks, which I wonder at,[215] 'tis of this country those are mostly, who carry about Raree Shows:[216] & a great number

---

[214]These gentlemen have not been identified, though are listed in Ingamells, *op.cit.*, 253

[215]In his journal, Pococke notes that "they say they have a powder which if taken inwardly when first they begin to swell will put a stop to it." Add. 22983, p.54

[216]Noted in the original letter (Add. 19939) as "the rary shows". The reference is obscure and alludes to some sort of public exhibition or entertainment

of Chimney Sweepers who [ ] a c[ ], take him home every [place]
going out in winter & return in summer...[217]

30. We set out from Aquebelle, the mountains begin to dwindle into
hills, the valleys are wider, the hills improved & covered with trees &
corn & the country pleasant enough. We dined at La Planese 7 leagues
about 14 miles the road better: we saw more swell'd necks this way, it
seems they generally apply a powder, which if not too far gone puts a
stop to it; the Inns much better yesterday & to day. The mountains
belong to the King, & those that improve any part, pay only a small
tax to the King. We came to Montmelian crossing to it the river Isere
into which the Arca runs a little higher, this town was well fortified,
but all destroyed by the late King of France; here the country greatly
improves, the hills covered with vines call'd montmelian wine, which
is very good; here the road goes to the left to Grenoble; we came in
good road 6 miles to Chambery, a pretty large City, the Capital of
Savoy, where the Dukes formerly resided, & where we saw their old
Castle. The Duke of Villars came in ½ an hour after us & parted next
morning before us for France. Prince Eugenes sister has a house here,
she is married to the Prince Carignan, who has a fine palace there.

July 1. We came 8 miles to Lechelles, bad road, & part is cut deep
thro' a rock by the Duke of Savoy in 1670 a great work, they cover
their houses here with shingle.[218] We came 7 miles bad road on the
side of a hill which is rocky to Pont Beauvosin, where is a bridge over
the river by which we entered into France; 'tis in a manner two towns,
the smaller of the Savoy side the other larger on the French side.[219]

---

[217]This note has been added, in Pococke's hand, and is difficult to decipher. It
does not appear in the original letter (Add. 19939). However, he adds a
similar note in his journal, "& many of the inhabitants turn beggars,
chimney sweepers, & go about with shows in France during the winter, &
come home in summer." Add. 22983, p.52

[218]In the original letter (Add. 19939), Pococke note that the houses are
covered with wood, "just like tiles as looks like 'em when turn'd brown
with the weather". Curiously, in his journal, he notes that they cover their
houses with shingles, and the next two lines are scored out. Add. 22983,
p.55

[219]The same observation marks the end of Pococke's journal, which
completes his journals for the first tour. Milles, however, continues to
record the journey until they reach London

Duke Villars having taken up all the Post horses, we waited here two hours leaving our Voiturin:[220] & at 7 set out about 12 arrived 25 miles at Burgoigne.[221]

2. Came 25 more to Lyons, which place we leave this afternoon. I send a short notice to be left at Mrs Fowlers in London, where we may possibly be Saturday the 29th of June, or I believe at the furthest Monday the 1st of July, & hope to meet you. I have writ so often lately, I need not be more particular. My most kind love to my Sister.

I am Dear Madam

Your most obedient & Dutiful Son

Richard Pococke

You need not send for ye letter in London in case you don't come for there is nothing [in] it[222]

---

[220]Noted also by Milles, Add. 60516, p.58

[221]Milles notes, in his journal, that "it being excessively dark, & there being a great deal of Thunder lightening, & rain, we could not think of going any further so we lay at Burgoin all night the next morning Friday July ye 2d we set forward about 7 of ye clock, & about 11 we arrived at Lyons wch is 4 posts & a half i:e: 27 miles. the country all ye way from Burgoin is exceedingly pleasant. we only staid at Lyons for three, or four hours to see somethings yt we had left unseen as we went thro' it before, ye acct of all wch I have given together in a former book." Add. 60516, p.81

[222]Scored out of the copy and reproduced from the original (Add. 19939)

Journal Essay by Milles on Italy & Savoy and the Italian People[223]

Italy is generally call'd ye garden of ye world, & look's upon as ye finest spot of ground in it: it lyes between 37, & 46 degrees northern latitude. it is undoubtedly a very rich, & fruitfull country. ye best parts of it are Lombardy, ye part of Tuscany, wch is between Florence, & Leghorn; ye Campania Felix, & some part of Romagnia. ye most barren parts of it seem to be between ye Sienna, & Rome quite down to ye Mediterranean ye Campania de Roma, & Sabina; but all these are very capable of improvement, & ye only reason why they are barren; is because people do not find encouragement to till them. indeed there are some rocks & mountains but there are few yt are so very barren but yt are planted either with vines or olive trees. Italy is principally divided between ye Vienna, & Rome quite down to ye Mediterranean ye Campania di Roma, & Sabina; but all these are very capable of improvements & ye only reason why they are barren; is because people do not find encouragement to till them. indeed there are some rocks & mountains but there are few yt are so very barren but yt the are planted either with vines or olive trees. Italy is principally divided between 4 Princes, & 2 Republicks viz The Emperour, The Pope; ye Duke of Tuscany, & ye Duke of Savoy, ye Republicks of Genoa & Venice. the former possesses all ye Kingdom of Naples; wch is all ye southern part of Italy; besides ye Dutchy of Milan, & Mantoua wth Orbitello, & Porto Longone, 2 little places in Tuscanny wch lay upon ye sea. The Pope is master of ye ancient Latium Sabina; what is now call'd ye Patrimony of St Peter, wch was formerly part of Tuscany; Picenum, now call'd Marca Anconitana; Romagha & ye Bolognese. The Duke of Savoy possesses ye country of Piedmont ye towns of Nice, & Villa Franca, & ye Marquisate of ONeglia on ye Mediterranean; besides Savoy wch is out of Italy. The Dukes of Parma, & Modena, & ye Republick of Lucca have small dominions ye other little principalitys are not worth naming. The Republick of Venice is more considerable yn yt of Genoua its territorys are bounded on ye North by Carinthia Carmiola, & ye Bishoprick of Trent, on ye East by Camiola & ye Adriatick, on ye South by ye Fenarese Manhian, & Cremonete, Y on ye West by ye Dutchy of Milan.

---

[223]Add. 60516, pp 58-80

besides wch they have ye Islands of ye country, Corfu, Zanthe, &
Dalmatia, out of Italy.[224] most of ye Venetian state in Italy is
prodigious fertile land, laying in ye plentifull vale of Lombardy. ye
Republick of Genoua possesses a mountainous, & barren tract of land
of about 20 or 30 mies in depth, & about 150 in length all along ye
Mediterranean sea, & what is properly call'd ye Gulph of Genoua.
Their hills all along ye sea shore, tho' for ye most part pretty barren,
yet are planted very thick with olive trees.

as to ye Government of these different states tho' some are
Monarchical, & some Republican yet it would be difficult to say,
whose subjects are ye happiest, & ye least burthen'd with taxes. all
their different maxims of Policy, & forms of Government seem to
agree in this resolution namely to oppress their subjects with very
grievous taxes. The Bolonghese seem'd to me to be ye happiest
people, for they did not absolutely give up their Libery to ye Pope, but
merely secur'd to themselves by articles some little powere; & liberty.
I had not sufficient time to examine into ye constitution of each
principality, but I thought yt ye Venetians, Genoese, & ye subjects of
ye Dukes of Florence & Savoy seem'd to be more oppress'd yn ye rest.
one cheif way yt they have in several of ye states in Italy, is for ye state
to buy up, & engross one or several commoditys & then afterwards
sell it out to ye people at a great advantage, obliging them to buy of
them. this method I know is practised in ye Republick of Genoua &
by ye Pope; & it may be so in several other states. indeed the Pope
does it out of a pretence of providing agst a famine, or scarcity, & yt he
may receive ye poor people, when they want bread, but some people
think yt it is done only with a view of raising money & enriching
himself thus much in General of ye government of Italy.

The cheif commoditys of Italy are corn, wine, oil, olives, silk, salt,
marble, wth several others wch are confin'd to particular citys. all
Lombardy & ye valley between Leghorn, & Florence is ye great
storehouse of corn for all Italy; about Florence, Naples, Monte
pulciano, Monte[ ], & Monte Fiascone, (wch 3 last places are in
Tuscany,) grown excellent wines; but common wines grown every

---

[224]The flow of this sentence is a little uncertain owing to the scorings out and
additions, above the line, of new words

where. Ye state of Genoua & yt country about Florence, & Lucca is remarkable for good oil, & olives. Bologna is ye cheif city for ye silken manufacture. (Footnote: Bologna is likewise famous for its sausages, & for ye shining stones wch are found thereabouts)[225] there is likewise a good deal at Genoua. the great Magazine for salt is near Cervia a little town on ye Adratick not far from Ravenna, where are vast quantitys of salt Pits. The yellow marble of Sienna, & ye black, & white of Brescia are esteem'd as ye best of ye Italian marbles. ye former is accounted more beautifull than ye Giallo antico or ancient yellow marble, tho' it has not hear ye hardness of it. if I remember right there is a good marble about Genoua too. Venice is remarkable for its glass, its treacle & its soap. all sorts of Chrystal & steel work are in perfection at Milan, Brescia is as remarkable for its fire arms; Turin for its silk stockings Florence for its essences, & p[erfumes, wch are made by ye Monks of Sta Maria Novella, & St mark; & for its stones wch are found about in ye mountains, & wch represent naturally trees, & ruins; these stones are call'd Dendrites; the work call'd marquetery is likewise in perfection there, wch is made wth several marbles or precious stones of different colours, so as to represent houses (&) %c: Genoua's best manufacture is its velvet, & silk, works; besides wch it is remarkable for dry sweetmeats, & for soap, & washballs. Rome is remarkable for its gloves, wch are counted ye best in Italy, thoi' they are not extroardinary [sic]. The Signor Rossi near ye church of ye Pace has a very large print shop, where are a great collection of cuts of ye churches palaces, ancient, & modern buildings in , & about Rome; likewise maps. he has a printed catalogue with ye prices affixed, so yt he never asks more nor takes less, yn ye settled price. Hamerani is remarkable for striking exceeding good medals in Gold, silver, & Copper; indeed I thi nk he is ye best workman in yt way, yt I ever saw. you may have there a collection of medals of all ye Popes; yt is from ye time yt medals were first struck of ye Popes.[226]

---

[225]Milles' footnote appears on the reverse of the page. According to Thomas Salmon (*op.cit.*), "And there is scarce a traveller but mentions the shining stones found about three miles from the city in the hill Paderni, which go by the name of Bologna Stones; but these I find, after they have been taken for some time out of the earth, lose their shining quality" (p.380)

[226]Ottone (Otto) Hamerani (1694-1768) came from a family of famous medallists and coin engravers and lived in Rome

The citys in Italy wch are remarkable for ye best painting are Rome, Bologna, & Venice, & Florence; for modern sculpture, Florence, & Rome, ye former had Sansovino, Michael Angelo Buonarotii, Baccio Bandinelli, Donatello, & John da Bologna to boast of. & ye latter Guglielmo della Porta, Cavalier Bernini, & Algardi, wth many others. Ye Architecture yt is most admird in Italy is at Vicenza Padoua & Venice, in ye Venetian State, & Florence & Rome. In ye former Palladio's buildings are admir'd in Florence Michael Angelo, Sansovino Architect to ye present G: Duke, & Galileo Galilei, & at Rome ....who was ye first reviver of Architecture[227] Balthazar Peruzio, Antheny Langaillo, Michael Angelo Buonarotti Carlo Maderno, Cavalier Fontania, & ye inimitable Bernini.[228]

As to ye trade of Italy, it is pretty large, ye most famous seaports for it, are Genoua, Leghorn, Civita Vecchia Naples (Gallipoli) Ancona, & Venice; at all wch places except Civita Vecchia, & I beleive Gallipoli we have consuls.

As to ye general character of ye Italians themselves, yt is so well known yt one need not mention anything of it. but I beleive whoever considers them well, & compares yr behaviour wth ye acct yt writers have given of them he will find them very different; especially in yt remarkable passion of Jelousy [sic]; wth wch they are so much branded having been us'd to such a number of strangers yt are continually amongst them; & seeing so much of ye French customs they have now pretty much given into them. & have a much freer carriage yn formerly. & so far are they from being Jealous of their wives yt allmost every married Lady has her gallant (wch in Italian is call'd Cisisbeu) even in ye sight & by ye permission of their husbands. & it is not to be doubted but yt ye husband in his turn provides himself wth some other Lady. The business of ye gallant is to squire them about & to find them in pin-money; & if you make your addresses to any married Lady, you have nobody to fear but ye

---

[227]It is impossible to decipher this name

[228]Milles appeared to have difficulty spelling many of the above names, the passage being full of errors and corrections. As a result, some of the names may have been incorrectly transcribed by the current editor

gallant, who perhaps it he is jealous of you may give you a stab; but
this never happens to any English Gentleman.[229]

As to ye manners, & behaviour of persons of quality they are generally
well bred, but pretty much on ye reserve, wch proceeds partly from
pride; & partly from a natural inclination it is true in ye parts of Italy
wch are nearest to France, as Milan Turin &c: they are more familiar,
& easy; but at Rome, & Florence they carry it pretty high. the Ladys
do not ordinarly converse with strangers, & in Rome, & Florence
particularly (I do not remember whether it was so any where else) ye
Ladys & Gentlemen do not go in ye same coach, but you shall see four
Ladys in one coach, & four gentlemen following in another. at
assemblys ye Ladys make a card table by themselves, & ye Gentlemen
by themselves.

The middling sort of people are very affable, & courteous; & I think
not inferior to ye French in their civilitys to strangers, unless it be yt an
Italians civility never carrys him so far as to put him to any expence.
They are vastly inquisitive, & ask every bodys name, country, religion,
& profession; nor are they less inquisitive about news;   & seem to be
all great Politicians.

The inferior sort of trading people seem to be very treacherous, &
deceitfull in their dealings; & will contrive all means to impose upon
strangers especially ye English of whose riches they form to
themselves strange & unaccountable notions. besides as they look
upon them as hereticks, they think it no sin to cheat thme; & generally
ask double, treble or five times more yn they will take; so yt one who
is not used to their ways, will at first be very much imposed upon.

The Italians have some virtues, & some vices peculiar to them; of ye
former they are very remarkable for their Temperance, Frugality, &
charity; their temperance in eating, & drinking is so great, yt they are

---

[229]See Richard Twiss, *op.cit.*, who, in his Appendix, designed to give advice
to potential Grand Tourists, notes: "It will be experienced that the
inhabitants of the southern climates are in general jealous of their
mistresses, but not of their wives; and that the women are there (and indeed
every where else) much easier to get at, than to get rid of , except by leaving
the place" (p.198)

never seen to drink a glass of wine between meals, & rarely at meals without mixing watger wth it. they eat very little flesh; & all other things very sparingly, & seldom make any supper at all; immediately as soon as dinner is over they drink a dish, or two of coffee; in ye morning they drink either coffee or chocolate for breakfast, but seldom, or never, eat with it, or put mik into their coffee. the common sort of people feed much upon macaroni, & upon soups made of different sorts of pulse, of wch they have great variety.

The Frugality of ye Italians is likewise very great & they are excellent oeconomists. the least expence of their [ ] is in eating & drinking for the greatest Princes in Italy never keep a table, or invite any body to dinner; even their servants are put to board wages, & some little trifling thing got for them & their family for dinner; it is said of y Princess Barberini at Rome yt she never spent abouve 18 pence for her dinner; all ye Italians in general live in this manner, there is no such thing ever heard of, as inviting either one another or strangers to dinner; & if you visit them, they never ask you to eat, or drink wth them, except when you are very well acquainted they may offer you a dish of tea, or coffee. as they are thus frugal, they cannot help wondering at ye excessive extravagance, & prodigality of most of ye English nobleman; whom they see so liberal of their money; & they make their advantage of them, & raise their price to every thing according to ye quality of ye Buyer. But tho' the Italians are so niggardly in some respects, in others they are very free of their money; especially in those things yt please their pride, & vanity. they will for instance lay out 2000 L on a very fine coach; I have seen one, or two such in Rome wch could not cost much less money. the very spokes of ye wheels were gilt, & there was a great deal of carved work behind, & about ye coach. in bying Pictures, statues, & medals they spare no money; for anything yt is curious in this way they will give almost as much as any body; & indeed most of ye Princes at Rome particularly have laid out vast sums of money on these things, tho' undoubtedly, they bought most of them very cheap. A fine equipage at ye Carnaval is what they delight in very much; where they will lay out a great deal of money in dresses for themselves, & their equipage the Italians (excepting those of ye highest quality) in some things are very mercenary; any body for instance yt has a collection of medals seals or any other valuable things will sell you any part or all of them for a good price: in short there is hardly any thing they have got, but what you might easily buy of them, if you would give them their own price.

The Charity of ye Italians both public, & private is certainly very great; of ye former, y emany noble Hospitals, & informarys, yt are all over Italy, is an instance; of ye latter ye prodigious number of beggars; who subsist very will upon ye alms they receive, is an instance; were their charity but well directed it would be of infinite service to ye country, but at present, ye only effect of it is, yt it makes ye country swarm wth Beggars; ye natural indolence, & inactivity of ye people; & ye great alms wch ye rich give away; makes ever poor idle fellow take up ye trade of begging. I have seen half a dozen beggars lye at a church door, where there was any feast, & beg people for ye sake of ye saint they were going to pay their devotions to yt they would give them an alms;. & allmost every body yt went in gave them some small matter; in this manner ye beggars ply about from church, to church. As to their Hospitals what vast sums of money have been bequeathed for ye founding, & supporting them, it is impossible for me to tell; but certainly they are such an instance of a well-placed Xtian charity, as cannot but make England blush; who has very few of these supports, & assistances for their poor, & sick people. & so extensive are these benefactions, yt anybody let him be ye greatest stranger in ye world, & of what religion he will, if he fall sick in any place where there is an hospital, is taken into it, & they attend him with a Physician & fid him in meat, & drink, & all things necessary till he is well.

If ye Italians have these virtues to recommend them, they have likewise some vices, wch make them odious. the most remarkable of whc is their violence of their passions & their insatiable thirst after revenge. a very little trifle will soon put them into a violent passion in many of wch they kill people instantly as for a weapon they allways carry a stiletto or a little dagger of about a foot long in their pockets, wch they can immediatly pull out, & do execution with. indeed these weapons are absolutely forbid to be carry'd by any body, nevertheless they always carry them about them. & what is worse, they do not soon forget injurys but avenge them a long time afterwards.

Their Jealousy is another remarkable vice, wch us'd to make them confine their wives so much; but it is hardly to be conceived, what an alteration there is in ye Italians within these 30 years; the intercourse they have had wth ye French, & ye vast quantity of Foreigners yt flock thither continually have taught them to be less reserved, & more free in their Behaviour than formerly; so yt you do not see now yt suspicious carriage & shyness, wch they formerly used to have. yet they have still some Jealousy in their temper, wch seems to be natural to them.

Lust is another remarkable vice among them, wch they indulge very much not only in ye nommon natural way, but also in yt horrid Bestiality for wch they are so famous. It is well known yt when Pope Sixtus Quintus expell'd ye common whores from Rome, he was forced to recall them soon after, because, the people had found out a worse way of gratifying their lusts. The Florentines are now said to be much addicted to this, as ye Venetians are to ye women.

The Italians are likewise too much addicted to swearing in common speech; & they have some most terrible, & bitter oaths, & imprecations likewise all their words yt are most commonly used by them are filthy.

As to religion they are as blind, & ignorant as you may imagine any people, giving a most implicit faith to every thing yt their priests tell them. & there is no absurdity so gross in religion yt they will not swallow down. & I have often thought yt their great credulity in religious matter, has mde them also credulous in every thing else; for the beleive all storys of witches apparitions & Ghosts; & I remember at Rome; a Dominican Father who was Confessor to ye Pretenders Lady, wth whom I happen'd to be acquainted shew'd me one day a little book wch treated of Palmistry, & Judicial Astrology telling me at ye same time yt he believed every thing in y book was true. they likewise entertain strange notions yt ye Devil has possession of all ye treasures under ground.

As to learning ye state of yt is at present very low in Italy. at Bologna, & Florence indeed there are some learned men; & at Venice likewise. but at Rome, where there ought to be a great number of learned men, as being ye place ot such all ye Clergy resort; there one finds ye least learning, & ye fewest learned men. the Canon Law indeed is studeyed

there because of ye Popes courts, but except yt branch of learning
there is very little else study'd except scholastic Divinity. & as this is
ye case ye Booksellers shops in Rome, are very poorly furnish'd. you
can find little else in them but decisions in ye canon law, & schoolmen;
they print but a few books at Rome of those are for ye generality very
ill done. at Venice they print ye most of any place in Italy, & ye
cheapest,; at Florence likewise they print very well. But hardly any of
them come up to ye old printing of ye Tiunti Giolito Tolentino, Bab
&c: there is a new press at Padoua, where they print better yn in any
other part of Italy; ye paper & letter being incomparably superior to all
ye rest; there is no press now at Ferara wch was formerly famous for
Gabriel Giolito's printing. at ye rest of ye citys they use a few presses,
but they are not remarkable either for ye beauty, or ye quantity of ye
Books they print. there is an Academy of virtuosi in allmost every city
in Italy, & in some of ye principal ones there are two, they affect to be
call'd by uncommon titles as ye Endormiti, Humoristi, ostinati, otiose,
Narscosti & several other odd names, one of wch each Academy takes
to itself as these Academy make very little noise in Italy, I conclude yt
their labours are neither very great, nor very serviceable to ye world;
yt at Verona seem'd to be ye most usefull, & best regulated; if I
remember, it is design'd for Musick, & ye members all themselves
Philarmonici.

As to ye language yt is spoken in Italy, tho' it is all in general call'd
Italian, yet there is a very great difference between ye dialect of everh
partcular people; ye best Italian is reckoned to be spoke at Sienna, &
in some parts of Tuscany ye purest Italian is call'd Tuscan, & the
Romans are reckoned to pronounce Italian ye best, so yt when the
language is spoke in perfection, it is as they call it Lingua Toscana in
bocca Romana i:e: Tuscan language in Roman mouth. at Florence, &
thereabouts they have a disagrable way of speaking in their throat, so
yt they turn a C, in t an ff, & when they should say casa, they say hasa;
at Rome they generally talk pretty well, but in ye Transtibertine region
on ye other side of ye river, they talk very bad. ye Bolognese ye
Venetians, the Bergamasa ye Genouse, Milanese, & ye Neopolitans
have all a barbarous dialect, peculiar to each country; but this is
talked only by ye poorer, & inferior sort of people; ye nobility in every
place speak good Italian.

As there are so many different states in Italy, & each state coins its own money, it is a little perplexing to change ones money so often, & to have so many sorts, yt one cannot remember all. indeed there are some gold, & silver coins wch are current all over Italy. at Florence, Rome, Genoua, & Venice, they coin sequins wch is a piece of Gold. those of ye 3 first states of about 50s or 50s & 8d value, yt at Venice is reconed about a shilling better. at Florence & Rome Milan they have crowns; half crowns festoons, & Pauls wch are good silver & are current every where. the Festoon is 18 value, & ye Paul 6d. as to all ye other peices of money they are current only in their own country, & upon borders of ye neighbouring ones. indeed at Milan they have hardly any money of their own except a few crowns, & some farthings, & therefore the Venetian Genoese Savoy, & all most all sorts of money are current.

The Italians imitate ye French in their dress; but ye citizens in every city have a very odd habit; they wear a sort of a short petticoat made of black cloath, wch is tyd about their middles under their westcoat, & they go all dress'd in black, wth a large band instead of a neck.

These few observations are what occurr'd to me, & therefore I chose to put them down least I should hereafter forget them.

DOVER
30 June, 1734
Letter from Pococke to his mother
Letter 22[230]

Honoured Madam,

I writ to you from Lyons on Friday July 2d N.S. We went to the Banker & to see some things we had over look'd when we were here before; as the Tauribile an ancient Altar - a mosaick pavement in figures of men &c: We set out between 4 & 5 in the Paris road by Dijon; the highest road is more west a better road but further about, this goes near the Soane to Chalons; we ascended a hill after we came out of Lyons & passed through a pleasant Country full of small hills 18 miles by Anse to Ville Franche, a middling town with one wide street in the middle where we lay.

3. We went by Mascon (where we lay when we came to Lyons in a boat, it is a pretty large city, the cathedral is small, but a very good light Gothick building, & by Furnes, a good middling town on the Soane as well as Mascon) to Chalons 54 miles.

4. We travelled by Beaume [sic] a fine situated town & Dijon to Thil [sic], 57 miles where we lay.[231] To Dijon is the same road we went to Lyons, now we are in a new road to Langres, you remember from

---

[230] Add. 22978. This is the thirteenth letter of the original collection (Add. 19939) and is addressed to Mrs. Elizabeth Pococke at Mrs. Fowlers in Sice Lane, London. The format of this letter differs slightly from the original in places, particularly in the last page, where Pococke dispenses with the numbering of each new day at the beginning of the paragraph, merging it into the text. However, Mrs. Pococke, when making the copy, sticks to the format she adopted from Letter 10, at the beginning of volume 2 of her son's manuscript

[231] In his journal, Milles notes, "ye people of Beaune are look'd upon by ye French as a very heavy sort of people; & a Gentleman who din'd with us there told us a merry story of them, yt once there happening a violent storm of rain a vast quantity of earth was carry'd down from all parts into ye fosse of ye town; upon wch ye people of Beaune send out a proclamation by beat of drum commanding every body to come & carry off their own ground out of ye fosse after dinner we set out again..." Add. 60516, p.83

Chalons we went in a boat to Lyons; the country from Dijon to Thil is
like that beyond Marlborough; mostly corn, but near Thil vineyards of
Champaign, into which country we came a league off, we drink all red
Champagne[232] which is much like Burgundy.

5. We went to Langres, a wine Country, a small city, the small
Cathedral has several old monuments in it of Bishops &c: with
couchant statues, some in stone there is one of Cardinal de Jeuvry
bronze kneeling, & one before the altar of 3 children of the Fornaci,
who were sainted; & there is a lamp always burning near these 3
couchant statues have wings like Angels & are gilt.[233] We went 18
miles to Chaumont, not a very little town, there we dined a corn
country; went 24 miles to Joinville, a little up & down hill, an open
Corn Country, some woods but no hedges, here we lay having
travelled 66 miles in a very rainy cold uncomfortable day but we went
the faster, the Postilions making hast[e] to get out of the wet: we were
so extravagant as to give 18d for a bottle of white Champain[234] & have
come to a resolution now we are going into the part of the country
where it grows, to drink no other wine till we come in to the Isle of
France, which will be the day after tomorrow.

6. We set out at 4 a very rainy windy morn & cold, we travelled 36
miles by 10 to Vitry, had champagne white with a little tinge of red,
we travelled 54 miles to Rheim in all 90, we should not have made so
great a journey in the morning if it had not rained very hard which
made the Postilions hasten, it cleared up in the afternoon & the reason
we run so far was the goodness of the road like a gravel walk, broad &
lately made & planted on each side with trees.[235] In the morn we

---

[232] Again spelled "Champaign" in the original letter (Add. 19939)

[233] As Milles explains, "there is before ye high altar tombs of the three twin
children who were massacred at ye foundation of ye church of Langres."
Add. 60516, pp 84-85

[234] Spelled thus in the original (Add. 19939)

[235] Milles comments on this road, too, noting, "I believe for 20 miles there is
but one turn in ye road; ye latter part of it is not made as yet. It was making
when we pass'd, & we were forced to turn aside into a by road & therefore I
cannot be certain, but I beleive when it is finished ye road will be all or very
near strait; what a beautifull effect must this have; to see a fine open
country before you; & to see ye finest road in ye world with only one bend
in it for 30 miles together." Add. 60516, p.89

passed through St Dizier I saw only a large street, the houses frames of wood with cage work as at Vitry where we dined & Chalons. Vitry is laid out very regular in strait streets across each other;[236] there is a church with a good front & a foss around the town as if designed for a modern fortification left unfinished. Chalons is the Capital of Champaign, the Cathedral & notre dame good Gothick buildings & good paintings in the windows of the latter;[237] Chalons in Burgundy we passed through two days ago, & before in our way into Italy, where we saw Mr Vincenois brother: we were out 17 hours, 13 of which only we ran & travelled 90 miles so that we might easily have made above 100 miles, & no more tired than when we set out, travelling in a Post: chaise is so easy. Rheimes is a large city some say 9, but I believe about 6 miles round, built as the others we saw with frames of wood & cage work.

7. At 4 we went to see a triumphal Arch or gate, now under the old fortifications of this city, of very rich Architecture,[238] we saw the magnificent Cathedral Gothick, I believe it is next to Amiens, here the King is crowned & consecrated with the Holy oyl of the Saint Ampoulle preserved at St Remi of the Benedictines here (a large old church) under the sepulchre of St Remi, there we saw it kept in a box of Gold sett [sic] with precious stones 'tis of the size & shape of a Spirit of Hartshorne [smelling salts] bottle of white glass, you know, they say it was brought from heaven, by an Angel in Shape of a Dove at Cloivisy is the Consecration, & the oyl is always sufficient. Another fine old church is St Remi.[239] We set out at 8 went 30 miles to Laons,

---

[236]According to Milles, this town was "one of ye prettiest laid out yt I ever saw", Add. 60516, p.86. He comments on the weather in his journal: "here [Vitry] we dined but we were first forced to dry ourselves; for we had now rode for a day & a half in incessant rain, wch had never once stopp'd & for ye month of July, I think I never felt heavier; ye rain had at last soak'd thro' ye chaise, so yt when we came to Vitry we were very wett; but by good luck it gave over ye afternoon, & we went four posts more to Chalons in Champagne, in as fine a country, & as good roads, as ever I desire to travell in." *Ibid.*, pp 87-88

[237]Milles notes this, too, though regrets that, "being in a good deal of hurry I forgot ye subject of ye painting." *Ibid*, p.89

[238]Milles also describes this antiquity in great detail (see *ibid.*, pp 92-95)

[239]Described by Milles as an abbey. He notes that as they were coming out of the church of St Nicaise somebody asked them if they would like to see the

half of the way bad & the other very bad; about 2 or 3 miles in the way we saw vineyards, the rest corn like common fields as every where, no trees, except about villages & here & there a wood. Laon is finely situated on the top of a hill, a small city not a mile round, the Cathedral is pretty large & in the inside one of the most beautiful Gothick buildings I ever saw. The Hill is planted with vines.[240] We went 15 miles by indifferent roads, to La fiere in Picardy, where the Duke Dura has a palace, 'tis a middling town on the river Ouse, which runs into the Seine; passing over another river between Rheims & Laon at Pontivere that runs into the Seine, we saw much wood for burning, floating down, they told us it was turned loose from Lorrain & that a boat follows it, to forward such as lodges by the way & so it goes to Paris. Half way between Rheims & Laon at the river we came into the Isle of France & a little before we came to Laon, in to Picardy.

8. We went to Ham a small town & then to Peronne, a pretty fortified town, where we dined, there is a good Gothick Collegiate Church. A little further we enter'd into Flanders came to Arras a strong fortified town, not very large but very beautiful, well built, a fine square with an ornamental cross, a fine tower; the Cathedral very handsome but old, we saw many women sitting at the door making lace: we came that evening by 12 to Betune [sic], a fortified town also not very large.[241]

9. We came by Aire a small town [and thence][242] to St Omer, where we dined; saw the indifferent cathedral[243] & St Martin belonging to the Benedictines not reformed, a very magnificent Gothick building, & the English College of 112 students under 30 Jesuits, a school as well as university or College; a handsome building of brick with Corinthian

---

sounding pillar, but being in a hurry and not knowing what it was, they didn't bother. See Add. 60516, p.92

[240] According to Milles' journal, they ate dinner at their inn

[241] As described by Milles, "but it being between 11, & 12 before we came there [to Bethune] we were forced to lodge in a little nasty house without ye town." Add. 60516, p.99. He further describes the town, which they saw they passed through the next morning, on p.100

[242] In the original but scored out in the copy

[243] Likewise described by Milles as "not a very beautiful building; nor very large". Add. 60516, p.100

Pilasters, they have a Theatre to act & fine dresses which we saw; with all other things very convenient for education; they are also taught musick, & the whole expence is full 25 a year. [244] We arriv'd at Calais about 7.[245]

10. Embarked at 7, had a little wind, then calm till 2, a tolerable wind for 2 hours calm again, & by the help of tide & a little wind we got to Dover by 10 at night. [I was sick in the afternoon once, went to bed & slept, cleard my stomack again just before we got out of the ship][246]

11. About 10 we are setting out for London, & to morrow, Monday 12 N.S. 1st of July Old Style we shall be in London where I hope to meet you; we shall go to Mrs Simpsons, & if you are there you will get us lodgings. [My fond love to my Sister][247]

I am Dear Madam, your most obedient & Dutiful Son

---

[244] According to Milles, this handsome college belongs "to ye English Jesuits, who educate 40 or 50 youths of ye three Kingdoms, in order to make some of them Ecclesiasticks, & others go there merely for education. they are all dress'd in ye same habits as the Jesuits, & when they come there they give them feigned names, yt it may not be known who they are. one of ye Fathers shew'd us very civilly all over ye college: they act plays here, & have a very large & handsome collection of dresses for ye young men..." *Ibid.* p.101

[245] Milles reckons they arrived "about 6, or 7 of ye clock yt evening." *Ibid.*, p.102

[246] Scored out of the copy and reproduced from the original letter. Milles gives further details of the crossing in his journal, as follows: "we set sail in a sloop one Westfeild ye captain about 8 of ye clock in ye morning; & as soon as we were got out of ye harbour we were becalmed; we had little or no mind till 7, or 8 of ye clock at night, when there sprung up a gentle gale, wch brought us within a league of Dover by ten at night; it being dark, & low water the ship could not come into ye port, so yt a wherry [a boat] came off, & brought us to shore. next morning Mr. Hart, Mr. Jeffrys; (two men of my acquaintance yt I had met at Calais, & who came over wth us) & Dr Pococke & I hired a coach for London. We dined ye next day at Dartfordk, & arrived safe in London on Monday July ye 1st O:S:. 12th N:S:" Add. 60516, pp 102-3. Thus ends Milles' journal

[247] Curiously, this sentence is scored out of the copy

Richard Pococke

We shall stay but 2 dais [&] ½ in London

Flanders is a fine country, but much like France towards St Omers more woody we pass'd by Arde in Picardy 9 miles from Calais, a little before this we came out of Flanders into France.

N.B. My Son calculated his return so exactly in his letter from Milan, for us to meet him in London July 1st 1734, that we were not arriv'd at Mr Simpsons in Pauls Churchyard above half an hour, where Mr Wood met us too, when he & Mr Milles came to the door in a coach. God be praised for his merciful preservation of them!

Novr 25th 1745[248]

---

[248]The tiny inscription inserted by Mrs. Pococke at the end of the manuscript, indicating that the volume of copy letters was completed on 25 November, 1745, almost twelve years after Pococke had returned from his first Grand Tour

HOLYHEAD
13 July, 1734
Pococke to his mother[249]

[This is the final letter in the collection of correspondence from the first Grand Tour. It will be remembered that Pococke had earlier "laid a scheme" to spend the winter with his mother in Newtown, a scheme requiring the permission of the bishop.[250] However, this was before the "Barbone affair" had come to light and clearly the request for further leave of absence was refused. We know, from his previous letter,[251] that the intention of the cousins was to spend two days in London, which means they should have set forth for Ireland on 3 July. However, they did not reach Holyhead, where they crossed over to Ireland, until 13 of the month, a curious delay given the urgency of the situation]

I writ to you from Chester on the 9th the day we got there, the 10th we set out for Holyhead stop'd at Holywell,[252] din'd at Rith Land [Rhuddlan?] & lay at Aberconway.[253] 11th we din'd at Beau Morris [sic] a way I had never been before a little clean town, Ld Buchley's [sic] seat close to it a fine situation & pleasant garden: [254] on the side of the hill, we saw the house & Gardens & a gentleman had us into the cellar & gave us beer & wine, there are 32 hogsheads of ale[255] on one side & 32 of beer on t'other good stables &c. My Lord & family are at

---

[249]Letter 14. Add. 19939. This short letter does not appear in the collection of copy letters (Add. 22978)

[250]See Letter 18. Add. 22978

[251]See Letter 22. Add. 22978

[252]In Flintshire, North Wales

[253]A medieval walled town in North Wales now known as Conwy

[254]The house was Beaumaris, in Anglesea, North Wales, and their host was Richard Bulkeley (1707-39), 5th Viscount Bulkeley of Cashel, County Tipperary, who died childless five years later. It will be noted that Pococke spelled both the name of the family and the house incorrectly, though he was a guest there

[255]Large casks holding particular quantities depending on the liquid. In the case of ale, the measurement was 54 gallons

his Ladies Grandmother in Merionethshire, the Lady is an heiress of the name of Williams.[256]

Mr Parker was not there he is a mixture of a Gentleman a Librarian & steward in some cases, has an exceeding good character is Mr Parkers 3d son Batchelors standing at Lincoln when his father died, & since has been with this Ld, I apprehend this submitting to such a condition is because he will not take the oaths,[257] heres a chapel in the house & prayers twice a day: His Ldship being an Irish peer I think Viscount of Cashil,[258] [he] is member for Beaumorris.[259]

We had with us 2 masters of ships German Hamburgers yt [that] talk'd english & diverted us much with their riding &c

We go off in the fastest packet boat about two a clock this afternoon.

My very kind love to my sister.

I am Dear Madam
Your most obedient & dutiful son
Richard Pococke

You may expect to hear from me in two or three ports.

---

[256]In 1732, just six years before his death, Lord Bulkeley married Jane Owen (daughter of Lewis Owen and Margaret Williams of Peniarth, Merionshire), with a fortune of £60,000

[257]This is rather an obscure passage, partly because of the punctuation, though it appears that the young Mr. Parker was a companion to Lord Bulkeley, having failed to progress in the legal profession on account of his refusal to swear the necessary oaths

[258]Cashel. This word is scored out but it makes better sense to leave it in

[259]He held the office of Member of Parliament (Tory) for Beaumaris between 1730 and his death, in 1739

Conclusion

It must be assumed that the first Grand Tour of Dr. Richard Pococke and Jeremiah Milles was deemed a success, though owing to various circumstances (some of which are obvious and others left un-stated) the travellers had to shorten their voyage, and in doing so failed to visit all the places originally planned. Milles, in particular, felt that his youthful experience in foreign travel had given him a good (though not altogether positive) understanding of French and Italian life, and both cousins were anxious to preserve and adapt their memoirs for future publication. The fact that plans were soon underway for a second, more intrepid voyage proves that they were not only good friends, but more importantly for Grand Tourists, were compatible travelling companions.

From the reader's point of view, the first trip yielded a fascinating collection of manuscripts which, though dealing largely with the same subject matter, are vastly different in their style and tone. While Pococke comes across as chatty and gossipy in letters to his mother, and at times flippant and a little irreverent in his views of the local nobility and the Roman Catholic hierarchy, he adopts a more formal and scholarly approach in his journals. Conversely, while Milles makes a deliberate attempt to prove his serious and studious nature in letters to the bishop, in his journals he tends to relax, talking about more mundane aspects of French and Italian life and eventually delivering his stylised essay on Italy and the Italian people. While there are few instances of bigotry in the latter's correspondence (which would not have gone down well with the bishop, who was criticised for fraternising with Papists), the unflattering comments in his journal essay mirror contemporary English views on the Catholic Church and are commonplace in the Irish travel accounts of his fellow countrymen.

The manuscript collections for the first tour also give a valuable insight into the political situation on the Continent, especially from a tourism perspective, and demonstrate the determined and intrepid nature of such travellers, who were willing to risk their lives by travelling in dangerous conditions to learn about the peoples of Europe and view the historical and cultural centres of Europe.

It is regrettable that the letters from their correspondents have not survived. However, we not only know precisely when Mrs. Pococke responded to her son's missives (usually within a day or two),[1] but many of the deleted passages refer to her remittances of money, her help in negotiating with his bankers and his colleagues, and thank her for her continued assistance and advice. Letters from Milles to the bishop also indicate how frequently replies are received from Waterford, and whether or not the former's requests for bills have been honoured.

On 26 April, 1736, the Rev. Jeremiah Milles (as he had become since his return from the first trip) arrived in Holyhead, whereupon he made his way to Oxford and then to Newtown, to collect Pococke for their second tour of the Continent. After a month's delay, owing to disturbing news from Waterford, they set out on the Canterbury Stage Coach which took them to Dover. The route they followed in France differed from that of their first tour, taking in the Low Countries, perhaps owing to Pococke's unfulfilled desire to see Flanders and Holland.

This voyage, which lasted from the summer of 1736 until the autumn/winter of 1737, and is recorded through a vast collection of letters and journals, is the subject of Volume 2.

---

[1]This information is provided in notes inscribed on the original letters

Appendix 1: Transcript of Bishop Milles' Last Will & Testament[1]

Rt Reverd Thomas Ld Bishop of Waterford & Lismore

In the Name of God Amen

I Thomas Milles Doctor in Divinity Bishop of Waterford and Lismore in the Kingdom of Ireland do ordain constitute and appoint this to be my last Will and Testament written in the manner and form following. In the first place I recommend my Soul into the hands of Almighty God my most Beautifull and Gracious and ffaithfull Creator thro the ...passion and Death of my most Dear Saviour and Redeemer Jesus Christ and in the Sanctification of the holy and the Blessed Spirit of God I do also order and desire that whensover it shall please God that I depart out of this Mortal Life my Body may be conveyed to High Clare [sic] near Newbury in Hampshire to be interred in the Chancell of the Parish Church there as near as conveniently may be to the Bodys of my ffather and Mother swiftly but with as little ffuneral Pomp as possible and over my Grave to be layd a Marble Stone with the following Inscription upon it: subtus jacet Thomas Milles S.J.P. Waterfordiensis & Lismorensis in Hibernia Episcopus... as to all my worldly substance moveable and immoveable real and personal of what kind or Nature soever whether in this Kingdom or Ireland or in that part of Great Britain called England I ... [hereby] bequeath and dispose of it as follows.

1 To my Nephew Thomas Milles the son of my Brother Isaac Milles I give and bequeath one thousand pounds.

---

[1]The National Archives of the UK, Catalogue Reference: Prob 11/717

2. To my two divers Daughters of my said Brother Isaac Milles I give and bequeath ffive hundred pounds to be equally divided between them.

3. To my Nephew Thomas Milles a son of my Brother Jeremiah Milles I give and bequeath two hundred and ffifty pounds .

4. To my Neice Elizabeth Pococke the Daughter of my sister Elizabeth Pococke alias Milles I give and bequeath two hundred and fifty pounds.

5. To my well beloved Sister Elizabeth Pococke alias Milles I give and bequeath the sum of ffive hundred pounds.

6. To my Servant Benjamin Robinson if living with me at the time of my decease I give and bequeath ffifty pounds over and above the Wages which may be due to him and I recomend [sic] it to him to transplant himself into England.

7. And whereas I paid to the Executors of my immediate Predecessor Dr Nathaniel FFoy Bishop of Waterford and Lismore at my first coming to the See the sum of ffive hundred thirty three pounds six shillings and Eight pence being two third parts of Eight hundred pounds sayd and Certified to have been by him layd out and Expended in repairing the Episcopal House at Waterford according to an Act of Parliament made in this Kingdom of Ireland one Anoioty of which sum of ffive hundred of which sum of ffive hundred thirty three pounds six shillings and Eight pence viz two hundred sixty six pounds thirteen shillings and ffour pence is to be repayed to my Executors Auditors or Assignd by my Solicitor according as by the aforementioned Act of Parliament (Special reference being had in thereunto) it is in this Case [stated] and provided [Now] I do give and bequeath the aforesaid sum of two hundred and sixty six pounds thirteen shillings and ffour pence when [desired?] to be paid into the hands of the Corporation of the City of Waterford in trust that the yearly Interest thereof shall be paid half yearly to a new Clergyman who shall be nominated appointed and Licensed by the Bishop of Waterford and Lismore for the time being to read Prayers and to preach the Morning and

afternoon Lecture on Sundays in St Olaves Church within the City of Waterford. And if should so happen that the said Lecture should drop or that the Lecturer should not be nominated appointed and Licensed by the said Bishop for the time being I do in this Case give and bequeath the yearly Interest of the said five hundred and sixty six pounds thirteen shillings and ffour pence to be payd half yearly as [?] aforesaid by the said Corporation to the Minister who shall officiate in reading of Prayers and preaching etc in the parish Church of St Patrick within the City of Waterford. And if the City of Waterford should refuse to Accept the above sum on the Conditions before specified I shall give and bequeath the said sum of five hundred and sixty six pounds thirteen shillings and ffour pence unto my Nephew the Reverend Richard Pococke Doctor of Laws. [However, the City did accept these conditions, which means Pococke did not receive this sum of money]

8. And whereas at the day of the date of this my last Will and Testament I have advanced expended and layd out the sum of one thousand and one hundred and seventy seven pounds and fifteen shillings and ffive pence in rebuilding repairing finishing and Ornamenting Seven Parish Churches within the Diocese of Waterford and Lismore namely the Parish Churches of St Patrick and St Olave within the City of Waterford, the Parish Churches of Drumcannon, Killoteran, Ardfinnan, Rathronan and Kinsalebeg within the Diocese of Waterford and Lismore besides and over above what I have from time to time out of the Rectorial Tythes of the Parish of Cahir given and bequeathed by the Right Reverend Hugh Gore D. D. and some time Bishop of Waterford and Lismore[2] by his last Will and Testament for the Rebuilding repairing etc of the Parish Churches within the Diocese of Waterford and Lismore since the said Rectorial Tythes came into my hands which was not till after the Death of Sir John Mason of the City of Waterford the [signing?] Executor of the said Bishop Gores Will and about the beginning of the year one thousand seven hundred and twenty three. Now I do hereby give and bequeath the above mentioned sum of one thousand and one hundred and seventy seven pounds

---

[2]Mayor of Waterford for the year 1696

and fifteen shillings and ffive pence or whatever shall appear to be due out of the said Rectorial tythes of Cahir over and above what I have [scribed?] be it more or be it less than the above mentioned Sum at the time of my Decease to my Dearly beloved Nephew the Reverend Richard Pococke Doctor of Laws and to my Dearly beloved Niece Elizabeth Pococke Sister of the said Richard Pococke to be divided equally between them.

9. And whereas I have let a Lease of about one fourth part of my Garden in Lady Lane, within the City of Waterford, to William Denis [Dennis][3] Choir Archdeacon of Lismore for a term of years many of which remain unexpired I do hereby forbid my Heir the Reverend Mr Jeremiah Milles Chantor of the Cathedral Church of Lismore his Heirs Executors Auditors or Assigns to sell alienate or otherwise to dispose of the said ffourth part of said Garden let as aforesaid and I also Expresly and straitly charge him and them not to renew the said Lease on any terms whatsoever.[4]

10. As for the History of England which I have drawn up as far as the Reign of King Stephen with the Greatest Care ffidelity and Exactness and if God grants me health and Life may sometime hereafter and of which I have two Copys one writ all with mine own hand in which are diverse [Margins?] and Interlineations the other transcribed by several hands and corrected tho but imperfectly by me My Will is that it if be thought proper in time to come to print and publish it that it be printed according to the Copy of my own hand writing and adding the Subjects of the

---

[3]The same Archdeacon Denis mentioned in Chapter 4, whose brothers were Mr. Dennis (London) and Monsieur Dennis (Paris). It is not clear why the bishop was so adamant that this lease should not be interfered with, but it was perhaps indicative of poor relations between Milles (or perhaps Pococke) and the Archdeacon

[4]This "Garden" is likely to have been a plot, rather than a garden in the modern sense of the word, and it is possible that there had been some move from the city to interfere with this lease, thus explaining the bishop's determination to leave it as it was

Paragraphs which are to be found in the Margin of the Transcript of this my History but are not in the Original.[5]

11. As to all the rest and residue of my Worldly substance Moveable and unmoveable Reall or personal of what kind or Nature whatsoever it may be after just Debts ffuneral Expenses and the above Legacys are duly discharged I do hereby in the fullest and amplest manner give and bequeath it all to my Dearly beloved Nephew Jeremiah Chantor of the Xchurch Cathedral Church of Waterford and Treasurer of the Cathedral Church of Lismore and his heirs for ever whom I do hereby appoint my sole heir of every thing that belongs to me or shall [be?] possessed of or have any just Right and Title to.

12. And I do hereby formally and Expresly revoke all former Wills by me made and do appoint the aforesaid Jeremiah Milles Chantor of the Cathedral Church of Xchurch Waterford &c and the Reverend Richard Pococke Doctor of Laws to be the sole Executors of this my last Will and Testament written this Eighteenth day of April in the year one thousand seven hundred and thirty Eight and Sealed with my own Seal. Tho. Waterford & Lismore Signed Sealed and Published..."

---

[5]As mentioned in Chapter 1, this manuscript has disappeared without trace

Appendix 2: Transcripts of two Manuscript Letters from Private Collections

[This letter was sent by the bishop to his sister shortly after his arrival in Waterford, and is one of the few letters surviving from him. It is particularly interesting as it gives details of his journey to Waterford, his friendly reception on arrival, and his desire to return home to Highclere almost immediately. It also includes a brief description of the Episcopal house and its furnishings, which is useful since nothing is otherwise known about this building, which was replaced with a new Bishop's Palace on his death]

Letter 1[1]

WATERFORD
12 May, 1708
The Bishop to Mrs. Pococke

My Dearest Sister,

Yours of the 27th of the last Month came to my hands about two days since, & was very acceptable to me, as every thing is that comes from you. I came to this Place the first instant, & was received with great ceremony, solemnity & kindness both by the Clergy & People. The former together with some of the chief of the Town met me in a Body at the Distance of five miles from this place,[2] & the latter crowded in vast numbers to see me land, after I had passed the Ferry, upon the Key, where the Mayor, Alderman,

---

[1]One of a collection of four manuscript letters advertised on Ebay, February, 2011
[2]Probably at Passage East, in County Waterford

& my Register, who is Sir John Mason,[3] received me, & after having given me a kind Welcome conducted me to my House. The House is very large, built college wise round a little Court, & was very neatly furnished by my Predecessor [Bishop Foy], all which furniture I find standing, & shall buy some part of it. I was inthroned last Sunday, which ceremony was performed with solemnity enough. Being in my Habit in the Dean's Stall (where I sat till I was inthroned) after the first part of the Morning Service was ended, the Verger lead me up the Choire to a Chair which upon this Occasion was placed near the Throne. I was followed by the Dean,[4] & the rest of the Clergy who stood round the Chair. Then I delivered my Patents, & the Act of my Consecration to my Register's Clerc who read them. Then the Dean lead me up into the Throne, & by a forme drawn up for the Purpose admitting me to, & gave me Possession of the United Dioceses of Waterford & Lismore, & then after I had received the respects of the Clergy, together with that of the Dean, he withdrew to the Altar & went on with the Service. My Cathedral is a very good one & has a very Good Organ in it, but no Quire. I found the Town was very agreeable, & shall be very happy if it pleases God to afford me Life & Health. I lodge in my own Palace, but eat generally abroad the Clergy & People of the Town inviting me almost every Day. The Thoreham Man of War [a sailing ship], on which I intend to go aboard is not yet come into this Harbour, so that it will hardly be possible for me to get into England by whitsontide. I am always glad to hear from you, but should be more so to see you at Waterford. Pray give my service to all the good People at Hampton, & believe me to be, Dear Sister, Your most Affectionate Brother Tho. Waterford, & Lismore

---

[3]He was Mayor of Waterford the following year, from 1709-10. His daughter, Jane Mason, married Rev. Alexander Alcock, who was appointed Chancellor of the Waterford Diocese in 1699 and Dean of Lismore in 1725. It will be remembered that Dean Alcock was "taken dangerously ill" while the travellers were in Italy, and this was one of the reasons why they were persuaded to return early from their Grand Tour

[4]Dean John Eeles, who occupied this position from 1699 to 1723

Letter 2[5]

SOUTHAMPTON
19 September [1725]
Mrs. Pococke to her son

My Dear Son!

This being the day which I conclude you are to be ordain'd I cannot but recommend you most earnestly to be the Guidance of Gods H Spirit, by which I hope you are & always will be chiefly influence'd; that you will consider the dignity of the Holy calling you under take, that your main design in all things may be to serve God, promote his Glory & Edifie his people, that you may be always ready to give a good account of your stewardship & at length save your own souls: these were my chief motives why I desired to see you one of that Holy Order; & I hope & trust they were & always will be yours. I have not receiv'd your letter mention'd by Hancock, but perhaps may to day. I thank God your Sister & I both are well again, & I hope the Irish air will agree with you, & then I shall have nothing to fear but the ill influences & temptations you may meet with in the course of your conversation there, as you might any where else; but I hope you are & will be by Gods assistance, proof against them, by Honest Virtuous & Couragious [sic] Principles

---

[5]One of a collection of four manuscript letters advertised on Ebay, February, 2011

Appendix 3: List of Grand Tour Letters Reproduced/ Quoted in Volume 1

Letters from Pococke to his mother:[1]

Letter 1	LONDON	28 August, 1733
Letter 2	CALAIS	1/12 September, 1733
Letter 4	PARIS	15/26 September, 1733
Letter 5	PARIS	25 September/6 October, 1733
Letter 6	PARIS	3/14 October, 1733
Letter 7	LYONS	18/29 October, 1733
Letter 8	NISMES	28 October/8 November, 1733
Letter 10	GENOUA	30 November/10 December, 1733
Letter 11	FLORENCE	19 December/2 January, 1733/34
Letter 12	ROME	24 January/4 February, 1734
Letter 13	ROME	1/12 March, 1734
Letter 14	ROME	21 March/1st April, 1734
Letter 15	ROME	11/22 April, 1734

[1]The letters are numbered here, as in Mrs. Pococke's volumes of copy letters (Add. 22978). The two letters in square brackets are the editor's numbering, as they come from the original volume of letters (Add. 19939)

Letter 16	ROME	30 April/11 May, 1734
Letter 17	VENICE	31 May/11 June, 1734
Letter 18	VENICE	13 June, 1734
Letter 19	MILAN	12/23 June, 1734
Letter 20	TURIN	15/26 June, 1734
Letter 21	LYONS	20 June/2 July, 1734
[Letter 21A]	LYONS	20 June/2 July, 1734
Letter 22	DOVER	30 June, 1734
[Letter 22A]	HOLYHEAD	13 July, 1734

Letters from Milles to the bishop:[2]

DOVER	31 August, 1733
CALAIS	1/12 September, 1733
PARIS	6/17 September, 1733
[PARIS]	7/18 September, 1733
PARIS	25 September/6 October, 1733
LYONS	22/29 October, 1733
AIX	18/19 November, 1733
ROME	11/22 January, 1734
ROME	14/25 February, 1734
ROME	No date [c. 28 February/11 March, 1734]

---

[2]These letters are not numbered in the manuscript

ROME	27 March/7 April, 1734
ROME	11/22 April, 1734
ROME	17/28 April, 1734
ROME	25 April/6 May, 1734
ROME	29 April/10 May, 1734
BOLOGNA	9/20 May, 1734
BOLOGNA	13/24 May, 1734
MODENA	15/26 May, 1734
PADUA	21 May/1 June, 1734
VENICE	30 May/10 June, 1734
VERONA	6/17 June, 1734
MILAN	12/23 June, 1734

Bibliography

(A) MANUSCRIPTS

Milles/Pococke Travel Correspondence

Jeremiah Milles, Register of Letters from J. Milles to Bishop of Waterford, copies (British Library, Add. 15773)

Jeremiah Milles, 3 Letters from J. Milles to Bishop of Waterford, originals (Gloucestershire Archives, Ref. D2663/Z8)

Richard Pococke, Letters to Mrs. Elizabeth Pococke, copies (British Library, Add. 22978)

Richard Pococke, Letters to Mrs. Elizabeth Pococke, originals (British Library, Add. 19939)

Milles/Pococke Travel Journals

Jeremiah Milles, "An acct of some remarkable places between Paris, & Rome" (British Library Add.15762)

Jeremiah Milles, "An Acct of My journey from Rome, to Venice" (British Library, Add. 15763)

Jeremiah Milles, "An Account of what I saw Remarkable between Venice & London" (British Library, Add. 60516)

Richard Pococke, "Travels Volume II From Antibes in France To Rome" (British Library, Add. 22979)

Richard Pococke, "Travels Vol III Being A Description of Rome" (British Library, Add. 22980)

Richard Pococke, "Travels Vol IV of The Places near Rome" (British Library, Add. 22981)

Richard Pococke, "Travels Vol. V. From Rome To Milan" (British Library, Add. 22982)

Richard Pococke, "Travels: Vol. VI Milan & from Milan to France" (British Library, Add. 22983)

Other Manuscripts in Public Archives

Al-Koran, the Minute Book of the Divan Club
(National Maritime Museum, London, Ref. SAN/V/113)

Last Will & Testament of Miss Elizabeth Milles, Spinster
(The National Archives of the UK, Catalogue Ref. Prob 11/999)

Last Will & Testament of Mrs. Elizabeth Milles
(The National Archives of the UK, Catalogue Ref. Prob 11/858)

Last Will & Testament of Isaac Milles
(The National Archives of the UK, Catalogue Ref. Prob 11/578)

Last Will & Testament of Jeremiah Milles
(The National Archives of the UK, Catalogue Ref. Prob 11/113)

Last Will & Testament of Thomas Milles
(The National Archives of the UK, Catalogue Ref. Prob 11/717)

Last Will & Testament of Richard Pococke
(National Library of Ireland, D. 27, 161)

Letters between Richard Pococke and Sanderson Miller
(Warwick County Record Office, 125B/801 and 8022)

Minute Book of the Egyptian Society (British Library, Add. 52362)

Minute Book of the Florists' Club with Names of Members, from its Foundation in 1746 to its end 1766 (Royal Irish Academy, 24 E 37)

Minute Book of the Physico-Historical Society [of Ireland]
14 April 1744-22 March, 1752 (Royal Irish Academy, 24 E 28)

Minutes of Waterford Corporation (Waterford City Archives)

Pembroke Estate Papers (National Archives of Ireland, 2/5/32)

Royal Society Citation for Jeremiah Milles (Ref: EC/1742/05)

Royal Society Citation for Richard Pococke (Ref: EC/1741/15)

Trinity College Dublin Board Register Volume (TCD/MUN/V/5/2)

Other Manuscripts Sources in Private Collections

Letter from Bishop Milles to Mrs. Pococke, dated 12 May, 1708
(http://cgi.ebay.ie/21-THOMAS-MILLES-BISHOP-WATERFORD-
LISMORE-LETTER-/270698824381)

Sealed document signed by Bishop Milles, dated 6 July, 1717
(http://cgi.ebay.ie/29-THOMAS-MILLES-BISHOP-WATERFORD-
SIGNED-DOCUMENT-/280622342548

Letter from Mrs. Pococke to Richard Pococke, dated 19 September [1725]
(http://cgi.ebay.co.uk/41-ELIZABETH-POCOCKE-MILLES-4-
LETTERS-1721-37-/270701658725)

(B) PRINTED BOOKS

Ahern Michael, *Figures in a Clonmel Landscape* (Clonmel, 2006)

Annis, M., "The First Egyptian Society in London (1741-1743)", in
Bulletin de L'Institut Francais D'Archaeologie Orientale 50 (1952)
99-105

[Anon.] *An Account of the Life and Conversation of the Reverend and
Worthy Mr. Isaac Milles, late Rector of High Cleer in Hampshire*
(London, 1721)

Barnard, Toby, *A New Anatomy of Ireland: The Irish Protestants, 1649-
1770* (Yale University Press, 2003)

Barnard, Toby & Fenlon, Jane (eds), *The Dukes of Ormonde, 1610-1745*
(Boydell Press, 2000)

Bartlett, John, R., "Richard Pococke in Lebanon, 1738", in *Archaeology & History in Lebanon*, Issue 16 (Autumn 2002) 17-33

Beaufort, Daniel Augustus, *Memoir of a Map of Ireland; Illustrating the Topography of that Kingdom, and Containing a Short Account of its Present State, Civil and Ecclesiastical, with a Complete Index to the Map* (London, 1792)

Bence-Jones, Mark, *A Guide to Irish Country Houses* (London, 2nd revised edition, 1990)

Benedetti, S., *The Milltowns - A Family Reunion* (Dublin, 1997)

Black, Jeremy, *The British and the Grand Tour* (Croom Helm, 1985)

Black, Jeremy, *The British Abroad: The Grand Tour in the Eighteenth Century* (Sutton Publishing Ltd., 1985, reprint 2003)

Black, Jeremy, *Italy and the Grand* Tour (Yale University Press, 2003)

Brewer, James, Norris, *The Beauties of Ireland being Original Deliniations, Topographical, Historical, and Biographical, of Each County*, Volume II (London, 1826)

Burke, Rev. William P., *History of Clonmel* (Clonmel, 1907, Reprint, 2011)

Carmichael, Catherine D, "Two Gentlemen Travelers in the Slovene Lands in 1737", in *Slovene Studies* 13/1 (1992) 19-26

Carter, Hazeltine, *Letters from Europe, Comprising the Journal of a Tour through Ireland, England, Scotland, France, Italy, and Switzerland*, Volume II (New York, 1827)

Cartwright, James Joel (ed.), *The Travels through England of Dr. Richard Pococke, successively Bishop of Meath and of Ossory during 1750, 1751, and later Years* (London, Camden Society, 1888-89)

Casey, Christine & Rowan, Alistair, *The Buildings of Ireland: North Leinster* (London, 1993)

Castle, Terry, *Masquerade and Civilization: the Carnivalesque in Eighteenth-Century English Culture and Fiction* (London, 1986)

Chaney, Edward, "Architectural Taste and the Grand Tour: George Berkley's evolving Canon", in *Journal of Anglo-Italian Studies* I (1991) 74-91

Chaney, Edward, *The Evolution of the Grand Tour: Anglo-Italian Cultural Relations since the Renaissance,* 2nd ed. (London, 2000)

Chetwood, W.R., *A Tour through Ireland In Several Entertaining Letters Wherein the Present State of that Kingdom is Consider'd and the most noted Cities, Towns, Seats, Rivers, Buildings &c. are described...* (London, 1748)

Cumberland, Richard, *Memoirs of Richard Cumberland written by Himself, containing an Account of his Life and Writings, interspersed with Anecdotes and Characters of several of the most distinguished Persons of his Time, with whom he has had Intercourse and Connexion* (London, 1806-7)

Delany (Mary Granville) a Memoir 1700-1788 (New York and London, 1900)

Doble, C. E. & Rannie, D. W. (eds), *Remarks and Collections of Thomas Hearne. Nine Volumes, covering the Years 1705–1714,* Volume 1 (Oxford Historical Society, 1885-98)

Early Printed Books, 1478-1840: Catalogue of the British Architectural Library Early Imprints Collection (K. G. Saur, 2005)

Ebert, F., *A General Bibliographical Dictionary, from the German of Frederic Adolphus Ebert, Librarian to the King of Saxony...* Vol. III (Oxford, 1837)

Ellis, D., *Newtown at the Millenium* (Newtown Parish Council, 2000)

Figgis, Nicola, "Artists, Dealers and Grand Tourists in Italy in the Eighteenth Century" (Unpublished PhD Thesis, UCD, 1994)

Finnegan, Rachel, *"The Classical Taste of William Ponsonby, 2nd Earl of Bessborough",* in *Irish Architectural and Decorative Arts. The Journal of the Irish Georgian Society,* Vol. VIII (2005) 12-43

Finnegan, R.J., *The Divan Club: an Eighteenth-Century Club for Travellers to the Ottoman Empire*): *Electronic Journal of Oriental Studies* IX (2006) 1-86

Finnegan, Rachel, "The Library of William Ponsonby, 2nd Earl of Bessborough, 1704-93", in *Hermathena*, No. 181 (Winter 2006) 149-87

Finnegan, Rachel, "Bishop Pococke's Improvements to St. Canice's Cathedral, Kilkenny", *in Irish Architectural and Decorative Studies: The Journal of the Irish Georgian Society*, Volume XI (2008) 12-55

Finnegan, Rachel (ed.) *A Tour in Ireland in 1775, Richard Twiss* (University College Dublin Press, 2008)

Fitzgerald, Elizabeth, *Lord Kildare's Grand Tour 1766-1769* (Cork, 2000)

Flin, L., *A Catalogue of the Library of the late Right Revd. Dr. Richard Pococke, Lord Bishop of Meath deceased* (Dublin, 1766)

Foster, J., *Alumni Oxonienses* (1887-92)

Fothergill, Brian, *The Mitred Earl: An Eighteenth-Century Eccentric: The Life of Frederick Hervey, Bishop of Derry* (London, 1974)
Gardiner, R.B., *Registers of Wadham College* (1889-1895), Vol. 1

Gentleman's Magazine: or Monthly Intelligencer for the Year 1734, Vol. IV (London, 1734)

Gough Nichols, J., *The Topographer and Genealogist,* Volume 1 (London, 1846) 409

Hartswick, Kim J., *The Gardens of Sallust: A Changing Landscape* (University of Texas Press, 2004)

Haskell, Francis & Penny, Nicholas, *Taste and the Antique*: *The Lure of Classical Sculpture 1500-1900* (Yale University Press, 1982)

Healy, John, *History of the Diocese of Meath,* Volume II (Dublin, 1908)

Hegarty, Maureen, "Dr. Richard Pococke's Travels in Ireland, England and Wales", in *Old Kilkenny Review: Journal of Kilkenny Archaeological Society* (1987) 388-98

Ingamells, John, *A Dictionary of British and Irish Travellers in Italy, 1701-1800* (Yale University Press, 1997)

Ireland, Aideen, "A Gentle Luxury: Collectors and Collecting in eighteenth century Ireland", in J.V. Luce et al, *The Lure of Greece: Irish Involvement in Greek Culture Literature History and Politics* (Dublin, 2007)

Ireland, Aideen, "Richard Pococke (1704-65), Antiquarian", in *Peritia*, Volume 20 (2008) 353-78

Jean-Etiènne Liotard, 1702-1789, Masterpieces from the Musees d'Art et d'Histoire of Geneva and Swiss Private Collections (Somogy Editions d'Art, Paris, 2006)

Kemp, Daniel William (ed.), *Tours in Scotland 1747, 1750, 1760*, 1747, 1750, 1760 (Edinburgh, Publications of the Scottish History Society 1, 1887; Reprinted Maryland 2003)

Kennet, Basil, *Romae Antiquae Notitia: or The Antiquities of Rome* (London, 1696)

Klima, Slava (ed.), *Letters from the Grand Tour* (Montreal & London, 1975)

Langford, Mr., *A Catalogue of a Curious Collection of Greek, Roman, and English Coins and Medals, of the Right Reverend Dr. Pococke, Lord Bishop of Meath, Collected by his Lordship, during his Travels* (London, May, 1766)

Langford, Mr., *A Catalogue of a Large and Curious Collection of Ancient Statutes, Urns, Mummies, Fossils, Shells, and other Curiosities, of the Right Reverend Dr. Pococke, Lord Bishop of Meath, Deceased: Collected by his Lordship, during his Travels* (London, 1766)

Leslie, J.B., *Ossory Clergy and Parishes: being an Account of the Clergy of the Church of Ireland in the Diocese of Ossory, from the Earliest Period, with Historical Notices of the several Parishes, Churches, &c.* (Enniskillen, 1933)

Luce, J.V., Morris, Christine & Souyoudzoglour-Haywood, *The Lure of Greece: Irish Involvement in Greek Culture, Literature, History and Politics* (Dublin, 2007)

Matthews, W.H., *Mazes and Labyrinths: Their History and Development* (New York, 1970)

McCarthy, Michael, "'The dullest man that ever travelled?' - A reassessment of Richard Pococke and of his Portrait by J.-E. Liotard", in *Apollo*, Volume 143 (1996)

McEneaney, Eamonn, *A History of Waterford and its Mayors from the 12ᵗʰ to the 20ᵗʰ Century* (Waterford, 1995)

McVeagh, John, *Richard Pococke's Irish Tours* (Irish Academic Press, 1995)

McVeagh, John, '"Romantick" Ireland: Pococke's tour of Cork and Kerry, 1758', in *Éire-Ireland*, 25:2 (1990) 69–95
Mead, William Edward, *The Grand Tour in the Eighteenth* Century (Boston & New York, 1914)

Messenger, Commander A. W. B., "An Eighteenth Century Dean of Exeter and his Family", in *Report and Transactions of the Devonshire Association for the Avancement of Science* Volume 83 (1951) 22-33

Milles, Jeremiah, and Pococke, Richard, Inscriptionum Antiquarum Liber Alter - a Supplement to Pococke's Inscriptionum Antiquarum Graec. et Latin. Liber (London, 1752)

Milles, Thomas, *The Happiness of those that suffer for Righteousness Sake: in a Sermon preached at St. Maries in Oxford, on the XXXth. Of January 1700/01* (Oxford, 1701)

Milles, Thomas, *Του εν αγιοις πατρος ημων Κυριλλου ... τα σωζομενα. S. patris nostri Cyrilli ... Opera, quæ supersunt, omnia; quorum quædam nunc primum ex Codd. MSS. edidit, reliqua cum Codd. MSS. contulit, plurimis in Locis emendavit, notisque illustravit Tho. Milles* (Oxford, 1703)

Milles, Thomas, *The natural Immortality of the Soul asserted: and proved from the Scriptures, and first Fathers: in answer to Mr Dodwell's epistolary Discourse, in which he endeavours to prove the Soul to be a Principle naturally Mortal* (Oxford, 1707)

Musson, A.E., & Robinson, E., Science and Technology in the Industrial Revolution (Manchester, 1969)

Nelson, Charles E., "The Dublin Florists' Club in the Mid Eighteenth Century", in *Garden History*, Volume 10, No. 2 (1982) 142-48

Nichols, J., *Illustrations of the Literary History of the Eighteenth Century, Consisting of Authentic Memoirs and Original Letters of Eminent Persons; and Intended as a Sequel to The Literary Anecdotes* Vol. II (London, 1814)

Nichols, J. & S. Bentley, S., *Literary Anecdotes of the Eighteenth Century*, Volume III (London, 1812)

O'Connor, Cynthia, *The Pleasing Hours: The Grand Tour of James Caulfield, First Earl of Charlemont (1728-1799), Traveller, Connoisseur and Patron of the Arts* (Cork, 1999)

Oxford Dictionary of National Biography (Oxford, 2001-2004)

Perry, Charles, *A View of the Levant: particularly of Syria, Egypt, and Greece. In which their Antiquities, Government, Politics, Maxims, Manners, and Customs, (with many other Circumstances and Contingencies) are attempted to be Described and Treated on)* (London, 1743)

Pococke, Richard, *A Description of the East and of some other Countries, Vol. I, Observations on Egypt* (London, 1743)

Pococke, Richard, *A Description of the East and of some other Countries, Vol. II. 1 Observations on Palaestina or the Holy Land, Syria, Mesopotamia, Cyprus and Candia; Vol. II. 2: Observations on the islands of the Archipelago, Asia Minor, Thrace, Greece, and some otherParts of Europe* (London, 1745)

Pococke, Richard, *A Sermon [on Thess. ii. 19, 20] Preached at Christ-Church, Dublin, on the 27th of June, 1762, Before the Incorporated Society, for Promoting English Protestant Schools in Ireland...* (Dublin, 1762)

Pococke, Richard, "An Account of some Antiquities found in Ireland; communicated by the Right Reverend Richard Pococke, late Lord Bishop of Meath", in *Archaeologia: or Miscellaneous Tracts relating to Antiquity*, Vol. II (Royal Society of Antiquaries of London, 1773) 32-41

Pococke, Richard, *Inscriptionum Antiquarum Græcae. et Latinae Liber. Accedit, Numismatum Ptolemæorum, Imperatorum, Augustarum, et Cæsarum, in Ægypto Cusorum, e Scriniis Britannicis, Catalogus...* (London, 1752)

Pococke, Richard, *The Happiness of doing Good : a Sermon [on Hebrews xiii. 16] Preached before the Right Hon. the Earl of Hertford, President; the Vice-presidents, Treasurer, and Governors of the Magdalen-House Charity, on Thursday the 12th of March, 1761, at the Parish Church of St. Brides, Fleet-Street...* (London, 1761)

Quane, Michael, "Pococke School, Kilkenny", *The Journal of the Royal Society of Antiquaries of Ireland*, 80 (1950) 36-72

Rennison, W., *Succession List of the Bishops, Cathedral and Parochial Clergy of the Dioceses of Waterford and Lismore, from the Earliest Times, together with some Hitherto Unpublished Records* (Ardmore, 1921)

Rizzo, B. (ed.), *The Early Journals and Letters of Fanny Burney, Vol. IV* (Oxford 2003)

Ryland, R.H. *The History, Topography & Antiquities of the County and City of Waterford : with an Account of the present State of the Peasantry of that Part of the South of Ireland* (London, 1824)

Salmon, Thomas, *Modern History or the Present State of All Nations* Volume II (London, 1745)

Shaw, Thomas, *A supplement to a book entituled Travels, or Observations, &c. wherein some Objections, lately made against it, are fully considered and answered: with several additional Remarks and Dissertations* (Oxford, 1746)

Shaw, Thomas, *Travels or Observations relating to Several Parts of Barbary and the Levant* (Oxford, 1738)

Smith, Charles, *The Ancient and Present State of the County and City of Waterford. Containing a Natural, Civil, Ecclesiastical, Historical and Topographical Description thereof* (Dublin, 1746)

Southampton City Council, *Historic Environment Record Listed Buildings in Southampton* (2010)

Southern, Pat, *Empress Zenobia: Palmyra's Rebel Queen* (Continuum, 2009)

Stanford, W.B. & Finopoulos, E.J. (eds), *The Travels of Lord Charlemont in Greece & Turkey, 1749* (London, 1984)

Stanford, W.B., "The Manuscripts of Lord Charlemont's Eastern Travels", in *Proceedings of the Royal Irish Academy,* Section C, Volume 80, Number 5 (1980) 69-90

Stokes, George Thomas (ed.), *Pococke's Tour in Ireland in 1753* (Dublin, 1891)

Strickland, Walter G., *A Dictionary of Irish Artists,* Volume II (Dublin, 1913)

Trease, Geoffrey, *The Grand Tour* (Yale University Press, 1991)

Twiss, Richard, *A Tour in Ireland in 1775* (London, 1776)

Waddell, John, *Foundation Myths: The Beginnings of Irish Archaeology* (Wordwell Ltd., 2005)

Warburton, William, *Remarks on several Occasional Reflections in Answer to The Rev. Dr. Middleton, Dr. Pococke... and others... Serving to explain and justify divers Passages, in the Divine Legation, Objected to by those Learned Writers...* (London, 1744)

Whiteside, Lesley, with Whiteside, Andrew, *Where Swift and Berkeley Learnt: A History of Kilkenny College* (Dublin, 2009)

Wilton, Andrew & Bignamini, Ilaria, *Grand Tour: The Lure of Italy in the Eighteenth-Century* (Tate Gallery Exhibition Catalogue, 1997)
Woods, Christopher J., "Pococke's Journey through County Down in 1760", in *Ulster Journal of Archaeology,* Volume 48 (1985) 113-15

Wynne, Michael, "Members from Great Britain and Ireland of the Florentine Academia del Disegno 1700-1855", in *The Burlington Magazine,* Vol. 132, No. 1049 (Aug. 1990) 533-38

Young, Arthur, *Gleanings from Books on Agriculture and Gardening* (London, 1802)

Index of Selected
People & Places